1974

This book may be kept

FOURTEEN DAYS

A fine will be charged for each day the book is kept overtime.

GAYLORD 142			PRINTED IN U.S.A.

DOSTOYEVSKI

IN RUSSIAN LITERARY CRITICISM

1846-1956

COLUMBIA SLAVIC STUDIES

A SERIES OF THE

DEPARTMENT OF SLAVIC LANGUAGES

COLUMBIA UNIVERSITY

Ernest J. Simmons, GENERAL EDITOR

DOSTOYEVSKI

in Russian Literary Criticism

1846-1956

BY

VLADIMIR SEDURO

1969

OCTAGON BOOKS

New York

*The preparation and publication of this study
were made possible by a grant from
the Research Program on the U.S.S.R.
(East European Fund, Inc.)*

*Reprinted 1969
by special arrangement with Columbia University Press*

OCTAGON BOOKS
A Division of Farrar, Straus & Giroux, Inc.
19 Union Square West
New York, N. Y. 10003

Library of Congress Catalog Card Number: 79-76006

Printed in U.S.A. by
NOBLE OFFSET PRINTERS, INC.
NEW YORK 3, N. Y.

to

IRENE

INTRODUCTION

THE ATTITUDE of the Soviet Union toward the work of Fyodor Dostoyevski has undergone those same vicissitudes and shifts to which the entire cultural life of the country has been subjected as a result of changes in Party policy.

During the 1920s the appearance in the Soviet Union of hundreds of critical and scholarly studies of Dostoyevski corresponded to the heightened interest in Dostoyevski in the West. In the years before the Second World War Dostoyevski scholarship remained productive, although there was a decrease in the number of books and articles published. Works on Dostoyevski appeared during and after the war, especially in connection with the celebration in 1946 of the 125th anniversary of the writer's birth. Thereafter the "Zhdanov reaction" in literature paralyzed Dostoyevski scholarship, and for almost a decade prevented the publication of new studies in the field. Then in 1956 another phase in the Soviet treatment of Dostoyevski, still not fully defined, was officially inaugurated with the observance of the 75th anniversary of his death.

Throughout the whole Soviet period Dostoyevski scholarship has been marked by a struggle between those who accept and those who reject the writer. Criticism has often alternated between sweeping apologia and denial of the significance of his writing and its ideological and philosophical value for contemporary society. In the views expressed we can usually discern the influence of Soviet policy in general and the zigzags of Party policy on literature and art in particular. The subordination of literary and scholarly thought to the tasks and policy of the Party, which was consummated in the last few years of Stalin's dictatorship, was a gradual process, however, and is less and less apparent the farther into the past we go.

For the sources of Soviet thought concerning Dostoyevski we

must consider the traditions of radical literary criticism in the nineteenth century and the beginning of the twentieth. Without a survey of the views of Belinski, Dobrolyubov, Pisarev, Mikhailovski, and, finally, the Marxist critics of the early 1900s, the full meaning of Gorki's articles on Dostoyevski is lost. And without an understanding of Gorki's work it is, in turn, impossible to understand Lenin's attitude, which to a great extent determined the subsequent development of Soviet criticism of Dostoyevski.

The revolutionary tendency to reject the heritage of past cultures went hand in hand with the reliance on the critical thought of the Russian radicals of the nineteenth century. We shall therefore begin our study of Dostoyevski in Soviet criticism with an analysis of the writings of Russian critics of the past.

VLADIMIR SEDURO

New York City
March, 1957

ACKNOWLEDGMENTS

THE AUTHOR wishes to express his deep gratitude to Ernest J. Simmons, Professor of Russian Literature at Columbia University, who not only encouraged him to undertake this work but who also followed its progress with sympathetic attention and was instrumental in arranging for its publication.

The author is also grateful to Alexander Dallin, first Associate Director of the Research Program on the U.S.S.R., under whose direction the work was begun, as well as to his successor, Robert M. Slusser, who helped to provide the conditions under which it was possible to complete and publish the work.

Mrs. Lois Weinert made the original translation; her contribution is hereby acknowledged with thanks.

The author's deepest obligation is due to Miss Louise Luke, Assistant Director of the Research Program on the U.S.S.R., who edited the work and whose exacting critical standard has been of inestimable advantage to the author in preparing the work for publication.

The author also wishes to thank Miss Barbara Melissa Voorhis of Columbia University Press, who supervised the publisher's editing of the manuscript and prepared it for printing.

The author alone, of course, assumes full responsibility for the content of the work.

V. S.

CONTENTS

PART I. Criticism before the Revolution

. 1 .

THE EARLY "RADICAL" CRITICS

VISSARION GRIGOR'YEVICH BELINSKI (1811–1848)

RECOGNITION OF DOSTOYEVSKI'S TALENT AND

CONFUSION OVER THE DOUBLE

Fyodor Mikhailovich Dostoyevski owed the swift recognition of his talent to "stormy Vissarion," the critic Belinski, whose opinions were heeded by all reading Russia. Immediately after the publication of Dostoyevski's first story, *Poor Folk* [*Bednye lyudi*] in *Petersburg Miscellany* [*Peterburgskii sbornik*] in 1846, Belinski gave it a prominent place in his long review of the collection.[1] With the same enthusiasm the writers Nikolai Nekrasov and Dmitri Grigorovich had felt when they sat up all night reading *Poor Folk* and at four o'clock in the morning went to the young author's apartment to congratulate him, Belinski welcomed it as "the first attempt at a social novel" [2] made in Russian literature. He warned against efforts to apply to Dostoyevski's fresh and original writing the ready-made critical formulas developed in the so-called "Gogol period," and against superficial comparisons between *Poor Folk* and the works of Gogol. While he noted traces of the latter's influence, Belinski pointed out the individuality of Dostoyevski's talent and predicted that Gogol's influence "will not continue and will soon disappear with his other faults, although Gogol will nonetheless always remain his literary father, so to speak." [3]

At first glance it is apparent that Dostoyevski's talent is not satirical, not descriptive, but to the highest degree creative, and that the predominant characteristic of his talent is humor. He produces his effect not by that knowledge of life and of the human heart which comes from experience and observation; no, he knows them—and knows them deeply—a priori, therefore purely poetically, imaginatively. His knowledge is talent, inspiration. We do not wish to compare him with anyone, because such comparisons are in general childish and do not lead to anything, do not explain anything. We shall say only that this is an extraordinary and original talent, which immediately, in his very first work, set him quite apart from our whole crowd of writers who are more or less indebted to Gogol for their bent and character, and therefore for the success of their talent.[4]

In Belinski's opinion the influence of Gogol might be spoken of only in regard

to details, to the turn of phrase, but not at all to the conception of the work as a whole or to the characterizations. In the last two respects Mr. Dostoyevski's talent shines forth in brilliant individuality.[5]

Behind the similarities between Dostoyevski's style and Gogol's, Belinski discerned the uniqueness of Dostoyevski's talent, although he was unable to define in what exactly it consisted. He felt that Dostoyevski had still not fully revealed himself as a writer in *Poor Folk*.

Belinski did not live to read the masterpieces—*Crime and Punishment* [*Prestupleniye i nakazaniye*], *The Devils* [*Besy*, also translated under the title *The Possessed*], *The Idiot* [*Idiot*], *A Raw Youth* [*Podrostok*], and *The Brothers Karamazov* [*Brat'ya Karamazovy*]. And knowing only the first few stories of Dostoyevski, Belinski showed extraordinary critical acumen in establishing that the young writer's work was fundamentally social in content.

Of the humanistic trend in Dostoyevski's writing, he said:

In Makar Devushkin he showed us how much beauty, nobility, and holiness there is in the nature of a very limited human being. Of course, not all poor people . . . are like Makar Alekseyevich with his good qualities, and we admit that such people are rare. But at the same time one cannot but admit also that little attention is paid to such people, little concern for them is shown, little is known about them. . . .

Honor and glory to the young poet, whose muse loves people in garrets and basements and who says of them to the inhabitants of gilded
palaces: These, too, are people; they are your brothers! [6]

Belinski came close to finding the very essence of Dostoyevski
in his combination of deep humanistic feeling and the pervasive-
ness of tragedy:

In general, the tragic element permeates this whole novel. And this element is all the more striking in that it is conveyed to the reader not
only in the words but also in the ideas of Makar Alekseyevich. To
amuse and to move the reader deeply at one and the same time, to
force him to smile through his tears—what skill, what talent! And no
melodramatic springs, no theatrical effects. Everything so simple and
ordinary, like that humdrum, everyday life which seethes around each
one of us.[7]

In the characters of *Poor Folk*, "people in garrets and basements," the critic asserted, Dostoyevski had revealed qualities
of high-minded humaneness, freedom from self-interest, self-
sacrifice, and selflessness which dwelt unperceived in the poor,
and which deserved human esteem and not merely pity and con-
descension.

His talent belongs with those which are not immediately understood
and recognized. In the course of his literary life there will appear many
talented writers who will be compared with him, but it will end with
their being forgotten at the very time when he reaches the height of his
fame.[8]

Even Belinski, however, was unable to comprehend fully all
the characters in *Poor Folk*. Concerning Varen'ka Dobrosyolova
he wrote:

All the characters are drawn so completely, so vividly . . . [except
that] the character of Varen'ka is somehow not completely defined and
finished; but apparently it is the fate of Russian women that Russian
literature is at odds with them, and that is all! [9]

On the other hand, Belinski did understand the many secondary characters, even less clearly drawn, such as Bykov, the mother and father of Varen'ka, the old and the young Pokrovski, Ratazyayev, the usurer, and other characters who appear only casually. But Varen'ka Dobrosyolova, with her abnormal pride, apparently remained incomprehensible to the critic. In her the pathological quickness to take offense, typical of many of Dostoyevski's future heroes, is evident. Devushkin's love seems to Varen'ka a manifestation of pity, which offends her and arouses the desire to torment her worshiper.

This exaggerated pride was a major stumbling block for Belinski in Dostoyevski's following works. In the article on the *Petersburg Miscellany*, when he came to the analysis of Dostoyevski's second story, *The Double* [*Dvoinik*], Belinski found himself puzzled by the dual personality of the hero. Giving its due to Dostoyevski's talent, Belinski nevertheless considered the character of Golyadkin abnormal. "The hero of the novel," he writes,

Mr. Golyadkin, is one of those resentful people, mad with *pride*, whom we so often meet in the lower and middle classes of our society. It always seems to him that he is being insulted by words and glances and gestures, that everywhere people are intriguing against him, that he is being undermined. And this is all the more amusing in that no one's envy can possibly be aroused by his fortune or his rank or his position or his mind or his capabilities. He is not intelligent and not stupid, not rich and not poor, he is very kind, and gentle to the point of weakness, and he might have had not at all a bad life in this world; but his morbid resentment and suspicion are the black demon of his life, which is fated to make a hell out of his existence. If you look around you more attentively, how many Mr. Golyadkins you will see —rich and poor, stupid and intelligent! . . . At the very beginning of the novel, in the conversation with Dr. Christian Ivanovich, it is not difficult to guess that Mr. Golyadkin is mentally disturbed. And thus the hero of the novel is a crazy man! The thought is daring and is carried out by the author with astonishing skill.[10]

Thus for Belinski, Golyadkin is the embodiment of the pride and self-love characteristic of all regardless of social position. Belinski failed to perceive in Golyadkin the tragedy of a poor and humble civil servant who had no rights and whose wounded pride, resentment, continual apprehension for himself and his position, and uncontrollable craving for justice and respect drove him to madness. He appreciated the artistry of the story, but he missed the psychological tragedy of the downtrodden man.

It is apparent at first glance that in *The Double* there is more creative talent and depth of thought than in *Poor Folk*. But meanwhile the consensus of St. Petersburg readers is that this novel is intolerably long-winded and therefore terribly boring, from which it follows that the author was trumpeted in vain and that his talent is nothing unusual! . . . Is this conclusion just? Without beating about the bush, let us say that on the one hand it is extremely false, and that on the other, there is a basis for it, as there always is for the judgment of a crowd which does not understand itself.[11]

This evasiveness, which reflected confusion about the nature of Dostoyevski's typical hero, was even more apparent in Belinski's appraisal of Dostoyevski's next story, entitled *Mr. Prokharchin* [*Gospodin Prokharchin*], in which the hero, one of the basement dwellers, becomes a miser out of fear of losing his independence. In the article "Review of Russian Literature in 1846" Belinski wrote:

The third of Mr. Dostoyevski's writings was published in the tenth issue of *National Notes* [*Otechestvennye zapiski*]—the story *Mr. Prokharchin*, which came as an unpleasant surprise to all those who admired Mr. Dostoyevski's talent. In it there are flashes from the bright sparks of a great talent, but they flash in such thick gloom that their light does not permit the reader to see anything. . . . It seems to us that it was not inspiration nor free and ingenuous writing that produced this strange tale, but something in the nature of—how shall we say it? —exhibitionism and pretension. Perhaps we are mistaken, but, if so, why is it so involved, mannered, and incomprehensible, as if it were an actual happening, but a strange and muddled one, and not a piece of fiction? In art there should be nothing obscure and incomprehensible.[12]

In his opinion of the long story *The Landlady* [*Khozyaika*], 1847, Belinski finally displayed his complete incomprehension of the essence and meaning of Dostoyevski's new work. The tone of his criticism is one of sarcasm and mockery: "If some unknown name were signed to it, we would not say a word about it."

What they said to one another, why they waved their arms, grimaced, attitudinized, swooned, sank into comas, and recovered consciousness we have no idea, because we did not understand a single word in all these long, pathetic monologues. Not only the underlying idea but even the general drift of this no doubt very interesting tale remains and will remain a mystery to our mind until the author publishes the necessary explanations and interpretations for this marvelous riddle of his capricious fantasy.[13]

Belinski, usually very sensitive to any development in literature, this time failed entirely to grasp Dostoyevski's meaning when the latter introduced into Russian literature the theme of the split personality—intended not merely as a fantasy but as a representation of the tragic duality of contemporary man. The critic of the 1840s was unprepared for what Dostoyevski himself called a "magnificent idea, the character of extreme social importance which I first discovered and heralded,"[14] for the theme of the split personality and the theme of the tragic conflict of the individual with society, the basic motif of all Dostoyevski's writings. The struggle of the noble and the lofty in man against man's double in the outside world of society who crowded out these qualities—in other words, the conflict of the real human "I" with its usurping double—and the tragic lot of the human personality—madness or death—escaped Belinski. Not understanding their purpose, he ridiculed the elements of Hoffmannesque split personality, the art of leading the reader into the realm of the subconscious, and the method, new to Russian literature, of illuminating the depths of man's spiritual life. "What is it," asked the puzzled critic in reference to *The Landlady*,

misuse or poverty of talent, which aspires to heights beyond its powers and therefore is afraid to proceed in the usual way and seeks a path that has never been used before? We do not know, but it does seem to us that the author was making an attempt to bring together Marlinski and Hoffmann, stirring into the blend a little humor in the latest fashion and then giving the whole thing a thick coating of distinctively Russian lacquer. . . . A strange thing! An incomprehensible thing! [15]

He did not take into account the total effect of Dostoyevski's enthusiasm for Pushkin, Gogol, Hoffmann, Schiller, Balzac, George Sand, and Eugene Sue; he did not trace all the ramifications of the Gogol tradition in *Poor Folk* and *The Landlady;* he did not satisfactorily explain the Hoffmannesque method of unmasking and penetrating into hidden psychological depths.

Belinski saw only one aspect of the unfamiliar rebellion of the poor man, of the protest of the individual against social injustice and human degradation, and that was the author's vindication of the little man (Makar Devushkin). Belinski, like Dostoyevski, was capable of admiring the unselfish pureness of heart of the poor folk, the loftiness of their dreams, and the hidden nobility of the people of the city street corners and hovels. But beyond this humane aspect of Dostoyevski's early works the critic could not go; the other new ideas, as well as the new form, remained unexplored. Had Belinski lived longer, he might well have repudiated his judgment of Dostoyevski.

Belinski's views nevertheless determined in many respects the further development of Russian critical thought in the nineteenth century. Lesser critics who were influenced by Belinski in writing of Dostoyevski were Pavel Vasil'yevich Annenkov (1812–87),[16] Aleksandr Vasil'yevich Druzhinin (1824–64),[17] and the "liberal censor" and professor Aleksandr Vasil'yevich Nikitenko (1804–77),[18] who was editor of Nekrasov's *Sovremennik* [Contemporary] in 1847–48. Moreover, Soviet critics of Dostoyevski still draw heavily on Belinski's ideas in the devotions required of them by the artificially stimulated cult of the *raznochintsy*[19] revolutionaries of the last century, primarily Belinski, Dobrolyubov and Chernyshevski. As a result, Belinski's writings, with all the defects of his mid-nineteenth-century critical method, the caprices of his personal taste and the dogmatism of his opinions, which are especially unsound in regard to Dostoyevski, even now carry great weight in Soviet criticism. In the extremely reactionary period after the Second World War —the "Zhdanov period"—the Party press attacked Dostoyevski's philosophy furiously and snatched at passages in which Belinski underestimated or failed to understand Dostoyevski as proof of the critic's great wisdom. To serve the purpose of the moment, the weaknesses and blunders of the first Russian professional literary critic were turned into virtues.

VALER'YAN NIKOLAYEVICH MAIKOV (1823–1847)

DOSTOYEVSKI AS PSYCHOLOGICAL ANATOMIST

Among the "radical" critics of Dostoyevski's early work, Valer'yan Maikov, brother of Dostoyevski's close friend the poet Apollon Maikov, was alone in his sure understanding of the new dimension added to Russian literature with the publication of *Poor Folk, The Double,* and *Mr. Prokharchin.* Valer'yan Maikov lived to read only these first three stories, but in them he took the measure of Dostoyevski's distinctive gift. Although a publicist like most of his fellow critics and in many respects a follower of Belinski, Maikov had a highly developed appreciation of purely literary values. He had welcomed the prospect of the development of the Gogol school, which for him promised a deflection of part of the attention of writers from social problems to the portrayal of man's inner world, and was therefore quick to respond to Dostoyevski. He wrote in 1847:

Mr. Dostoyevski's writings stabilize the reign of the aesthetic principles which Gogol introduced in our literature, demonstrating that even a very great talent cannot take a different road without violating the laws of art. Nevertheless, the creative method of Mr. Dostoyevski is original in the highest degree, and he is the last one who may be called an imitator of Gogol. If you were to apply this term to him you would be obliged to call Gogol an imitator of Homer and Shakespeare. In this sense all true artists imitate one another, because beauty is always and everywhere subject to the same laws. . . .

Both Gogol and Mr. Dostoyevski portray actual society. But Gogol is primarily a social writer, and Mr. Dostoyevski primarily a psychological writer. For one, the individual is significant as representative of a certain society or a certain circle; for the other, society is interesting insofar as it influences the personality of the individual.[20]

The young critic was free of Belinski's confusion over the arrogant pride of Dostoyevski's characters. In Varvara Alekseyevna, as well as in the other characters of *Poor Folk*, he found "an extraordinarily true picture, taken from human nature" and "tremendous significance for psychology." [21] He accepted *The Double* with none of Belinski's consternation:

In *The Double*, Dostoyevski's method and his love for psychological analysis are revealed in all their fullness and originality. In this work he has penetrated so deep into the human soul, has gazed so fearlessly and feelingly into the innermost workings of human emotions, thoughts,

and affairs that the impression produced by reading *The Double* may
be compared only with the experience of a man of inquiring mind who
has penetrated into the chemical composition of matter. Strange! What,
you say, can be more down-to-earth than a chemical view of reality?
Nonetheless the picture of the world illuminated by such a view always
seems to the man flooded with a mystic light. From what we ourselves
have experienced and from what we have been able to conclude from
the impressions of most of Mr. Dostoyevski's admirers, in his psychological studies there is that same mystic gleam which is in general
characteristic of the representation of profoundly analyzed reality.

Before our eyes *The Double* anatomizes a soul destroyed by the realization of the discord of personal interests in a well-ordered society.
Think of this poor Golyadkin, sick with pride, constantly apprehensive
about himself, constantly tortured by determination not to lower himself
under any circumstances nor to any one and at the same time constantly
undone even in the presence of his rascally servant Petrushka, constantly
ready to give up his claims to individuality if only he may have *his
rights.* Think how the slightest stir in nature seems to him an evil
portent of enemies of every kind plotting against him, enemies who
devote themselves totally and indivisibly to harming him, enemies who
are constantly keeping watch on his unfortunate person, who are
steadily and persistently intriguing to undermine his petty little interests. Think of all this and ask yourself: Isn't there in you yourself
something of Golyadkin, to which no one wants to confess but which
is fully explained by the amazing harmony prevailing in human society? . . . However, if you were bored reading *The Double,* despite
the impossibility of failing to sympathize with the character of Golyadkin, there is still nothing surprising in that. Not to everyone is analysis
endurable. Was it so long ago that Lermontov's analysis gave many a
jab in the eye? Is it so long ago that an insufferable element was seen
in Pushkin's poetry? [22]

Golyadkin's split personality did not suggest madness alone to
Maikov. As if in deliberate retort to Belinski, he derided the
opinion that the story was boring and long drawn out.

Again, as if in reply to Belinski's criticism of *Mr. Prokharchin,*
Maikov offered the opinion that Dostoyevski had paid too much

attention to objections that *The Double* was dragged out and in the new story had sacrificed valuable qualities for the sake of brevity. Whereas Belinski had regarded *Mr. Prokharchin* as "involved, mannered, and incomprehensible," "strange and muddled," Maikov saw "the terrible wasting away of the powers of Mr. Prokharchin in avarice, which had developed in him as a result of brooding on his insecurity." Maikov advised Dostoyevski to pay less attention to the critics and to follow his own bent:

If even a third of the labor spent on Golyadkin had been put into the modeling of [Mr. Prokharchin], the outcome of the story could not possibly have escaped the reader, and there would have been no arguments about its idea. We cannot but wish that Mr. Dostoyevski might have greater faith in the powers of his own talent than in the observations of outsiders, no matter who they may be. However, it is easy to give advice.[23]

NIKOLAI ALEKSANDROVICH DOBROLYUBOV (1836–1861)

THE *RAZNOCHINETS* APPRAISAL

Soon after the publication of a two-volume edition of Dostoyevski's works in 1860 and of the novel *The Insulted and Injured* [*Unizhonnye i oskorblyonnye*] in 1861, Dobrolyubov's critical review "Downtrodden People" appeared in *Sovremennik*.[24]

Although Dobrolyubov, too, died before Dostoyevski's masterpieces were written, he was acquainted with several works which were produced after Belinski's lifetime. Furthermore, the social development of Russia, the increase in the number of *raznochintsy* among the intelligentsia, and the progress of social thought during the movement to end the feudal system made possible a deeper and more faithful interpretation of Dostoyevski's work.

From Dobrolyubov the stories that followed *Poor Folk* did not evoke Belinski's bewildered exclamation: "A strange piece! An incomprehensible piece!" On the contrary, he displayed extraordinary sensitivity toward the characters in Dostoyevski who have exaggerated pride and discerned in them hidden sparks of that flame of protest which blazes in the souls of "downtrodden people." Those utter derelicts, as they seemed, who, when put to test, proved capable of fighting "for their rights" were especially understandable to him.

In "Downtrodden People" he wrote of Dostoyevski:

The truth of life did not escape him, and he very aptly and clearly placed a boundary line between the official frame of mind, between outward bearing, the man in uniform, and that which constitutes his inner being, that which is hidden in the secret recesses of his nature and which only at times, when he is in a particular mood, shows for a moment on the surface.[25]

For Dobrolyubov the problem of the split personality did not turn solely on its extreme manifestation, the madness of Golyadkin. On the contrary, he tried to give a social explanation even for this madness, seeking its cause in the fact that the "downtrodden people" actually had no rights in society:

I do not know whether I understand the basic idea of *The Double* correctly; in explaining it, no one, so far as I know, has been willing to get into it more than to say that "the hero of the novel is crazy." But it seems to me that if there must be a reason for every madness, then for madness about which a talented writer relates a story for 170 pages, all the more so. . . .

Something rose up from the bottom of his soul and was expressed in grim protest, of the only kind of which the unresourceful Mr. Golyadkin was capable—madness. . . . I do not say that Mr. Dostoyevski developed the idea of this madness in an especially artistic manner. But it must be acknowledged that his theme—the split personality of a weak, characterless, and uneducated man, fluctuating between timid uprightness of action and unrealized proclivities for intrigue, a duality under

the weight of which the reason of the poor man finally goes to pieces
—this theme, in order to be executed well, requires very great talent.[26]

Dobrolyubov saw in Dostoyevski the faculty for detecting living people with living souls in his dulled, numb heroes:

The spark of godliness nevertheless smolders in them, and as long as a man lives, there is no way whatever of extinguishing it. A man may be ground down, turned into a filthy rag, but still somewhere, in the filthiest folds of this rag, feeling and thought are preserved—voiceless and obscure as they may be, they are nonetheless feeling and thought.[27]

Even in Dostoyevski's earliest fiction Dobrolyubov found the one feature which runs through all Dostoyevski's work to the end, namely, compassion for man. The realization by man of his legitimate right to be himself and to find genuine, complete, and independent expression of his personality was the driving force in the behavior of Dostoyevski's heroes. The impossibility of preserving their individuality leads them to bitterness, withdrawal from the world, or even to madness, but more often "simply to quiet torpor, to the suppression of human nature in themselves, to the frank recognition that they are something much lower than a man." [28]

This is the merit of the artist: he discovers that the blind man is not completely blind; he finds in the stupid man flashes of very clear and sound reasoning; in the downtrodden, lost man who is deprived of individuality, he searches out and shows to us the living, never-stifled aspirations and needs of human nature, draws out of the very depths of the soul the hidden protest of the personality against external, violent suppression and offers it for our judgment and sympathy.[29]

Neither before nor after Dobrolyubov did Russian critical thought of the nineteenth century rise to such a height of keen penetration into the secret of Dostoyevski's writings. The character of Golyadkin and his heroic madness, which was the self-

sacrifice of a zealot in behalf of the lofty estate of man, a protest against the unjust conditions of life, an explosion of the
insulted human dignity lying hidden in his secret inner world,
found their interpreter in Dobrolyubov.

Dobrolyubov's classification of Dostoyevski's characters carried through into Soviet literary criticism. It is obvious that
V. F. Pereverzev, whose interpretation of Dostoyevski enjoyed
almost exclusive recognition from the Marxist point of view in
the 1920s, borrowed from Dobrolyubov the division of Dostoyevski's heroes into two main types: the meek and the embittered. Dobrolyubov wrote in "Downtrodden People":

> The former make no protest; they bow under the weight of their
> circumstances and seriously try to convince themselves that they are
> zero, nothing, and that, if his excellency speaks to them, they should
> consider themselves lucky and favored. The others, on the contrary,
> seeing that their rights, their legitimate demands, that which is sacred
> to them, that with which they entered the world, are trampled upon
> and disregarded, wish to break with everything around them, to have
> nothing to do with it, to be sufficient unto themselves and to ask nothing
> of anyone in the world, to accept no favors, no brotherly feeling, no
> kind look. It is self-evident that they do not succeed in standing firm,
> and therefore they are eternally dissatisfied with themselves, curse them-
> selves and others, plan suicide, and so forth.
> Between these two extremes there is another category of people, who
> perhaps might well be classified with the first type: those who have lost
> the full awareness of their human rights but have replaced it with a
> narrow fiction of conventional prerogatives, who have become con-
> vinced of the truth of this fiction and treasure it. At any moment when
> such gentlemen imagine that their personal dignity is in danger, they
> are ready to repeat, for example, "I am a titular counselor," "Vasili
> Petrovich himself shakes hands with me," "The wife of staff-officer
> Pokhlestov knows me," and so on. They are also cowardly people,
> suspicious, stickling, unconscionably quick to take offense, and they
> themselves suffer most of all from their touchiness.
> From observation in our society of the so-called "little people," one

knows that the meek and submissive are sometimes also touchy people and sticklers. This depends on the circumstances. In the presence of the chief of the division, an assistant to the head clerk is blotted out and completely subdued, but with the other assistants he considers himself "within his rights" and holds on to his rights jealously and sullenly. The latter aspect is developed by Mr. Dostoyevski in *The Double*.[30]

A radical thinker of the sixties, who had made his profession of faith in the people and who shared the democratic hopes and dreams of the urban lower classes, the working people, Dobrolyubov was interested not so much by the formal aspect of Dostoyevski's fiction—the still not fully developed art of the novel—as by the author's extraordinary insight into the previously unknown world of the insulted and injured man of the time. In his keen and subtle analysis of the complex psychology of Dostoyevski's characters, with their tangled lives and their gloomy feeling about life, the critic expressed concern for the lot of the downtrodden people and anxiety over the failure of efforts to curb the forces striving to extinguish the sparks of human dignity.

"Within the limits imposed by nature," wrote Dobrolyubov in "Downtrodden People,"

absolutely every man should be a complete, independent human being and, when he enters into the complex pattern of social relations, should bring to them his own individuality. And when he takes up suitable work, even the most humble, nevertheless he should in no way conceal, destroy or stifle his manifest human rights and demands. This seems to be clear. But why, then, does this Makar Alekseyevich Devushkin "hide himself, conceal himself, tremble," why is he continually ashamed of his life, why does he "now look around with a confused look, now strain to overhear every word," and find his only consolation in the fact that he is a small, insignificant man? Why is this Gorshkov so pitiful and sickly that his knees shake, his hands shake, his head shakes, he is shy, afraid of everything, walks to one side? And why does Golyadkin —in agonizing and vain attempts to gain his rights and to go his own

way—give up the last vestiges of his actual rights, and finally, unable
to endure the idea in his weak mind that everyone is undermining his
rights, become deranged? And why, too, was Mr. Prokharchin a miser
for twenty years and why did he live in poverty all that time because he
thought he was needy and finally become ill and die because of this
idea? Why does this young civil servant, Shumkov [*A Faint Heart
(Slaboye serdtse)*] consider himself a monster of humanity and rave
that they will send him into military service because, carried away by
his affection for his betrothed, he could not copy the papers within the
time allotted him by his superior? Why does little Netochka so humble
herself before Katya [*Netochka Nezvanova*]? Why does Rostanev
surrender his own will to Foma Fomich and consider himself utterly
unworthy of the love of Nasten'ka, the governess, whom he loves passionately [*The Village of Stepanchikovo and Its Residents (Selo Stepanchikovo i yevo obitateli*, published in English translation under the title
Friend of the Family)]? Why does Natasha lose her will and reason,
and Ivan Petrovich respectfully step aside before the weathercock Alyosha? Why is the old man Ikhmenev, suffering all possible tortures of
a father's love, unwilling to forgive his daughter, lest he appear to be
making a concession to the prince and his son? Why does little Nellie
respond so strangely to Ivan Petrovich's kindness and go to beg alms
in order to buy him a cup with the money she collects [*The Insulted and
Injured*]? What is the reason for all these preposterous, astonishingly
strange relations among people? What is the root of the incomprehensible discrepancy between what should be, according to the natural,
reasonable order of things, and what happens in fact? No one character,
no one story, of Dostoyevski's by itself gives a direct answer to such
questions. In order to find the answer, we must group them and explain one according to the others.[31]

The critic regarded Dostoyevski as an impartial artist, de-
tached from controversies and theories of the day, who observed and depicted reality "without thinking at all whom this
will benefit, for what idea it will prove useful." [32] On the other
hand, the transmutation of facts of life into art gives them such
force as a generalization that "afterwards there can be no doubts
whatever in respect to the entire range of similar phenomena." [33]

Proceeding from this premise, Dobrolyubov, here as much publicist as literary critic, grouped the personalities and types of
characters found in Dostoyevski and arrived at answers to the
questions raised throughout his writing.

In his examination of the character of Ikhmenev in *The Insulted and Injured* and of the ineffectuality of the latter's protest
against the injustice inflicted upon him by the prince, who was
protected by "connections and the police regime," the critic
prompted the reader to seek a way out of the circumstances that
had been created for Dostoyevski's heroes:

Does it thus follow that the position of these unhappy, downtrodden,
insulted, and injured people is completely hopeless? Can they do nothing but keep silent and endure, and, reduced to the condition of a dirty
rag, tuck away their unvoiced feelings in its most obscure folds? [34]

Dobrolyubov's radical trend of thought had brought him to
unequivocal answers, but censorship forced him to hedge at
this point, to say that he would not enlarge upon the subject
and that it would be naïve to expect him to answer these questions, which were fraught with the accursed and still vexed problems of the times. He deliberately limited his task to the classification of the downtrodden, insulted, and injured characters,
pointing out that there were many of them in the middle strata
of society, that they had a hard life in both the moral and physical sense, that underneath their apparent outward resignation
they never ceased feeling bitter over their circumstances, that
their irritation and protest were easily aroused, and that they
longed for a way out.

The critic's conclusion is full of sincere indignation, sympathy, and desire to help shape a consistent philosophy of life
out of the feelings which Dostoyevski's characters had about
their world. In the muffled beat of life among them Dobrolyubov,
filled with dreams of a better Russia, heard precisely what he

yearned to hear. Restraining himself from forecasts too far beyond the bounds of literary criticism, he nevertheless found re-
assurance in the actual trends of his time—the emergence into
the social and cultural arena of extraordinary forces from the
people, chiefly the middle classes, as represented by Dobrolyubov himself, those of similar persuasion among the men of the
sixties, and even Dostoyevski; and the heartening signs that
new masses were awakening and coming to a realization of their
cultural, social, and political role:

Since the appearance of Makar Alekseyevich and his kin, life has already accomplished a great deal, but this great deal has not yet been
made into habitual practice. We have noted, among other things, a
general tendency to restore human dignity and full civil rights to each
and every one. Perhaps here a way out of the grievous situation of the
mistreated and the downtrodden is already being found, not, of course,
by their own efforts, but with the help of persons who are less affected
by the oppressive and crushing hardships of such circumstances. And
for these people, who possess some amount of initiative, it is a good
thing to look into the state of affairs, to know that a large part of these
downtrodden people, whom they have perhaps considered done for and
morally dead, still harbor within them a living soul, strong and deep,
although in hiding even from themselves, and an eternal consciousness
of their human right to life and happiness, a consciousness not to be
put to rout by any sufferings.[35]

With a wary eye on the censor, he called cryptically upon his
readers to give themselves to the revolutionary current:

The most important thing is to follow the unbroken, harmonious,
mighty, never-to-be-arrested current of life, and to be alive, not dead.[36]

As a *raznochinets*, Dobrolyubov clearly alluded to those like
himself who were less crushed by their circumstances, and ap-
pealed to them to look more closely at this third force coming
to life among Dostoyevski's characters. Here to a certain extent
the political thinker in Dobrolyubov involuntarily gained the

upper hand over the critic, as in the case of all those writing for the journals of the 1860s. Dobrolyubov was the leading exponent of such social and publicist critical literature of the period. His great interest in public affairs, coupled with a deeply analytical mind, contributed much to his understanding of the complexities and contradictions of Dostoyevski. Dobrolyubov was the first to open up the new world of Dostoyevski for later Russian scholarship and, indeed, it may be that no other Dostoyevski critic has ever surpassed him in insight.

In the discussion of Dobrolyubov we have been concerned here only with the basic trends and ideas in the article "Downtrodden People," leaving out many minor observations, which are to be explained by the journalistic critical practices of the time and which are now outmoded.

DMITRI IVANOVICH PISAREV (1840–1868)

INTERPRETER OF RASKOL'NIKOV

Pisarev, an outstanding critic of the 1860s, wrote two articles on Dostoyevski, "The Perished and the Perishing," [37] 1865, and "Struggle for Life," [38] 1867. The first was a comparative analysis of Dostoyevski's *Notes from the House of the Dead* [*Zapiski iz myortvovo doma*] and N. G. Pomyalovski's *Seminary Sketches* [*Ocherki bursy*, 1862–1863] from the educational point of view. As literary analysis, the second article, a magnificent treatment of *Crime and Punishment*, is the more significant.

At the beginning of the article Pisarev explains his methodology. He is concerned neither with the partisan sympathies and antipathies of the author nor with the development of his writing and the trends which run through it; as critic, he is guided primarily by the principle of the truthful reflection of objective reality, "of the phenomena of social life":

If these phenomena are faithfully noted, if the raw facts which constitute the basic fabric of the novel are completely true to life, if in the
novel there are neither aspersions on life nor a false and cloying
touching-up nor internal incongruities—in a word, if living people who
bear the stamp of actual social conditions act and suffer in the novel,
struggle and make mistakes, love and hate, then I treat the novel as I
would an authentic account of events that have really happened. I observe and ponder these events, trying to understand how one derives
from the other, trying to explain to myself to what extent they are
caused by the general conditions of life, and in doing this I completely
leave aside the personal views of the narrator, who may convey facts
with great accuracy and detail but still explain them in a highly un-
satisfactory manner.[39]

In this definition of the task of literary criticism it is at once
obvious that Pisarev was influenced by Dobrolyubov, who in the
article "Downtrodden People" had referred to the function of
criticism as that of disclosing and explaining the reality depicted
in an artistic work, freeing it from the prejudices and biases of
the author's philosophy. For both critics the criterion of the value
of a genuine work of art is the degree to which it corresponds to
reality.

In accordance with this basic position, Pisarev attempted
first to explain Raskol'nikov's thoughts and actions as due to the
external circumstances in which he finds himself and which in-
exorably determine his whole make-up. Like Dobrolyubov, he
definitely rejected the assumption that Dostoyevski's heroes are
mad. According to Pisarev, Raskol'nikov could not behave otherwise because of the tragic circumstances of his life.

In detail, step by step, following the life of Raskol'nikov in all
its vicissitudes, the critic showed even the slightest nuances of
his psychology as produced by the circumstances of his life.
He considered Raskol'nikov's exhaustion from the unsuccessful
struggle for existence, enumerated the events jarring upon his

overwrought nerves, deliberated the effect on Raskol'nikov of the meanness and callousness of the people around him, and then took up the question of freedom of choice and Raskol'nikov's responsibility for his actions:

The vast majority of people setting out to steal or rob go through the same phases through which Raskol'nikov passes. The crime described in Mr. Dostoyevski's novel differs from many ordinary crimes only in that the hero is not an uneducated, wretched creature, completely undeveloped intellectually and morally, but a student, capable of analyzing in minute detail all the impulses of his own soul, able to construct large and elaborate theories to justify his actions, and retaining even in his wildest delusions the quick and many-sided susceptibility and the moral sensitivity of a highly cultivated man. For this reason, the tonality of the crime is changed to a certain degree, and the process of preparing for it is more easily observable, but the basic motive remains unchanged. Raskol'nikov commits his crime not exactly *in the same way* in which a poor untutored wretch would have done it, but he commits it *for the same reason* as that for which any untutored wretch would do it. In both cases, poverty is the main, compelling motive.[40]

The ideas and the plan which sprang to Raskol'nikov's mind were not the controlling factor in his actions but were themselves born of the abnormal conditions of his life:

The crime was committed not because Raskol'nikov, in bouts of philosophizing, convinced himself of its lawfulness, rationality and necessity. On the contrary, Raskol'nikov began to philosophize to this effect and convinced himself only because circumstances drove him to crime.[41]

Pisarev emphasized that in a situation such as that of Raskol'nikov all the best powers of a man turn against him and draw him into conflict with society:

The holiest feelings and the purest aspirations which ordinarily support, encourage and ennoble a man become harmful and destructive passions when he lacks the possibility of satisfying them legitimately. It was

Raskol'nikov's desire to show his affection for his old mother and to
take care of her at any cost to himself, to provide for her those modest
comforts of life which she needed, to deliver her from the distressing
worry about daily bread; he also wanted to see his sister protected for
the present against the insolence of the various Svidrigailovs, and in
the future against the fate which had befallen Sonya Marmeladova. . . .
But these imperatives remain lawful, reasonable and laudable only so
long as Raskol'nikov has the material means with which he can in
actual fact take care of his mother and save his sister from dishonor.
So long as Raskol'nikov has property, capital, or work, he is accorded
his full rights, and he is even charged with the holy obligation to love
his mother and sister and to protect them from deprivation and indigni-
ties. . . . But as soon as his material means are exhausted, then Raskol'nikov at once loses, together with his resources, the right to bear
human feelings in his breast. . . . Love for his mother and sister and
the desire to care for and to protect them become unlawful and antisocial feelings and aspirations from the moment when Raskol'nikov is
turned into a hungry and ragged pauper. If a man cannot feed and
clothe himself like a human being, then he is not to think and feel like
a human being. Otherwise, human thoughts and feelings produce behavior which leads inevitably to a clash between the individual and
society. . . . When he had landed in his exceptional situation, Raskol'-
nikov found himself at the crossroads told about in fairy tales, where
one road promises ruin to the horse, the second to the rider, and the
third to both. It seems to Raskol'nikov that he must either deny everything that is dear and holy to him in himself and in the world around
him or else enter into a desperate struggle against society for those
things which are sacred to him—a struggle in which it would no longer
be possible to pick and choose the methods.[42]

The desire to care for and protect his sister and mother only
drove him on and brought him near the realization of the "accursed dream."

In discussing the problem of free will Pisarev declined to
apply to Raskol'nikov the copybook maxims of accepted morality. He admitted that he was perplexed by this difficult question
and unable to give a definitive answer:

In life there are situations which convince a dispassionate observer that
suicide is a luxury, attainable and allowable only for well-to-do people.
Finding himself in such a situation, a man learns to understand the
eloquent saying: "Wherever you turn, you're cornered." In such a situation the rules and injunctions of the generally accepted moral code
prove inapplicable. In such a situation the exact observance of any such
excellent rules and injunctions leads a man to a kind of glaring absurd-
ity. That which under ordinary circumstances would be a sacred obligation begins to appear to a man in an exceptional situation as contemptible cowardice or even as a clear crime; that which under ordinary
circumstances would arouse horror and revulsion in a man begins to
seem to him a necessary step or a heroic deed when he is under the
stress of his exceptional situation. And it is not only the man himself,
crushed by the exceptional situation, who loses the ability to decide
moral questions as they are decided by the great majority of his contemporaries and compatriots; the dispassionate observer also, ponder-
ing such an exceptional situation, halts in perplexity and begins to have
the feeling that he has come into a new, strange, completely fantastic
world, where everything is done topsy-turvy and where our usual concepts of good and evil can have no binding force.[43]

The critic also casts doubt on the possibility of condemning
Sonya without taking into account the special circumstances
of her life:

What will you say, indeed, about the behavior of Sof'ya Semyonovna?
What feeling does her behavior arouse in you, contempt or reverence?
What do you call her for this behavior, a filthy prostitute, casting her
sacred honor as a woman into the mire of the streets, or a noble
heroine, accepting with quiet dignity her martyr's crown? Which voice
should this girl heed as the voice of conscience: that which says to her,
"Sit at home and suffer to the end, die of hunger with your father, your
mother, your brothers, and your sisters, but preserve to the last minute
your moral purity," or the voice which says to her, "Don't feel sorry for
yourself, don't spare yourself, give everything you have, sell yourself,
disgrace and contaminate yourself, but save, comfort, support these people, nourish and warm them, if for no more than for a week, at any
cost." [44]

Although in his article Pisarev never explained Dostoyevski's characters immanently, on the basis of their psychology alone, but always etiologically, he was in no way the forerunner of the sociological interpretation of Dostoyevski. In his writing psychology was not reduced to a social or class factor, but, on the contrary, was highlighted, took on special cogency, and found its justification in actual conditions. Pisarev's clarification of the apparent confusion and involvement of psychological motives in *Crime and Punishment* is exemplified by the passage in which he speaks of Raskol'nikov's dualism during the time when his plan was ripening:

As his mind succumbed to exhaustion, it no longer had sufficient strength to wipe out the accursed dream by calm and cool reflection. He could only be terrified, shudder, and experience fits of convulsive horror for those vile things to which this accursed dream impelled him. His terror and revulsion could at times reach such proportions that the accursed dream began to appear to him completely unrealizable and consequently not dangerous. At such moments he could rejoice in his liberation from the evil spell and look upon nature and himself with the eyes of a man who was recovering health. But terror and revulsion, no matter how strong, could not serve as substitute for calm reflection and change the pattern of what had long since been constructed in his mind by persistent and laborious thinking along false and dangerous lines. As soon as circumstances squeezed him to the wall with a crucial question demanding an immediate answer, he at once became the unprotesting slave of his accursed dream.[45]

A radical thinker, a leader of the *raznochintsy* of the 1860s, believing in the natural sciences and work as the sole panacea for all ills, Pisarev could not but condemn Raskol'nikov as an individualist who had turned his back on the society in which he lived. Raskol'nikov's argument that crime is allowable and justified for great people did not accord with Pisarev's ideals, and Raskol'nikov by no means fitted into the category of Pisarev's "thinking realist":

Raskol'nikov's theory has nothing in common with those ideas which constitute the philosophy of the enlightened people of today. He worked out the theory in the sinister silence of deep and agonizing solitude; this theory bears the stamp of his personal character and of that exceptional situation which gave rise to his apathy.[46]

Nonetheless the critic expressed sorrow for a man who, in tormented solitude, conscious of his own powerlessness, can never fulfill his potentialities. While Dobrolyubov sought a solution to the tragic situation of Dostoyevski's heroes in the operation of a third force, in the rising force of democracy, Pisarev, placing his reliance in the enlightened man of the time, the "thinking realist," also displayed a tendency to seek a solution in Raskol'nikov himself. And then, in the passages in which he advised Raskol'nikov to try to improve his situation through all-saving work, without transgressing the laws of existence, the deliberations of the critic took on the character of somewhat abstract and sententious maxims, and his tirades on "passionate love of any honest work, no matter how exhausting, inane or humble," [47] are suspended in a vacuum.

In this lapse from his basic method of considering characters in close connection with the concrete circumstances which determine their behavior, Pisarev's thoughts have the sound of a priori reasoning applied to Raskol'nikov and fall somewhat below the level of Dobrolyubov's understanding of Dostoyevski. In contrast to Mikhailovski and Merezhkovski, who subsequently carried this a priori trend to greater lengths, Pisarev in general held consistently to the view that psychology and behavior are determined by objective factors of social and personal life, and his occasional lapses are mere inadvertence.

Pisarev's article was the high point of Russian critical thought at the end of the 1860s, and his interpretation of the personality of Raskol'nikov takes its place, with Dobrolyubov's "Downtrodden People," among the best pages of literary criticism of the nineteenth century.

NIKOLAI KONSTANTINOVICH MIKHAILOVSKI (1842–1904)
THE LEGEND OF THE "CRUEL TALENT"

The *narodniki*[48] of the 1870s and 1880s, incensed by the "libel" in *The Devils* upon the generation of revolutionaries to which they belonged, condemned Dostoyevski through their strongest voice, Mikhailovski, and for a time, with considerable force, through Pyotr Nikitich Tkachov (1844–85).[49]

Mikhailovski's most significant articles on Dostoyevski are "Commentaries on *The Devils*"[50] and "A Cruel Talent" (1882).[51] His article entitled "On Pisemski and Dostoyevski"[52] and the tenth section of "Letters from an Outsider to the Editors of *National Notes*"[53] are also of interest.

Mikhailovski's opinion of Dostoyevski carried great weight not only with his contemporaries who wrote of Dostoyevski, such as Mikhail Alekseyevich Protopopov (1848–1915)[54] and Aleksandr Mikhailovich Skabichevski (1838–1910),[55] but also with subsequent generations of critics. Indirectly, through his influence on Maxim Gorki, Mikhailovski set the tone for much of the Soviet critical literature on Dostoyevski. The tendency to discredit Dostoyevski as a reactionary, to condemn *The Devils* as a slander on young revolutionists, to reject Dostoyevski's basic concept of man, and to criticize his methods of depicting social reality in art stem from Mikhailovski. The ambivalence later characteristic of Soviet criticism of Dostoyevski was displayed by Mikhailovski in his simultaneous recognition of a great talent

and his violent attack on the basic philosophical ideas of Dostoyevski's writings. Mikhailovski did not, of course, go to the extreme of interpreting the writer as a whole solely on the basis
of his "all-explanatory" petit-bourgeois class origin, as did later
Marxist literary scholars using their "sociological" method. On
the contrary, Mikhailovski went to the other extreme, explaining everything by the individual personality traits of the writer
himself, in accordance with the so-called subjective method in
sociology, which he introduced into the field of literary analysis.
His system shifted the explanation of literary phenomena entirely to the level of the individual personality and conscience
of the writer, which constituted, in his opinion, the main factor
in literature. His attempt to unlock all the secrets of the author's
writing through the personality of the writer alone was far from
successful in clarifying the characteristics of Dostoyevski's work
and producing an objective scholarly explanation of its genesis,
nature, and meaning.

In 1882, when Mikhailovski published his "Cruel Talent" on
the occasion of the publication of the second and third volumes
of Dostoyevski's complete works, the glorification of Dostoyevski
had reached its height. Devoted critics like Orest Miller were
burning incense to his name, and Vladimir Solov'yov was pronouncing him the prophet and spiritual leader of the Russian
people.

For the apologists of Dostoyevski, his fiction and publicist
writings were important in their entirety. Mikhailovski, however, as a *narodnik*, although acknowledging the originality
and great "literary interest" of Dostoyevski's fiction, simply
wrote him off as a publicist:

As a publicist, he was nothing more than a hodge-podge, which everyone would have recognized as a hodge-podge had it not been for the
political maneuvering of some and the slavish devotion of others. But,

on the other hand, his talent in belles-lettres was whetted to the glitter and sharpness of a knife.[56]

Even in Dostoyevski's fiction, Mikhailovski found reprehensible features which had not been noted by other critics. To a certain extent he accepted Dobrolyubov's definition of the basic trend of Dostoyevski's writing as humanistic in regard to *Poor Folk* and *The Insulted and Injured,* in which "the main tenor at least is compassion for the humiliated man and a careful search into his soul for glimmerings of human dignity and protest," [57] but reproached his predecessor for overlooking the evidences, even in the early works, of Dostoyevski's cruelty and inclination to enjoy suffering. In the article "On Pisemski and Dostoyevski" Mikhailovski called attention to the mixture of compassion for the insulted and injured man with the opposite feeling, bordering on delight in human degradation, and to the fact that preaching of meekness and suffering came to replace the feeling of personal dignity and protest:

Formerly Dostoyevski grasped with special sensitivity that driving motive in the soul of the insulted and injured which said, "I am no worse than others!" And although this motif, because of the intimidation and maltreatment of the insulted, came through incoherently, in comic ugliness, the author nevertheless recorded this welcome but inept outburst with obvious compassion in his heart. Later, on the contrary, he began, even with much more avidity, to search the human soul for the consciousness of sin, the consciousness of one's own worthlessness and loathsomeness, and the corresponding thirst for atonement of sin through suffering. [58]

Mikhailovski assiduously ferreted out signs of the coming shift in Dostoyevski's early work, noted the gradualness of the process and found three reasons which had brought the writer to the passionate exaltation of suffering: respect for the existing social order, the eagerness for personal confession, and the cruelty of his talent.

In his detailed analysis of the last feature, in "A Cruel Talent," Mikhailovski's methodological approach to Dostoyevski is utterly different from that of Dobrolyubov. The latter had observed the downtrodden people in the environment which gave rise to their psychology, prompted their behavior and actions, and impelled their minds to strange and extravagant deductions and theories; that is, he saw the very reality which Dostoyevski depicted as playing its part in forming the whole complex of a character's psychology. The critic included in the humanistic category not only the stories about the meek, but also those of the embittered, the two main types into which Dobrolyubov divided Dostoyevski's characters. Mikhailovski, on the other hand, tracing the literary evolution of Dostoyevski's heroes, found a hypertrophy of bitterness in them. He asserted that cruelty—the proclivity to torture—had always absorbed Dostoyevski, and, moreover, by virtue of the sensual pleasure which seemed to be involved in torturing:

No one else in Russian literature has analyzed the sensations of a wolf as it devoured a sheep with such thoroughness, depth, and, we may say, love as Dostoyevski, if we can really speak of an attitude of love toward the feelings of a wolf. And he was very little interested in the elementary, primitive kinds of wolfish feelings, in simple hunger, for example. No, he burrowed into the profoundest depths of the wolf's soul, in search of subtle, complex things—not simple satisfaction of appetite, but sensual enjoyment of anger and cruelty. This predilection of Dostoyevski is too obvious to disregard. . . . Taking into consideration Dostoyevski's whole literary career, we shall be obliged to come to the conclusion . . . that he simply loved to bait the sheep with the wolf, the sheep having been of especial interest to him during the first half of his career, and the wolf during the second half.[59]

Declaring Dobrolyubov's viewpoint outmoded, Mikhailovski emphasized that, strictly speaking, in Dostoyevski's writing there was no great and sudden change:

There was no great about-face. Dostoyevski did not burn the object of
his worship, and did not worship what he burned. There was simply a
gradual shift in interests and the distinctive components of his talent;
that which formerly was of secondary importance became of primary
importance, and vice versa.[60]

The world of Dostoyevski's heroes seemed to Mikhailovski to
be a menagerie of beasts of prey, in which the writer was assigned the role of cruel trainer:

The whole thing is a very carefully kept menagerie, a whole nursery of
various breeds of wolves, whose owner does not even boast of his rich
collection and has even less thought of deriving direct profit from it.
He knows his business so thoroughly and loves it so much that the study
of the wolf's nature is for him a thing sufficient in itself. He purposely
teases his animals, shows them a sheep or a piece of bloody meat, beats
them with a whip and a red-hot iron, in order to observe one detail or
another of their anger and cruelty—to look for himself and, of course,
to show it to the public.[61]

In Mikhailovski's opinion, the development of Dostoyevski's
talent seemed to parallel the development of his cruelty; once
he had realized the power of artistic torment, he was so cap-
tivated by the "sport" that, like the underground man in the
episode with Liza, he became more and more skillful in stab-
bing the heart of his heroes and readers. Dostoyevski's talent,
cruel by nature and as a result of his upbringing, Mikhailovski
stated, found the sphere in which it was most at home and there
developed with great brilliance. The lack of a social ideal and
a deficient sense of moderation allowed Dostoyevski to slip along
an inclined plane from simplicity to pretentiousness, from a
humanist bent "to a not quite overt twitching at the nerves until
they quiver," [62] then to "gratuitous and aimless torture." [63]

To support his argument Mikhailovski used an epigraph to
"A Cruel Talent" composed of quotations from Dostoyevski's
writings: "Man is a despot by nature and loves to be a tor-

turer" (*The Gambler* [*Igrok*]); "Tyranny is a habit which becomes an addiction" (*Uncle's Dream* [*Dyadyushkinyi son*]); and several passages from *Notes from the Underground* [*Zapiski iz podpol'ya*] and *The Crocodile* [*Krokodil*].

Producing an almost hypnotic effect by variations on this motif of cruel torture which he found in all of Dostoyevski's works, Mikhailovski labored to inspire in the reader a feeling of disgust. At the end, however, this characteristic and dominant feature of Dostoyevski's work remained unexplained. Finding no "reason or purpose," and at a loss to give a satisfactory interpretation, the critic fell back upon the peculiarities of an author who chose to depict cruelty for its own sake. Mikhailovski said of "that section of the menagerie which is called *Notes from the Underground*": [64] "The hero tortures because he wants to, he likes to torture. There is neither reason nor purpose here, and, in the opinion of the author, they are not at all necessary, for absolute cruelty, cruelty *an und für sich* is interesting." [65]

Golyadkin, in *The Double*, a victim of caste inequality, whose suffering made him a split personality and a madman, in Mikhailovski's interpretation was forced to undergo all his misfortunes at the will of the author. For Golyadkin's double, "whose appearance adds immeasurably to the suffering, neither nature nor history is to blame, but the author alone," [66] whose cruel fantasy had taken a situation so unusual as to be implausible and made it into a "source of suffering for a human being who is already miserable." [67] Dostoyevski brought the second Golyadkin into the story "for 'sport,' for the sake of playing cruelly on the nerves." [68]

Even Dostoyevski's most fully-drawn characters remained incomprehensible to Mikhailovski. The Soviet critic Pereverzev has aptly pointed out Mikhailovski's failure in regard to Raskol'nikov:

In comparison with what Mikhailovski says about [Raskol'nikov], Pisarev's article is the extreme of profundity. The tragedy of Raskol'-nikov, this overwrought torturer, tossing about from frenzied crime to frenzied confession, was completely beyond Mikhailovski's understanding. He was unable to comprehend the inevitability of the crime as retaliation for unjustified suffering nor the inevitability of punishment as retribution for unjustified crime, which constitute the tragedy of the "downtrodden man," powerless before the blind force of the social order. According to Mikhailovski, Raskol'nikov resorts to crime and is imprisoned not because he is powerless to destroy the order which is outraging his human dignity, but because the writer, at pains to keep this order inviolate, and at the same time with an inclination to torture, punishes him with penal servitude for his arrogant and, moreover, stupid outrage upon the order.[69]

For Mikhailovski, Raskol'nikov was an a priori phenomenon, unrelated to specific conditions of life, through whom Dostoyevski was solving abstract moral problems:

The first one to have submissiveness preached to him and to have visited upon him the punishment of conscience and of prison is the insulted and injured Raskol'nikov. At first glance this is strange, incomprehensible. But remember that, properly speaking, there are no insulted and injured, but there is a general order which is inviolable, and there is a moralist who is called upon to pronounce judgment on the individual and only on the individual; that is, other than the insulted and injured, there is no one to be brought to judgment. Moreover, Raskol'nikov is not a simple insulted and injured man. He has dared to rebel, he has touched blasphemously on the general order, both in theoretical thinking and in practical action (quite senseless action, however). And it is for this that his conscience torments him, for this he goes to prison, and only there in prison, humbled and finally confirmed in faith, does he at last find peace of mind.[70]

Elsewhere Mikhailovski wrote:

[When] a man himself loves to be a torturer and on the other hand himself loves to suffer, [he finds] a twofold justification for the existence of torturers. Therefore, the general order of things, which creates torturers and tortured, represents something holy and inviolable, and Dostoyevski in various ways persecuted all those who in word, deed, or thought infringed upon this inviolable general order.[71]

Mikhailovski objected to what he called Dostoyevski's arbitrary treatment of his heroes in characterizing those who protested against the social order as morally warped and mentally ill and in endowing them with his own philosophy of suffering. The earlier attempt, which Dobrolyubov had ridiculed, to interpret Dostoyevski's strange heroes as madmen, was in part repeated by Mikhailovski when he placed them on "the borderline between reason and madness, between a normal and an abnormal condition of the will": "They are either people who are in an extremely excited state or monomaniacs who are given a chance to think up and preach exceedingly high-flown theories." [72]

Dostoyevski stuffs his heroes' heads with his own ideas and solves "moral problems" by means of these "psychiatric characters." "He plays moral and political motifs on the strings of mental illness." [73]

In *The Devils*, as well as in *Crime and Punishment* and *The Idiot*, he organizes whole orchestras of this kind. He does this in two ways. Either he takes a psychological motif, for instance, the feeling of sin and the desire for atonement (a motif which especially interests him), and sets it to work in a character. You see, for instance, that a man has sinned, that his conscience is tormenting him. He finally takes [penance] of some sort upon himself and thereby attains peace of mind. This is one method. It is used by Dostoyevski in *Crime and Punishment*. In *The Devils* Stavrogin represents an unsuccessful attempt of this kind. The other method consists in putting the solution of some moral problem into the mouth of a man who is tormented by mental illness. In *The Devils*, unfortunately, the second method predominates. I say "unfortunately" because this method is obviously not suitable in art. One of the characters in Dostoyevski's last novel [*The Devils*] says: "I did not devour my idea, but my idea devoured me." A great many of Dostoyevski's heroes might say this about themselves. This type is without doubt highly interesting and instructive. But it is one thing to show him as a type, as a living character really being devoured by his idea before the eyes of the reader, and it is another thing to make a man hold forth indefatigably concerning an idea that has been pinned on him. But such is the case with most of the main characters in *The Devils*. . . . They are devoured by their idea in an entirely different sense. The thing is that Dostoyevski has such a huge store of eccentric ideas that he simply overwhelms his heroes with them. . . . In general, then, instead of characters representing *people who are driven by their own ideas*, in *The Devils*, characters are portrayed *who are driven by ideas imposed upon them by the author*.[74]

Mikhailovski denied that the young people portrayed in *The Devils* were in the least typical of the progressive youth of the time, for whom the critic considered himself the ideologist, and maintained that theories such as those of Shatov, Kirilov, and Stavrogin had only a "microscopically small place" among young people:

Where did Dostoyevski hear young Russians of today greeting one another and taking leave with the questions: Are you an atheist? Did you light a lamp [before an icon]? Have you become a believer? And, furthermore, where did he hear from the lips of young people such ideas as "The people is the body of God," "The Russian people is the bearer of God," and the like? I do not dispute the fact that he may even have heard [such remarks], but merely on this basis he has, of course, no right to put these traits in the foreground as characteristic and typical. . . . If Dostoyevski had deliberately set out in search of a milieu in which mystical theories were completely out of place, he would have found it in contemporary Russian youth.[75]

Mikhailovski accused Dostoyevski of seizing upon the Nechayev affair—an anomaly, a grievous and criminal mistake—as a pretext to represent radicals and revolutionaries as eccentric and pathological cases, and deplored the fact that he had ignored the really progressive young people, those "who give the tone to the times," who represented the Russia of the future, and who were "worthy of being portrayed" by a great artist "with a crystal-clear and resolute conscience"; in short, the revolutionary *narodniki* of Mikhailovski's camp. Dostoyevski had missed "the most interesting and the most typical features of our time"; "he missed much, he missed everything." [76]

In every one of [the characters in *The Devils*] we again see only more deviations. To begin with, people who are psychologically abnormal hardly furnish grounds for drawing a generalization. And since the people in *The Devils* are for the most part only props for eccentric ideas, then it becomes even more difficult to take the point of view that they can all be merged into the concept of a herd of possessed swine. The eccentric idea—if the expression may be pardoned—fairly bristles at you all the time. It has nothing in common with noneccentric ideas and other eccentric ideas, and therefore the assemblage of props for eccentric ideas does not permit a synthesis; it is impossible to add them together in one sum. And therefore, no matter how Dostoyevski strove for logic, he did not attain it. [77]

The novel seemed to Mikhailovski "a many-centered thing, dissolving and spreading," "a series of dramatic situations fitted together by force, in which it is extremely difficult to orient oneself." [78]

To the *narodnik* Mikhailovski, the greatest evil was the capitalist development of Russia, which, in his opinion, would lead the people off their true path of popular socialism, corrupt them with the devilish desire for wealth, and ruin the peasantry by destruction of the *obshchina* (communal land tenure) system —the nucleus of socialism—and of the moral virtues linked with it. Dostoyevski had made the noxious mistake of disregarding the really terrible devils of approaching capitalism:

Russia, this sick and bedeviled Russia which you have depicted, is girdled with railroads, studded with factories and banks—and in your novel there is not one trace of this world! You concentrate your at-

tention on an insignificant handful of madmen and good-for-nothings!
In your novel there is no demon of national wealth [capitalism], a demon which is most widespread and which, less than any other one,
knows the boundaries between good and evil. Swine overcome by this
devil will not, of course, fling themselves from the cliff into the sea. No,
they will be more cunning than your favorite heroes. If you had noticed
them, they would have adorned your novel. You did not seize upon these
devils. The devil of service to the people [the program of the *narodniki*]
—let it be actually a devil, cast out of the sick body of Russia—thirsts
in one or another form for atonement; this is its very essence. But it is
best for you to disregard it entirely, if you can see its pathological forms
only.[79]

Mikhailovski's criticism was in some respects the forerunner
of that Party criticism which examines each work of art from
the point of view of the correspondence between the opinions
it expresses and Party doctrine, and pronounces judgment accordingly. Polemic political purposes prevailed over the purposes of aesthetic criticism. Seeing in *The Devils* an attempt to
discredit *narodnik* ideology, and, in fact, a repudiation of all
revolutionary aims, the critic rejected sharply the entire world
of its characters and denied its validity.

The literary tradition of condemning Dostoyevski on political
grounds, which began with Mikhailovski's attacks and was continued by other radical and revolutionary critics, has long hin-
dered Dostoyevski scholarship.

. 2 .

DECADENTS, SYMBOLISTS, AND MYSTICS

DMITRI SERGEYEVICH MEREZHKOVSKI (1865–1941)
IDOLATRY OF THE "PROPHET"

During the later 1880s the critical principles of the *narodniki*
had little influence on Russian literature. After the defeat of
their social and political program, their long-held authority in
the field of art was soon challenged. No one school dominated
the literary scene in the eighties, but two factions were gathering
their forces: on the one hand, the "modernists" or "decadents,"
who later evolved into the symbolists and impressionists, and,
on the other, the Marxists. The forerunners of modernism, protesting against the civic demands made upon literature by the
older generation of critics, against the emphasis on duty and
the sacrifice of the individual personality for the advancement
of social purposes, rose to the defense of "pure art" and asserted their interest in idealistic philosophy and religion. The
leader of the decadent movement during the 1890s, D. S.
Merezhkovski, wrote extensively on Dostoyevski. Like the other
outstanding Dostoyevski critics of the time, Rozanov and Shestov, as well as Aikhenval'd, who wrote slightly later, Merezhkovski was indebted to the philosophical interpretation of Dostoyevski by Vladimir Sergeyevich Solov'yov in the 1880s [1] and was
strongly influenced by Nietzsche. For Solov'yov's followers, as
for Solov'yov himself, the writings of Dostoyevski were less
a subject for objective scholarly study than material for justifying their own views.

In 1893 Merezhkovski published a collection of essays entitled *On the Causes of the Decline and the New Trends in Contemporary Russian Literature,* in which he hailed the beginning

of a new idealism in the works of Turgenev, Goncharov, Dostoyevski, and Tolstoi, and proclaimed Dostoyevski "a prophet unprecedented in history," whom the Russian realist critics were incapable of comprehending:

Some regarded him as a humanitarian preacher on the order of George Sand and Dickens, others as "a cruel talent," something like a literary Torquemada. Both groups stood before the mysterious phenomenon of poetry, the living creation of God, like people with bare hands, without a ladder, before a sheer granite cliff. They did not even suspect whom they were up against. Their subtle aesthetic and moral standards, fragile as glass, break on this primeval boulder. Poor realist critics! [2]

Merezhkovski himself accepted all of Dostoyevski, whose "soul was woven of contrasts, of contradictions, of entangled and unresolvable knots," [3] of divinity and baseness. Dostoyevski had no fear of approaching the extreme limits of doubt, comprehended its ultimate consequences, dared to infringe upon the sanctities of duty and faith. At the same time the critic noticed "the gentle and chaste beauty of his female figures," "his Russian tenderness for children," and "his fanatic, burning compassion for people." "There is no depth of vice where he would lose sight of the charm, the angelic beauty of virtue." [4] The reading of Dostoyevski, according to Merezhkovski, is extremely beneficial morally; it makes one aware of the two worlds of good and evil, arouses the conscience of the indifferent, and reveals the struggle of opposing principles in the depths of the soul.

In this essay Merezhkovski's efforts to interpret Dostoyevski do not go beyond excited questioning and exclamation, touching, it is true, upon the essential qualities of Dostoyevski but giving no explanation of the factors outside the mere personal characteristics of Dostoyevski as a man:

Who then is he himself? Who is he, our tormenter and friend Dostoyevski? An angel of darkness or an angel of light? Where, then, is the
heart of the artist? In the Christian humility of Father Zosima or in
the pride, bordering on madness, of the nihilist Kirilov, in the chastity
of Alyosha or in the sensuality of Stavrogin, in the compassion of the
Idiot or in the Grand Inquisitor's scorn for humanity? Where is he?
Neither here nor there. Or perhaps both here and there! It is terrible
that in a human heart there can exist side by side such abysses of good
and evil, such unbearable contradictions.[5]

Merezhkovski discussed Dostoyevski more fully in a long
article first published, in 1890, under the title "On Dostoyevski's
Crime and Punishment," [6] and reprinted in Merezhkovski's collected works under the title "Dostoyevski." [7]

In 1900 the journal *Mir iskusstva* [The World of Art] began
serial publication of Merezhkovski's long study *L. Tolstoi and
Dostoyevski: Life, Writings and Religion*, which was republished many times.[8] Merezhkovski's other major critical pieces
were *Prophet of the Russian Revolution*,[9] 1906, written for the
twenty-fifth anniversary of Dostoyevski's death, and "Gorki and
Dostoyevski" in the collection *Past and Future*, 1915.[10] Cursory
treatment was also given Dostoyevski in several articles dealing
with other writers in Merezhkovski's *Eternal Companions*[11] and
elsewhere.

The study *L. Tolstoi and Dostoyevski* had a strong influence
on subsequent Russian criticism of the two writers, even in the
early years after the revolution. Merezhkovski contrasted Tolstoi,
the great pantheist and pagan, "seer of the flesh," and Dostoyevski, the great Christian, "seer of the soul." By implication the
book conveyed Merezhkovski's dislike for the sober realism of
Tolstoi and his unqualified acceptance of Dostoyevski, with
whom he associated the messianic role of Russia in the coming
Christian regeneration of mankind. Formerly a Westerner in all

his aspirations and interests, the critic now veered from the European West to justify and defend the Russian version of Christianity as reflected in the writings of Dostoyevski.

Merezhkovski's earlier study entitled "Dostoyevski" is more interesting for our present purposes. It contains in concentrated form the essence of his views on Dostoyevski. Displaying, like his other writings, literary erudition, brilliance, and a lively cleverness in exposition, this study is also marred by Merezhkovski's unconscionable addiction to antithesis, shown in the artificial attempt to mark out poles of opposition, to resolve complex and unique phenomena into their opposites, and to arrange the whole living fabric of Dostoyevski's writings in accordance with the critic's own philosophical scheme. Often his categorical and almost geometrically exact sophistries respecting the contrasts, the rise and fall in Dostoyevski's work, are strained and confusing.

From the very beginning, however, the great stumbling-block to an understanding of the essence of Dostoyevski was that apologetic attitude, that absolute and ecstatic acceptance to the point of self-oblivion, which characterized all Merezhkovski's criticism of Dostoyevski. The Christian ideals embodied in Dostoyevski's heroes corresponded more closely than those of other writers to Merezhkovski's symbolist principles. Of the three giants of the Russian novel—Turgenev, Tolstoi, and Dostoyevski—the critic proclaimed the last "more our own, closer to us." [12] He felt a special reverence for Dostoyevski as the mentor of the human heart to whom the deepest secrets might be confided. The artist's portrayal of the tragic problems and hopeless position of the "downtrodden people" in a society of class inequality did not move Merezhkovski. In Dostoyevski's treatment of the problem of duality, which the critic transferred from the social plane to the abstract psychological plane, he saw limitless possibilities of delving into the labyrinth of this dark world and sharing with the author the poignantly painful pleasure of mute and chilled contemplation of the abysses into which the human conscience falls and from which it again ascends. In studying the world of Dostoyevski, decadent criticism perceived no dividing line between object and subject. Everything was merged into an intimately harmonious revelation and a mutual confession. Merezhkovski wrote:

He lived among us, in our sad, cold city; he was not afraid of the complexities of contemporary life and its unsolvable problems; he did not try to escape our troubles or the taint of our times. He loves us simply, as a friend, as an equal—not in the poetic distance, like Turgenev, and not with the arrogance of a preacher, like Lev Tolstoi. He is ours, in all his thoughts, in all his sufferings. *"He drank with us from a common cup; like us, he was poisoned and great."* Tolstoi is too contemptuous of the "rotten" society of the intelligentsia, feels too deep an aversion for the weaknesses of the erring. He repels and frightens by his scorn and his blunt condemnation of what will still remain dear and holy to the people whatever attacks are made upon it. Dostoyevski is at some moments closer to us than those with whom we live and whom we love, closer than our relatives and friends. He is a comrade in sickness, a partner not only in good but also in evil, and nothing draws people closer together than common failings. He knows our most intimate thoughts, the most criminal desires of our hearts. Often when you read him you are aghast at his omniscience, at his deep penetration into the conscience of another. You are confronted by the secret thoughts which you would hesitate to voice not only to a friend but even to yourself. And when such a man, hearing the confession of our hearts, nevertheless forgives us, when he says "Believe in good, in God, in yourselves," this is more than aesthetic delight in beauty, greater than the haughty sermon of a strange prophet.[13]

Merezhkovski acknowledged that Dostoyevski had neither the harmony and classical proportion of Pushkin and Turgenev nor Tolstoi's elemental force and direct bond with nature, but, on the other hand, he found in Dostoyevski a clot of human sufferings, the heavy surge of life lived with tears in the eyes, the shuddering pulse of human tragedy. To Merezhkovski the greatest gift of all was Dostoyevski's ability to force the reader to live through and suffer, to repeat, the experience of his heroes, so that an indelible trace was left on the heart.

The critic called attention to Dostoyevski's device of juxtaposing, in sharp contrast, the divine and the diabolic, the mystic and the real. To Merezhkovski the sense of mysterious and tragic fate conveyed by means of the endless coincidences and chance events in the plot was linked with the mystic strain in Dostoyevski. In his analysis of other characteristics of the novelist's art—the unity of time in the classical sense and the swiftness of action, the preponderance of the dramatic element over the descriptive, the predominance of psychological description over the depiction of nature, and his role as prophet of the city dwellers—Merezhkovski little by little proselytized in behalf of his own symbolist faith and finally treated Dostoyevski as a full convert:

A great realist, and at the same time a great mystic, Dostoyevski senses the illusoriness of the real. For him life is merely the apparent, like a shroud behind which is hidden the inscrutable, forever concealed from the mind of man. As if on purpose, he wipes out the boundary between dream and reality. . . . In the common, petty details of life there are revealed such depths, such secrets, as we have never suspected.[14]

Once Merezhkovski had turned away from all the concrete social problems and ideological questions of Dostoyevski's time and confined himself to the pure spirit of Dostoyevski, little remained but to perform exercises in theological sophistry. His appeals to the eternal verities of conscience, good and evil, while not devoid of interest, did little to explain the work of art under consideration. Of *Crime and Punishment* he wrote:

The eternal struggle of the Angel and the Demon takes place in our own conscience, and the most terrible thing of all is that we never know

which of them we love more, which one we prefer to win the victory.
The Demon appeals to us not only through pleasures but also through
his deceptive seemliness. We wonder whether he is not a part of the
truth that has not been understood, one of its unrecognized aspects. A
weak, proud heart cannot but respond to the rebellion, disobedience and
freedom of Lucifer. . . .[15]

All three main plot lines which develop parallel in the novel—the
drama of Raskol'nikov, of Sonya and of Dunya—lead to essentially the
same end: to show the mysterious, fateful mixture of good and evil in
life.

Raskol'nikov strives for good through evil, breaks the moral law in
the name of the general good. But does not his sister Dunya do the very
same thing? She sells herself to Luzhin in order to save her brother.
Just as Raskol'nikov sacrifices the life of another out of love for people,
so she, out of love for him, sacrifices her conscience. . . . Raskol'nikov
sees Dunya's mistake clearly, but he does not realize that this is his own
mistake, too, that he has also resolved upon an evil act for a good end.
. . . Sonya Marmeladova is also a martyr. She sells herself to save her
family. Like Raskol'nikov and Dunya, she has "broken the law" and
sinned in the name of love; she too wants to attain good through evil.
. . . Sonya is a criminal but there is also the saint in her, as there is
the martyr in Dunya and the ascetic in Raskol'nikov. . . .[16]

Potentiality of evil and crime is revealed in a pure and saintly girl—
in Dunya; like Sonya, she is prepared to sell herself. In a dissolute,
abandoned man—in Svidrigailov—is revealed the potentiality of kindness and a heroic deed. Here is the same basic motif of the novel—the
eternal mystery of life, the mixture of good and evil. . . .[17]

Dunya, Raskol'nikov, Sonya, Marmeladov, Svidrigailov—how can one
decide what they are, good or evil? What follows from this fatal law of
life, from the inevitable mixture of good and evil? When you know
people as does the author of *Crime and Punishment*, is it possible to
judge them, is it possible to say, "This one is a sinner and that one is
righteous?" Are not crime and holiness blended in the living soul of
man in one living, insoluble mystery? It is impossible to love people
for their righteousness, because no one is righteous except God; in a
pure soul such as Dunya's and in a great self-sacrifice such as Sonya's,
there is a germ of criminality. It is impossible to hate people for their

depravity, because there is no degradation in which the human soul would not preserve a reflection of divine beauty. It is not "measure for measure" nor justice which is the basis of our life, but love for God and mercy.[18]

To Merezhkovski, Dostoyevski was not only the great realist, who sounds the depths of human suffering, madness and vice, but also the great "poet of evangelical love." For the critic every book of Dostoyevski's breathed of love; love was "its fire, its soul and its poetry." [19]

As Merezhkovski himself confessed, however, the explanation of the behavior of Dostoyevski's characters and of the startling contrasts and contradictions in their philosophy was for him an eternal secret, a mystery beyond the power of human mind to decipher, and in his powerlessness the critic turned to prayer:

In every one of us, in the good and the evil alike, in the stupid painter Mikolka, seeking for some cause for which to "suffer," in the debauched Svidrigailov, in the nihilist Raskol'nikov, and in the prostitute Sonya— in everyone somewhere, sometimes far from life, in the very depths of the soul, there is hidden one impulse, one prayer, which justifies mankind before God. This is the prayer of the drunkard Marmeladov: "Thy kingdom come." [20]

In his criticism of Dostoyevski, Merezhkovski's justification of evil, as inherent in man together with good, proceeded from his philosophy of irrationalism and amoralism, which was developed in his youth under the influence of Nietzsche and which was characteristic of the decadents.

LEV SHESTOV (1866–1938)

RELIGIOUS PHILOSOPHER

Lev Shestov, author of *Dostoyevski and Nietzsche: The Philosophy of Tragedy*, 1903,[21] applied Nietzscheism more consistently in his interpretation of Dostoyevski. Like Nietzsche,

Shestov found in Dostoyevski a great mystic who rejected human ethics and morality, and sought the true God, irrational and amoral. In Shestov's treatment Dostoyevski was finally stripped of the content of reality and transferred into the field of purely speculative philosophy. Thus at the end of the nineteenth and beginning of the twentieth century, a time of general confusion and dejection among the Russian intelligentsia, the decadents were often led to extreme forms of mysticism and irrationalism in their attacks on the positivists and the rationalists, and departed farther and farther from objective scholarly study of Dostoyevski.

VASILI VASIL'YEVICH ROZANOV (1856–1919)
RELIGIOUS MYSTIC AND INDEPENDENT CRITIC

Like Merezhkovski and Shestov, Rozanov approached Dostoyevski steeped in philosophical and religious thought, a mystic and a relentless opponent of positivism and rationalism, and, again like his two contemporaries, he produced one of his most brilliant works on the subject of Dostoyevski. Unlike Merezhkovski and Shestov, however, Rozanov avoided interpreting Dostoyevski on the basis of his own preconceived ideas, and his work was therefore not marred as was theirs by dogmatism. In fact, his book *F. M. Dostoyevski's "Legend of the Grand Inquisitor":* *An Essay in Critical Commentary*, 1890,[22] was the first serious attempt at a searching scholarly analysis of Dostoyevski's mind and art. The information which Rozanov's former wife, Apollinaria Suslova, had been able to contribute from the years of her intimate relationship with Dostoyevski was of no little value to the critic.

Like Mikhailovski, but with a completely different approach, Rozanov found clues to an understanding of all Dostoyevski's

writings in *Notes from the Underground,* in which the underground man first voices Dostoyevski's running criticism of the
idea that it is possible, by means of reason, to erect a perfect
edifice of human society designed to make life comfortable for
mankind, to crown its history, and to abolish suffering. In Rozanov's opinion, the underground man, through solitary observation of human nature and criticism of the utopian rationalists, attained a deep understanding of human imperfection as a
law of nature and of history and became convinced that man, by
his very essence, is an irrational, incomprehensible being, endowed in the act of creation with the capacity for suffering and
rejoicing, and for profound emotional experience of his vicissitudes, but whose intellect has not been given the possibility of
understanding and explaining the essence of man. In their reliance on reason, all rational sciences are equally powerless to
unravel the secret of man. The understanding of man can come
only through irrational, mystical penetration into the essence of
things, that is, through religion.

In *Crime and Punishment,* which, Rozanov considered, began
the second and main period of Dostoyevski's writing, the idea
of the absolute, and not the relative, significance of the individual was first developed completely. In the book Dostoyevski
set forth in full detail and with great artistry the irrational nature of man and the illusoriness of all final causes, such as utopian
socialism, anarchism, and the like, to which thousands of need-
less and meaningless sacrifices are made and which inflame hostility among men and class struggle. Irrational processes took
place in Raskol'nikov's mind. He himself was unable to understand their meaning and to control his actions. In committing
murder, Raskol'nikov disregarded the mystic origin and the
nonrational aspect of man, and broke the law that every living
human individual, as an image of God, his creator, is absolute

and inviolable. He tore the mystical, impalpable knot binding him to all other human beings; the holiness faded from the countenance of man and nature; he lost touch with people around him, and life became a genuine hell. Rozanov pointed out that in Dostoyevski's analysis of crime the secret of human nature and the law that man is absolute and not to be trespassed against were also revealed. Behind outward actions, desires and words —all manifestations of the personality which are clear and comprehensible to the individual himself and to others—there is hidden something primary and unknown, and it is this that constitutes the true essence of man. Everything else is merely a distortion of the natural or, in any case, highly imperfect and transitory. Without thinking of the existence of this primary thing in every human being, even the contemptible old money-lender, Raskol'nikov murdered her. And only then came the disclosure of what he had failed to surmise. Thus, only by trespassing against the individual, by breaking the law of the absolute value of man, is it possible to approach an understanding of the irrational, mystical significance of the individual. Yet the state to which Raskol'nikov was brought by his guilty conscience and his final repentance testify to the futility of such an experience and the baneful consequences of yielding to its temptations. The individual is an end in himself and cannot be used as a means of executing the designs of someone else.

Rozanov discusses the "Legend of the Grand Inquisitor" in *The Brothers Karamazov* in connection with the problem of the individual. The critic believed that only in religion is the true significance of the human personality revealed. In law the individual is defined in terms of contractual obligations, property rights and qualifications, and other conventions. Here individuality is a fiction. In political economy the individual completely disappears and is replaced by the concepts of labor force and surplus value. In a word, science overwhelms the individual and, if he has faults and behaves badly, treats him with contempt. The relativity and unsoundness of the historical concepts of the individual are apparent from the fact that "for the Greeks all barbarians were bad, for the Romans all noncitizens, for the Catholics all heretics, for the humanists all obscurantists, and for the people of 1893 all conservatives." [23] Only in religion is every individual treated as the equal of every other individual.

Rozanov differed fundamentally from Merezhkovski's view that good and evil are inseparably united in man, and, in refutation, cited the suffering and repentance that follow every sin committed and every untruth told. Rozanov considered the evil in man to be a perversion of the principle of good, merely evidence that, in the process of being given outward expression, the thought or desire of man is subjected to a distorting influence. Thus suffering itself is explained as a consequence of the discord between the evil done and man's nature, which is good. The design of the Grand Inquisitor for arranging man's life on earth, however, ignores the predominance of the principle of good in man as an image of God and is dictated by historically transient defects and conflicts in human society, because of which the Inquisitor sees man's exercise of freedom as not in accord with his inner weaknesses. The Inquisitor violates the principle of true freedom, which is a condition of harmony between inner impulses and external actions, the latter resulting from the former. Thus Rozanov saw as the core of the "Legend" Dostoyevski's condemnation of attempts to order mankind's life on earth by taking advantage of the weaknesses of man.

Rozanov's reflections on the "Legend" as a criticism of Roman Catholicism took the form of a passionate defense of Russian Orthodoxy, which had preserved the evangelical spirit of faith long since lost by the West. He considered the general and enduring feature of Catholicism to be the striving toward universalism, and the striving toward individualism to be peculiar to Protestantism, and explained the difference as a result of racial difference between the Roman, with his all-embracing social and political interests, and the introspective German: "Just as Catholicism is the Roman concept of Christianity, and Protestantism the German, so Orthodoxy is the Slavic concept." [24]

Although the intention of the "Legend" was to censure the Catholic ideal—a "correction" of Christ's work, a debasement of his teaching in order to make it understandable to man, an accommodation of the divine to the human—Dostoyevski himself, Rozanov was constrained to point out, harbored germs of Catholicism, concealed in the strictures of the Grand Inquisitor and Ivan Karamazov on the imperfections in the ordering of human life and in the teaching of Christ.

The passages in which Rozanov defined Dostoyevski's place in Russian literature and compared him with other writers are highly original and interesting. Far from continuing the Gogol tradition, Dostoyevski and all subsequent Russian writers of the nineteenth century had rejected Gogol's reliance on external forms which had neither substance nor soul behind them. Rozanov contrasted Tolstoi, depicter of life in its definite, discrete, fixed, and final forms, with Dostoyevski, analyst of all the indeterminate in life, depicter of what is coming to birth and what is disintegrating. Thus Dostoyevski's heroes are disturbed and seeking, destroying or creating, and the human soul is analyzed in terms of its various, changing states of suffering—the actual pattern of thought in process rather than the passive contemplation of Tolstoi.

Despite his subtle and felicitous insights, however, Rozanov's criticism was, on the whole, so abstract and speculative in nature that it contributed little to an understanding of the concrete so-

cial, cultural, and historical factors which influenced Dostoyevski's development and which explained his personality and writing.

YULI ISAYEVICH AIKHENVAL'D (1872–1928)
IMPRESSIONIST

Akim L'vovich Volynski (pseudonym of A. L. Flekser; 1863–
1926), one of the early "moderns" and "decadents," and Yuli
Isayevich Aikhenval'd continued the critical principles of symbolism and impressionism through the first decade of the twentieth century. In his book *F. M. Dostoyevski: Critical Articles* [25]
Volynski attacked the positivism and utilitarianism of the radical critics of the nineteenth century and eliminated social and
political questions as irrelevant to the core of Dostoyevski's art.

Volynski's impressionism was carried even further by Aikhenval'd, who, decrying Belinski's views, maintained that an artist
must be free of any social function. As the deputy of God on
earth, the artist continues God's work, embodying in art His
fundamental design. Creation was not completed, and the poet,
the high priest of art, is entrusted with the great mission of carrying it further, of developing the preliminary sketches of the
deity, of filling in the outlines of nature. The creative act, like
a sacrament, is performed in the soul of the artist himself, independent of history, outside time and space. The art of fiction
is by its very essence irrational. Attempts to consider a writer in
relation to his historical and literary milieu were, therefore, in
Aikhenval'd's opinion, fruitless and meaningless. For him there
were no literary schools nor trends, just as society and environment do not exist for the creative individual. Above all else
there was the personality of the writer, unique, never to be repeated, and it was that personality which stamped every work

of true art. The tasks of the critic lay in self-contained aesthetic contemplation, in closed and intimate communion with the work of art.[26]

These are the critical principles underlying Aikhenval'd's article "Dostoyevski," later retitled "The Night of Russian Literature," [27] which is brilliant in its insights but rather abstract. Aikhenval'd considered Dostoyevski the greatest expression of the spirit of the age, a genius voicing the unceasing anxiety, confusion and spiritual chaos in the man of the period, permeated by consciousness of the guilt of all mankind. In Dostoyevski's books the critic saw opening up, one after another, "Dantean circles of moral lacerations and anguish." Dostoyevski's characters, like mankind in actuality, are incurably ill:

> The novels of Dostoyevski present a spectacle which has no equal in all world literature. They are filled to such a degree with suffering and ailment that one is somehow ashamed to apply to them a purely aesthetic criterion, although he is a great artist, a rare master of portrayal, although he combines nervous bursts of writing with a feeling of moderation and an astonishing power of circumspection, so that he artistically and skillfully weaves together all the delicate loops of his broken narrative, never becomes confused himself, forgets nothing, and confidently makes all the numerous ends meet. He is passionate, but he is also clever. He writes as if he would not allow his readers to think for a moment that he is composing, that he is inventing. This is because in his writing, much more than in that of any other writer, all the characters and scenes represent merely an objectification, a personification of his own inner state.
>
> All this is psychology, his own psychology in the characters. All this is a sick disclosure of his unprecedented soul. A brother of the brothers Karamazov, a co-murderer with his murderers, he merely revealed himself personally, his sun and his night, his Madonna and his Sodom, in the involved, complicated, fantastic texture of his work.[28]

Aikhenval'd felt in every book of Dostoyevski the "disturbances of his own heart," and heard the "echoes of all human dramas." "All his writings present only a panorama of his soul, express its dark and gloomy essence in people and events," [29] in the "living knot of human hearts, the tangle of souls which he creates." [30]

Aikhenval'd called attention to Dostoyevski's characteristic devices of "encounters and conflicts," "conversations and disagreements"; Dostoyevski is the psychologist not of the crowd, but of the individual, for it is not mankind that serves his purposes, but man.

Independent in his opinions, which were in general the very antithesis of Mikhailovski's positivism, Aikhenval'd was nevertheless apparently influenced by Mikhailovski's argument in "A Cruel Talent." For Aikhenval'd, too, Dostoyevski's pictures of suffering and grief made his books frightful. Pushing to the utmost extreme his portrayal of the contradictions of life, focusing on the "intolerable and lamentable," where "all the crags and abysses of existence" are sharply exposed, where nothing is softened and nothing is smoothed over, where every baseness is fearlessly turned inside out, Dostoyevski became in Aikhenval'd's eyes "a demon writer," a symptom of "the night of Russian literature, full of oppressive phantoms and confused apparitions." "The night enveloped Dostoyevski," concluded the critic: "Dostoyevski poisons everything, he ruins everything around him, and if there is so little nature around him, so little greenery, then it is because it fades and wastes away from his accursed approach." [31] Aikhenval'd compared Dostoyevski to Pushkin's upas tree, which not only kills others with its poison but itself languishes from it in solitude, and he magnified the cruelty in Dostoyevski to far greater proportions than had Mikhailovski:

Dostoyevski, scourging us with the fiery serpents of his evil gift, himself suffers unbearable torture from his pageants, himself ascends the pyre of his victims. Tormentor and martyr, the Ivan Grozny of Russian literature, he tortures us with the savage torture of his words and then, like Ivan Grozny, this human upas tree murmurs and prays, and calls on Christ. And Christ comes to this madman and sage, this holy fool, and then he weeps bloody tears and rapturously lacerates himself with his chains, with his prison fetters which people put on him and which he has never been able to cast off his tormented soul.[32]

In the pale, emaciated face of Dostoyevski's portrait, in which he saw morbid passions lurking in the features, and in the fiery eyes, full of agony and cruelty, Aikhenval'd found confirmation of his surmise that the tragedy of the Grand Inquisitor's fateful meeting with Christ occurred in the soul of the writer himself, that God and the Devil struggled for the soul of Dostoyevski himself. Like Merezhkovski, Aikhenval'd asserted that good and evil were inseparably joined in Dostoyevski, and in this union he saw the key to that trait of fanatically cruel love of suffering for its own sake which he ascribed to Dostoyevski. An apostle of the sensual delight of suffering, eagerly taking to himself "the cup of Gethsemane, writhing with pain," the embodiment of "the inquisitorial principle in the world," "the grand inquisitor of his own soul and those of others," "a witness of darkness," "a fiery Gehenna, aflame with devils," [33] "a martyr to the black sickness" [34]—such was Dostoyevski in Aikhenval'd's interpretation.

Aikhenval'd's approach to the problem of the double in Dostoyevski was equally unscholarly and injudicious; to him the problem was simply that of sanctity and Sodom in the conscience of the author, reflecting the eternal irrational, "wild, lawless, and meaningless" elements of life. The inclination toward crime, hidden in everyone from time immemorial, Aikhenval'd dismissed as a result of "evil spells," "the bewitchment of crime." [35] The temptation of crime is so strong in every man that its commission depends on the chances of encountering something on which we may vent our criminal impulses: "It is not that we kill accidentally; it is accidental that we do not kill." [36] In this respect completely under the influence of Nietzsche—who had bowed to Dostoyevski for his depiction of the battle in the human soul between the defiance and obedience of which man is created and which in their struggle produce in every man both a Prometheus and a criminal—Aikhenval'd saw the ground prepared for crime in the very self-will of Dostoyevski's heroes and their ability to protest.

Unable to discover objective laws for Dostoyevski's writings, Aikhenval'd found no more convincing explanation of the novelist than his inner visions of the abyss. These visions of conflicts, doubts, and horror, of a Dantean hell, came to him in the moments when he awaited execution, then in the prison camp and during the sickness and death of his wife and child, as well as in the early years of his joyless childhood behind a hospital fence and in government school. His turning toward God, as well as his search for chaste, harmonious beauty, Aikhenval'd explained as a need to find escape for a soul exhausted by its own disharmony. The same need, according to Aikhenval'd, explained the pull upon Dostoyevski—as he himself expressed it in his Pushkin speech—which was exerted by Pushkin's sunny, human, all-embracing talent and by Tat'yana, that purest embodiment of the Russian responsiveness to all mankind.

Aikhenval'd could not synthesize Dostoyevski; for him, the writer's soul, embittered by the suffering and crime he had seen in the world, remained unintegrated and unhealed, and his works were "nervous and shattered." At one moment of brilliant clarity Aikhenval'd seemed to be on the verge of grasping the laws that governed the art of the "evil genius" when he wrote that Dostoyevski could not have "created works other than those which lie before us." [37] But at once the critic slipped back to his beaten path of abstract explanation in terms of the eternal laws of humankind, and Dostoyevski's genius was again enshrouded in mystery, which Aikhenval'd left to future generations to solve.

Nevertheless, he acknowledged Dostoyevski's enormous influence on Russian literature, saw his "great shadow" cast "over the whole expanse of Russian literature":

With heavy step, with pale countenance and fiery gaze, this great prisoner, clanging his chains, passed through our literature, and to this day it has been unable to come to its senses and recover from his frenzied passage. He set some still undeciphered signals on the summits of Russian consciousness, he pronounced some prophetic and ill-boding words with his burning lips, and we now puzzle them out without him. And he remains an oppressive mystery to us, pain personified, the black sun of suffering. The deep mysteries of humankind were known to him, and he is no chance phenomenon or frightful short-lived mirage, but a persistent and grievous category of the soul, so that every soul must undergo the sickness that is Dostoyevski and, if possible, overcome it. This is a hard ordeal, for he himself was like a living Divine Comedy; and in it there is no Hell more powerful or more terrible.[38]

In this concluding definition of Dostoyevski's world as a hell and in his confessed inability to "puzzle out" its meaning, Aikhenval'd demonstrated the blind alley in which the decadent critics found themselves early in the twentieth century.

VYACHESLAV IVANOVICH IVANOV (1866–1949)

AN APPROACH TO MODERN SCHOLARSHIP

Meanwhile, however, the dean of the "second generation" of symbolists, the poet-scholar V. I. Ivanov, was developing a new and original method for the study of Dostoyevski. The publication in 1911 of his "Dostoyevski and the Tragedy-Novel" [39] laid the foundation for a truly scholarly interpretation of Dostoyevski. Brilliant and erudite, gifted as poet, historian, philologist,

philosopher, professor, and critic, Ivanov, for several years
after the 1905 revolution, was the leading theorist and poet
of the St. Petersburg symbolists, who assembled at his home
for weekly literary discussions and readings—the celebrated
"Ivanov Wednesdays." In opposition to the theories of the early
decadents and symbolists, as well as the individualism of Nietzsche, which he had first embraced and then repudiated under the
tutelage of Solov'yov, Ivanov expounded a new symbolism based
on the principles of *sobornost'* ("togetherness").[40] He argued
that individualism must be overcome by an organic fusion of the
individual with the collective and that the principle of art for
art's sake must be discarded in favor of theurgic art. The true
poet of the future would be not a writer of esoteric visions for
the few, but a teacher, the voice of the people. For his mythopoeic
art—a signification of a higher reality, a cosmic reality, that of
the life of the spirit of humanity—the new symbolism was to be
a preparation. Ivanov regarded Dostoyevski as the great creator of
myths in the present period. As model for the future syncretic
religious art, Ivanov proposed medieval art, not of the West but
of Byzantium, more closely related to the Slavic world and
linking it with Hellenism. The focus of this art of the future age
of "organic culture," as well as the focus of religious and social
life, was to be the synthetic art of the theater, in which there
would be no passive spectators but in which all would participate.

    In "Dostoyevski and the Tragedy-Novel" Ivanov made the first
significant attempt in Russian criticism to deduce the ideas and
world-view of Dostoyevski by the method of beginning with an
analysis of the formal structure of the novels and then proceeding to an analysis of the ideological content. In the first part of
the study, entitled "The Principle of Form," Ivanov dealt with
the technique of Dostoyevski's novels against a background of

the theory of classical and world tragedy. He regarded the entire conception, as well as the plot development, of Dostoyevski's novels as essentially that of dramatic tragedy. One of Ivanov's most brilliant insights was the discovery that, in his architectonics of tragedy, Dostoyevski applied to the novel the method of contrapuntal development of the theme in music, and that in the novels a simultaneous movement of several independent worlds, or voices of the characters, forms one harmonious whole. Ivanov's idea of the polyphony of Dostoyevski's novels, incidental in his analysis and not fully elaborated, nevertheless was a fresh contribution and an aid to future scholars. In part, Ivanov anticipated the thesis of M. M. Bakhtin, who, in his book of 1929, *Problems of Dostoyevski's Writing* (to be discussed later), used the term "polyphonic novel" for the form which Dostoyevski originated.

According to Ivanov, all the components of the Dostoyevski novel were grouped about one main event, around which, as around a planetary body, all the action moved toward catastrophe:

It is as if we look at tragedy through a magnifying glass and see repeated in its molecular structure the stamp of the same tragic principle by which the entire organism is governed. Every cellule of this tissue is a small tragedy in itself; just as the whole is catastrophic, each unit is a catastrophe in miniature. Hence that peculiar law of epic rhythm in Dostoyevski which turns his writings into a system of strained muscles and taut nerves and makes them so exhausting and at the same time so powerful in their effect on us.[41]

Although the "cruel talent," in Ivanov's opinion, allowed the reader no enjoyment, he could not but go through the entire hell of the novel in order finally, through pity and fear, to attain catharsis in the rebirth which the characters experience. The ending of a Dostoyevski novel is designed to leave lucidity in the

mind of the reader after the catastrophe and to suggest definitely
the philosophical import. This final idea is implicit in the development of the action even before the occurrence of the main
event of the tragedy. And the real Dostoyevski, that is, the central
interest in the novel, begins at the point where, through catharsis,
the characters and the reader renounce the ideas that were the
ground, the premises, for catastrophe. Thus the critic likened
Dostoyevski's tragedy-novel to a theorem-novel, in which, from
the first propositions of its syllogism, the conclusion follows.

Ivanov found a certain monotony in Dostoyevski's devices,
which seemed to result from "a direct transfer of the technique
of the stage to fictional narrative":

the artificial bringing together of persons and circumstances in the
same place and at the same time; the predetermined clash between
them; the introduction of dialogue which is less characteristic of reality
than fitting for the stage; the depiction of psychological development
in the same manner, by means of endless catastrophic shocks, violent
and frenzied outbursts, and revelations of people placed in circumstances that, though theatrically effective, are implausible in the action
itself; the use of pure *coups de théâtre* in order to round off individual
scenes as the culmination of the action; and the anticipation of the truly
catastrophic before it has yet taken shape, when it is still too soon for
it to break, in scenes of brawl and uproar that are caricatures of catastrophe.[42]

Ivanov saw three causes of the central catastrophic action, or
catastrophe of crime, in Dostoyevski: the metaphysical antinomy
of the individual will (God and the devil struggling in the hearts
of men); psychological pragmatism (the development of pe-
ripheral states of consciousness from the chain of emotional
experiences—that surface ruffling of the elemental surges that
finally bring a man to temporary insanity and to crime); and the
pragmatism of external events (living conditions and so forth,
producing the logic of the crime). Ivanov also pointed out that

this threefold explanation of human behavior in the novels of Dostoyevski was applicable to society and that the will of the individual was joined with the collective "will of whole legions of the God-fighting host." [43]

The thematic development of the plot, the psychological motivation, the depiction of the characters, and the style of the language are all functionally dependent on the occurrence of the main catastrophic event. The enormous role attributed to crime in the life of man gives an excessively criminological tone to the novels and accounts for the nervous excitability of Dostoyevski's characters and the immoderate emphasis of the emotional element at the expense of objective narration. The fatal outcome of events makes it necessary to introduce legal protocol, reports, investigations, and the like, which contribute to the illusion of authentic reality and obscure the fact that the world depicted is one of Dostoyevski's imagination. For the richness and grandeur of his invention and for his talent in tempering invention for the reader by adapting it to the rhythm and outlines of reality, Ivanov called Dostoyevski the Russian Shakespeare.

The critic commented also on the extraordinary exactness and power with which Dostoyevski handled the language of his characters, the speech of ordinary city folk primed to revolutionize the conventional, stiff, polished, affected language of the literary salons.

Ivanov compared Dostoyevski to an explorer and hunter in the darkness of the soul who had no need of the general lighting of the material world which was indispensable to Tolstoi:

Dostoyevski is like Rembrandt, all in the dark shadows that gather in the corners of sealed dungeons [or] all in the bright illumination of deliberately contrived light. . . . His lighting and the color tones of his light, as in Rembrandt, are somber. Thus he moves with a torch through the labyrinth, exploring the vaults of the spirit, passing in the light of his torch hundreds of faces that flicker in the flickering flame, and gazing into their eyes with his grave, denuding, penetrating gaze.[44]

In the second part of his study, entitled "The Premise of His World-View," Ivanov explained his opinion that Dostoyevski was a philosophical realist. The basis of his realism was not cognition as such, which presupposes the existence of an object of cognition apart from the subject, the thinking agent. The critic considered Dostoyevski's realism to be based on "insight," which lies not so much in the cognitive sphere as in that of the instinctively creative principle of life, which exercises supremacy over the rational principle.

In defining Dostoyevski's realism as consisting mainly in his penetration into the ego of another, the emotional experiencing of this other ego as a fully valid, independent, and original world, Ivanov came close to Bakhtin's definition of the polyphony of Dostoyevski's novels, in which each character is an independent entity, a separate world independent of the will of the author, with its own separate logic and cogency. Ivanov, however, stopped midway and turned to philosophical argumentation to the effect that God is postulated in the open penetration into the world of another ego, as "a reality, more real than all these absolutely real beings, to each of whom he said with all his will and with all his conviction, 'Thou art.' " [45]

Ivanov regarded this penetration into the ego of another as a great act of love and the ultimate attempt to overcome the element of individualism; this principle of Dostoyevski's world-view derived from his belief that every man shared in the guilt of all, and for everything, a belief which, in the critic's opinion, could have its basis only in mystical reality.

The catastrophic nature of Dostoyevski's writings was also to be explained by his own spiritual life. Resorting to the biographical method at this point, Ivanov maintained that during the moments when Dostoyevski stood at the scaffold awaiting execution, on the border between life and death, between the eternal and the temporal, the inner man was born in him. His personality was split into two, one part empirical and external, opposed to the other, which was internal and metaphysical, one with all mankind. The intricacy of his fiction technique reflects the labyrinthine and vacillating outer personality; but the loftier metaphysical plane, that of the clear vision of the inner man, is no longer marked by complexity but by utter simplicity, for it is here that Dostoyevski makes the supreme decision—whether to exist in God or to exist in nonexistence. This is the realm of supreme tragedy in his writings, the expression "of the heights or depths of the tragedy in the ultimate self-determination of man." [46]

Thus, resting his argument on Dostoyevski's universalization of guilt, Ivanov removed the tragic from the bounds of art to the sphere of the purely metaphysical.

Despite the nature of his conclusions, in his methodology of combining formalistic, philosophical, and biographical analysis, Vyacheslav Ivanov was a pioneer of modern Dostoyevski scholarship.

. 3 .

THE EARLY MARXIST CRITICS

During the last decade of the nineteenth century the swift rise of the Marxist movement as a political force among the intelligentsia and the working class was accompanied by a much slower growth of influence in the literary field. The Marxist journals of the period were devoted to polemics against the *narodnik* social program, almost to the exclusion of questions concerning the application of Marxist doctrine to the criticism of belles-lettres.

YEVGENI ANDREYEVICH SOLOV'YOV (1866–1905)

One of the first to essay the method of "economic materialism" in the analysis of literature and to trace the development of Russian literature on the basis of the class origin of its writers was Yevgeni Andreyevich Solov'yov, who wrote under the pseudonym Andreyevich. His approach was, however, by no means consistent, for a large residue of traditional *narodnik* ideology remains in his work. In his book *F. Dostoyevski: His Life and Literary Activity*, first published in 1891 and reprinted many times,[1] Solov'yov endeavored to explain many of the characteristics of Dostoyevski's art as a result of his social position, that of a literary proletarian, which sharply differentiated him from well-to-do writers of the nobility, such as Tolstoi, Turgenev, and Goncharov. They wrote solely from the urge to create; Dostoyevski, hard pressed by poverty and debts, wrote also from economic necessity. Not for him was the luxury of putting the finishing touches to his writings; he worked in a feverish hurry for the sake of money:

For this reason, with very few exceptions, nothing in Dostoyevski has been worked out to the end or allowed to season. Sometimes an entire hundred pages produce the impression of mere verbiage, and only suddenly, at the end, does genius, overcoming fatigue, appear in all its power, just as lightning erupts from the clouds and lights the whole scene with a fantastic, wonderful flash. Usually, however, there are thousands of unnecessary details, dozens of extraneous complications heaped one upon another, frequent shifts in theme, sudden appearances of new heroes and heroines. All this in a hurry, hastily, by fits and starts, with straining and creative crises, with lightning flashes of genius and a despondent grinding out of words. But it could not have been otherwise. Dostoyevski could not accumulate money and often took advance payment not on a novel but on a blank sheet of paper, signing a contract in which "the swindler publishers" protected their own interests with various forfeits for breach of contract on his part. Open Dostoyevski's correspondence and you will find one and the same motif, "Money, money, money." And the man who feels and thinks to the slightest extent will understand what tragedy was taking place in the soul of the great writer who had to prepare a certain number of pages without fail within a given period of time. . . .[2]

Dostoyevski's life is a tragedy-filled struggle of genius with the market.[3]

Solov'yov mentioned the unevenness, quick temper, irritability, nervousness, and capriciousness of Dostoyevski's writing. His approach to his theme was an assault; he described the most complex characters with one sweep. Detailed description was not his forte, but he was a master of psychological analysis. He lived and suffered with his characters. He was all nerves, torment and suffering, passion and seething, love and hate, curse and blessing. "Dostoyevski is the greatest of psychopathologists." [4] In explanation the critic cited the fact that Dostoyevski was a *raznochinets*, from the class of government employees, a nervous son of the city and the educated proletariat; the psychopathic traits of Dostoyevski's heroes and their hysteria were likewise linked with their environment, also the world of petty officialdom, the intelligentsia and the city proletariat.

Accepting Dostoyevski's own words about himself and his contemporaries as writers, "We have all emerged from under Gogol's *Overcoat*," and regarding Gogol's story as a protest against the social order, Solov'yov found at the core of Dostoyevski's work—both in the period before his term of penal servitude, when he concentrated on the depiction of human suffering and injury, and in the period after imprisonment, when he stressed the "self-will" of man—a plea for the rights of the oppressed, in keeping with the general philanthropic tendencies of the time. Driven underground by injured dignity, Dostoyevski's characters emerge in seizures of anger and despair, to take vengeance on other people and themselves:

Here in Dostoyevski is the very deep psychology of the contemporary proletarian, yearning toward life and ruthlessly pushed back from it, sometimes by the prerogatives of the nobility, sometimes by the shameless arrogance of the powerful, sometimes by something preterhuman which takes on the dimensions of fate.[5]

The cardinal question of whether man is destined for freedom or slavery inspired all his writing:

He understood that you cannot do away with man's freedom, that there is nothing, in the last analysis, before which it will bow down. For the sake of his freedom, the individual is capable of going against prudence and advantage, and even against God himself. To assert his freedom, his self-will, even in the wildest and most reckless form, is a necessity, one of the deepest necessities of man, even though, as in Raskol'nikov and Svidrigailov, it be through murder or through blasphemy. But then, in his hypostatization, the individual encounters God, the idea of the Deity. And then, too, Dostoyevski is appalled at the solitude of man and is again ready to put him under the yoke, which he has only just thrown off, of conscience, suffering, faith—in a word, of everything which has its real sanction in God. Therefore, the personality of man, striving for un-

bounded freedom, feels that this is its great obstacle, the main stumbling
block to its desires. For this reason religious questions are always in
the foreground. Everything revolves around them, and for Dostoyevski
they are, of course, in the center of the stormy movement of the 1860s
and 1870s.[6]

Solov'yov adumbrated the theses of several Soviet scholars when
he wrote of Dostoyevski's philosophical duality: "He could not
reconcile himself to the 'horror' of freedom and faith, although
to the end he was equally unable to escape their fascination." [7]

As evidence that Dostoyevski's views in respect to the Russian
people were akin to those of the Slavophiles, the critic cited
Dostoyevski's speech at the dedication of the Pushkin monument and his idea of the people as the God-bearer, and likened
his mystic populism to that of the Slavophile theorists Khomyakov, Konstantin and Ivan Aksakov, and N. Ya. Danilevski. The
critic found sympathy for the people developed to the point of
zealotry in Dostoyevski's early activities and in his pronouncements against serfdom as the most loathsome phenomenon in
Russian life. Only later, frightened at the anarchism of freedom,
did he begin to preach suffering and coercive measures although
he hated such punishment and shuddered at it. He called upon
the proud, egotistical unbeliever of the intelligentsia to humble
himself and throw in his lot with the people, who alone, despite
their lowliness and corruption, preserved in their souls the inner,
lofty truth. Apart from the people there is no worthy work nor
a truly righteous life. Raskol'nikov, the educated man who is
alienated from the people, Dostoyevski condemns to prison, so
that there his heart may finally be cleansed of conceit, pride and
imperious self-will.

On the basis of Dostoyevski's contention that in the West science, the acknowledgment of historical necessity, and the judicial
prevail, while in Russia the belief in love, which will destroy

all barriers and establish a new life without "the economic contradictions" of capitalism, reigns, Solov'yov claimed Dostoyevski for the *narodnik* camp:

Dostoyevski is first and foremost a *narodnik* because, of all the facts of
Russian life, he considered the plain folk the most important, the greatest. It is a force destined to transform everything and to solve all our
problems with one great principle, achieved through much suffering—
love.[8]

Thus, after beginning with a "sociological" interpretation of
Dostoyevski from the Marxist point of view, Solov'yov shifted his
position and concluded with encomiums to the writer as a
narodnik.

In 1891 Solov'yov as a literary critic was still on the border
between *narodnichestvo* and Marxism.

In the course of the 1890s the Marxists gained ascendancy
over the *narodnik* faction, which, at the beginning of the decade,
had rallied from the defeat of the 1880s and had vigorously
opposed Marxism in its journal *Russkoye bogatstvo* [Russian
Wealth], edited by Mikhailovski. Partly in reply to his articles,
in which he castigated the Marxists for breaking with the traditional Russian program of social reform through an alliance
between the intelligentsia and peasantry, and accused them of
making common cause with capitalism, the Marxist theorists
published a barrage of books attacking the sociological and
economic premises of *narodnichestvo* and setting forth the doctrine of historical materialism as it pertained to Russia. In 1894
P. B. Struve's *Critical Notes on the Economic Development of
Russia* [*Kriticheskiye zametki k voprosu ob ekonomicheskom
razvitii Rossii*] appeared. The book by G. Bel'tov (pseudonym
of G. V. Plekhanov), *On the Question of the Development of
the Monistic View of History* [*K voprosu o razvitii monisti-*

cheskovo vzglyada na istoriyu], was published in 1895 with the authorization of the censor and became the gospel of the radicals of the time. *The Development of Capitalism in Russia* [*Razvitiye kapitalizma v Rossii*] by Vladimir Il'in (V. I. Lenin) appeared in 1899. Karl Marx's *Das Kapital*, first published in Russian translation in 1872, came out in several new editions during the 1890s. From 1897 to 1901 the Marxists had their own literary journal or, rather, series of journals, one after another being banned by the censor. The wave of strikes in Russian industry, fostered by propaganda and organizational work of the Marxists, strengthened their cause and commanded general attention to their program. By the beginning of the twentieth century, Marxism, both as a revolutionary and literary movement, had a strong grip on young Russian radicals.

GEORGI VALENTINOVICH PLEKHANOV (1856–1918)

The father of Russian Marxism and the greatest theorist of its application to art was G. V. Plekhanov, who perhaps contributed more than any other theorist to the development of "scientific" Marxist aesthetics. Possessing a sharp encyclopedic mind, extraordinary erudition and aesthetic taste, a brilliant prose style, and humor, he quickly became the leading literary critic and publicist in Marxist circles and won a reputation as "the omniscient George Plekhanov." A *narodnik* in his youth, he soon became disillusioned and turned to Marxism. In 1883 he was one of the founders of the Marxist "Liberation of Labor" group.

On the basis of the Marxist doctrine that existence determines consciousness and that social relationships arise from the mode of material production, Plekhanov attempted to lay a solid scientific foundation for the study of literature as a reflection of the life of society. Seeking the key to the laws of art in the laws of the historical development of society as formulated by Marx and Engels, he studied the economic factors on which attitudes and opinions depend and investigated the question of which art forms correspond to a given stage of social development. Instead of abstract criteria for the interpretation and judgment of artistic phenomena, instead of a normative aesthetics, Plekhanov called for a sociological analysis of the content and devices of art as historically determined. Plekhanov's own thought was rigorously held within the framework of the Marxist dogma of productive forces and relationships, division into classes, the economic structure of society and the superstructure, political organization and psychology of social groups, and class ideology as the crux of social psychology. In the final analysis, everything boiled down to the reflection of social existence in the consciousness of the artist.

Furthermore, in Plekhanov the practice of literary criticism was inseparable from his political convictions and the revolutionary movement. His evaluation of contemporary and recent Russian writers tended to rest on their attitude toward the development of capitalism and the class struggle in Russia, which was, in Plekhanov's opinion, a historical necessity in the transition to socialism. Thus, despite his admiration for the radical publicists of the nineteenth century, he criticized Belinski and Chernyshevski for failure to share his views. Belinski was taken to task for his romantic dreams and the subjectivity of his belief in the power of truth without regard for the actual historical process, for the abstractness of his ideals and his inability to see that objective conditions necessitated the transition of the bourgeois organization of society into the socialist. Chernyshevski was criticized as an "enlightener" who believed in the power of individual initiative and ideas, who had a utopian faith in the efficacy of the heroic deeds of progressive people. Plekhanov, on the other hand, pinned his hopes not on the initiative of the hand-

ful of enlightened intelligentsia but on the Europeanization of
Russia, the consolidation of the working class, and a mass struggle of the latter with the oppressing classes.

Plekhanov's definition of the social role of art in *The Proletarian Movement and Bourgeois Art*, 1905,[9] served as a weapon
against the idealist and impressionist critics, such as Merezhkovski and Aikhenval'd, both before the revolution and afterwards,
when efforts were made to eradicate all vestiges of their influence.
In fact, despite Soviet repudiation of much of his thought, Plekhanov supplied the theoretical basis for many stock ideas in
postrevolutionary literary criticism.

Although Plekhanov wrote extensive individual studies of innumerable other Russian writers, he devoted no special work to
Dostoyevski, who, in all his attitudes and psychology, could not
but arouse antipathy in the Marxist critic. Aksel'rod, who knew
Plekhanov intimately, states flatly in her memoirs: "Of Russian
writers, his favorites were Pushkin, Gogol, Tolstoi, and Uspenski.
He clearly disliked Dostoyevski." [10]

Plekhanov did, however, make a few incidental comments on
Dostoyevski, particularly in *The Russian Worker in the Revolutionary Movement*, in which he refers to *The Brothers Karamazov*
and *The Devils* to point up the problems of morality in the crucial years of transition. Speaking of the mental processes by
which a workman fresh from his patriarchal village arrives at
antisocial views in the prevailing atmosphere of social change,
Plekhanov indicates his disapproval of Dostoyevski's treatment
of sociopsychological problems. "I knew a young factory
worker," Plekhanov says,

a perfectly decent fellow as long as he was untouched by revolutionary
propaganda. As soon as he heard the socialist outcries against exploit-
ers, he turned to mischief and found excuses for cheating people belonging to the upper classes. "So what? They've been robbing us," he

replied when his fellow workers tried to shame him. Had the late Dostoyevski known of this case, he certainly would not have failed to use it
to prick the revolutionaries—either in *The Brothers Karamazov*, where
he would have shown this young fellow next to Smerdyakov, that victim
of "educated" freethinking, or in *The Devils*. . . . Curiously enough,
the man's friends, who had probably never read Dostoyevski, nick-
named the thieving young fellow "The Devil." But they did not blame
the intelligentsia in general, or socialist propaganda in particular, for
his exploits. They [simply] tried, by their influence, to put the finishing
touches, so to speak, on the moral personality of this young man, and
to teach him to fight the upper classes not as a cheat and a thief but as
a revolutionary agitator.[11]

Lenin, too, who expressed his admiration for Tolstoi in many
articles, joined with Plekhanov in the conspiracy of silence as to
Dostoyevski. Lenin once replied angrily when asked a question
about Dostoyevski: "I have no time free for such trash." [12] A few
other remarks show the same spleen. He once censured a writer as
"an ultra-bad imitation of the ultra-bad Dostoyevski" and
pounced upon writers who tried "to paint horrors, to frighten
their own and the reader's imagination, to beat themselves and
him 'to a pulp.' " [13]

During the period of reaction following the failure of the 1905
revolution, a strong revulsion against Marxist doctrine and all
revolutionary activity was evident in literature. Disenchanted
symbolists, impressionists, and other decadents clutched at
Dostoyevski as at a strong remedy. Preaching the futility of
efforts at social reform, they sought quietude in religious mysticism, and in this vein wrote many of the studies of Dostoyevski
which were discussed earlier. Another more militant group of the
intelligentsia, repudiating their former allegiance to various
revolutionary programs, in 1909 published a book serving as
manifesto—*Landmarks* [*Vekhi*], a collection of essays by seven
authors—in which they characterized the whole Russian intel-

ligentsia as deceived by the illusions of *narodnichestvo* and Marxism, as irreligious, unphilosophical, inept in politics, and working against the interests of the nation. This group, too, had recourse to Dostoyevski, alluding to his treatment of the revolutionaries in *The Devils:* "The legion of devils has entered into the gigantic body of Russia and shakes it convulsively, tortures and cripples it." [14]

For Marxists also, in their attempt to stem such retrograde tendencies in literature, Dostoyevski in a sense became a cynosure of critical attention.

V. V. VERESAYEV (PSEUDONYM OF VIKENTI VIKENT'YEVICH SMIDOVICH; 1867–1945)

V. V. Veresayev, who was by no means fully committed to Marxist doctrine but who came under its strong influence in the 1890s and early 1900s, joined in the effort to revive flagging spirits and overcome the general aversion for civic activity. In his study "Man under a Curse," [15] first published in 1910 and later incorporated in his book *Living Life*,[16] in which he discussed Tolstoi and Dostoyevski, he condemned Dostoyevski as a writer preoccupied with sick and lonely people and blind to the beauties of nature. According to Veresayev, Dostoyevski's characters are consumed by an idea, and their life is martyrdom and zealotry in the cause of the devil. They live a phantom life, of a dull yellow, ghastly color, not the life of the living. In Dostoyevski man is under a curse, he lives by logic, his instincts are dormant, he is blind to nature, everything alive passes him by, his soul is incapable of life. For antidote, Veresayev turned to Tolstoi, the lover of life, the very antithesis of Dostoyevski.

Veresayev's criticism of Dostoyevski was by no means Marxist in the full sense of the word, even by the criteria of the time, inasmuch as it omitted sociological analysis of the genesis of his writing. Nevertheless, his views on Dostoyevski coincided with those of Marxist critics, in that both deprecated Dostoyevski and opposed to his philosophy their sanguine views on man and man's power to reform society. In large measure Veresayev's study of Dostoyevski was intended to counteract the exaltation of "the great seer of hearts" by the decadents and symbolists and to restore enthusiasm for the social cause, the road to "living life," which the symbolists had forsaken.

VLADIMIR BORISOVICH KRANIKHFEL'D (1855-1918)

Among the early critics of Dostoyevski who followed Marxist principles as interpreted at the beginning of the century were A. V. Lunacharski, Maxim Gorki, L. N. Voitolovski, V. F. Pereverzev, V. B. Kranikhfel'd, N. A. Rozhkov, V. M. Shulyatikov, and N. I. Korobka.[17] The first four were prominent in the Soviet period, and we shall therefore consider their work later. The others, oversimplifying Plekhanov's theories, were primarily concerned in their criticism with establishing the social genesis of a writer's work, that is, his ideology, and thus explaining all his characteristics. Rozhkov[18] and Shulyatikov[19] baldly reduced their sociological analysis of Dostoyevski to a direct correlation between his ideology and economic causes or to the position of the writer in a class society.

Kranikhfel'd in his 1911 article "Overcoming Dostoyevski,"[20] calling himself a continuator of the "real" criticism of Dobrolyubov, tried to deepen and broaden the latter's interpretation of Dostoyevski on the basis of the newer "materialistic" methods of research. In opposition to Merezhkovski and Aikhenval'd, who interpreted the behavior of Dostoyevski's insulted and injured characters on the abstract, metaphysical plane,

Kranikhfel'd took up the same behavior—the endless wavering between compassion and cruelty, between God and Satan, good and evil, heaven and hell—and explained it as a result of actual conflicts in the social relations of real life; that is, the tragedy of Dostoyevski's characters is the tragedy of the *raznochintsy* intelligentsia of the nineteenth century, humiliated by their dependence upon the wealthy and the powerful.

Whereas Dobrolyubov looked to the progressive *raznochintsy* or thinking individuals to reform an estate structure of society and free the insulted and injured from their predicament, the Marxist Kranikhfel'd looked to the proletariat to overthrow the capitalist system and assigned to the intelligentsia an ancillary role. As satellite to the new, rising class, the previously isolated social group of the intelligentsia would finally find material support and cease to be "an eternal wanderer," tossing about agonizingly between good intentions and degrading behavior. The intervention of the proletariat would build a social system in which there were no insulted and injured, and would put an end to the intelligentsia's tragic view of life. Kranikhfel'd's theses were nothing but the theses of earlier Marxist theorists respecting the inevitable future development of Russian society, mechanically taken over by the literary critic and offered as solution for the tragic plight of Dostoyevski's heroes.

. 4 .

CRITICISM ON THE EVE OF THE REVOLUTION

Criticism of the nineteenth and early twentieth century in many respects delineated the basic lines for the study of Dostoyevski. In addition to the most influential critics already considered, there were many others who made minor contributions, often derivative and merely serving to elaborate the opinions of the leader of their school, but in several cases—notably that of Apollon A. Grigor'yev—highly original and still worthy of attention on their own merits.

Grigor'yev (1822–64), Dostoyevski's associate in publishing the journal *Vremya* [Time], 1861–63, and chief critic of its successor *Epokha* [Epoch], had a very large part in the cult of *pochvennichestvo*, of which Dostoyevski himself was the chief exponent. In Grigor'yev's theory, a work of art is an "organic product" of the whole age and of the entire nation, rising from the infinite depths of national life (the *pochva* [soil], from which the untranslatable word *pochvennichestvo* is coined), where falsities and artificialities are renounced and the "immediacy" of life is found in the organic wholeness of being. Literature, Grigor'yev believed, is written less by the author himself than by the people to which he belongs and the age in which he writes. A poet is the voice of his people, the crier of great truths and the great secrets of life, the bearer of the word which serves to reveal an age and a people to the understanding. Grigor'yev's critical theories, which he had developed during the 1850s, were carried further by the editorial staff of *Vremya*. In Dostoyevski's prospectus for the journal he announced that one aim was to work for elimination of the division, which had been created by the reforms of Peter the Great, between the educated class and the folk principles; new forms of literature were to be sought, native forms, taken from the native soil, from the spirit of the folk. Writers of the new trend were later given the name *pochvenniki*, from Dostoyevski's frequent adjurations to the intelligentsia to find its own "soil." [1] Grigor'yev wrote very little on Dostoyevski himself,[2] but his theories stirred heated debates which reverberated throughout Dostoyevski criticism even into the Soviet period.

Maksim Alekseyevich Antonovich (1835–1918), who succeeded Dobrolyubov as critic for the *Sovremennik* and who regarded himself as the continuator of Dobrolyubov's views, incorporated much of his criticism of Dostoyevski in sharp polemics concerning *pochvennichestvo* with the journals *Vremya* and *Epokha* during the 1860s.[3]

The philosopher and critic Nikolai Nikolayevich Strakhov (1828–96), contributor to *Vremya* and adviser to Dostoyevski in his publishing venture, accepted Grigor'yev's aesthetic theories enthusiastically and became a zealous *pochvennik*. Strakhov's "Reminiscences of Dostoyevski," in the book published by Orest F. Miller and Strakhov under the title *Biography of F. M. Dostoyevski, Letters, and Notes from His Notebook*, 1883, is the most valuable contribution to the prerevolutionary biographical literature on Dostoyevski.[4] Several of Strakhov's reviews elsewhere contain astute criticism of Dostoyevski's work.[5] Miller (1833–99), a literary historian and folklorist, treats Dostoyevski with extravagant praise in his book *Russian Writers after Gogol*, 1886.[6]

The other main biographical materials published during the late nineteenth and early twentieth century are contained in the reminiscences of Aleksandr P. Milyukov,[7] Vsevolod Solov'yov,[8] and Anatoli F. Koni.[9] The most important prerevolutionary reminiscences of Dostoyevski, as well as part of his letters, are collected in the volumes published by Ch. Vetrinski in 1912 and 1914.[10]

V. F. Chizh's study *Dostoyevski as a Psychopathologist*, first published in 1884, was one of the earliest investigations in its field.[11] In 1911, L. N. Voitolovski attempted to analyze Dostoyevski's writings in Freudian terms.[12]

Except for these few studies, which are outside the main stream of prerevolutionary criticism, and for the work of the "decadents" and symbolists, almost all critics of the nineteenth century and the first decade of the twentieth approached Dostoyevski from the point of view of political ideology. Successive generations of critics reduced his characters to a common denominator, and pronounced judgment on the author in accordance with their approval or disapproval of the views, motives, behavior, and spiritual world of his heroes. Criticism therefore was concerned with sharp "civic" controversy centering on Dostoyevski, rather than with literary values. Of the major critics, only Dobrolyubov and, to a lesser degree, Pisarev made an attempt to understand the laws that dictated the nature of Dostoyevski's writing. At the beginning of the twentieth century almost no scholarly study had been made of Dostoyevski's literary provenance and style, his genres, plots, language, syntax, epithets, similes, and other formal elements.

It was not until the eve of the First World War that a Russian scholar, Vyacheslav Ivanov, undertook a well-rounded study of Dostoyevski, formal and technical as well as philosophical. Although the formal aspect of the novels was not to be investigated systematically until the postrevolutionary period, Ivanov's pioneer effort in 1911 was followed during the war years by several analyses of Dostoyevski's style and comparative studies of his relation to purely literary trends: for example, L. P. Grossman's articles of 1914 to 1917, "Balzac and Dostoyevski," [13] "Hoffmann, Balzac, and Dostoyevski," [14] "The Russian *Candide:* On the Question of the Influence of Voltaire on Dostoyevski," [15] "Dostoyevski and Europe," [16] "Composition of Dostoyevski's Novels," [17] and "The Problem of Realism in Dostoyevski"; [18] the studies of V. L. Komarovich entitled "Dostoyevski and Heine," [19] and "Dostoyevski and the Men of the Sixties"; [20] and S. I. Rodzevich's article "On the History of Russian Romanticism: Hoffmann in the Thirties and Forties of Our Literature." [21]

Vyacheslav Ivanov's innovations in Dostoyevski criticism and the monumental erudition he brought to bear on the subject are symptomatic of the revival of Russian cultural life in the early twentieth century.

The heightened scholarly interest in Dostoyevski from the eve of the First World War through the revolutions of 1917 was matched by an extraordinary interest on the part of the general reading public of Russia, which turned eagerly to the writer who had predicted and to a large extent defined the character of the approaching cataclysm. Sharp alternations between enthusiasm for Dostoyevski and indifference on the part of Russian readers in different periods, as well as the rise and fall of critical interest, have often been observed.[22]

In the 1860s and 1870s, when the opinions of Dobrolyubov and Pisarev were dominant in criticism, interest in Dostoyevski was sustained at a high level. From the mid-1880s general interest waned, and a negative critical attitude, initiated by Mikhailovski, prevailed. In the 1890s the decadents rekindled enthusiasm, but even then Dostoyevski remained somewhat in the shadows until the eve of the 1905 revolution, when numerous new studies appeared. At times of upheaval and turmoil, interest in Dostoyevski has always grown. The lull following 1905 ended with the swift flaring of general and critical atten-

tion to Dostoyevski as the catastrophes of war and revolution
approached. The Bolshevik revolution turned the study of
Dostoyevski in a new direction, but at the same time postrevolutionary scholarship at its best is in many respects heir and continuator of the achievements of the three quarters of a century
during which Dostoyevski criticism had developed under conditions of relative freedom.

PART II. Soviet Literary Criticism

. 5 .

MAXIM GORKI (1868–1936)

Maxim Gorki's ambivalent attitude toward Dostoyevski, displayed most conspicuously in 1913, when a dramatization of *The Devils* was produced by the Moscow Art Theater, to a great extent determined the trend of postrevolutionary Dostoyevski scholarship.

Much earlier, however, Gorki's antipathy for Dostoyevski was perceptible. While living on the island of Capri, 1906–13, Gorki began a popular history of literature, which was never completed. Although the manuscript remained in rough draft and part of it was lost, in 1939 the work was published in book form by the Gorki Institute of World Literature in Moscow under the title *A History of Russian Literature*.[1] In it are apparent Gorki's waverings between the humanistic traditions of Russian culture, for which he had a deep respect throughout his life, and Marxist ideology, with which he was becoming more strongly imbued through association with revolutionary leaders of the Russian Social-Democratic Labor Party and his own political activity. From their correspondence it is obvious that Lenin esteemed Gorki's opinions of literature,[2] and it may be assumed that they influenced each other's literary judgments. At any rate they both refused to accept Dostoyevski.

In his *History of Russian Literature* Gorki did not single Dostoyevski out for special attention; in fact, he gave Tolstoi a far more prominent place. The discussion of Dostoyevski begins with an analysis of *Notes from the Underground*, which to Gorki epitomized the author's "very tormenting and barren" writing: "[It] clarifies nothing, does not exalt the positive in life, but, dwelling on the negative aspects only, fixes them in the mind of man, always depicts him as helpless amid a chaos of dark forces, and can lead him to pessimism, mysticism, etc." [3]

Clearly influenced by Mikhailovski, Gorki expatiated on the propensity of Dostoyevski's characters to torture one another. He did not deny the presence of cruelty in the Russian people, but was disposed to attribute it to the long bondage under the Tatars and to serfdom, and, furthermore, he considered that the traits of cruelty were outweighed by the gentleness, kindness, and compassion inherent in the people.

In opposition to Mikhailovski, who saw in the cruelty of Dostoyevski's characters a revelation of the author's own personality, Gorki, seeking an explanation in social forces, found that the traits of cruelty were vestiges of the feudal mentality, of the brutality of masters who flogged their serfs and branded them with a red-hot iron: "It was inevitable that a man should appear who in his soul would personify the memory of all these human tortures and who would reflect this terrible memory—and this man is Dostoyevski." [4] Dostoyevski thus became the voice of conscience and of the protest of the oppressed against the enslavement of the past, the voice of the *raznochinets* struggling in behalf of human dignity and individuality.

The characteristics of Dostoyevski's writing which Gorki decried at this time were those to which he also objected in Tolstoi: "the complete autonomy of the personal element, the need for harmony, the recognition of some supraterrestrial, superhuman will, and, finally, even the famous do-nothingness, which is tossed in in passing." [5]

As a revolutionary, a proponent of action, believing that the world must be transformed in accordance with the demands of reason and the doctrine of the Social Democrats, Gorki was especially repelled by Dostoyevski's conviction that harmony cannot be brought into life through reason, his preaching of irrationalism, and his criticism of the "doer" as a limited and empty man and of the crystal palaces of socialism as contravening the individualistic nature of man. The same extreme confusion, hasty conclusions, "nervous shrillness, and melancholy despair" [6] which Gorki found in Dostoyevski he discovered also in the other great writers of the nineteenth century, regardless of their different births and stations—a result of the conflicts of the time.

In the years of reaction after the 1905 revolution, Gorki's efforts to combat the influence of the literary decadents prompted him to deprecate Dostoyevski, whom they apotheosized. Behind all their panegyrics to Dostoyevski, Gorki detected nostalgia for the old, primitive, backward, Asiatic Russia of which he himself was an irreconcilable enemy.

In his publicist writings from 1905 to his death in 1936, when Gorki discussed Russian literature, he almost always resorted to polemics against Dostoyevski in one form or another. His first strictures were contained in "Remarks on the Petit Bourgeoisie," originally published in 1905 and then included in a 1918 collection of Gorki's articles with extensive commentaries in which he stated his basic position in respect to Dostoyevski.[7] By and large these views remained unchanged in later years.

It was as "a social pedagogue" that Dostoyevski, like Tolstoi, was unacceptable to Gorki. Humility and sufferance he regarded not only as doubtful virtues but as offensive qualities, damaging to the cause he served and thus, in his eyes, harmful to the country. As a revolutionary he could brook no passivity or fatalism. Never for a moment, however, did Gorki impugn the stature of Dostoyevski as an artist:

> Tolstoi and Dostoyevski are two very great geniuses. They shook the whole world with the power of their talent and turned the astonished attention of all Europe to Russia. Both entered the ranks of the great

as equals along with those who bear the names Shakespeare, Dante, Cervantes, and Goethe. But at one time they rendered a disservice to their dark, unhappy country. . . .

"Have patience!" said Dostoyevski to the Russian public in his speech at the unveiling of the monument to Pushkin. "Perfect yourself," said Tolstoi, and added "Do not oppose evil with violence!"

. . . There is something inordinately wrong and shameful, something close to mockery in this preaching of patience and nonresistance to evil. For the two world geniuses lived in a country in which the abuse of human beings had already reached shocking dimensions with its licentious cynicism. Despotism, drunk with its own impunity, made the whole country a dark torture-chamber where the servants of the regime, from the governor to the village policeman, arrogantly robbed and tortured millions of people, playing with them like a cat with a mouse it has caught.

And they said to these tormented people, "Do not oppose evil!" "Have patience!" And they sang beautiful praises to their patience. And this sad example shows very clearly the true character of Russian literature in its relationship to the people. All our literature is an importunate teaching of a passive attitude toward life, an apologia for passivism. And this is in the nature of things. The literature of the bourgeoisie cannot be otherwise, even when the bourgeois artist is a genius.[8]

In branding Dostoyevski a petit-bourgeois writer, Gorki gave a catchword to subsequent Marxist critics, both prerevolutionary and Soviet.

Gorki attacked "Dostoyevskiism" still more sharply in the 1913 articles entitled "On Karamazovism" and "More on Karamazovism." Written more or less as a protest against the production by the Moscow Art Theater of a dramatized version of *The Devils* (under the title *Nikolai Stavrogin*), these articles had loud repercussions and initiated a heated press discussion. At this time another leading theater had announced that it would produce *The Idiot. The Brothers Karamazov* had been staged a few years earlier. Gorki deplored this popularization of Dostoyevski, particularly of *The Devils*, as serving to lull the civic conscience. In his eyes it was detrimental to the interests of the public to concentrate attention on the warped and morbid traits of the national psyche.

Following Mikhailovski's formula of the "cruel talent," Gorki took up arms against Dostoyevski for his implication that the sadistic cruelty of the utterly disillusioned nihilist and the masochism of the downtrodden man who relishes his own suffering are typical phenomena. In Dostoyevski he saw a preoccupation with the bestial and the vile—the Karamazov element. To Gorki all Dostoyevski's characters were to some degree repetitions or variations of Fyodor Karamazov, in whom he found depicted only the dark aspects of the Russian soul, formless and motley, cowardly and insolent, morbidly evil:

the soul of Ivan the Terrible . . . of the landowner who set his dogs on children, the soul of the muzhik who beats his pregnant wife to death, the soul of that bourgeois who raped his betrothed and then gave her to a crowd of hooligans to rape. It is a very perverted soul, and there is nothing to admire in it.[9]

Even Dostoyevski's positive heroes—Prince Myshkin and Alyosha Karamazov—despite their contrast to the anarchists and sensualists, are "half dead fatalists." [10]

All these traits of character must be conquered, Gorki argued, by creating a healthy atmosphere in which there would be no place for such psychological ills, through a fundamental reorganization of the sociopolitical life of the country and thus also of the psychological life. Propaganda of social pessimism, absorption in the higher "needs of the soul," which contribute nothing to ethical improvement, and the negative results of church and religious education must be counteracted by greater concern for the needs of life itself, by the cultivation of spiritual health, cheerfulness, and belief in the creative forces of the mind and the will. As example of a salutary influence in literature, Gorki mentions Gogol's writing, which, under the tutelage of Pushkin, a man acquainted with Russia's past but not poisoned by its dark aspects, itself became healthy and powerful. The dramatization of *The Devils,* of dubious value even from the aesthetic point of view, was, from the social point of view, a menace.

Gorki's attack rocked literary circles and civic groups. Many writers retorted in the press, labeling Gorki's article an insult to Russian culture.[11] Only the leftist press, particularly the Bolshevik, agreed with Gorki's position.[12]

In answer to his writer-critics Gorki wrote the article "More on Karamazovism," in which he explained that he had objected not to Dostoyevski's novels themselves but only to their theatrical production. He saw less harm in reading Dostoyevski than in seeing his heroes on the stage. In his opinion, the reader could detect the reactionary tendencies and correct the thoughts of the characters for himself. The theater-goer, however, was enthralled by the performance of the actors. The human being Dostoyevski had created "in the form and likeness of a wild and vicious animal" was thus given a greater opportunity to stifle critical thought and to take possession of the audience, which succumbed easily "to all kinds of infections." [13] The stage prevented the spectator from arguing with Dostoyevski and, by suggestion and hypnosis, transported him into a world of Karamazovian emotions. And here the harm was done: the audience was persuaded by Dostoyevski's "genius for generalizing the negative symptoms and traits of the Russian national character" [14] that these emotions and actions were typical.

In maintaining that it was inadvisable to dramatize Dostoyevski, Gorki was motivated not by narrow Party aims, but by democratic ideals, above all, by the earnest desire to guide the development of the Russian people along the path of European progress and culture:

> Man is not a wild and vicious animal, and he is much simpler and kinder than the Russian sages imagine him.[15]
> . . . [The Russian] has no need now to be shown Stavrogins, but something else. The teaching of courage is needed, spiritual health is needed—action, and not self-contemplation; a return to the source of energy is needed, to democracy, to the people, to civic activity, and to science.
> There has already been enough self-sneering, which with us takes the place of self-criticism, enough mutual insults, senseless anarchism, and convulsions of every description. Dostoyevski is great, and Tolstoi a genius, and all of you, gentlemen, if it pleases you, are talented and intelligent. But Russia and its people are more important, dearer than Tolstoi, Dostoyevski, and even Pushkin, not to mention all of us.[16]

These articles of Gorki's were not, of course, intended as scholarly criticism of Dostoyevski, but merely as comments on issues of the day.

Upon his return to the USSR at the end of the 1920s, after long residence abroad, Gorki was received in government circles as the dean and arbiter of Soviet literature, and his words concerning Dostoyevski established the criteria of current criticism. As before, in his criticism and publicist writings he consistently placed Dostoyevski's novels—those "marvelously fashioned coagulations . . . of thought, feeling, blood, and of the bitter, burning tears of this world" [17]—among the greatest works of world literature, and remained as consistently intolerant of Dostoyevski's ideology. Returning to *The Devils*, he called it "the most talented and the most evil of all the countless attempts to defame the revolutionary movement of the 1870s." [18] With no suggestion of rebuke, he noted the influence of Dostoyevski on many Soviet writers as exemplified in the structure of their novels, in the methods of characterization, and in the language, especially in Leonid Leonov's novel *Vor* [The Thief], but nevertheless warned them of the danger of being influenced by "the anarchistic ideology of the defeated," [19] as he defined the philosophy of Dostoyevski's *Notes from the Underground*.

In the last years of his life, when Gorki spoke of Dostoyevski, he often resorted to the formulas of Mikhailovski and even of Merezhkovski. He reiterated that he felt intolerable fear as he contemplated the dark depths of Dostoyevski's own soul. What truth was contained in his writing seemed to Gorki ambiguous. Dostoyevski's man seemed to him to be opposed to society and his immediate environment, to the whole world. The doubles were incomprehensible to Gorki, and in characterizing them he fell back upon the words of Merezhkovski and spoke of the struggle between God and the devil. He failed to speak of the meaning behind the sufferings of Dostoyevski's heroes. For the doctrinaire Gorki, suffering for its own sake was incompatible with the task of reforming society; it was a sickness which must be cured. Only the normal aversion to suffering, in Gorki's opinion, could arouse the people to combat the source of suffering, that is, the unjust social order; the teaching and acceptance of martyrdom led to the fanatic theories of Nietzsche and to fascism.

In Gorki's address to the First All-Union Congress of Soviet Writers on August 17, 1934, in which he surveyed the Soviet literary heritage, he furnished Soviet critics with a serviceable interpretation of Dostoyevski and his characters, particularly the hero of *Notes from the Underground*. In the interpretation there were strong echoes of Mikhailovski's "cruel talent." Dostoyevski was characterized as an offspring of the inhuman capitalist system, and the underground man as a superbly portrayed egocentric and social degenerate. The sufferings of the hero Gorki con-

strued as the means by which the reactionary older Dostoyevski
took revenge for the misfortunes of his revolutionary youth:

With the triumph of one who is insatiably taking vengeance for his personal misfortunes and sufferings and for the enthusiasms of his youth,
Dostoyevski showed in the person of his hero to what lengths the individualists in the class of young people cut off from life in the nineteenth and twentieth centuries can go in their whining baseness. This
man of his combines traits of Friedrich Nietzsche and of the Marquis
des Esseintes, the hero of Huysmans' novel *A Rebours*, of *Le Disciple*
of Bourget, and of Boris Savinkov—[both] the author and the hero of
his work—of Oscar Wilde and Artsybashev's Sanin, and of many other
social degenerates who were created by the anarchic influence of the
inhuman conditions in a capitalist state.[20]

To Gorki's mind, capitalism inspired and completely justified
the ideas held by Dostoyevski's underground man, and the
teaching that the individual self-will is not responsible for word
and deed, that man is a despot by his very nature and loves to
torture and suffer, and that unlimited freedom of action should
be accorded him performs the shameful service of justifying a
society of class inequality. Because he accepted a world of degrading and meaningless suffering, Dostoyevski was accused of
seeking and finding the essence of man in the brute element,
which Gorki considered largely a product of bourgeois society.
Acceptance of man's need to manifest the beast in himself was
to Gorki equivalent to acceptance of a cat's need to play with
a mouse in order to exercise its muscles. The fascist who breaks
a worker's spine by a kick of his boot "is not a beast, but something incomparably worse than a beast—a mad animal that
should be destroyed, the same sort of odious animal as the White
officer who cuts stripes and stars out of the skin of a Red Army
man." [21]

In his speech Gorki took pains to mention other reactionary
vagaries of Dostoyevski, such as the opinion he had once voiced

that Belinski was a disgraceful and stinking phenomenon in
Russian life, his insistence that it was necessary to take Istanbul
away from the Turks, his remark that serfdom was conducive
to an ideal moral relationship between the landowners and the
peasants, and his deference in matters of religious doctrine to
Konstantin Pobedonostsev, the most reactionary public figure
in Russia in the second half of the nineteenth century.

At the Writers' Congress in 1934 it was unmistakably the
intention of the Party to discredit Dostoyevski's ideology and to
end his recognized influence on Soviet literature, against which
all the earlier pin-pricks of Communist criticism had been un-
availing. For this purpose the Party brought into action its
heaviest artillery, Maxim Gorki himself. But, schooled to respect Russian literature and revering its giants, Gorki was still
unable to deal a critical blow to Dostoyevski as an artist, and
limited himself to representing Dostoyevski as the ideological
culprit for the turn to the right taken by the Russian intelligentsia
after the 1905 revolution. In the concluding part of his speech
Gorki again revealed his ambivalent attitude toward Dostoyevski:

> Dostoyevski's genius is indisputable. In power of portrayal his talent
> can be compared only to that of Shakespeare. But as a personality, as
> a "judge of the world and of men," he may very easily be imagined in
> the role of a medieval inquisitor.
>
> I have given so much attention to Dostoyevski because without the in-
> fluence of his ideas it is almost impossible to understand the sudden turn
> of Russian literature and of a large part of the intelligentsia after 1905–
> 1906 from radicalism and democratism toward the preservation and de-
> fense of the bourgeois order.
>
> They began to be carried away by Dostoyevski's ideas immediately
> after his speech on Pushkin, after the destruction of the *Narodnaya volya*
> [The People's Will] party, which tried to overthrow autocracy.[22]

Whatever the effect upon his audience of writers—and it is
reasonable to assume that his tribute to Dostoyevski's genius car-

ried more weight with them than the abuse which might well be dismissed as a capitulation to Party demands—Gorki's speech gave the Party new weapons for its campaign against "reactionary ideology" not only in Dostoyevski but in all literature, past and present, Western and Russian. In the use made of Gorki's pronouncements, his own original ideas were often submerged and his genuinely humanitarian purposes defeated, to the great detriment of subsequent Dostoyevski scholarship in the USSR. However, his unstinting admiration for Dostoyevski as artist also served as bulwark for Soviet scholars who, relying on his authority, were able to pursue their studies and to achieve notable successes, particularly during the 1920s.

. 6 .

SURVEY OF SOVIET STUDIES OF DOSTOYEVSKI

After the revolution the secret archives of the tsarist government, which contained among other things documents and materials dating back to Dostoyevski's youth, were made available, and scholars quickly seized their new opportunities. A certain re-evaluation of Dostoyevski occurred, and for a time at
least his place in Russian literature was not denied him. Once
the Bolsheviks were in power, Dostoyevski may have appeared
less dangerous to the revolutionary cause. In any case, Lenin
—a self-admitted layman in questions of art and literature and
relying upon the judgment of Anatoli Vasil'yevich Lunacharski,[1] People's Commissar of Education, who strove devotedly to
preserve the Russian cultural heritage—refrained from rash
measures in regard to the literature of the past. The influence of
Maxim Gorki was also apparent. Although from Lenin's correspondence it is known that in 1913 he attentively followed the
controversy over staging *The Devils* and that he shared Gorki's
views,[2] Dostoyevski was granted a period of grace by the revolutionaries. *Izvestiya* of August 2, 1918, published a list of the
names of persons to whom it was proposed to erect monuments
in Moscow and other cities of Soviet Russia. In second place
among the writers, after the name of Lev Tolstoi, was that of
Fyodor Dostoyevski. Authorization for the project was signed
by Lenin himself as chairman of the Council of People's Com-
missars. The monument to Dostoyevski, on the Tsvetnoi Boule-
vard in Moscow, was unveiled in November of the same year. In
the speech by the official representative of the Moscow Soviet,
Vladimirski, as well as in the main speech by Vyacheslav Ivanov,
Dostoyevski was represented as forerunner and prophet of the

revolution, voice of its spirit of rebellion against the complacency and compromising of the bourgeoisie.

During the 1920s and the early 1930s biographical studies of Dostoyevski, his correspondence, and a definitive edition of the collected works, as well as new critical appraisals, were published in large volume in the USSR. Russian émigré scholars began publication in Prague of a three-volume collection of articles on Dostoyevski.[3] Until the end of the NEP period and the beginning of the First Five-Year Plan, in 1928–29, there was relative freedom of thought in Russia. Lenin's 1905 article entitled "Party Organization and Party Literature"[4] was still regarded as an inconspicuous piece of Party journalism from the polemics of the past, rather than a pretext, as it became in later years, for regulating literature in accordance with Communist objectives. New ideological interpretations were made and expressed, without hindrance, by the outstanding Marxist critics Lunacharski, Pereverzev, Gorbachov, and L'vov-Rogachevski. Although the Pereverzev school was undoubtedly dominant until 1930, all the critics named followed their own bent during the early period, before creative thought was stifled even in the formerly "orthodox," and their views are a genuine and sincere expression of the opinions of convinced Marxists concerning Dostoyevski. As such they will be given detailed consideration in later chapters devoted to individual critics. A rather sketchy compendium of the work of the leading Marxist critics of Dostoyevski during the 1920s is available in a book of selected passages published in 1928.[5]

Throughout the Soviet period investigations of Dostoyevski's style—plot, genre, devices, vocabulary, syntax, epithets, metaphors, and so on—have been neglected in favor of biographical research, ideological analyses, and the editing and publication of the letters and manuscripts. Like prerevolutionary critics,

orthodox Soviet critics have been hypnotized by the psychology
of Dostoyevski's heroes and, although following new interpretations of Marxism, have limited themselves mainly to consideration of the social and philosophical views attributed to
the heroes with little regard for the interrelationships among the
characters and the attitude of the author himself toward them.
Of such criticism B. Engel'gardt said in the 1920s:

It does not dominate the material presented, but the material completely
controls it. It keeps seeing things through the eyes of Ivan Karamazov
and Raskol'nikov, Stavrogin and the Grand Inquisitor, becoming entangled in these contradictions in which they are entangled, stopping in
perplexity over problems they did not solve, and showing respectful
deference to their involved emotional sufferings.[6]

In the 1920s, however, the critical study of Dostoyevski was
put on a genuinely scholarly basis by formalists or literary his-
torians such as L. P. Grossman, Yuri N. Tynyanov, V. V.
Vinogradov, A. S. Dolinin, G. I. Chulkov, and B. V. Tomashevski. Political considerations hampered this group to some extent but, on the whole, their work was very fruitful up to the
mid-1930s; taking advantage of the attempt by the Marxists themselves to place Dostoyevski among the precursors and prophets
of the revolution, non-Marxist specialists were able to pursue
their own course with little restraint.

Major Soviet literature on Dostoyevski during this period includes the three large volumes of source materials and studies
edited by A. S. Dolinin,[7] the collection of studies under the
editorship of N. L. Brodski,[8] the volume of articles and materials edited by L. P. Grossman,[9] the papers published by the
literature section of the State Academy of Arts,[10] and the materials contained in the sixth issue of Zven'ya [Links].[11]

A shift in general policy at the end of the 1920s and beginning of the 1930s put an end to the formalist, historical, and

comparative trends in literary scholarship, and the so-called "dialectical-materialist" method was imposed as the exclusive method for the Soviet study of literature. Formalist criticism almost ceased to appear, and in general the number of critical studies was curtailed. The publication of factual materials and documents concerning Dostoyevski, however, continued intensively even during the thirties, and non-Marxist critics were driven into the field of biographical and textological work. The few ideological studies they attempted encountered far greater difficulties than had the work done during the 1920s.

The most important ideological studies of the non-Marxists in the thirties are those in the volume which was published by Dolinin in 1935, *F. M. Dostoyevski: Materials and Studies*, and Chulkov's book *How Dostoyevski Worked*.[12]

In the policy change at the end of the twenties Pereverzev's approach was condemned as Menshevik, and the Pereverzev school dissolved. Thereafter the influence of Gorki became especially marked in Soviet literary theory and practice. In April, 1932, "socialist realism" was proclaimed the sole method of Soviet literature. Following Gorki's critical re-evaluation of the literature of the past and his ambivalent pronunciamentos on Dostoyevski at the First All-Union Congress of Soviet Writers on August 17, 1934, two opposing trends developed in Soviet Dostoyevski scholarship. One group of critics, the more orthodox, devoted themselves to condemnation of Dostoyevski's ideology, applying Gorki's ready-made formulas. At the end of the thirties the chief representative of this trend was V. V. Yermilov. The second group, echoing Gorki's praise of Dostoyevski's artistic power, strove to reclaim Dostoyevski from the Soviet limbo, to which he had been relegated as reactionary and out of harmony with the new, revolutionary, proletarian writings, and to restore him to contemporary life by representing him as ideologically akin. At the end of the thirties O. V. Tsekhnovitser represented this type of criticism.

After the outbreak of the Second World War Dostoyevski was rehabilitated and pressed into service. The government and Party press referred to him only to extol him as one of the great patriotic writers of Russia. His animadversions on the Germans were quoted copiously by *Pravda*.

In 1946, in connection with the 125th anniversary of Dostoyevski's birth, several critical articles, predominantly ideological in character, appeared, and in 1947 three book-length studies were published: Professor V. Ya. Kirpotin's *F. M. Dostoyevski* [13] and *The Young Dostoyevski*,[14] and Dolinin's *In Dostoyevski's Creative Laboratory*.[15] In these three books the effort to vindicate Dostoyevski by casting him in the role of a forerunner of socialism reached its high point.

The ideological climate of the "Zhdanov period," which began with the resolution of the Central Committee of the Communist Party on the journals *Zvezda* [Star] and *Leningrad* in August, 1946, effectively silenced all serious Dostoyevski scholars in the USSR during the late 1940s and first half of the 1950s. The few scattered articles that appeared were either completely tendentious attacks on the "reactionary Dostoyevski" in comparison with "progressive" revolutionary writers, or perfunctory and jejune pieces on occasions when mention of Dostoyevski was unavoidable, as in the second edition of the *Large Soviet Encyclopedia*.

Before this time, however, postrevolutionary scholars had succeeded in producing a sizable body of useful, often highly original, and rewarding Dostoyevski studies. The remaining chapters will treat their work in detail and trace the course of their struggle in behalf of genuine and unbiased literary scholarship.

. 7 .

DOCUMENTARY RESEARCH
AND PUBLICATION OF THE MATERIALS

Among the biographical studies of Dostoyevski that multiplied rapidly after the revolution, Leonid Grossman's work was especially prominent. In his book *The Path of Dostoyevski*,[1] 1924, he traced Dostoyevski's ideological development, making use of the mass of new materials which became available after 1917, such as the correspondence of Dostoyevski's parents, the memoirs of his wife, diaries, manuscripts, and letters. Grossman's *Dostoyevski on Life's Path*, 1928, is a valuable compilation of memoir materials.[2] He also wrote a detailed work on Dostoyevski's relations with government circles in the 1870s [3] and on his legal status of "civil death." [4]

Grossman's main biographical work on Dostoyevski was *Life and Work of F. M. Dostoyevski: A Biography in Dates and Documents*, published in 1935.[5] It contains a complete list of Dostoyevski's published work and of all the unpublished archival materials concerning him. The detailed summary of biographical materials arranged according to date constitutes a full chronological record of Dostoyevski's life. In its scope and exhaustive treatment this work still remains unsurpassed in the biographical literature on Dostoyevski. Leonid Grossman was also the first Soviet writer to interpret Dostoyevski in fictional biography.[6]

In producing his comprehensive work of 1935, Grossman was assisted by many studies of smaller compass published after the revolution by other writers. V. L. Komarovich had investigated little-known aspects of Dostoyevski's early years—the books he read with enthusiasm in the 1840s, his friendship and break with Belinski, his correspondence with A. N. Pleshcheyev, and so forth—and in his articles "The Youth of Dostoyevski" [7] and "World Harmony" [8] dealt with the young writer's world-view as a reflection of his actual experiences and with the form in which he remembered these experiences later in life.

A. S. Dolinin's numerous studies contributed valuable biographical data, although his conclusions are often disputable. In "Dostoyevski and Herzen," for instance, on the basis of the meeting between the two writers in 1862, Dolinin argued that Dostoyevski's *pochvennichestvo* (see page 76) was his own brand of Herzenism and that he never deviated from the views he owed to Herzen.[9] Other biographical studies by Dolinin include "Dostoyevski and Suslova" [10] and "Dostoyevski in the Petrashevski Circle." [11]

Also of use to Grossman were M. P. Alekseyev's *An Early Friend of F. M. Dostoyevski,*[12] 1921, and K. K. Istomin's "From the Life and Work of Dostoyevski in His Youth." [13] The latter is interesting in its method of explaining Dostoyevski's characters and plots by the writer's own experiences.

The early research of L. K. Il'inski on Dostoyevski and Gleb Uspenski [14] and of Ye. Pokrovskaya on Dostoyevski's part in the Petrashevski circle [15] deserves mention. From the work of the latter it is evident that Dostoyevski was dissatisfied with the passivity of the Petrashevski circle and therefore joined the more radical group of Sergei Durov.

Modern Dostoyevski scholarship owes much to Nikolai Fyodorovich Bel'chikov (1894–), thanks to whose efforts over a period of two decades many archival materials and documents concerning the relationship of Dostoyevski to Pobedonostsev and Chernyshevski, the trial of the Petrashevtsy, and Dostoyevski's methods of work were published.[16] Bel'chikov prepared for publication in 1931 the record of the testimony given before the commission investigating the Butashevich-Petrashevski case in

1849. The statements made during the inquiry, especially those of Dostoyevski himself, shed new light on the personality of the writer.[17]

On the basis of Dostoyevski's deposition alone, P. N. Sakulin had concluded in his book of 1922 that Dostoyevski had not been a Fourierist but had occupied an isolated position in the Petrashevski circle. In Sakulin's opinion, Dostoyevski in the 1840s looked upon socialism as artificial and imposed, not applicable to Russia, and none of his fictional characters revealed a trace of socialist thinking.[18] The testimony published by Bel'chikov, however, indicated that Dostoyevski was close to Sergei Durov, Aleksandr Pal'm, and Aleksei Pleshcheyev of the revolutionary Petrashevski circle, as well as to the most radical members, Vasili Golovinski and Pavel Filippov. Filippov had copied Belinski's letter to Gogol "from Dostoyevski's copy" [19] in order to circulate it and had brought Dostoyevski into the Durov circle.[20] Between him and Dostoyevski there was "a similarity of ideas and tastes." [21] From a letter of Apollon Maikov to Professor Viskovatov it is apparent that Dostoyevski even shared in Filippov's scheme for an underground press. Dostoyevski brought Golovinski, who was prepared to see the establishment of a revolutionary dictatorship for the emancipation of the peasants, into the Petrashevski circle. The opinion expressed during the inquiry, that Dostoyevski was considered "one of the most important" [22] members of the group, tallies with his own later statements in *Diary of a Writer*.

These official records point to several prototypes of characters and settings that occur in Dostoyevski's writing. For example, there is a certain correspondence between Konstantin Timkovski of the Petrashevski circle and the monomaniac Kirilov in *The Devils*. In his testimony Dostoyevski said of the former: "Timkovski is one of those exceptional minds which, when they accept any idea, accept it so that it predominates over all others, to the detriment of the others. The element of beauty in Fourier's system struck him." [23] In the police information contained in the records, Dostoyevski's address is given as "First District, Second Ward, on the corner of Malaya Matrosskaya and Voznesenski Prospect in the house of Shil'." [24] This "house of Shil'," in which Dostoyevski was arrested in 1849, became, almost twenty years later, the residence of Rodion Raskol'nikov in *Crime and Punishment*.

Other studies of Dostoyevski's early years published up to the mid-1930s are K. Chukovski's "Dostoyevski and the Pleiad of Belinski," [25] Georgi I. Chulkov's "Dostoyevski and Utopian Socialism" [26] and S. N. Kulikov's article dealing with the period of penal servitude.[27]

The publication between 1921 and 1930 of various reminiscences and diaries by Dostoyevski's wife,[28] daughter,[29] and younger brother,[30] and by Apollinaria Suslova [31] rendered an invaluable service to biographical study.

The question of Dostoyevski's genealogy was investigated by S. Lyubimov and M. V. Volotskoi. Their findings are of uncommon interest. In his first article on the question of Dostoyevski's origin, published in 1923, Lyubimov shared the opinion of the time that the Dostoyevski family was of "south Russian" (Ukrainian) origin and belonged to the middle nobility (*szlachta*) of Podoliya and Volyn' in the former Polish Ukraine.[32] Further research brought Lyubimov to the conclusion, set forth in an article of 1925, that "the original homeland of the Dostoyevskis was not Podoliya, but first the Pinsk region and later, from the first half of the seventeenth century on, Volyn'." [33]

In 1933 Mikhail Vasil'yevich Volotskoi (1893–) published his book *Chronicle of the Dostoyevski Family, 1506–1933*,[34] in which, on the basis of voluminous documentary evidence, he reconstructed the genealogy of the Dostoyevskis without a break from 1506 to 1655, chronicled the activities of the family through six generations in the Pinsk and Minsk area, and established convincingly that they belonged to the native Slavic population of Byelorussia, then part of the Grand Duchy of Lithuania. The name Dostoyevski was derived from that of the village of Dostoyevo (in the south of present-day Byelorussia), which was granted in perpetuity to Danil Ivanovich Irtishchev (or Irtishch, Rtishchevich, Artishchevich) and his successors by the Prince of Pinsk, Fyodor Ivanovich Yaroslavich, and his wife, on October 6, 1506. The Irtishchev family, in accordance with custom, then took the new surname from the name of the landholdings.

One of the branches of this family was later found, in the seventeenth and eighteenth centuries, in the Ukraine; and, as Lyubimov pointed out, it is to Yarosh Stefanovich Dostoyevski, a member of this branch, that the lineage of Fyodor Mikhailovich Dostoyevski is to be traced.

In the light of the material presented by Volotskoi and Lyubimov, it is evident that the traditions of the nobility which, according to F. M. Dostoyevski's daughter Lyubov' in her book *Dostoyevski As Portrayed by His Daughter L. Dostoyevskaya*,[35] were still preserved even in her parental home, were those of the Slavic Byelorussian nobility and not those of the Lithuanian nobility, as she assumed—an understandable confusion in view of the fact that the predominantly Slavic population and culture of the Grand Duchy of Lithuania had frequently been disregarded and that even within the Grand Duchy itself the designations for the various nationalities were most imprecise. The non-Slavic Lithuanians themselves did not use the collective term "Lithuanians" but referred to themselves by the names of the local principalities, and the Byelorussians and Ukrainians called themselves "Russians." Furthermore, the Ukrainian and Russian population often designated Byelorussians as "Lithuanians."[36] Despite Lyubov' Dostoyevskaya's misunderstanding of the ethnic origin of her family through the assumption that historical Lithuania was entirely a non-Slavic country and that the Dostoyevskis who moved southward from Byelorussia in the seventeenth century were Lithuanians in the contemporary meaning of the word, her book, of course, is of perennial value to students of Dostoyevski. The intimate details of family life which she recounts are of interest in themselves and, in combination with the scholarly findings on the origin of the family, serve to explain certain characteristics of Dostoyevski's writings.

Volotskoi and Lyubimov called attention to the fact that both Orthodox and Catholics were found among Dostoyevski's ancestors and considered the influence on the population of competing religions and cultures—the Western Latin and the Eastern Orthodox—in the regions where the various branches of the Dostoyevski family lived from the sixteenth to the eighteenth century.

The fixing of the homeland of the Dostoyevskis on the territory of present-day Byelorussia has, as might be expected, given rise to claims to Dostoyevski as a Byelorussian writer, notably in an article by the Byelorussian historian and literary critic Vatslaŭ Lastoŭski.[37]

During the second half of the 1930s and up to the Second World War Dostoyevski biographers continued to publish recently discovered documents and facts and their new interpretations, several of book length. Bel'chikov's lengthy treatise, *Dostoyevski in the Trial of the Petrashevtsy*, appeared in 1936.[38]

How Dostoyevski Worked, one of the most provocative and soundly documented Soviet studies of Dostoyevski's life and work, written by the non-Party scholar Georgi Chulkov, was

published in 1939.[39] In accordance with the practice of the
1930s, approximately two thirds of Chulkov's book consists of
painstakingly gathered facts, excerpts from letters and manuscripts. In determining the history of the texts from notes and
drafts, Chulkov displayed exceptional skill and talent. From
his rich factual material, much of it previously unknown, the
author reconstructed a rather complete picture of the course
of Dostoyevski's life and work. *How Dostoyevski Worked* will be
discussed more fully in later chapters.

In the same year, 1939, V. S. Nechayeva's *In the Family and
Homestead of the Dostoyevskis* was published.[40] The monograph
The Sixties, edited by N. K. Piksanov and published in 1940,
once more provided biographical data and letters unknown up
to that time.[41]

The occasional tendentiousness in the commentaries and interpretations supplied in the publication of these biographical materials in no way impairs the value of the documentary data.

Before the revolution no one had specialized in the subject
of Dostoyevski's correspondence; only part of the letters had
been published, scattered through various collections of materials: Orest F. Miller's and Nikolai N. Strakhov's *Biography
of F. M. Dostoyevski, Letters, and Notes from His Notebook*,
1883;[42] S. Sharapov's *Moscow Miscellany*, 1887;[43] two issues
of the periodical *Severnyi Vestnik* [Northern Courier] of
1891;[44] and Vetrinski's *Dostoyevski in Reminiscences of His
Contemporaries and in Letters and Notes*, 1912–14.[45]

After the revolution serious work began on the assembling,
systematization, and publishing of the correspondence in separate cycles. For instance, Dostoyevski's letters to Pobedonostsev
appeared in 1922,[46] his letters to his wife in 1926,[47] and his correspondence with Turgenev in 1928.[48] Despite the interest in

the hostile relationship between Dostoyevski and Turgenev (indicated, for example, by Yuri Nikol'ski's book *Turgenev and
Dostoyevski: The Story of an Enmity*, written in 1917 in Russia
and published in 1921 in Sofia, Bulgaria),[49] until the publication of their correspondence in the 1920s only eight of Turgenev's letters to Dostoyevski were known.[50] Only in 1921 were
the letters of Dostoyevski removed from the Turgenev archive
in Paris, in the possession of Pauline Viardot's heirs, and published there in that year.[51] I. S. Zil'bershtein prepared these letters for publication in 1925 in the collection *Dostoyevski: Articles and Materials*, edited by Dolinin.[52] Several letters from
Turgenev and one from Dostoyevski, not included in the Viardot
archive, had appeared in 1923.[53] All these letters were collected
in Zil'bershtein's 1928 edition, and, after a delay of more than
forty years, publication of the Dostoyevski-Turgenev correspondence was finally completed. In his annotations the editor quoted
valuable collateral material, such as letters from P. V. Annenkov and Mikhail Dostoyevski to Fyodor Mikhailovich.

In *Letters of Russian Writers to A. S. Suvorin*, edited by
D. I. Abramovich and published in 1927, two previously unknown letters of Dostoyevski to Aleksei S. Suvorin were made
public.[54]

Finally, the urgently needed comprehensive collection of
Dostoyevski's letters was published under the editorship of A. S.
Dolinin, who assembled all the published letters and the unpublished letters available in government and private archives,
systematized them, verified the texts of previously published
letters with the originals, and prepared an all but complete
annotated edition in three volumes, publication of which began in 1928.[55] The editor's work in establishing definitive texts
and in dating the letters is irreproachable. With the exception
of a few cases in which the autographs were missing, all texts

were collated with the originals—90 percent of the letters in the first volume and practically all in the second. Many passages which had once been censored by the wife of the writer were restored. It was a stroke of fortune that the non-Party Dostoyevski specialist Arkadii Semyonovich Dolinin (1885–), well known for his conscientious and scrupulous work, was the editor of this collection. Despite the fact that he was compelled to adapt himself to the current Marxist ideology and methodology in his commentaries, the publication of the letters in a single collection was a great event in the development of Dostoyevski scholarship.

The first volume covers the period 1832–67, and the second the period 1867–71; the two volumes contain a total of 393 letters—which is, as the Soviet writer V. L. Komarovich has correctly pointed out, three times the number for the same period in the prerevolutionary edition of Miller and Strakhov, which contains only 125.[56]

Unfortunately, the publication of the first two volumes of Dolinin's edition preceded the publication of the *Reminiscences of Andrei M. Dostoyevski* (1930), previously cited, which included several new letters formerly in the possession of the writer's younger brother and not available to Dolinin for his edition. It will therefore be advantageous to consider the first two volumes of Dolinin's collection in conjunction with the *Reminiscences of Andrei M. Dostoyevski* in order to survey the letters in chronological order.

In Dolinin's first volume there are six letters written to his parents during Dostoyevski's childhood, four of which appear for the first time. In the *Reminiscences of Andrei M. Dostoyevski* there are three more childhood letters, dating from 1834 to 1835.

From the Petersburg period of 1837–49, Dolinin provided

18 letters missing from the Miller and Strakhov edition, eight
of which were published for the first time. For the same period
the *Reminiscences* contain eight additional new letters, four of
them written jointly by Dostoyevski and his older brother
Mikhail Mikhailovich, including the previously unknown beginning of a letter of March 10, 1839, to their father, which
had been published in part by Miller and Strakhov. This opening passage, written as it was on the eve of the father's tragic
death, throws light on the reasons for Dostoyevski's feeling of
guilt in respect to his father and on the time when it arose.
The first of the four letters to his brother Mikhail during this
period reveals the emotions produced in the young Dostoyevski
by the death of his father. The new letters of 1846 give much
information concerning his relationship with Belinski. The letter of December 22, 1849, to Mikhail, written a few hours after
the countermanding of his death sentence, describes the agony
experienced in Semyonov Square, which had, until publication
of the letter, been known only in the fictional transmutation
of the experience in *The Idiot* and in the form of later recol-
lections in *The Diary of a Writer* for 1873.

Dostoyevski's letters to family members in Moscow which
appear in the *Reminiscences* strongly suggest that his personal
background served as material for *Poor Folk*. The hero, Makar
Devushkin, feels toward the marriage into which his Varen'ka
is forced just as the young Dostoyevski felt toward the marriage
of his sister Varvara Mikhailovna, whom he calls Varen'ka in
his letters. The personality of P. A. Karepin, Varvara's husband,
as portrayed in Dostoyevski's correspondence during the dispute
over money and the division of the inheritance, particularly in
the letter of September 19, 1844, cannot but bring to mind the
landowner Bykov in *Poor Folk* and the subsequent series of self-
satisfied, predatory characters (the old man who marries the

young girl in "A Christmas Tree and a Wedding," 1848, the heroes of the comic sketches "Another Man's Wife" and "The Jealous Husband"—both published in 1848 and later combined in "Another Man's Wife and the Husband under the Bed"— and the husband of Mme M. in "The Little Hero," written in 1849) which culminates in Luzhin, the unloved fiancé in *Crime and Punishment* (1866). Again, in *Crime and Punishment* the distress of the young Dostoyevski on his sister's behalf colors the sufferings of Rodion Raskol'nikov in a similar situation. Other echoes of Karepin's faults displayed in the correspondence of 1843–44 and of the family dissension at the time are heard in "Uncle's Dream" (1859), in which Karepin's comic distaste for Shakespeare, once mentioned by Dostoyevski in a letter, is revived in Mar'ya Aleksandrovna Moskaleva, and in "A Gentle Spirit" (1876), in which the hero resigns his army commission, like Dostoyevski himself in 1844, just at the time when his sister's husband in Moscow has "squandered" the small family property, leaving the hero "on the streets without a penny."

Dostoyevski's correspondence from the time of his imprisonment until he left Russia in 1867 for a four-year residence abroad is represented in Dolinin's collection by 205 letters, as against the 50 published by Miller and Strakhov. Fifty-nine of the 205 appeared in print for the first time; the remainder came from other published sources.

Dolinin's second volume contains 129 letters written in 1867–71 while Dostoyevski was abroad (44 from the Miller and Strakhov collection, 16 previously unpublished, and 69 garnered from other publications).

Of the letters dating from 1872 to 1877, Dolinin assembled 219 in the third volume, of 1934 (8 previously published by Miller and Strakhov, 30 appearing for the first time, and 181 collected from other published sources. In addition to the interesting letters to his wife, there are letters in Volume III (especially the one of June 7, 1876, to V. A. Alekseyev) which aid the reader's understanding of Dostoyevski's intention in *The Brothers Karamazov*, particularly the "Legend of the Grand Inquisitor."

Despite Dolinin's painstaking efforts, his edition of the Dostoyevski letters up to 1877 remains incomplete in that not all Fyodor Mikhailovich's letters to his father are included and the correspondence with Karepin is missing. It is regrettable that the final volume has never been published.

In his introduction to the third volume, Dolinin wrote that, for the attempt to reconstruct the general tenor of Dostoyevski's thought from the fragments of correspondence which have survived, the letters in Volume III were especially valuable, for the years covered, 1872 to 1877, were years of wavering views and zigzags of opinion. In 1875, by invitation, Dostoyevski published the novel *A Raw Youth* in *Otechestvennye zapiski* [National Notes], the organ of the revolutionary *raznochintsy* and *narodniki*, headed by Saltykov-Shchedrin, Nekrasov, and Mikhailovski. Despite the hostility aroused among the *raznochintsy* intelligentsia by *The Devils* in 1871–72, *A Raw Youth* was favorably received by the editorial staff of the journal. Mikhailovski himself, who had fiercely attacked *The Devils* and who a few years later was to describe Dostoyevski as a "cruel talent," in an editorial preceding the opening instalment of *A Raw Youth* justified its appearance in his journal by stating that in the new novel Dostoyevski repudiated the preconceived ideas of *The Devils* and made an effort to understand the new generation.

In Dostoyevski's reconciliation with this group of radical ideologists and in the extensive correspondence which he carried on with progressive young people during the mid-1870s,

Dolinin found a basis for asserting that Dostoyevski did not frown upon the revolutionary goals of these years. Shielding himself with Marxist terminology, Dolinin spoke of the "dual nature of this genius who represents the urban petit bourgeoisie," [57] doomed to waver between revolution and reaction without finally joining either side. "The constant agitation, sincerity, and honesty" [58] of his efforts to find a way out of the dilemma created a bond between Dostoyevski and the searching youth of the time, who addressed huge numbers of letters to him appealing "for advice, consolation, and precepts on how to live":

The majority of the petit-bourgeois intelligentsia, of the same dual nature as his, lacked the strength to make a sharp break with the old world, but, already captive to the new, they could not but feel in Dostoyevski a kindred soul and see in him a spokesman of their thoughts and sufferings.[59]

Dolinin, of course, did not deny that Dostoyevski opposed revolution by violence, regarded the revolutionary whirlwind sweeping Europe as a menace to Russia, and looked to love and universal forgiveness for the establishment of social justice, but, in extenuation, the editor asserted that the revolutionary forces in Russia ceased to seem diabolical to him:

The eagerness for reform, the sincerity and legitimacy of it—that is what he recognized during these years in all young people without exception, including the "nihilists." [60]

Dolinin intimated that Dostoyevski's reversion in the mid-1870s to the ideals of his youth was by no means a passing phase but part of a long, completely logical and inevitable process which continued to the last days of his life. As evidence, he quoted a passage from *Diary of a Writer* written not long before Dostoyevski's death:

Our bright, fresh youth will immediately, before anyone else, give its heart to the people. . . . Therefore I place my hopes first of all on young people—they also suffer from "the search for the truth" and long for it, and they are most akin to the people and will immediately understand that the people also seek the truth. And becoming so well acquainted with the soul of the people, they will give up those extremist delusions which have nearly led astray so many of them who imagined they had found the truth in extremist European doctrines.[61]

To counteract not only this quotation, in which the "extremist delusions" must be read only as an attack on the socialism of his day, but also the editor's apologia for Dostoyevski, a second preface, "From the Publishers," was added. It was evidently written by Lev Borisovich Kamenev, who, not long before the publication of the third volume in 1934, had been put temporarily in charge of certain phases of Soviet publishing in order to remove him from the Kremlin inner circle.

In January, 1934, Kamenev announced publication plans for the year in an article in *Pravda*. Among the books to be published by the "Academia" publishing house, he mentioned a new edition of *The Devils*, which would contain a lengthy introduction demolishing the ideas of the novel from the point of view of Communist ideology. *The Devils* did not appear in 1934, nor has it been republished subsequently in the USSR (up to the end of 1955). Evidence that the new edition was being prepared in 1934 and indications of the nature of the planned introduction remain, however, in the statement by the publishers in the third volume of letters: "Our point of view will be developed in greater detail in the introductory articles to Dostoyevski's *The Devils*, which is to be published by 'Academia.' " [62]

"From the Publishers" expresses in concentrated form the Communist attitude toward Dostoyevski. On one hand, in accordance with tradition, he is recognized as one of the greatest figures in world art of the nineteenth century, largely because "he was never able to rid himself of the thought that socialism and revolution are the central problems of human history and culture." [63]

On the other hand, though in his early years an ardent admirer of the utopian socialist Fourier, he had become an opponent of socialism and revolution in the latter half of his life, and in his writings had erected a towering structure of reactionary ideology. Dolinin was reproached for exaggerating the importance of Dostoyevski's change of publisher from Katkov's *Russkii vestnik* [Russian Courier] to *Otechestvennye zapiski* of Nekrasov, Mikhailovski, and Saltykov-Shchedrin, which the editor had offered as evidence of a shift in ideology, and for minimizing the reactionary elements in Dostoyevski's philosophy of life after his return from prison. Allied with the forces of counterrevolution, Dostoyevski had fawned on the imperial house of the Romanovs and written "crude lampoons" on the revolutionaries: "If his work had been limited to [these things], interest in it could only have equaled the interest in the work of the not inconsiderable number of ideological sycophants of the rising bourgeoisie; that is, it would have approached zero." [64] But Dostoyevski, unlike other "bourgeois" thinkers and writers, was not to be so lightly dismissed. His work retained interest as "the most significant and the most profound" of all the arguments that could be offered "in the way of ideology against socialism during the second half of the nineteenth century." [65] Dostoyevski was "one of the greatest figures of the class society which has already perished in our country and which is perishing throughout the whole world," [66] "the last of the thinkerartists who were able to depict the dying world of feudal and bourgeois culture in the face of oncoming socialism." [67]

The task of Dostoyevski scholarship is therefore to expose and combat "the illusoriness of the artistic and ideological system which he erects in art":

To reveal the inner poverty of the ideal which at the end, as a result of agonizing quests, he set against the shining ideal of socialism is to force out of the consciousness of contemporary man once and for all the last remnants of those petit-bourgeois illusions with which dying capitalism is still capable of infecting him.[68]

In their anxiety to dissociate themselves from the reactionary views expressed in Dostoyevski's letters and to conform with the recently promulgated directive of the Second Five-Year Plan on overcoming the survivals of capitalism in Soviet minds, the publishers went far beyond the immediate subject of concern— the new edition of the letters—into a pronouncement on Dostoyevski's writing as a whole. Only toward the end of the piece did they turn to the new publication itself and offer a few generalizations to which there could be no objection. "An event which scholarship both in the USSR and abroad has long awaited . . . the publication of the first complete collection of Dostoyevski's letters in the Soviet Union from now on gives solid ground for genuinely scholarly study of the biography, belles-lettres and publicist writing of one of the greatest figures." [69]

Readers of the three-volume edition of Dostoyevski's letters may omit the publishers' introduction with good conscience. It adds nothing to—nor can it destroy the value of—the rich factual material in the letters.

The first careful collation of the printed texts of Dostoyevski's writings with the originals and the insertion of previously banned or omitted sections began after the 1917 revolution. The pre-revolutionary editions of the complete works of Dostoyevski simply duplicated the first posthumous edition (1882–83), which was by no means definitive.[70] It was essential to collate the texts used in this edition, the texts of all the separate works published during Dostoyevski's lifetime both in periodicals and in book form, and the manuscript texts in order to eliminate variant readings, misprints, orthographic and stylistic "improvements" introduced in publishing, and to find and incorporate the final revisions made by the author himself.

B. V. Tomashevski and K. I. Khalabayev edited the thirteen-volume Soviet edition of Dostoyevski's complete works (exclusive of the correspondence), which was published from 1926 to 1930, with full annotation tracing the course of textual changes and giving variants.[71] Among the main restorations were a section entitled "Old Times in the Petrashevski Circle" [*Starina o petrashevtsakh*] which had been omitted from *Diary of a Writer* for 1877, and "Stavrogin's Confession" [*Ispoved' Stavrogina*] consisting of three chapters eliminated from *The Devils* and first published, in two variants, in 1922–23.[72] In the Tomashevski and Khalabayev edition the two texts are presented in composite form. The editors also collected and combined in one volume (XIII) the unsigned and miscellaneous criticism and publicist writings of Dostoyevski, which up to then had been scattered through various journals and anthologies published during the author's lifetime. Authorship was established both by thematic and stylistic indications and by reference to data in office records of Dostoyevski's journals *Vremya* [Time] and *Epokha* [The Epoch]. Through such methods the errors of earlier scholars were corrected, and the number of articles of doubtful authorship substantially reduced. The final volume contains a bibliography of the postrevolutionary literature on Dostoyevski and a good index of names. This edition owes much of its sound scholarly character to the editor-in-chief, B. V. Tomashevski, a non-Party member of the formalist school, textologist, and author of several books on the theory of literature published in the twenties. Out of political considerations Dostoyevski's writings have never again been published in full in the Soviet Union.

During the 1920s and at the beginning of the 1930s many of Dostoyevski's manuscripts and notebooks were also published. In addition to the three chapters of "Stavrogin's Confession" already mentioned, manuscripts and notebooks for *The Double*,[73] *Netochka Nezvanova*,[74] *Crime and Punishment*,[75] and *The Idiot*,[76] an unpublished short story entitled "House Demon," [77] manuscript variants of *Diary of a Writer* for 1876,[78] a new version of *A Gentle Spirit*,[79] unpublished pages of *Notes from the House of the Dead*,[80] and draft materials for *The Brothers Karamazov* [81] were published in the USSR. In addition, the Soviet scholar V. L. Komarovich published in Germany, in a German translation, manuscript materials for *A Raw Youth* [82] and *The Brothers Karamazov*. [83] The notebooks containing materials for *The Devils*, from the collection of the Central Archives, were not published until 1935,[84] although they had been prepared for publication in the 1920s. The plan for the unwritten novel "Life of a Great Sinner" was published in 1921.[85]

In the notebook materials and early drafts of *Crime and Punishment* and *The Idiot*, one may trace step by step the tortuous course of the planning of these novels and the many changes involved before the whole design was formulated and writing might proceed.[86]

The variant readings from *Diary of a Writer* for 1876 throw new light on the relationship between Dostoyevski and Turgenev, in which the editor of the publication, N. F. Bel'chikov, saw the conflict of a "prickly plebeian" and a "proud noble."

The manuscript of *The Brothers Karamazov*, published in German translation, with excellent commentaries, indicates the prototypes for Dmitri Karamazov and other characters of the novel.

The very interesting manuscripts of *A Raw Youth*, which have not yet been published in full in the original Russian, are quoted abundantly in Chulkov's *How Dostoyevski Worked* and in Dolinin's book *In Dostoyevski's Creative Laboratory*, 1947.[87] Although *A Raw Youth* is in some respects the culmination of Dostoyevski's work and the manuscript materials are so copious that, in the opinion of Dolinin, the main steps in the writer's creative process can readily be traced, up to this time scholars have had to be satisfied with second-hand excerpts.[88]

Thus the publication of the Dostoyevski manuscripts, which began auspiciously, was halted short of completion.

. 8 .

STYLISTIC AND HISTORICAL STUDIES

In stylistic analysis, Marxist critics, preoccupied with questions of ideology and the "sociological" interpretation of literary phenomena, have been conspicuously weak, and almost all Soviet studies of Dostoyevski in this field have been written by non-Marxist members of the historical and formalist schools.

In preceding chapters we have already mentioned several studies, both prerevolutionary and Soviet, dealing with the influence of various writers on Dostoyevski. Leonid P. Grossman published a great deal in this field, beginning in 1914 and continuing into the 1930s. In his "Balzac and Dostoyevski," first published in 1914,[1] and in his book *Dostoyevski's Library: From Unpublished Materials*, 1919,[2] Grossman analyzed the epistolary and *feuilleton* style of Dostoyevski, and compared the style of Dostoyevski's translation of Balzac's *Eugénie Grandet* with that of *Mr. Prokharchin* and the style of Balzac's *Père Goriot* with Dostoyevski's in *Crime and Punishment*. Comparisons of Dostoyevski with Pushkin, Gogol, Tolstoi, Shakespeare, Cervantes, Voltaire, E. T. A. Hoffmann, Edgar Allan Poe, Victor Hugo, Charles Dickens, George Sand, and others shed new light on Dostoyevski's reading and on the role of traditional plots in his writings.

Grossman's book *Dostoyevski's Style*, published in 1925, brought together a number of his studies which had been published previously.[3] In them Grossman refuted the traditional opinion, current since the beginning of the twentieth century, that Dostoyevski was predominantly a great psychologist, thinker, and prophet, and not an especially brilliant stylist; that, in his feverish haste, under the pressure of poverty and debts, he had no time to put the finishing touches on his novels; and that their intricate and involved composition was a resulting defect. Even the seasoned scholar Dolinin once remarked that not one of Dostoyevski's major works "satisfies the requirements of form as a definite artistic task." [4] Leonid Grossman, however, like Vyacheslav Ivanov, recognized that the composition of Dostoyevski's novels was dictated by their own internal laws and marvelously designed to serve a higher artistic truth. Violating the conventional unities of material and action, Dostoyevski introduced new principles into the European novel: whirlwind movement of plots, characters, and actions around a single idea, the achievement of a coherent and integral effect by linking together heterogeneous elements, and the fusion of variegated particles and fragments into the single whole of the novel. In "The Art of the Novel in Dostoyevski," one of the pieces in the book, Grossman defined the diverse genres which Dostoyevski combined in the construction of his novels as the autobiographical novel in the form of letters or diary, the detective story, and the horror tale.

He also discussed the style of Dostoyevski's novels in his sketch "The Path of Dostoyevski," published in 1921 in *Dostoyevski's Writing*,[5] a collection of articles and materials edited by Grossman, and again in his 1924 book entitled *The Path of Dostoyevski*, an expansion and reworking of the sketch.[6] Grossman treated the subject of Dostoyevski's language in an article published in his *Seminar on Dostoyevski*, 1923.[7]

In many respects Grossman extended and deepened Vyacheslav Ivanov's ideas on Dostoyevski's style, and his work in this field constitutes a notable achievement of modern scholarship. His criticism will be discussed more fully in later chapters.

In 1921 a very interesting brochure entitled *Dostoyevski and Gogol: On the Theory of Parody*[8] was published by Yuri N. Tynyanov (1894–1943), a young critic and theorist of the formalist school, later to be well known for his biographical novels. In the two articles contained in the brochure, "Parody Stylization" [*Stilizatsiya-parodiya*] and "Foma Opiskin and *Correspondence with Friends*" [*Foma Opiskin i* Perepiska s druz'yami], Tynyanov, using all methods of stylistic analysis, offered the first well-founded interpretation of Gogol's influence on Dostoyevski as indicated by the latter's novels.

The opinion had long prevailed—confirmed by Dostoyevski's own statement that all writers of his generation had emerged from under Gogol's *Overcoat*—that Dostoyevski followed in the footsteps of Gogol. Nekrasov had spoken to Belinski of Dostoyevski as a new Gogol. Belinski had called Gogol "the father of Dostoyevski," and the critic Pyotr Aleksandrovich Pletnyov echoed him. Only Strakhov had recognized, in the 1880s, that Dostoyevski had made "a revision" of Gogol. Then Rozanov had spoken of Dostoyevski's opposition to Gogol. Tynyanov concluded that Dostoyevski did not simply continue Gogol's style, but rather moved away from it, surmounting Gogol's influence by parodying his style. Tynyanov was of the opinion that the process of literary succession consists mainly in resistance, destruction of the old totality, and building anew from the old elements, and he gave illustrations to show that Dostoyevski broke with Gogol and at the same time retained Gogolesque devices of using catchwords and masks for his characters (for instance, the appearance of Svidrigailov, Stavrogin and Lambert). Dostoyevski was not bound to these devices, but was able to rise above them by means of parody or stylization suggestive of parody. In *The Village of Stepanchikovo*, for example, Dostoyevski boldly and successfully parodies and caricatures Gogol's personality as disclosed in *Correspondence with Friends*, his appearance, his homilies and literary style, in the character of Foma Opiskin, a failure as a littérateur, sponger, cheat, bigot, hypocrite, and Tartuffe. The

behavior of Foma with the Rostanev family is analogous in many
ways to the behavior of Gogol with the Aksakov family. In appearance there is a strong resemblance between Gogol and Foma
as described in the story—a short, insignificant-looking man,
with aquiline nose and blond hair, dressed in a frock-coat down to
his heels. In Foma's speech Dostoyevski parodies Gogol's vocabulary in *Correspondence with Friends:* he uses foreign words
with comic effect and incorrect plural forms, separates traditional epithets from their nouns and applies them to other words,
and is given to mechanical repetition. The characters in the story
often parody one another. As Tynyanov pointed out, the device
of parody for outright lampooning in fiction, which Dostoyevski
used for the first time, with comic effect, in *Village of Stepanchikovo,* he repeated on a much larger scale in *The Devils* in the
characters of Karmazinov (Turgenev), Verkhovenski (Granovski), the younger Verkhovenski (Nechayev), and Stavrogin
(Bakunin, in the opinion of Grossman).

M. P. Alekseyev, analyzing the same story more or less in
accord with the theories of Vyacheslav Ivanov concerning Dostoyevski's "tragedy-novel," saw evidence that the plan for a play
had served as basis for the plot. He supported his argument by
reference to Dostoyevski's earlier plans, never realized, to write
tragedies entitled "Mary Stuart" and "Boris Godunov" and a
comedy *"Zhid* Yankel' " [The Jew Yankel']. Alekseyev enumerated the characteristics of drama present in *The Village of
Stepanchikovo:*

For all [its] skillful treatment as narrative, the fact that it was
originally in the form of a comedy is felt at once. The characteristic
lively and gay dialogue certainly prevails throughout the work; the
sentences connecting the dialogue often remind one of an author's stage
directions; the rounding off of individual scenes as culmination of the
action, as for instance the appearance of Foma and Korovkin, is espe-

cially marked. Finally, notwithstanding the considerable scope of the work, all the events of his story take place in two days.[9]

The influence of Molière's *Tartuffe* is obvious in the main characters and in the pattern of the plot development:

Dostoyevski follows Molière's example in full. He slowly prepares the reader for the meeting with Foma, fully acquainting him with the latter's biography, and almost gives the effect of dawdling in the endless preparations for the meeting. The hero of the tale hurries to Stepanchikovo to see this villain or freak as soon as possible. On the road he meets Bakhcheyev and the peasants. Foma's name is on everyone's lips. But, having arrived at Stepanchikovo, burning with impatience to see Foma, he does not succeed immediately, for Foma is at prayer. On all sides the talk is of him, and you feel him approaching. Dostoyevski had fully realized the value of this device of Molière's for building up tense interest in the development of the action. For deliberate contrast, Dostoyevski, like Molière, uses the long, slow-paced dialogues of Foma, confident of his power, the calmness and moderation of his behavior and movements. These very qualities create the impression of the calm before a storm, which forces one to await tensely the sudden denouement.[10]

The relationship of Dostoyevski's style to Russian literary traditions is explored in A. I. Beletski's paper "Dostoyevski and the Natural School [11] in 1846," [12] published in 1922, and in the anthology *The Creative Path of Dostoyevski*, edited by N. L. Brodski and published in 1924.[13]

One of the most interesting articles in the latter volume is V. V. Vinogradov's, in which the distinguished linguist classified Dostoyevski's *Poor Folk*, on the basis of stylistic characteristics, as a product of "the natural school," affected, as was his early work in general, by the style of "civic sentimentalism," which had developed by that time. According to Vinogradov, Dostoyevski violated both the canons of sentimentalism and the stereotypes of the "natural school" and went on to the realistic psychological novel.[14] Vinogradov's later work entitled *The Evolution of Russian Naturalism: Gogol and Dostoyevski* also contains interesting passages on this subject.[15]

In another study included in the volume edited by Brodski, A. P. Skaftymov investigated the "Thematic Composition of the Novel *The Idiot*," [16] in many respects following Vinogradov's "functional-immanent" method of analysis. In their comparative study of genre, plot, and linguistic style, both scholars treated the development of form within strictly literary and linguistic bounds without regard to extrinsic factors.

The same volume contains K. K. Istomin's study of *Mr. Prokharchin* and *The Landlady*; [17] A. Gizetti's "Proud Pagans," [18] a discussion of Dostoyevski's women characters; M. G. Davidovich's "The Problem of Interest in Dostoyevski's Novels"; [19] and D. Darski's "Dostoyevski as Thinker." [20]

An early work of Aleksander G. Tseitlin, *Stories about Dostoyevski's Poor Civil Servant: On the History of a Plot*,[21] traced the theme of the "poor civil servant" in the work of many second-rate writers of the 1840s and suggested that Dostoyevski's heritage from Gogol came not only directly but also through numerous insignificant writers, Gogol followers of the "natural school."

Two of Tseitlin's later articles furnish especially interesting illustrations of the effect of Marxist "sociology" on the analysis of the formal aspects of Dostoyevski's writing: *"Crime and Punishment* and *Les Miserables:* Sociological Parallels," [22] and "Time in the Novels of Dostoyevski." [23]

The two volumes of *Dostoyevski: Articles and Materials*, edited by A. S. Dolinin and published in 1922 and 1925, contain many studies of Dostoyevski's style. Such articles in the first volume are "Dostoyevski's Aesthetics" by I. Lapshin,[24] "An Unwritten Poem of Dostoyevski" by V. L. Komarovich,[25] and "Style of the Petersburg Poem *The Double*" by V. V. Vinogradov.[26]

In the second volume S. Askol'dov, in his essay "Psychology of the Characters in Dostoyevski," [27] systematized the characters in Dostoyevski's novels according to their psychological kinship and offered a new interpretation of the relationship of Stavrogin to the other characters. B. Engel'gardt maintained that Dostoyevski's novels were ideological, in opposition to Vyacheslav Ivanov's definition of the "tragedy-novel." [28] The subject matter of V. L. Komarovich's contribution "The Novel *A Raw Youth* as an Artistic Unity" is apparent from the title.[29] The author examined the extent to which in writing *A Raw Youth* Dostoyevski had drawn upon his plan for the unwritten novel "The Life of a Great Sinner." In Komarovich's opinion, the latter would have had the same relation to Dostoyevski's work as a whole which *Dead Souls* has to the body of Gogol's writings. Until the publication of V. Sidorov's piece in this collection, Dostoyevski's *Diary of a Writer* had been treated mainly as political journalism. Sidorov, however, argued that many pages displayed art of a high order.[30] L. P. Grossman's "The Stylistics of Stavrogin," published in his book *Dostoyevski's Style*, also appears in this volume.[31]

Other pieces in these two volumes, although chiefly of biographical interest, also provide information concerning Dostoyevski's literary sympathies and antipathies and the question of influences.[32]

The volume entitled *Dostoyevski*, published by the literature section of the State Academy of Arts, which has become, in retrospect, one of the most interesting of the many compilations of the 1920s, includes several papers on Dostoyevski's style: V. S. Nechayeva's "Comparisons in Dostoyevski's Early Stories," [33] M. A. Petrovski's "The Composition of *The Eternal Husband*," [34] and S. N. Durylin's "On One Symbol in Dostoyevski." [35] The following papers are interesting from the point of view of literary history: V. S. Dorovatovskaya-Lyubimova's

"Dostoyevski and the Men of the Sixties," [36] F. F. Berezhkov's "Dostoyevski in the West," [37] P. S. Popov's "The Ego and the Id in Dostoyevski's Writing," [38] and Georgi I. Chulkov's "Dostoyevski's Last Word on Belinski." [39] Popov attempted a philosophical analysis and an interpretation of Dostoyevski's style in the vein of Vyacheslav Ivanov, but with an effort to provide a Marxist explanation. Chulkov expressed the opinion that the dialogue between Kolya Krasotkin and Alyosha Karamazov in *The Brothers Karamazov* was a parody on the disputes between Belinski and Dostoyevski.

The very publication of this volume, in which the authors range from the extreme formalist M. A. Petrovski to the Marxist "sociologist" I. N. Kubikov, all under the aegis of the State Academy of Arts, demonstrates the ideological liberalism which still characterized Soviet scholarship in 1928.

The analysis of Dostoyevski's style made by Pereverzev before 1930 is outstanding in this field and will be considered later in the chapter dealing with Pereverzev's work as a whole.

The theories of M. M. Bakhtin set forth in his book *Problems of Dostoyevski's Writing*, 1929,[40] which represents the most exhaustive and original treatment of Dostoyevski's style in Soviet criticism, will also be examined in a separate chapter.

With the inauguration of the First Five-Year Plan in 1928–29 and the literary hegemony of RAPP (Russian Association of Proletarian Writers) [41]—particularly after the bitter intra-Party theoretical controversies of 1930 and the overthrow of the Pereverzev school—the formalists, as well as many scholars of the historical and comparative school, were obliged to abandon their stylistic investigations of Dostoyevski and turn to other fields.

The few articles specifically dealing with Dostoyevski's style and creative process which appeared from time to time during the thirties included L. Pogozheva's "Composition of the Novel

Crime and Punishment" [42] and "Dostoyevski's Skill in Creating Atmosphere," [43] and B. G. Reizov's "More on the History of the Conception of *The Brothers Karamazov*." [44]

No full-length books devoted to purely technical analysis of Dostoyevski's work were published during the thirties. Not because all of the problems of his literary forms had been solved in the preceding decade—merely because the political climate required other pursuits.

. 9 .

THE QUESTION OF DOSTOYEVSKI
AND REVOLUTION

The very mention of Dostoyevski's name in connection with revolution has always aroused sharp differences of opinion, but neither the critics of the right nor the radicals, whatever their opinion of his stand on the subject, have questioned Dostoyevski's preoccupation with the theme.

Merezhkovski in "Prophet of the Russian Revolution," written during the revolution of 1905, aptly phrased the thesis embraced by many subsequent critics when he said that Dostoyevski "was revolution pretending to be reaction."[1] His imagination fired by the revolutionary upsurge of the time, Merezhkovski assailed the autocracy as "legalized lawlessness, terror congealed, anarchy frozen into ice"[2] and turned toward the "God-bearing people," the Russian people, whose genius lay not in statehood, in devising forms of government—witness the "monstrous chimera" of the Russian autocracy—but whose mission was to create a living body of the church and Godmanhood. "Predominantly non-state-minded, anarchic, composing a religious society, theocratic," the Russian people had an unconscious and undying "longing for the coming tsar-Messiah, who will reconcile earthly truth with heavenly truth."[3] To Dostoyevski Merezhkovski ascribed the great role of prophet of a theocratic rebirth through suffering and service to all mankind. Father Zosima's words "So may it be, so may it be!" Merezhkovski interpreted as Dostoyevski's own prediction.

The actual experience of revolution, however, disillusioned Merezhkovski and caused him to re-examine his mystical faith in revolution for Russia and the import of Dostoyevski's prophecy.

His characterization of Dostoyevski as "revolution pretending
to be reaction" might nonetheless have served as epigraph for
Pereverzev's essay "Dostoyevski and Revolution," published in
1921.[4] The Marxist Pereverzev did not trouble himself with the
apocalyptic aspect of Dostoyevski's writing. For him the novels
constituted a huge panorama of the psychology and world-view of
one social group. Contrary to the traditional protest of Marxist
critics against Dostoyevski's depiction of revolutionary forces,
Pereverzev found in *The Devils* and elsewhere in Dostoyevski a
faithful rendering of the essence of the revolutionary upheaval,
an elemental revolt of the petit bourgeoisie.

Pereverzev began his analysis with the statement that Dostoyevski's writing was especially vital in the post-1917 period, in
view of the fact that the problems he had raised had not yet been
disposed of:

To speak of Dostoyevski for us still means to speak of the most burning
and profound questions of our current life. Seized by the whirlwind of
the mighty revolution, spinning amid the problems it poses, passionately
and painfully aware of all the vicissitudes of the revolutionary tragedy,
we find ourselves in Dostoyevski, we find in him such a painfully passionate treatment of the problems of revolution that it is as if the writer
were living through the revolutionary storm with us.[5]

Pereverzev pointed out Dostoyevski's ambivalence toward
revolution, his fierce criticism of the underground movement
coupled with sympathy and justification, his conservatism combined with rebellious outbursts. In the camp of the conservatives
and opponents of the revolution he seemed a strange ally and an
enemy at the same time. At odds with the revolutionaries, he felt
a kinship against his will and suffered pangs of conscience over
the estrangement. The atmosphere of revolution, which had fas-
cinated him in his early years, never ceased to perturb him. He
saw clearly all the misery and sorrow involved in putting into

effect a revolutionary program for the reconstruction of the world, and often in his writing his own struggle against the allurements of revolution is felt:

Dostoyevski was a revolutionary and a reactionary at one and the same time; in him both revolutionary and reactionary strains sounded with equal verve. In his writing there is always something reminiscent of that "amusing little piece" which one of the characters in *The Devils*, Lyamshin, composed for the piano. "The piece . . . began with the stern strains of the *Marseillaise:* 'Qu'un sang impur abreuve nos sillons!' A bombastic challenge was heard, the intoxication of coming victories. But suddenly, mingling with the masterly rhythm variations of the anthem, somewhere to the side, underneath, in the corner, but very near, were heard the nasty strains of *Mein lieber Augustin*. The *Marseillaise* pays no attention to them—the *Marseillaise* is at the peak of intoxication with its own majesty—but *Augustin* becomes stronger, *Augustin* is more and more impudent, and now suddenly the beats of *Augustin* begin to coincide with the beats of the *Marseillaise*. . . ." In the spirit of Dostoyevski, the author, there is the sound of the piano under the fingers of Lyamshin. Here [too] the stern strains of the *Marseillaise* are tangled in a weird snarl with the nasty strains of *Mein lieber Augustin;* the melody of the anthem, with its call to freedom—"Arise, accursed of the earth"—is tangled with the slave melody "God Save the Tsar." In [Dostoyevski] revolution is always fraught with reaction, and reaction fraught with revolution.[6]

Availing himself of the freedom which existed in the early years after the revolution, Pereverzev often drew an explicit analogy between events in *The Devils* and Bolshevik practice.

In Pereverzev's opinion, Dostoyevski demonstrated superbly in this novel that the basis of the revolution is not great pity, as the sentimental idealists imagined, but the great anger, self-assertion, and self-will of the oppressed. There is no idealization of the revolution in Dostoyevski; revolution offers an outlet to the destructive desire for revenge that has built up in the oppressed and injured:

Revolution is cruel and immoral; it treads over corpses and bathes in blood; it prefers torture, scoffing. . . . Revolution brings with it horror, terror, and despotism, because it is the purpose of those who were formerly held in fear and submission to inspire fear and submission, to become despots and terrorists. He who fears despotism, terror, blood, and corpses is not a revolutionary and calls upon the name of revolution in vain. The real revolutionary is not the noble defender of the weak and the oppressed who is inspired by pity, but the grim man who seizes power, inspired by self-will. Such is Pyotr Verkhovenski in Dostoyevski's *Devils,* and likewise Stavrogin in his revolutionary phase.

Thus the psychological mechanism of revolution reduces to an attempt by the oppressed to become oppressors, an attempt by slaves never permitted to assert their will to become self-willed despots.[7]

Although the revolution brings to those who have been insulted, injured, and enslaved "the undeniably purifying, humanizing fire of freedom,"[8] Pereverzev pointed out that it also opens dizzying opportunities for action freed of all legal, moral, or ethical restraints. The urge of the unfettered slave, intoxicated with freedom, to crush his recent enemies may become an urge to crush all dissidents as well. Everything returns to its starting point, except that the roles of slaves and despots are now reversed. The new order may be no better than the old, perhaps even worse. Thus in freedom, potential despotism and the attendant terror, bloodshed, and massacre are inherent; otherwise freedom does not exist. "Without despotism," says Pyotr Verkhovenski in *The Devils,* "there would be neither freedom nor equality."

Pereverzev's own disillusionment in revolution as he had seen it with his own eyes was unwittingly betrayed in his analysis of Dostoyevski's position:

In revolution there is something diabolically cunning, devilishly sly. The horror of revolution does not lie in the fact that it is immoral, spattered with blood, drunk with cruelty, but in the fact that it offers gold from the devil's treasures which turns into broken shards after all manner of cruelties have been committed for the sake of this gold.

The revolution is seductive, and the almost maniacal passion for it is completely understandable.[9]

Pereverez saw Dostoyevski's characters as repeating the author's own experience. Like him, they throw themselves headlong into the revolution, taste the ecstasy of self-will and unlimited freedom, and come to grief in the abyss. As the phantoms of freedom vanish into air and the monster of unlimited tyranny steps forth from behind, accompanied by the inevitable informers, spies, and murderers, fascination gives place to disillusionment and disgust. They fling themselves from the embrace of revolution to the arms of reaction, cursing their past as a diabolical delusion. Just as freedom bears potential despotism in it, Pereverzev generalized from Dostoyevski's life and from *The Devils*, so revolutionary energy may be transformed into the most profound reaction. Dostoyevski was, the critic asserted, the expert anatomist of the revolutionary underground who disclosed its secrets to the world and revealed features still unseen even by the leaders of the revolution themselves.

In the agonizing doubts and vacillations of the author and his characters, Pereverzev, as a Marxist, saw reflected the conflict-ridden existence of the petit bourgeoisie in Russia. The social and economic position of this class, Pereverzev stated, produced the psychological duality which Dostoyevski probed to the depths and thoroughly understood.

Everything has come true as Dostoyevski predicted. He even foresaw their disillusionment, depicting the revolutionary rebels "who could not endure their own revolt." Thus Dostoyevski, decades removed from the present revolution, has much more understanding of its mechanics than many contemporary revolutionary ideologists of the petit-bourgeois stamp. It is this that makes Dostoyevski so akin to the present.[10]

In adding the qualification that Dostoyevski had of course not known the proletarian revolution of 1917, Pereverzev at the same

time admitted that this revolution had drawn in a large admixture of the rebellious petit bourgeoisie and its characteristics.
Therefore

what [Dostoyevski] said about revolution is for us up to the present
time the most profound interpretation of its essence insofar as it is the
fruit of petit-bourgeois rebellion. In Dostoyevski one can learn much,
can understand much, and can make a sound judgment of many things
in the revolution which is proceeding before our eyes.[11]

Thus by his "objective scientific" method of considering literature as a reflection of specific social conditions, Pereverzev res-
cued Dostoyevski's *Devils* from opprobrium as a slander against
the revolution and brilliantly reappraised it as a mirror of the
revolution, a wise, instructive, and prophetic book, putting readers on guard against the degeneration of the revolution into a
terroristic, totalitarian, despotic dictatorship of a small group of
professional revolutionaries consolidating their power by destroying and murdering their own adherents.

Pereverzev neither censured nor praised Dostoyevski. He
simply stated and explained objectively the laws governing the
course of revolution as they are represented in Dostoyevski's
writing and as they appear in actuality, pointing out the similarities. In Dostoyevski the revolution could read itself and take its
own measure.

During the comparatively liberal NEP period, Pereverzev's
interpretation was subjected to only mild criticism by such orthodox Marxists as Gorbachov, and a third edition of Pereverzev's book *Dostoyevski's Writing* was published in 1928. In 1930,
however, the campaign to discredit him as a "Menshevik critic"
began. The RAPP critic S. Shchukin utilized a chapter of his
book *Two Critiques: Plekhanov and Pereverzev* [12] to attack the
"apologia" for Dostoyevski in the essay "Dostoyevski and Revolution," which had again served as introduction to the third edi-

tion of Pereverzev's book. Many times afterwards his opponents singled out the same piece as particularly cogent evidence of the non-Marxist character of Pereverzev's views and methodology.

The fiftieth anniversary of Dostoyevski's death at the beginning of 1931 was observed under the slogan "For a Class Reevaluation of Dostoyevski's Writing." [13] In an article that appeared in the special anniversary number of *Literaturnaya gazeta* [Literary Gazette], February 9, 1931, Aleksandr G. Tseitlin firmly pegged the author of *The Devils* as a political renegade. To explain Dostoyevski's transformation from a *raznochinets* writer and apparently enthusiastic participant in the Petrashevski circle into a bitter and virulent opponent of revolution, Tseitlin employed the "sociological" method, dividing the petit bourgeoisie of the mid-nineteenth century into the radical-socialist wing of Belinski, Dobrolyubov and Chernyshevski, on one hand, and the downtrodden and submissive strata of city dwellers who could not bring themselves to discard the remnants of patriarchal psychology and take the revolutionary path of political struggle, on the other. Dostoyevski belonged to the second group:

The Dostoyevskis had no desire to come to terms with reality. This reality was too hopelessly difficult for them. They could not find in themselves the strength to fight to the finish for realization of their ideals. They lacked the necessary political hardness. It remained for them to strike a balance between these two forces. This was the bourgeois humanism of [Dostoyevski's] early work.[14]

The critic reproached Dostoyevski for preferring psychological sentimentalism to sociological analysis and for stubborn reluctance to touch upon social background in his portrayal of "poor folk." He cast doubt on the genuineness of Dostoyevski's revolutionary views even in the Petrashevski period, asserting that they amounted to no more than a love of humanity and visionary Fourierism. Prison showed Dostoyevski that the Russian people looked upon plans for revolutionary reform with indifference and even hostility, as a wild scheme of the nobility or a flippant rebellion of the intelligentsia. Then Dostoyevski called upon the intelligentsia, who were cut off from the people, to forget the delusion of socialist utopias and turn toward the people and the truth residing in them. Tseitlin remarked that, by sentencing Dostoyevski to penal servitude, the autocracy cured in him its own incurable social disease.

After prison and exile, Dostoyevski threw himself into the fight against nihilism, the revolutionary intelligentsia and the trifling liberalism of the nobles, Slavophilism. His hostility to Chernyshevski was, in Tseitlin's opinion, part of his battle with all varieties of utopian socialism. In his critical and publicist articles of the 1860s, Dostoyevski struck at the "civic" aesthetics of the *raznochintsy*, who advocated "natural" portrayal and repudiated the theory that art is the transmutation of the world in the aesthetic consciousness of the artist. In *Notes from the Underground* Dostoyevski scoffed at "crystal palaces" and the enchanted birds of utopian phalansteries. In *Crime and Punishment* he subjected the ethics of nihilism to devastating criticism. In *The Crocodile* Chernyshevski was ridiculed in the story of a man who was swallowed by a crocodile but continued to dream about bettering the lot of mankind and to work out his own new economic theory. Dostoyevski's hatred of revolution culminated in *The Devils*, which Tseitlin lumped with the most reactionary novels of the time: *Vzbalamuchennoye more* [The Turbulent Sea], 1863, by Pisemski, *Nekuda* [No Way Out], 1864, and *Na nozhakh* [At Sword's Point], 1871, by Leskov, *Marevo* [Mirage], 1864, by Viktor Klyushnikov, and *Panurgovo stada* [The Herd of Panurge], 1869, by Vsevolod Krestovski.

Practically every important segment of Russian society of the time was lampooned in *The Devils,* Tseitlin observed. In Stepan Trofimovich, the liberalism of the nobles in the 1840s is ridiculed. In the sybarite Karmazinov, political sycophancy to the revolutionaries is stigmatized. Stavrogin represents the anarchist Bakunin. The use of the fanatic Sergei Nechayev as model for the character of Pyotr Verkhovenski is a rabid attack on young Russian revolutionaries.

In his notebooks at the end of the 1870s Dostoyevski defended the autocracy, preached the primacy of the Orthodox Church among other Christian religions, advocated the expansion of Russia to the east, and castigated socialism. Dostoyevski's publicist articles became a reference book for the ideologists of the Russian Black Hundreds.[15]

Criticizing Pereverzev's views, Tseitlin denied that Dostoyevski was a revolutionary and a reactionary at the same time. No deep gulf separated Dostoyevski from other reactionary writers of the 1860s, such as Avseyenko, Krestovski, and Leskov. They were all united by hatred of the revolution, the difference being that Dostoyevski expressed their hatred more eloquently and artistically. Tseitlin also rejected Pereverzev's theory concerning the dual nature of the petit bourgeoisie and argued that it had simply split into a radical wing, the *raznochintsy,* and the faction of the reactionary bourgeoisie. "Dostoyevski was *always* an ideologist of the second group, never for a moment in the ranks of the first." [16]

Disguising Dostoyevski in the toga of a "prophet" of the proletarian revolution ("Everything has come true as Dostoyevski [predicted] . . .") especially exasperated Tseitlin. Such an effort, in Tseitlin's opinion, was unconvincing and politically harmful:

A genius in depicting . . . the psycho-ideology of the petit-bourgeois apostasy, chronicler . . . of the history of bourgeois renegadism,

Dostoyevski still remains, both in his social ideals and in the methods of attaining them, most profoundly hostile to those who made [the October Revolution] and who are at present laying the foundation of socialist society.[17]

The critic called upon Dostoyevski scholars to fight against reaction, using all the weapons of the Marxist-Leninist method, to investigate the logic of the social development of Dostoyevski's writing and put an end to the vaporing and unctuousness of the anniversary celebration. Well-aimed and frequent gunfire against reactionary tendencies should characterize the work of the scholar, in ideological analysis as well as in detailed study of style. In Tseitlin's opinion, proletarian writers of the Soviet period—in contradistinction to Leonid Andreyev and M. P. Artsybashev, and, for that matter, Ilya Ehrenburg—had nothing to learn from Dostoyevski "except the usual devices of the technique of the novel." [18]

The same number of *Literaturnaya gazeta* contained several excerpts from Dostoyevski's notebooks and comments on them by N. L. Brodski, in which he pointed to evidence in the notebooks that Dostoyevski had had Chernyshevski's personal life and arrest in mind when he wrote *The Crocodile*. Chernyshevski had become a yardstick of Soviet critics for measuring the rapport of his contemporaries with the revolutionary movement. Accordingly, Brodski damned Dostoyevski as a maligner of Chernyshevski and therefore a class enemy:

Dostoyevski lied when he denied in *The Diary of a Writer* [1873] the rumors that this sketch was a "civic" allegory on Chernyshevski, pointing out that he bore no "hate because of convictions." A fundamental, implacable hatred for the class enemy exudes from the notebooks of Dostoyevski, who as early as 1861 had become a complete obscurantist. The standard-bearer of reactionary social groups, the ideologist of the enemies of socialism, of whatever stripe, Dostoyevski, in fear, displays his malice toward "the revolutionary party." The October Revolution,

which admirers of Dostoyevski abroad accuse of spilling streams of
blood, is the clearest, sharpest, most direct answer to the class partisans
of Dostoyevski.[19]

The editors of *Literaturnaya gazeta* expressed their agreement with Tseitlin and Brodski both in their use of a phrase
from Brodski—"Dostoyevski's Undercover Fight against Chernyshevski"—as the headline for the entire issue and in their
introductory note, which read:

The extracts being published from the notebooks of Dostoyevski are of
the highest degree of interest. These pages, unknown up to now, reveal
a new feature of Dostoyevski's biography on which little light has
been cast—his political maneuvering. The outspokenness, passion, and
malice of the tone of these notes for his own use, these day-to-day
jottings of secret thoughts and desires, only more sharply emphasize
their naked class significance. Not even the open class enemies of
Chernyshevski—Katkov and others—went to such lengths of unbridled,
hate-blinded attack on socialism, the revolution, and the representative
of the revolutionary movement of the time, Chernyshevski. In the years
from which the notes date (1861–1863), Dostoyevski is still not prepared to make an open attack upon the beloved leader of the young
generation of revolutionaries. But here, privately, to himself, Dostoyevski
gives vent to his raging hatred, that of a traitor, a "betrayer" of the
revolution. The publication of the excerpts once again and in a new
way emphasizes the point that all theories concerning Dostoyevski's
"dichromatism" are theories of our class enemies. These pages from
the notebooks first of all demolish the Menshevist conception of
Pereverzev, who tried to "split apart" Dostoyevski's imaginative and
publicist writing and represented him "as a revolutionary among reactionaries and a reactionary among revolutionaries." The notebooks
are damaging to the theories of Pereverzev's followers, especially Bespalov, who metaphysically differentiates between world-view and world-
perception.[20]

In the same issue of *Literaturnaya gazeta*, considerable space
was given to an article by Mikhail Yul'yevich Levidov (1892–)
entitled "The Myth About Dostoyevski: Random Thoughts," in

which the author contended that, for all the talk about it, Dostoyevski's reactionary ideology was nothing more than a myth. Dostoyevski had no ideology, just as he had no fixed point of view. He was ideologically irresponsible. It was likewise a myth that he had a distinct publicist personality, for he had no talent for philosophizing on life and no philosophy of life. The substance and diversity of the ideas in his novels belonged to the characters only, and not to the author himself. Dostoyevski made use of some of them, borrowing them from the Shatovs, the Ivan Karamazovs, the Versilovs, and other characters. Either the idea saddled them, or they saddled it and raced along at the mercy of fate. The relationship was simply that between a reckless gambler and his luck:

Dostoyevski's so-called philosophy of life—that is, the abundant and diverse ideas of the characters in his novels—played a most important role in the artistic design of the novels: these ideas were purely *a plot device, a literary contrivance, a lever moving the story—but no more than that.*[21]

In Lev Tolstoi, on the contrary, Levidov recognized a genuine philosophy of life for which he was ready to fight. In Dostoyevski there was only a well-stocked wardrobe of ideas from which he borrowed the necessary ideological costumes and properties for the setting of his novels:

Tolstoi wrestled with the idea of the state, and it has become customary to think that Dostoyevski wrestled with the idea of atheism. But could Tolstoi have cried out about his fight: "In Europe there is not and never has been such powerful agitation for the state as mine!" He could not, of course. But Dostoyevski asserted: "In Europe there are not and have never been such powerful expressions of atheism. . . ." This power was needed only in order to lend more significance to Ivan in the plot, to increase the complexity of his composition.[22]

Levidov concluded with the observation that there was no "Dostoyevski-ism" and there were no "Dostoyevskians" in the sense of Tolstoi-ism and Tolstoians, for Dostoyevski was not a writer with a powerful and integrated philosophy of life, not a prophet and teacher, not a thinker and publicist. The legends to such effect were to be explained only by the myth-making of Russian and foreign critics. Dostoyevski was an unprecedentedly gifted writer with an unconscious talent which he himself was unable to control.

The editors of *Literaturnaya gazeta*, who saw in Levidov's argument an attempt to deal with Dostoyevski from the formalist point of view, and to conceal his ideology under the cover of "art," referred to his article as "bourgeois contraband." Nevertheless, at the beginning of 1931 it was still possible to publish an article which expressed opinions at variance with those of the editors; Stalin's letter to the editors of the historical journal *Proletarskaya revolyutsiya* [Proletarian Revolution], which put an end to such criticism, appeared only later in the same year.[23] In February, 1931, the editors of *Literaturnaya gazeta* merely deemed it necessary to dissociate themselves from Levidov's views by means of a note which read: "M. Levidov has completely 'declined' even to hint at a sociological explanation of Dostoyevski's writing. And in this sense, the article is itself a curious example of the masked opposition of the petit-bourgeois consciousness to the oncoming revolution."[24] To be categorized along with Dostoyevski among the "petit-bourgeois" opponents of the revolution portended no good for Levidov, and he finally disappeared from the literary scene.

The pressure that forced critics to censure Dostoyevski was heaviest in 1931 and early 1932. It was slightly relieved after the liquidation of the RAPP in 1932 and the partial rehabilitation of the classics of Russian literature which accompanied the canonization of "socialist realism" as the sole method of Soviet literature.

By 1935, when the voluminous monograph *F. M. Dostoyevski: Materials and Studies* was published, a milder approach to the question of Dostoyevski's attitude toward revolution was possible. In the introduction and commentaries the editor, Dolinin, returned to this subject, which he had touched upon in his introduction to the third volume of Dostoyevski's letters. He now spoke of Dostoyevski's ideology as fluid and everchanging. Again he referred to a major shift in Dostoyevski's position beginning in mid-1874—a departure from his reactionary convictions toward reconciliation with radical *narodnik* views, as indicated in *A Raw Youth*. In dealing with Dostoyevski, Dolinin made an effort to apply the same type of historical analysis of the period as that used by Lenin in, for example, the latter's article "Lev Tolstoi as Mirror of the Russian Revolution," [25] and also strove to examine Dostoyevski's work from the point of view of the social conditions in which his genius developed. Like Lenin, Dolinin regarded Tolstoi as reflecting mainly the distress and suffering of the peasants. Dostoyevski, on the other hand, dealt with the down-and-out masses of the cities, who had sunk to the lowest level of the petit bourgeoisie. Dolinin wrote:

As the author of *The Brothers Karamazov*, this work which is the culmination of his writing, he is great for the very reason that he depicted in it the great idea of the Russian revolution with all its contradictions in that precise historical period when everything in Russia was in upheaval and the new bourgeois order was still only taking shape. At that time the urban petit bourgeoisie, no less than the peasantry, suffered the miseries which are characteristic of periods of upheaval. In any case the petit bourgeoisie, or its most progressive element, took a more active part in the class struggle than the peasantry. And herein lies the reason why the revolution was expressed much more clearly, much more powerfully, in Dostoyevski than in Tolstoi. But at the same time the nature of the petit bourgeoisie was always to be reckoned with— basically hesitant, fainthearted, longing for changes and in such fear of them.[26]

Unable to avoid mention of Dostoyevski's teaching of universal reconciliation and forgiveness, his cult of Orthodoxy, faith in the messianic role of the Russian people, and rejection of socialism as a godless, impractical path toward social reconstruction, foreign to the Russian people, Dolinin at the same time tried to single out for emphasis the features which indicated Dostoyevski's profound interest in the coming revolution: the portrayal of the temper of the suffering millions, their torments, their hatred for the court bureaucracy of Russia, and their still greater hatred for the "moneybags" and capitalists.

Dolinin developed the thesis that the revolutionary aims which were deeply ingrained in Dostoyevski in his early years had been merely transferred to the plane of art and were again embodied in *The Brothers Karamazov*. All the characters of this novel are symbols or bearers of definite social ideas. Father Zosima influences Ivan Karamazov's thoughts; at times they share the same critical attitude toward reality, and at other times they break over the program of social reconstruction. Alyosha Karamazov is sent by Father Zosima into the world of sin with the difficult mission of re-educating man. On the other hand, all the force of logic and conviction in the "Legend of the Grand Inquisitor" is given not to Christ, but to the Inquisitor, the rational spirit, in other words, to godless socialism. On the realisitic plane, in the scene in which Ivan Karamazov converses with the devil, the devil is more persuasive.

From the strong social criticism in Dostoyevski's last writings, Dolinin concluded that in the period of *The Brothers Karamazov*, and immediately before, Dostoyevski was "a revolutionary in many respects, despite all his preaching of religion." [27]

In view of the fact that Dostoyevski's attitude toward the revolution to a large extent determines the fate of his books in the Soviet Union, almost every Dostoyevski scholar has felt obliged to touch on this theme. In periods of lowered ideological tension the tendency is to interpret Dostoyevski as predominantly revolutionary in attitude; at times of greater ideological stress it becomes necessary to offer evidence that he was a reactionary, a mystic, an enemy of revolution. Communist critics have followed both courses, and they, too, have been indebted to Merezhkovski for the formula that Dostoyevski "was revolution pretending to be reaction."

. 10 .

V. F. PEREVERZEV (1882–)
THEORIST OF THE SOCIOLOGICAL SCHOOL

The strongest influence on Soviet literary scholarship during the 1920s was undoubtedly that of Valerian Fyodorovich Pereverzev. Until he was deposed from the seat of authority in 1930, almost all Dostoyevski specialists in Soviet scholarship adopted his general views and methodology. He was head of the literature section of the State Academy of Arts in Moscow, conducted courses in literature for graduate students of RANION,[1] lectured in the First and Second Moscow Universities, and rallied around himself a large group of young scholars, including G. N. Pospelov, U. Fokht, V. Sovsun, I. M. Bespalov, and A. I. Zonin. Critics who had studied at the Institute of the Red Professoriate followed his views and methodology in their work published throughout the USSR, both in Russian and in the languages of the national minorities. In fact, up to 1930 the Pereverzev school exercised almost a monopoly in Soviet Marxist literary scholarship.

The first open criticism came in reviews by G. Ye. Gorbachov, L. I. Timofeyev, and A. Gurshtein after publication in 1928 of the collection *Literary Scholarship*,[2] under the editorship of Pereverzev. At that time Pereverzev's adherents still had the ascendancy over his opponents. Early in 1929, however, at the Moscow conference of littérateurs, A. V. Lunacharski himself and P. I. Lebedev-Polyanski began the full-scale campaign. In the fall of 1929, at the plenum of the board of directors of RAPP, Leopol'd Averbakh and Yuri Libedinski attacked Pereverzev. Opinion was still divided. Just as the campaign was reaching its climax in the RAPP journal *Na literaturnom postu* [On Literary

Guard], even *Pravda*, the newspaper of the Communist Party, acknowledging occasional mistakes of Pereverzev, nevertheless called upon the "On-Literary-Guardists" to learn from him the Marxist approach to literature and the scientific method of its study. Then, at the end of 1929, in an address delivered to the Institute of Literature, Art, and Language of the Communist Academy under the title "Plekhanov and Pereverzev," S. Shchukin branded Pereverzev as anti-Marxist, and a resolution of the Presidium of the Communist Academy passed in 1930 condemned Pereverzev's theories as Menshevik.

The Pereverzev school collapsed. Pereverzev himself, however, made no public recantation of his views and methodology. The entry on Pereverzev published in 1934 in the Soviet *Literary Encyclopedia* states:

Embracing all the basic problems of literary study, [Pereverzev's] system is definitely opposed to the Marxist-Leninist doctrine in respect to art, revises it and, eliminating its revolutionary, materialist Partyism, endeavors to emasculate it.[3]

A brief outline of Pereverzev's methodology follows.

Pereverzev offered a very clear and concise exposition of his methodology for the study of belles-lettres in the two articles "The Necessary Premises of the Marxist Study of Literature"[4] and "Problems of Marxist Literary Scholarship."[5]

As a Marxist, Pereverzev considered literature a function of social life, subject to social necessity. The method of studying literature must therefore be the sociological or, more precisely, the historical-materialistic method. For Pereverzev the determining factor in a work of art was not subjective thought, but objective reality; in other words, being determined the consciousness of the artist. Accordingly, the scholar should, unlike the idealist critics, seek explanation of literary phenomena not in the subjective ideas and thoughts of an author but in his relationship to material reality. In Pereverzev's opinion the "creative history" of a writer—the development of his ideas, psychology, dreams, and so on, as reflected in letters, diaries, rough drafts, and similar documents—no more explained his writing than did his biography. The task of literary investigation was to disclose the objective existence, the being, which, rather than idea, underlay every work of art and determined its character and structure. Pereverzev used the term "being" to denote a unity of object and subject, of the object portrayed and the portraying subject, of the reality depicted and the personality of the artist. He differentiated between the "reality" which nineteenth-century critics demanded in literature and the "being" which determined the character and the structure of a piece of fiction. The naïve, so-called "real" critic of the nineteenth century, understanding fiction as a representation of life, had reduced reality to a passive object of perception and representation. The role of the critic consequently was reduced to pronouncing judgment on the themes touched upon in the work. The "real" critics informed the reader what the subject matter was, and then began to deliberate thereon, presenting their own views and in general adding to or correcting the author's interpretation of facts. Genuine literary scholarship, on the contrary, must

feel its way in a work of art to that point where objective representation shades into the subject, where the object portrayed and the portrayer form an organic whole. It is at this point that we come to that being which underlies a work of art, to that social reality where, in the living production process of society, the object and the subject, the concrete world of objects and the concrete man, are organically fused.[6]

The first obligation of the scholar, to find the portrayer in the thing portrayed, Pereverzev considered a very difficult task, requiring intent and careful study of all the elements of structure, minute attention to the smallest details of the texture, research and deep thought, a sensitive nose, sharp eyes, and insight. The investigator must have the ability to detect in a complex set of characters the personality of the writer, the subject in whom this set of characters had been organized and through whom objective existence became consciousness. Only through him could the laws governing existence be known.

The old methods of studying literature through an interpretation of the problems, the life, and the personality of the author, his environment and his contemporaries, through tracing the creative process and digging up biographical details, through a search for prototypes, and so on, not only did not bring the scholar to the heart of literature but often only blinded him to the object of his study. His method, however, Pereverzev described as one of "moving through literature, and not past it." [7]

Pereverzev regarded the writer as an involuntary mirror of his environment, reflecting the characteristics peculiar to it; the fictional characters he portrays are a projection of the type of social character inevitably formed by the social milieu from which the writer has come. Hence, inevitably one central character is present in all the works of a writer. Produced by a single social milieu, they form that structural unity which is called style, and the style reveals the conditioning factors and the laws governing the work of art:

No one has the power to shed a style because no one has the power to depart from a determined circle of images. It is for this reason that every writer moves in a vicious circle of images, that one general character is common to all the writings of an author, that they all form a single style, a single body of creative work. The basis of this unity lies not in the personality of the author, but in the social conditioning of the character which is projected in [his] images. Since they are projections of a single social character, the writings of an author form a single body of creative work, a single style. This style is not the attribute of one individual only, is not confined to the writing of one author only. The writings of many authors are generically related, inasmuch as they rest on a single social base and on variants of a single social character expressed in the images of which the system of each writer's body of work is made up. Style is thus the generic category in respect to the body of work, and the latter is the generic category in respect to the individual work. Every individual work represents a single example of one variety of creative writing, which [in turn] forms a variety of one and the same style. From this point of view, to study a work of art means to find out the social factors which have determined it by classifying it under the general categories of writing and style, for it is style which, in art, is the equivalent of the laws of social development. From this point of view, for a scientific interpretation of literary phenomena it is useless to dig into the personal biography of a writer, because the secret of style does not lie in the personality of the writer. . . . The real basis of style must be sought where the source of social laws lies, in those production relationships in which the social character which is being projected in the images [of art] is formed.[8]

In Pereverzev's thesis that a writer cannot go beyond the fixed circle of his own themes and characters, predetermined by his social nature, that a writer cannot truthfully portray social groups other than his own—the characters from a different environment which he attempts to create being nothing but disguised images of the one social character he can portray—Party ideologists at the beginning of the First Five-Year Plan found a denial of the possibility of re-educating the fellow-traveler writers. For if it is impossible to go beyond a closed circle of socially determined images, if the writer is not free within himself to create according to his own discretion—political convictions, literary influences, and world view having no effect in this sphere—then the creative process becomes a mechanical reproduction of the author's own character, an autogenous image, and it is meaningless to talk of enlisting fellow-traveler writers in the tasks of socialist construction and of liquidating the remnants of capitalism in their consciousness.

Accused of ignoring the class struggle in art, of denying the role of the individual, of divorcing scientific, logical thought from artistic perception, of dismissing the educational role of literature, of disregarding the importance of the political and philosophical convictions of a writer, of denying consciousness in art, of Menshevist preaching of spontaneity and biologism, of rejecting Party opinion, of isolating art from politics and reducing art to entertainment, and of revising Marxism in the field of literary scholarship, Pereverzev was silenced as arbiter of Soviet literary theory. After 1931, he limited himself exclusively to teaching, without ever repudiating his views in the press. An avowed Marxist, Pereverzev had little in common with Bolshevik Marxism in its later manifestations. The Party made literature into a weapon of ideological warfare; Pereverzev did not.

The main fruits of Pereverzev's long study of Dostoyevski were his books *Dostoyevski's Writing* [9] and *F. M. Dostoyevski* [10] and a long article published in the Soviet *Literary Encyclopedia* in 1930.[11] The most important parts of *Dostoyevski's Writing* were republished in the second book, in which the earlier detailed treatment of Dostoyevski's basic types and characters is abridged, the chapters on his creative process and the style and content of his writing are repeated *in toto*, and a short biographical sketch is added.

Like Pereverzev's work in general, despite his controversial methodology, his studies of Dostoyevski bring to bear much knowledge, well-ordered thought, penetrating insight, and skill in generalization and in organization of his abundant material. Their main defect is the mechanistic reduction of the whole com-

plex of Dostoyevski's ideas and characters to a reflection of one
social group, the narrow sociological interpretation of psychology.

According to Pereverzev, Dostoyevski was the great genius
writing in the literary style of the *meshchanstvo* during the
breakup of the feudal social order and the birth of capitalism.
By *meshchanstvo* Pereverzev understood the social group included in the urban bourgeoisie which lived by private work, the
self-employed craftsmen and tradespeople or intellectuals. All
the characteristics of Dostoyevski's style, Pereverzev argued,
were explained by the disintegration of this social group.

To support his argument that the nature of Dostoyevski's
writing was determined by his social origin, Pereverzev relied
on his analysis of the writings themselves and adduced biographical data only to confirm his conclusions. He saw the
meshchanstvo, which engendered the style of Dostoyevski, placing upon it the stamp of dark tragedy. A humble caste, eco-
nomically insecure, deprived of civil rights, it was forced to
balance itself precariously between the bourgeoisie and the
lower depths of the city. Competition forced many of its members down the social pyramid into the dregs of society. If they
freed themselves from the yoke of class humiliation, they fell
under the yoke of poverty.

The eternal theme of Dostoyevski's novels is the hysterical
struggle for honor of characters whose human dignity has been
degraded and who are filled with resentment. The struggle often
takes on strange and morbid forms. In order to be completely
independent, to feel themselves fully men, to avoid injury from
others, the characters must themselves injure, insult, and torture
others:

Man is independent in the full sense of the word, he stands above any
injury and humiliation when he can do anything, when he dares to

break all laws, all juridical barriers and ethical standards. And in order to prove that everything is allowed to him, that he can do anything, Dostoyevski's hero will resort to crime. True, crime inevitably involves punishment, cruelty inevitably involves suffering, but this is acceptable suffering. This is lawful retribution, which does not wound the dignity of man. It is necessary not to avoid such suffering, but humbly to bear it. One must even seek it, love it, as a sign of the highest virtue of man. Thus the pathological inclination to wound, to torture, to injure, to commit crime, goes along with the equally morbid inclination to suffer, to endure injury. Insulted and injured, bursting to humiliate and to insult, a martyr thirsting to torture and a torturer in search of suffering, an evildoer and a criminal seeking to have evil done him and to be punished—here is the pivotal character around which all of Dostoyevski's writing revolves, the character of the *meshchanin* writhing under the double pressure of class injustice and capitalist competition.[12]

For all Dostoyevski's duality and contradictoriness, his sick, strained dissonance and ambivalence, Pereverzev discerned an organic unity in the complex world of Dostoyevski's characters, a well-ordered and carefully thought-out system. He classified Dostoyevski's heroes into the three main categories of the doubles, the self-willed, and the meek characters.

Most often in Dostoyevski—in *Poor Folk, The Double, The Village of Stepanchikovo, Notes from the Underground, The Gambler, Crime and Punishment, The Eternal Husband, A Raw Youth,* and *The Brothers Karamazov*—the central character is a psychological double. In Dostoyevski's early work the doubles display a still primitive emotionality. Makar Devushkin in *Poor Folk* alternates between outbursts of hysterical exasperation and humility. Opiskin in *The Village of Stepanchikovo* is tortured by lack of faith in himself and, seeking this faith, tortures and causes suffering to those around him. Like Golyadkin in *The Double,* the other doubles have a moral feeling, but they still have no moral consciousness. They have a feeling of their own individuality, but they still lack consciousness of it.

In *Crime and Punishment,* however, Raskol'nikov is an analytical, psychologically complex double, gifted with a keen critical mind. He is half criminal and half ascetic. From the point of view of his own duality he sees the world as a clash between self-will and humility, and faces the dilemma of choosing unbounded power or utter submissiveness. According to Pereverzev, the *meshchanin* Raskol'nikov could not be other than a double, could not perceive the possibility of harmony between the interests of society and the individual will; only if he had been born in a different environment could he have understood.

Ivan Karamazov represents a further development and deepening of the character of the philosophizing double. In him Dostoyevski's philosophical searchings are expressed in their most complete form. Ivan Karamazov projects his own duality, the contradiction between self-will and passivity, not only to the relations between the individual and society, as did Raskol'nikov, but also to the relations between the world and mankind. Unable to understand the possibility of harmony between the world and man, Ivan Karamazov faces the dilemma of choosing either the unlimited dominance of man and his will or the primacy of the world over man, the rule of the irrational and the inscrutable and the necessity of submission to it. The aberrations of Ivan's philosophy derive from the contradictions of his own nature, the inner struggle between pride and humiliation—contradictions which are not to be resolved for the reason that they are rooted in the social nature of the character. Ivan could resolve the metaphysical contradiction only by overcoming the disharmony of his own duality. Like all the doubles, Ivan Karamazov is obsessed by the craving for inner harmony, but two irreconcilable principles, that of self-will, of the man-god, and that of God and passive resignation, struggle for possession of his soul. His tragedy lies in the fact that he is not wholly possessed either by the devil or by God:

In the heart of Ivan Karamazov struggle the same Ormazd and Ahriman who waged a struggle in the heart of Devushkin. The mind, tortured by this eternal struggle without victory, exhausted by unsolved, inner contradictions, cannot hold out, and Karamazov ends in insanity.[13]

Pereverzev points out that Golyadkin and Ivan Karamazov, the two doubles who represent the beginning and the end of Dostoyevski's writing, demonstrate its inner unity and the consistency of its evolution. Golyadkin and Ivan Karamazov are only different stages of development of one and the same type, and moreover, of one and the same individuality. Golyadkin is the embryo, and Karamazov is the double gigantically developed both mentally and morally. Golyadkin's nervous system is shattered, and his dualism produces agonizing hallucinations. Each half of Golyadkin leads an independent existence. In the end he loses his equilibrium and goes mad. Ivan Karamazov, the culmination of the series of analytical doubles, is also psychically deranged, his inner duality is objectified in hallucination, and he too ends in madness.

In the character of Ivan Karamazov it seems that Dostoyevski is trying once more to embody the dream of his early fiction—to create a double in the narrow and exact sense of the word—a dream which the youthful powers of Dostoyevski fell short of realizing but which he so brilliantly realized at the fullness of his creative powers.[14]

The two sets of attributes with which Dostoyevski endows the doubles are separated and used independently in the other characters, who may be divided into the self-willed and the meek. Both types appear in Dostoyevski's first story, *Poor Folk,* in the characters of Bykov and Varen'ka. Bykov, in whom the traits of cruelty are still only adumbrated, is later developed into the torturers and criminals like Orlov, Petrov, and Luchka in *Notes from the House of the Dead*, Svidrigailov in *Crime and Punishment*, Valkovski in *The Insulted and Injured*, Verkhovenski in *The Devils*, and old Karamazov and Smerdyakov in *The Brothers Karamazov*.

Varen'ka Dobrosyolova began the line of meek sufferers, including Vasya Shumkov in *A Faint Heart*, Sonya Marmeladova in *Crime and Punishment*, Prince Myshkin in *The Idiot*, Makar Ivanovich Dolgoruki in *A Raw Youth*, and Alyosha Karamazov and the Elder Zosima in *The Brothers Karamazov*. In contrast to Voltaire, who makes fun of his optimistic hero Pangloss, Dostoyevski always sympathizes with his meek optimistic characters who believe only in the good with which God has endowed man. Pereverzev classifies them as people who have no part "in the process of social production and take no active part either in the creation of social capital or in its appropriation." [15]

Dostoyevski's religious pilgrims and ascetics Pereverzev also saw mainly as people divorced from the production process and *déclassés*, living on charity. They are the meek among those at the bottom of society, who have submitted and bless their lot, in contrast to the self-willed, who perish with a protest and a curse on their lips.

The Elder Zosima in *The Brothers Karamazov* is the personification of meekness and strict asceticism, the complete suppression of personal desires. In youth a sinner, like most of his kind, in his old age he makes humility and poverty the law of his nature. For him such a life is not a stern necessity dictated by circumstances; on the contrary, having made poverty and humility his calling and the purpose of existence, he feels great spiritual freedom and inspiration. "For Zosima," wrote Pereverzev,

the social order is just as inviolable, just as exempt from criticism and protest as the ordering of the world. Over all life a wise providence rules, by which even social relations are established. The apparent abnormality of these relations is the result of our short-sightedness. Amid suffering and want, the humility and faith which hold the promise of future universal harmony and happiness are developed. In suffering and poverty are forged meek and devoutly religious characters, and it is the "meek" who inherit the earth. Rebellion against such social relations not only leads to no betterment, but, on the contrary, is only a further disturbance of harmony and a moving away from it, a sin before God, the natural consequence of which is suffering.[16]

Zosima does not share what he considers the Western European belief in the rule of force. He opposes the class struggle in Europe, which leads only to bloodshed and in no way improves the life of the people. Anger and bitterness he deplores as incompatible with the sole way of salvation, the people's faith in God and the idea of humility. Most of all he condemns rebellion against the injustices of the world and the incitement of desire for revenge. All are guilty, and therefore everyone is called upon to give light to others in their striving to expiate their sins by the acceptance of suffering. Zosima's philosophy has its pragmatic aspect: he preaches poverty and humility, resignation, obedience, fasting, and prayer, which he upholds as the highest form of man's earthly existence, the sole source of freedom and happiness. The ideal of life is a loving unity of people without regard to station, origin, wealth, or poverty. Moral redemption for all rests on deeds of charity and love. The social order, based on submission, is inviolable. The world order was established by a benign providence and holds for man the hope of harmonious unity and grace through mercy and universal love.

Pereverzev, as a Marxist, regarded Zosima's religio-democratic optimism as a philosophy of inaction and poverty, a philosophy for those weak in spirit and body, a sign of the waning of the forces of life among the meek in the lower depths of society.

Although Pereverzev's classification of Dostoyevski's characters is a refinement upon Dobrolyubov's scheme of dividing them all into two types, the meek and the bitter, Pereverzev did not go beyond Dobrolyubov in explaining their genealogy. As long as the reader grants his premises, Pereverzev's strictly reasoned analysis is cogent and persuasive, but at the end his extreme sociological determinism has merely scratched the surface of Dostoyevski's characters and even tends to vitiate his frequently brilliant and penetrating interpretation of their enigmatic motivation and behavior. With all its shortcomings of oversimplification and schematization, however, Pereverzev's work is of lasting value to the student of Dostoyevski.

His observations on Dostoyevski's fictional technique were a highly original contribution at the time of their first publication. He pointed out that the characteristic manner of narration is not to follow the chronological order of events but to begin *in medias res* with a hurly-burly of unmotivated incidents. Action is always in the foreground. Dostoyevski relates events before the circumstances which have prepared them, depicts relations between people before he introduces the people themselves, and describes the behavior of characters before the characters. Thus he creates a mood of mystery and irreality. The behavior of the heroes seems fantastic, the relations between them tangled, the events haphazard. No other novels in world literature have the plot tension, the dark catastrophic quality, the whirlwind unfolding of the story found in Dostoyevski's. Their dynamism and suspense, chaotic disorder and unexpected turns have a stunning effect. Dostoyevski handles a plot in an extremely short period of time. In the novels of Tolstoi or Goncharov events drag on for years, while in Dostoyevski's novels they develop and are resolved in a few days. To intensify the dynamism, Dostoyevski resorts to a supercharging of events, piles up sudden, unexpected incidents that end with a catastrophic denouement. To impart a darker coloring to the events, he concentrates the action in the twilight and nocturnal hours. He leads the reader over devious paths of intrigue and confusion, whetting his curiosity by thrilling encounters and clashes.

Dostoyevski avoids lengthy digressions or descriptions. There are only genre paintings of city slums, apartments, and streets through which his characters ramble. Action, gestures, dialogue, and events hold sway. The heroes themselves are rarely described. More often, they themselves in their confessions portray their own characters and tell about their past. This method frees the author from the necessity of interrupting the action with descriptions and characterizations. The confessions of the characters serve to develop the action, revealing the secret springs which move and motivate it. Dostoyevski never speaks his thoughts as from himself; he puts them into the mouths of his innumerable characters.

The speech of the characters is shot through with the same chaotic dynamism. They speak quickly and nervously, piling up word upon word in a hurry-scurry manner; their speech is a mixture of long, awkward sentences and short, jerky phrases. In the nervous syntax of their speech Pereverzev heard the strained language of the high-strung, nervous, and harassed denizen of the city's lower depths. The poetic semantics adds to the dark character of Dostoyevski's style. Epithets, metaphors, similes, and other stylistic elements are, in Pereverzev's opinion, drawn from the cheerless and grim back streets of the city. Everywhere the face of the city man is seen. Everything in Dostoyevski —this classic of the new style of modern literature—is in nervous motion. His style is profoundly democratic, in both form and content. It is filled with social protest, with understanding of the man degraded in society, and with deep sympathy for him, and is charged with socially progressive energy.

In the concluding chapter of the book, "Dostoyevski in the History of Russian Belles-Lettres," Pereverzev defined Dostoyevski as a conscious antagonist to the writers of the landed aristocracy and their literary canons and as the initiator of a new bourgeois style. In his fiction itself Dostoyevski engaged in polemics against the old style, Pereverzev pointed out, citing examples given earlier by Beletski. In *Poor Folk* the letters of Makar Devushkin parody the *beau monde* style of Marlinski (A. A. Bestuzhev) and Mikhail Lermontov ("Why am I not a bird, not a bird of prey"), Zagoskin's manner in historical fiction (*Yermak and Zyuleika*), and Gogol's local-color style ("Story of Ivan Prokof'yevich Zholtopuz"). Dostoyevski's *The Double* is also the antithesis of Gogol's *Notes of a Madman*. While he is working on *Netochka Nezvanova* Dostoyevski writes in a letter to his brother on December 17, 1846, that he is taking action against all Russian literature. In 1859 he carries on the battle in *The Village of Stepanchikovo* by parodying Gogol's *Correspondence with Friends* and Gogol himself in the character of Foma Fomich Opiskin. The ridicule of landed-gentry literature continues in *The Devils*, in which Karmazinov is a parody on Turgenev. And in May, 1871, in a letter to N. N. Strakhov, Dostoyevski makes explicit his dislike for the writing of the landed gentry and asserts the urgent need for a new, nonaristocratic word in literature. Acknowledging Tolstoi to be the highest expression of the word of fiction, he nevertheless calls him "the last word of the landed aristocracy." The need for a new literature was proclaimed by the appearance of writers from the people, the Reshetnikovs, but they expressed them-

selves crudely. Obviously Dostoyevski professed himself the
representative of the new literary style. Through him, according
to Pereverzev, petit-bourgeois fiction made its way from the
lower levels of literature to the upper and opened a broad,
smooth road for itself. He was followed by a long line of writers
who created, to counteract the Pushkin-Gogol school of fiction,
a Dostoyevski school: Leonid Andreyev, Artsybashev, Sergeyev-
Tsenski, Remizov, and others. Chekhov, Korolenko, and Gorki
were also partially under the influence of Dostoyevski. Pereverzev enumerated various stories by Korolenko which depict a
world of spiritual stresses and strains akin to that in which
Dostoyevski's characters live. In Chekhov's comedy Pereverzev
found no trace of Gogol's style but instead saw a resemblance to
Dostoyevski's comic vein in "Novel in Nine Letters," "Another
Man's Wife and the Husband under the Bed," and "An Unpleasant Predicament." Even in Gorki, Pereverzev found "sometimes the wolf's bared teeth, sometimes the sheep's look of the
embittered and meek heroes of Dostoyevski." [17]

There is a sizable kernel of truth in Pereverzev's view of
Dostoyevski's influence on subsequent literature, but his analysis
of Dostoyevski's relationship to Pushkin is disputable. Pereverzev maintained that the lineage of all modern Russian petit-
bourgeois literature might be traced back to Dostoyevski, and
all literature of the landed gentry to Pushkin, that the two
writers represented diametrically opposed and antagonistic
styles of Russian nineteenth-century literature, and that the
struggle for supremacy between these styles was a reflection in
literature of the struggle of aristocratic Russia with bourgeois
Russia. The rise of Dostoyevski signified the dying out of
aristocratic culture and the appearance of a new class, the
bourgeoisie, at the front of the social stage.

Thus carrying his sociological argument to the extreme,

Pereverzev discounted the power of great art to transcend social barriers, to portray, and to hold meaning for, not a single class but the entire nation, and, indeed, to surmount the boundaries of nations and of continents. Aleksandr Pushkin belongs to the entire nation; Dostoyevski belongs to the world. Pereverzev's attempt to place Dostoyevski in opposition to Pushkin also discounted Dostoyevski's veneration for Pushkin, his boundless admiration for his clarity and coherence, his endless desire to write in the Pushkin manner. Reading Pushkin's prose, he was often sickened by the realization of his own seeming inability to overcome the confusion and complexity of his plots. In his notes for *A Raw Youth* he speaks of his yearning to "stick to Pushkin's consistency in developing the action, to hold myself tight in the pincers of his wise restraint in word and plot." [18] But, as N. N. Strakhov put it, "Dostoyevski was constitutionally unable to tone down his writing, to drop the subtlety of his analysis, to stop at one character and ten scenes instead of at twenty characters and one hundred scenes." [19]

Pereverzev, of course, would have explained this inability by the irrelevance of the author's own convictions and criteria. He wrote elsewhere: "Inspiration is the voice of class . . . all that subconscious sphere of the psyche which in itself has the power to determine the creative process, often even against the conscious purpose of the man. . . ." [20]

Other critics are unwilling to dismiss so cavalierly Dostoyevski's own words in his speech at the dedication of the Pushkin monument in 1880:

All these treasures of art and of an artist's insight are left by our great poet by way of guideposts for artists to come after him, for future workers in the same field. It may be said positively that had there been no Pushkin there would not have been the writers of talent who followed him. At least, however great their gifts, they would not have manifested themselves with such power and clarity as that with which they have been able to express themselves afterwards, even in our days.[21]

Nor did Dostoyevski consider himself a writer of one definite social group in contradistinction to Tolstoi and Goncharov, although he called them writers of the mid-upper circle. Certain that life as he depicted it was not the exception but the general rule, he regarded his work as of universal significance: "Future generations, who will be more dispassionate, will be convinced of this; I will [prove to] be in the right—I have faith in this." [22] In his notebooks Dostoyevski defined his innovation as an attempt to represent in his novels the spiritual phenomena above and beyond social practice, to resolve the contradictions of human psychology in terms of true, eternal, and unchanging "humanness," regardless of social position. He strove "to find the man in man": "They call me a psychologist. It is not true. I am only a realist in the higher sense; that is, I portray all the depths of the human soul." [23]

. 11 .

GEORGI YEFIMOVICH GORBACHOV (1897–?)
DOSTOYEVSKI AS A WARNING
AGAINST INDIVIDUALISM

During the 1920s Georgi Yefimovich Gorbachov was regarded
as one of the most orthodox Marxist critics. He was active in the
so-called "proletarian literary movement" and in the mid-1920s
joined the leftist "On-Guard" (*Na postu*) group. His book
Capitalism and Russian Literature, published in 1925, contains
a lengthy section on Dostoyevski.[1] In 1922 he had published the
article "The Revolution and Dostoyevski," [2] and in 1924 "The
Social Roots of Dostoyevski's Teaching." [3]

Gorbachov's approach to Dostoyevski was in many respects
similar to that of Pereverzev, although in the last article named
he had made the first criticism of Pereverzev, accusing him of
disobeying the basic requirement of Marxist methodology—the
necessity of beginning with an analysis of the concrete historical
situation. He agreed with the definition of Dostoyevski as a
writer of the down-and-out *meshchanstvo* but reproached Pereverzev for failure to make clear to what country and period
Dostoyevski's *meshchanstvo* belonged, what the concrete circumstances of the writer's life were, and what his attitude was
toward the dominant trends of social thought. Disregard of the
cultural, historical, and literary influences of the 1860s "makes
Pereverzev's interesting work one-sided and greatly oversimpli-
fied." [4]

Gorbachov objected to Pereverzev's use of the label "down-
and-out *meshchanstvo*" for all of Dostoyevski's characters, including "the typical degenerate nobles, Stavrogin, Myshkin, and

even Svidrigailov." [5] Raskol'nikov, Kirilov, Verkhovenski, and Ivan Karamazov, all cropped to the same sociological haircut in Pereverzev's criticism, lost their clearcut individuality. In comparison with Pereverzev, even the early Marxist critic Kranikhfel'd seemed to Gorbachov to be on firmer ground, in that he approached Dostoyevski as the product of a concrete historical and social milieu despite his addiction to large, loose generalizations.

Gorbachov also condemned the "broad" sociological interpretation by P. N. Sakulin as idealistic. In Sakulin's opinion, Dostoyevski and Tolstoi were among those great writers who, although they are the product of definite social conditions, nevertheless grow out of their socially predestined bounds, spiral upward above the level of their surroundings and become the possession of all.

Gorbachov himself was essentially a member of the sociological school and, like Pereverzev, first of all sought the social roots of Dostoyevski's writing; but, while Pereverzev concentrated his attention on an analysis of the psychology of the double and a classification of the characters, Gorbachov concerned himself mainly with the social and philosophical content of Dostoyevski's work as a whole. His theoretical principle that a work of literature must be analyzed as an organic unity of content and form was discarded in his actual practice. Style was completely neglected in favor of ideology.

Like the majority of Soviet critics of the 1920s, Gorbachov by no means denied the significance of Dostoyevski for the new epoch and the new generation of readers. In "The Social Roots of Dostoyevski's Teaching" he advocated knowledge of Dostoyevski and criticism of him as a means of reinforcing the new revolutionary ideology:

We must make use of this heritage ourselves and destroy the legend that in Dostoyevski's works there is a very powerful criticism of socialism, that Dostoyevski is a writer who, from the revolutionary point of view, is "harmful" and "dangerous" and cannot but seduce [his readers].[6]

It does no harm to the young people of the revolution, who are gnawing on the granite of science, to harden their teeth by gnawing through Dostoyevski too until they understand him.[7]

In Gorbachov's opinion, Dostoyevski paints a ruthlessly realistic picture of the tragedy of social individualism and offers profound criticism of utopian socialism and petty groups of conspirators isolated from the genuinely democratic revolutionary movement and from the popular masses.

Gorbachov's definition of the world of Dostoyevski's characters was the usual one of Marxist critics: the world of the petit bourgeois, on the verge of becoming the *Lumpenproletariat* and its shady fringes. In the fact that Dostoyevski had found his medium here in the dregs of society, Gorbachov discerned a "proletarian" or "democratic feeling" in Dostoyevski himself. From Dostoyevski's enmity for the nobility and the Slavophile aristocrats, his sympathy for the *raznochintsy*, and his faith in the peasantry, Gorbachov concluded that Dostoyevski was and always remained a democrat: "Even when he became a reactionary, his sincere, prayerful idolatry of the truth in the people and of their suffering did not stop." [8] His early faith in utopian socialism was not a firm conviction, but a momentary enthusiasm tinged with doubts. His testimony at the trial revealed an ironic attitude toward utopianism, and prison cured him of it forever. The anti-historical rationalism of the utopians and their admission that in the future it would be necessary for society to use compulsion and force on the individual disillusioned Dostoyevski as to their practical political program, but on the

moral and religious plane socialism never lost its appeal for
him. Shigalovism in *The Devils*, was, according to Gorbachov,
a caricature merely of utopian socialism. Dostoyevski's criticism
was wide of the mark in respect to scientific socialism, which he
did not know; it was only the European forms of socialism
which he rejected.

The prime reason why Dostoyevski turned from socialism,
Gorbachov stated, was his individualism. The individualistic
solution of the problems of freedom and the meaning of life led
inevitably to belief in the immortality of the soul and in personal
bliss in a future life. In the Russian peasant he thought he perceived his own faith in future harmony through universal Christ-
like love, and thus he became

an ideologist of the feudal and petit-bourgeois reactionary fear of
capitalism and protest against it. The reactionary nobles and the reactionary *narodnik* of the intelligentsia joined hands in idealizing the
backwardness of the petit-bourgeois, patriarchal countryside.[9]

To Gorbachov, Dostoyevski epitomized the tragedy of the
intelligentsia, who had lost their social ties and moral principles
and were isolated from revolutionary events. Dreaming of
patriarchal harmony, fearing "the beast in man" and the capitalism which was descending on Russia, he turned to the past and
fled into the arms of reaction. At the same time in his incessant
longing for social harmony, he expressed sentiments which, in
the opinion of the critic, were sometimes very similar to the
principles of communism. In *Winter Notes on Summer Impressions*, for example, Dostoyevski argued that with true social
harmony there would be no compulsory sacrifices and duties.
The individual would say to society: "Take everything from
me and do not give much." Gorbachov matched this phrase with
the formula of communism: "to each according to his needs,
from each according to his abilities."

In tracing the manifestation of Dostoyevski's ideology in his major novels, Gorbachov characterized Raskol'nikov as an individualist, a *déclassé* member of the intelligentsia, who does not take into account the collective interests of any group, takes no side in the struggle, and solves all problems in solitude. Society, as he sees it, is the sum of separate personalities, and he repudiates social decisions on the general welfare in favor of the higher value of the individual.

Prince Myshkin, according to Gorbachov, represents a criticism of rationalistic Christianity, individualistic ethics, and the neo-Christianity akin to Tolstoiism. Dostoyevski is apparently saying that the precept of the individual is powerless and sometimes even ludicrous in the face of real life with its wild human passions. Although in the novel *The Idiot* everyone agrees with his preaching of love, nevertheless in the heat of human passions they all torture and tear one another to pieces. At the same time Dostoyevski seems to be bowing to the mystical intercession of Christ.

In *The Devils* Gorbachov saw a portrayal of the hideous corruption of the conspiratorial intelligentsia, cut off from the masses and paving the way for the dictatorship of the minority with their provocations, demagogy, and stifling of those who disagreed. Verkhovenski is a product of the aristocratic liberalism of the 1840s. The rootlessness, disillusionment, and degeneration of the nobility are personified in Stavrogin, who takes up revolution out of boredom. For him revolution is simply a novel sensation after the depravity, mysticism, and nihilism which he has outlived—pastimes reminiscent of those of the degenerate ruling circles at the end of the Roman Empire. Yet in Stavrogin's personal charm and influence on others, Gorbachov glimpsed Dostoyevski's devotion to and envy of the ancient culture of the nobility. Himself depicting unsettled, haphazard families, Dostoyevski always envied Tolstoi for his power to portray aristocratic families, and this envy is reflected in Dostoyevski's ambivalence toward Stavrogin.

Again in *A Raw Youth* Dostoyevski contrasts the Christian truth of the people, as represented by Makar Dolgoruki, and the aristocratic liberalism and humanism of the cosmopolitan, in Versilov. The theme of the novel Gorbachov defined as the decay of an aristocratic family under the influence of the money relations of the new world.

The most powerful picture of the crisis of feudal society is *The Brothers Karamazov*. The character of Fyodor Karamazov serves as exposé of the serf owners. Ivan Karamazov is poisoned by the philosophy of European materialism and individualism. His disbelief and nihilism are embodied in the figure of the devil. Ivan's ethical ratiocinations constitute the most striking pages of the novel. The burden of the consciousness of sin leads Ivan to madness.

Mouthing maxims of Communist doctrine to justify terror and violence, Gorbachov attacked what he understood to be Dostoyevski's position in the "Legend of the Grand Inquisitor":

Socialism combats the sophistical dialectics of Dostoyevski with genuine dialectics; force and coercion are unavoidable as a means for attaining freedom. The path to freedom is class struggle arising from material needs, but the results of social struggle are complete, all-embracing social and personal freedom and the power of society over the economy—the reign of freedom. Only the idea of absolute individualism, and even the cutting up of the life of the individual into separate, disconnected, fleeting moments, could have produced in Ivan Karamazov his denial of progress.

. . . Capitalism prostitutes, starves, tortures in wild pogroms, and, by the bombing of cities, kills millions of children. Therefore, if the shells of the revolution accidentally injure and doom to agonizing death thousands of children or if revolutionary decrees give occasion for provoking an unnecessary pogrom, still the revolution proceeds to this, and it is right.[10]

Gorbachov, a typical Communist critic at this time, was surprisingly weak in his political analysis of Dostoyevski. His attempts to define the symbolic characters which persist throughout Dostoyevski's fiction also seem pale and schematic in comparison with Pereverzev's brilliant interpretation. In order to emphasize the fact that Dostoyevski merely revolved in a circle of the same social, moral, religious, and historical ideas, Gorbachov divided all his characters into five categories: the serf-owning noble, predator, egotist, and voluptuary; the liberal noble; the protesting man of the intelligentsia; the *raznochinets* sot; and the meek type. Gorbachov almost completely ignored the double.

Dostoyevski's characters interested Gorbachov only insofar as he was able to apply to them the Marxist yardstick of class. Pereverzev's statement that with the appearance of Gorbachov's criticism the interpretation of Dostoyevski "fell into good hands" [11] is an amusing bit of literary logrolling.

Gorbachov nonetheless stands out favorably among Communist critics of Dostoyevski because of his ability to rise above the level of arbitrary censure. He tried to understand Dostoyevski's writing as a product of definite historical conditions and, if only by dint of stressing the inadvertent merits of his novels as a lesson in the dangers of individualism, held the door to Dostoyevski open for Soviet readers during the 1920s.

For a while at the beginning of the 1930s Gorbachov remained prominent as a literary critic and took part in the campaign against Pereverzev. But soon he too was accused of Trotskyism, was removed from his position as assistant director of the Institute of Russian Literature of the Pushkin House in Leningrad, and disappeared. His books were then withdrawn. His work on Dostoyevski, of little intrinsic value as literary criticism, thus retains only a certain historical interest as documentation of a stage in Soviet literary development.

. 12 .

V. L'VOV-ROGACHEVSKI (1874–1930)
AND LEV NAUMOVICH VOITOLOVSKI (1876–)
DOSTOYEVSKI IN SURVEYS
OF RUSSIAN LITERATURE

Several surveys of Russian literature published in the 1920s
contain chapters on Dostoyevski which are of more than textbook interest, notably those of V. L'vov-Rogachevski and L. N.
Voitolovski. The former's *Modern Russian Literature*,[1] first
published in 1922, was used in many higher educational institutions and secondary schools and was widely read by the
educated public. Like his anthology of modern Russian literature, the book was frequently republished until its suppression
in the 1930s during the campaign against "bourgeois liberalism"
and "Menshevism" in scholarship. At the same time Nazarenko's
History of Russian Literature in the Nineteenth Century,[2] which
had been used even more extensively in the schools, was "un-
masked" as anti-Marxist. Nazarenko's treatment of Dostoyevski
was largely derivative, L'vov-Rogachevski's relatively independent and original.

Although he ostensibly embraced Soviet Marxism, L'vov-
Rogachevski's deep respect for literary tradition made him oppose the Soviet tendency to discard the classics.

Like his fellow critics, he looked upon Dostoyevski's writing
as a prologue to modern urban literature, in contrast to that of
Tolstoi, which was the epilogue to the literature of the aristocratic period. Against the epic calm, the majesty, the aristocratic
country estates of Tolstoi, Dostoyevski set the uneasy, stormy,

humbled poverty of the city intelligentsia, and against the non-resistance of Karatayev, the rebelliousness of Ivan Karamazov.

His whole life, all the vicissitudes that he experienced shaped him for the end of opposing the country-estate Oblomovs, Tentetnikovs, and Lavretskis [3] with his nervous, down-and-out, epileptic heroes, always slightly mad, always unbalanced and hysterical, people of the noisy city, harassed by social conflicts, stepping over the line or already over it, fighters against God and penitents, people in hospital and prison garments, his Raskol'nikovs, Rogozhins, Verkhovenskis, Stavrogins, Karamazovs, Smerdyakovs. . . . No one came so close to our turbulent and nervous, catastrophic and dynamic epoch as this contemporary of Gogol, Grigorovich, Turgenev, and Tolstoi.[4]

As evidence of Dostoyevski's challenge to the literature of the gentry, L'vov-Rogachevski again pointed out the caricatures of Turgenev and Granovski in *The Devils* and the parody on Gogol in the *Village of Stepanchikovo*, adding that the character Shchedrodarov in an article entitled "Fragment from the Novel 'Shchedrodarov' " [5] was a parody on Saltykov-Shchedrin.

It fell to Dostoyevski "to say a new word in imaginative literature—not that of the great estate nor of the peasant village nor of the country house, not anything *raffiné* and elegant." [6] He also expressed the need for a new word by breaking the old aesthetic canons. His ideas of beauty grew out of the bustle and commotion of the city, the tempo of its traffic. Nine tenths of Dostoyevski's life was spent in the city, while Tolstoi spent seventy-five of his eighty-two years in the country. Tolstoi disliked telegrams and city newspapers, but newspapers with their reports of crime were Dostoyevski's mainstay. Working in bursts of inspiration, nervously, feverishly, Dostoyevski caught in his novels the cinematographic flashes of incidents and characters of the city, read the swift-passing faces in the city kaleidoscope at the moment when persons were in a state of greatest tension. Not to depict the time-ingrained characteristics

passed from generation to generation, but to portray the dynamics of life, the developments which were putting an end to
the old rural mode of life—such was Dostoyevski's forte and
the essence of his new word.

The very composition of his stories is determined by the city.
Into the boiling whirlpool of the streets, the writer brings events
from the criminal news of the day, sharpens the clashes, and
imparts to his account of swift-running life a strange atmosphere
of chance and fate. The slow and measured flow of events in the
fiction of Gogol, Turgenev, Tolstoi, Goncharov, and Aksakov
disappears. In contrast to the chronological succession of childhood, adolescence, youth, and maturity, Dostoyevski portrays a
strained and terror-struck world where characters clash during
a brief snatch of time. The reader is plunged immediately into
the very midst of events and is carried down to the nether world
of the city:

In the streets of the city which this tragic artist has immortalized there
is a smell not of ancestral lindens but of blood. The novels of Dostoyevski, this uniquely tragic writer of Russian literature, have no air
of philosophy through a dream nor of the stories of an old nurse "about
old times" nor of the sweet tales of grandmothers lulling the Oblomovs
and the Hamlets of Shchigrov District [7] to sleep, but of storms and
tempests. Even the children in these novels—the Ilyushechka Snegiryovs
and the Netochka Nezvanovas—pass before us as heroes of tragic events.
Is not Ilyushechka, the son of Staff-Captain Snegiryov, who was man-
handled by Mitya Karamazov and whom the schoolboys call "wisp of
tow"—is not this little martyr, with his tragic childish wail, "Papa,
how he humiliated you," the embodiment of the tragedy of city life?
The novels *Crime and Punishment, The Idiot, The Devils, The Brothers
Karamazov,* and *A Raw Youth* are a complicated tissue of tragic events;
in them, what is crime in a cheap thriller is turned by this Dante of our
day into a divine comedy, or, rather, a tragedy of the contemporary
city, and has taken on prophetic, significant meaning. The brilliant

dialogue on religious and philosophical themes, the very subtle psychological analysis, the complex motivation of human behavior, the revelations and insights of a genius have turned Dostoyevski's tangled, action-packed criminal records into the greatest achievement of our time.[8]

Resorting to an old un-Marxist biographical method and quoting statements of Dostoyevski's daughter as evidence, L'vov-Rogachevski explained the "predilection for bloody, tragic events" [9] by the history of the family in which the writer was born and grew up, the unfortunate heredity from his father, and the memories of his father's violent death. Fyodor Mikhailovich's daughter had written: "He remembered [it] all his life and analyzed the reasons for this terrible death." [10] Life in prison then fed his interest in human criminality. Simultaneously, "the new artist, flesh of the flesh and bone of the bone of the poverty of [Petersburg]," [11] he immortalized both the romanticism of ghostly, foggy St. Petersburg with its white nights and the humdrum life of the basements, garrets, and stuffy furnished rooms which housed the unbalanced, eccentric "intellectuals of the proletariat, solitary people, dreaming in their corners of becoming Rothschilds or Napoleons." [12]

For Dostoyevski himself "poverty stood at his cradle in Moscow, poverty accompanied him to St. Petersburg and into the capitals of Europe." [13] He was a "true proletarian of the intelligentsia" who, writing of his own kind, the "isolated proletarians, perishing under the yoke of eternal, crying need," [14] demonstrated the necessity of re-ordering life. In Dostoyevski's own poverty, his membership in the Petrashevski circle and testimony during the investigation, and in his article on George Sand in Diary of a Writer for 1876, L'vov-Rogachevski found grounds for representing Dostoyevski as a champion and precursor of the Russian revolution:

The new word of Dostoyevski was not the word of the city, of the proletarian, intellectual; it was a new attempt in Russia to express new hopes, new ideals of radical social reform. And even though later Dostoyevski changed from Paul to Saul and cursed socialism, he was the creator of the social novel and he forced people to feel the full sharpness of social conflicts.[15]

In Dostoyevski's revelation of the injustice of the world through the sufferings of his characters, L'vov-Rogachevski sees the ascendancy of the artist over the philosopher:

None of Dostoyevski's metaphysics, none of the accusations against the nihilists and socialists could drown out the cry of the hungry child. The wan, blue-hued face of this child, pressed to the shriveled breast of the mother, black with hunger, came through the fogs of mysticism, through the preaching of submission and humility. The dream of Mitya Karamazov was more powerful and more convincing than the Slavophile teachings of the Elder Zosima.[16]

It is true, L'vov-Rogachevski says, that in Dostoyevski's first period, when he was interested in social problems, his heroes appeared to be victims of social disorder, and that in the second, as a result of his own personal catastrophe, religious and moral problems dominated his life and work. But even in the first period the writer continually turned to religious questions, and in the second period the defects of the social order never ceased to harass him.

L'vov-Rogachevski compared Dostoyevski's return to St. Petersburg from penal servitude in 1859 to "the return of [a Lazarus] who had been in the power of death for many long years." [17] Dostoyevski had been saved by the Gospel given him in Tobol'sk by the wife of a Decembrist. The symbol of the cross and the head, about which Prince Myshkin speaks in the fifth chapter of *The Idiot*, epitomizes the significance of Dostoyevski's writing after prison, "when the exhausted, deathly pale, despairing man stretches out his blue lips to the cross, as to the last refuge." [18]

Like Dolinin, L'vov-Rogachevski saw Dostoyevski's spiritual reversal as completed in the fall of 1863. At this time Dostoyevski, while abroad, conceived the ideas for *Notes from the Underground* and *The Gambler*. The first of these L'vov-Rogachevski regarded as a parody on the writer's own former socialist views. In the following years Dostoyevski's personal experiences—his relationship to Apollinaria Suslova, the deaths of his brother Mikhail and his first wife in 1864, the forced suspension of his journal *Vremya* [Time] and the difficulties with its successor *Epokha* [Epoch], his bondage to his creditors, his attacks of epilepsy—all left their immediate mark on his fiction. In *Crime and Punishment* (1866) the hero takes the way of the cross, and Sonya Marmeladova reads a chapter about the resurrection of Lazarus to Raskol'nikov. During his stay abroad in 1867–71, Dostoyevski reasoned out the destiny of Russia on the basis of his observations in Western Europe and faced the problem of theodicy which tortures Ivan Karamazov. There, too, the idea for an epic novel, to be the culmination of his work and life, was conceived. Its central figure was to have been a man who succumbed to many temptations and finally found Christ, the Russian land, and God. In the end the idea was splintered among other novels—*The Devils, A Raw Youth*, and *The Brothers Karamazov*.

L'vov-Rogachevski joined the Marxist chorus of condemnation of Dostoyevski's reactionary religious ideology in the last fifteen years of his life, but at the same time found objective reasons for it—the course of revolution in the West (the rout of the Paris Commune in 1871), the Nechayev affair, and atheistic socialism in Russia:

Disillusioned, rootless, deep in the spiritual underground, in the last fifteen years of his life the artist becomes a *pochvennik,* a nationalist, a Byzantine. He joins the crusade against nihilism. At one time the pupil of Belinski, he now curses Belinski, and in a letter to N. Strakhov in 1871 he calls Belinski "a disgraceful and stinking phenomenon in Russian life." Politically he adheres to V. Meshcherski and K. P. Pobedonostsev, and philosophically he goes along with Apollon Grigor'yev, N. N. Strakhov, Konstantin Leont'yev, and Vladimir Solov'yov. The mysticism of [Solov'yov], then still "a young philosopher," more and more lays hold of Dostoyevski.[19]

In his mind atheism is identified with the formula: "There is no God, therefore everything is permitted." The degenerate Smerdyakov grows out of the atheist Ivan Karamazov, just as previously Fed'ka the convict had grown out of the atheism of Pyotr Verkhovenski. In opposition to the Napoleonic supermen— Raskol'nikov, Pyotr Verkhovenski, Stavrogin, Kirilov, Ivan Karamazov, all atheists divorced from the life of the people— Dostoyevski offers Sonya Marmeladova with her Gospel (in *Crime and Punishment*), the old religious pilgrim Makar Ivanovich (in *A Raw Youth*), Shatov, who renounces atheism (in *The Devils*), the God-fearing Alyosha and the wise Elder Zosima (in *The Brothers Karamazov*). The meek, all-forgiving Christ is contrasted to the Grand Inquisitor, snared in the dream of ruling the earth. The trip with Vladimir Solov'yov in 1878 to Optina Pustyn' and the conversations with the Elder Amvrosi strengthened Dostoyevski's faith in the religious traditions of the people. He ends his Pushkin speech with an appeal to the haughty intelligentsia to humble themselves and unite with the people.

"In all that F. M. Dostoyevski wrote, like a terrible phantom, a tormenting nightmare, there arises the familiar picture of the last step . . . the cross . . . and the head of the man condemned to death." [20]

For partial explanation of Dostoyevski's "frenzied" religiosity, L'vov-Rogachevski resorted to the writer's ancestors, citing S. Lyubimov's article in which the latter had pointed out that several generations of the Dostoyevski family, living in the Grand Duchy of Lithuania, on the territory of present-day Byelorussia and the Ukraine, had been forced to fight for their Eastern Orthodox belief against the influence of Rome.[21]

L'vov-Rogachevski characterized Dostoyevski as an extreme individualist, incapable of understanding that, apart from the fear of God, the individual might find salvation in the awareness of the organic link between him and his social milieu, of his unity with people. Dostoyevski had refused to see the fact that the nonbelievers Belinski, Chernyshevski, and Dobrolyubov were the loftiest of idealists, to whose level he himself could not rise, and that these selfless public workers had never subscribed to the atheist slogan, "Everything is permitted."

Instead of revolutionaries of pure strain such as Vera Figner, Sof'ya Bardina, and Veimar, Dostoyevski had chosen Nechayev, a man deplored by the *narodnik* intelligentsia. Yet, even while accusing Dostoyevski of inconsistency when he criticized the revolutionaries in the name of Christ, L'vov-Rogachevski again attempted to bring this "martyr of God" into rapport with contemporary Soviet life: "No other Russian artist has given so much material for, or so much prodding toward, revolutionary atheistic thought as did this Byzantine." [22]

L'vov-Rogachevski considered the salient feature of Dostoyevski's writing to be the duality—manifested both in his own outlook and in that of his heroes—which is characteristic of periods of decay and disintegration. Like Pereverzev, L'vov-Rogachevski regarded *The Double* as an overture to all Dostoyevski's subsequent work, and, like Belinski, he referred to the personality disintegration in the double as strange and incomprehensible madness. In general, Dostoyevski's characters are

"bearers of spiritual discord and disintegration, clear precursors of the decadents in the writings of Leonid Andreyev and
Fyodor Sologub." [23]

An eclectic critic, L'vov-Rogachevski occasionally borrowed
heavily from the ideas and phrases of other authors. Like
Merezhkovski, he spoke of "God and the devil" fighting for the
soul of Dostoyevski.[24] And the ·following passage is strongly
reminiscent of Gorki's ideas, as well as those of Belinski and
Mikhailovski:

With them "Thought" is both a rapier and a serpent. And it is difficult
to say for what they argue more convincingly—the existence of God
or atheism, repudiation of the revolution or its affirmation. All these
martyrs and torturers, at one moment submissive and at another rebellious, at one moment trembling creatures and at another daring
Napoleons in their attitude toward women and in their frenzied love,
with elements of both sadism and masochism, are strikingly similar in
their basic traits, as Grushen'ka and Nastas'ya Filippovna are strikingly
alike in their traits. Morbid cruelty, nervous excitement, hysteria, de-
pression, fits, madness—such is the mournful chart of the gloomy, isolated inmates of this hospital for the poor erected at the expense of
F. M. Dostoyevski for his doubles.[25]

On the other hand, L'vov-Rogachevski was also capable of
challenging the critics whose opinions he purveyed. In one of
the early criticisms of Pereverzev, he objected to Pereverzev's
disregard for the individual traits of the writer and his reduction of the dual psychology of Dostoyevski's characters to
merely a social basis, finding such an interpretation an abuse of
the sociological method. L'vov-Rogachevski himself ascribed
many of the distinctive characteristics of Dostoyevski's writing
to his epilepsy.

In the final analysis L'vov-Rogachevski evaluated the significance of Dostoyevski in terms of universal humanity rather
than of the class struggle:

He painted a shocking picture of social disorder, he showed how the poor man was insulted, injured, and wronged. A preacher of humility, with his vivid characters he called for human dignity and for active struggle for the brotherhood of man. A nationalist, he prophetically welcomed in the Russian man the inclination toward universal brotherhood and universal happiness. This was the other countenance, the other hypostasis of the soul of Dostoyevski, a hypostasis deeply human and deeply humane. Compassion for man and the force of great anger and burning love were perceived in the books of Dostoyevski by the poor of the contemporary city, the downtrodden, insulted, and injured. And this wronged folk, after it had revolted, erected in Moscow at Trubnaya Square, not far from the hospital for the poor, a granite monument to the writer of the insulted and injured, whom he summoned from human suffering to universal brotherhood.[26]

In the 1920s L'vov-Rogachevski, a Marxist, dared to acknowledge that the criteria of his own tendentious and prejudiced time were not suitable for application to Dostoyevski:

Of all the artists of our time, F. M. Dostoyevski is most of our time, no matter how paradoxical this sounds. The time has not yet come for an objective study of his work. The question is still put too tendentiously and in too publicist a manner: whether or not Dostoyevski was on the same road with Soviet Russia. But now, as never before, abundant materials have been accumulated which are preparing the ground for a scholarly, historical-literary study of his amazingly rich work.[27]

L'vov-Rogachevski, aware of the defects of bald sociological analysis, tried to combine the Marxist method of the time with those of the formalist school, which also erred, in his opinion, by examining only a writer's devices and disregarding his ideology.

After the death of L'vov-Rogachevski in 1930, his work was branded as un-Marxist and Menshevik, "a product of the opportunist petit bourgeoisie attaching itself to the workers' movement." With his "impotent, spineless, petit-bourgeois liberalism," [28] he was declared unable to distinguish between the friends and the enemies of the revolution—an accusation per-haps referring to his favorable attitude toward Dostoyevski as a precursor of the revolution. In the 1930s L'vov-Rogachevski's textbook *Modern Russian Literature*, as well as his other books, disappeared from the shelves of the public libraries in the USSR.

L. N. Voitolovski, a physician by profession, began work as a literary historian only in his mature years. His sketch of Dos-toyevski, first published in 1911 [29] and then reworked for in-clusion in his *History of Russian Literature in the Nineteenth and Twentieth Centuries* [30] (1926), is of interest chiefly by virtue of the fact that it was the first attempt by a Russian writer to apply the methods of Freudian analysis to Dostoyevski's work. Although Voitolovski's effort was countenanced in the 1920s and the study was even included in a volume published in 1928 in the series *The Classics in the Light of Marxism*,[31] almost no other Soviet scholar has ventured to follow in his footsteps.

In the prevailing Marxist mode, Voitolovski contrasted Dos-toyevski, the writer of a new social milieu and a new word, to Tolstoi, the voice of the nobility—the two poles of Russian literature. Tolstoi stood for the settled, patriarchal way of life, Dostoyevski for a furious succession of events, hurly-burly hysterics, and catastrophes. Tolstoi's heroes always know their role and place in life and never startle the reader by suddenly stepping out of character. Dostoyevski's heroes are a constant astonishment, behaving not at all as the reader expects them to. In Tolstoi, the characters are clear, distinct, and positive. In Dostoyevski, they are pure figments of the imagination, con-cealing their vices and sinfulness behind a mask of apparent virtue. In Tolstoi, the heroes love healthy and beautiful women with an unshakable, enduring love, and they live in beautiful houses. In Dostoyevski, they inhabit slums and often love freaks and cripples. The fate of Tolstoi's heroes is portrayed during the course of their entire lives, while Dostoyevski winds up the action in a very short time, sometimes half an hour. Tolstoi's heroes have a steady income, wear elegant dress, have refined manners and speech, and have an irreproachable past. In Dostoyevski, the heroes are selected from indigent students, prostitutes, and criminals with the manners of the street; they speak the coarse language of their environment.

Like Kranikhfel'd and Pereverzev, Voitolovski interprets Dostoyevski's writing as a response to the new spirit of capitalism:

In Dostoyevski money is the breath of capitalism, a breath which like a subtle poison steals through the veins of his heroes and fills them with eternal unrest. Tormented by a thirst for money, by a thirst for the terrible opportunities offered by gold, they are confused, act like madmen, smash idols and barriers, fall, rise, and again plunge into the slough of sorry nightmares. Thus in a mad chaos of contrasts the capitalistic psychology of the city dweller is hammered out in Dostoyevski, the psychology of the Raskol'nikovs, the Stavrogins, and the Karamazovs.[32]

Were it not for their priority in time, Voitolovski observed, the baffling characters in Dostoyevski's novels might well have been patterned upon the theories of Freud, except that sex plays a lesser role. In Dostoyevski everyone has myriad secrets, concealed desires and passions, usually buried deep and well covered by the mask of everyday living. In the depths of the soul are deposited all the distress, all the injuries and the insults heaped upon man by life around him. Thus there is unconsciously built up "a second world," in which man seeks salvation from all the conflicts of life, between emotion and duty, between the interests of the individual and his obligations to society. Depending on their individual inclinations, people find an outlet in art, in gambling, or in vice. The second world is usually a contrast to the external existence, and in it shy, modest people may abandon themselves to unrestrained passions or, on the contrary, natures that are crass in their everyday manifestations may be ennobled to the point of extreme sensitivity. The impressions of daily life, relegated to the sphere of the subconscious, sometimes break through to the surface in the form of strange and sudden actions, like Raskol'nikov's murder of the old woman in *Crime and Punishment* or Lyamshin's tour de force with the *Marseillaise* in *The Devils*. Voitolovski finds in all Dostoyevski's characters the "dry rot" compounded of wanton Karamazovism, "Lyamshinism" and "Smerdyakovism." [33] Every one of Dostoyevski's heroes has his "double" with traits of "Lyamshinism." Yet the heart must confess openly in order to cleanse itself. "All of Dostoyevski's novels are spilling over with cries of repentance." [34] At the same time, even in the heroism of confession there is an admixture of "Lyamshinism":

The "Augustin" of self-debasement grows stronger, "Augustin" becomes more and more confident, more and more insolent. And our sinner in search of purification has not time to recover himself before every trace of heroic repentance is gone, and the Stavrogin of yesterday feels in his despondent breast the despicable, mean soul of Lyamshin and Smerdyakov.[35]

Voitolovski dealt at some length with what he called Dostoyevski's "international style." He objected to attempts of Western critics to see in Dostoyevski an expression of the Slavic soul and to assertions that the author himself and his own dark life story are reflected in his writing. For the Marxist Voitolovski these points of view were subjective and idealistic. Nor did

Voitolovski entirely accept Pereverzev's opinion that the petit
bourgeoisie in the process of breakdown was the sole determining factor in Dostoyevski's writing. According to Voitolovski, Dostoyevski raised the problem of the alarmed *raznochinets*
or "critically thinking individual," that is, the intellectual
divorced from the masses and feeling his responsibility to history, in whom the moving force was hatred for the feudal order
and consciousness of his role in the new bourgeois order coming
into existence. The need to solve the problem of the individual
and the right to resort to deception and force determined the
behavior of many of the characters. Everywhere Dostoyevski
appears to condemn the feudal order, but he censures the individual for self-will and violence. The weight can be removed
from a world which has been defiled by violence not by a
Napoleon, but by Sonya Marmeladova.

In giving his own definition of Dostoyevski's style, Voitolovski began by saying that, as a *raznochinets*, Dostoyevski expressed the very rhythm of capitalist life. The mechanizing and
leveling action of his city results from the impersonal and unlimited sway of money in the capitalist world. Dostoyevski's
characters live in constant fear of something unknown and fatal
—a psychology engendered on one hand by the desire to make
money, to collect interest, and, on the other hand, by a fear of
competition. The endless anxiety and fear, temptation, and
struggle against the world and against themselves explain not
only their duality and fluctuation between confession and
secretiveness but also Dostoyevski's style and language. Voitolovski designated his style as "international" in that it conveys the
dark pits of the spirit into which people fall during the capitalist phase and asserted that it was by virtue of this "international" quality that Dostoyevski had become a widely read
and highly honored writer in the West.

Thus, holding to Marxism, Voitolovski again arrived at the mechanistic explanation of human psychology by economic causes.

Voitolovski's sole innovation was his attempt to consider Dostoyevski from the Freudian point of view, an inconsistent and rather elementary attempt. Apparently his medical training and keenly analytical mind came into conflict with the demands of his Marxist sociology.

. 13 .

LEONID PETROVICH GROSSMAN (1888–)
FROM APOLOGETICS TO ACCUSATION

The shift in emphasis and tone of Leonid Grossman's criticism is a clear example of the enforced adaptation of literary scholars to the Soviet ideological requirements of the 1930s. Grossman was an erudite, brilliant, non-Party scholar, master of a lively and distinguished prose style which made his work interesting and enjoyable to the general reader as well as to the Dostoyevski specialist.

In his book *The Path of Dostoyevski*, written during the NEP period when relative freedom of thought was still possible, Grossman expressed his own convictions concerning Dostoyevski's philosophy. At this time he saw Dostoyevski's work in its entirety as a philosophical drama, the core of which was a search for faith and a unitary system of thought; in his novels Dostoyevski was examining ideas, which were realized in action, movement, and struggle. These ideas were never categorically established final truths. In the novels the author's disturbed and agonizing search for truth, the doubts and waverings, persist in the unending conversation and dispute in which different points of view dominate in turn, and the thoughts and emotions of the characters are a fiery lava, eternally precipitated.

The moral demands of a sick conscience, suffering from the sight of evil in the world, give rise to both his religious views and his social ethics, which center upon the individual in his relationships with his environment, society, and the state.

Believing in the unlimited right of every individual to independent spiritual growth and complete freedom to develop his gifts, Dostoyevski fervently sought a solution which would allow the individual to remain free in relation to society with its immutable laws. In his youth he was inclined to give priority to the rights of the individual will as the highest spiritual value. But throughout his life he was also deeply concerned for the rights of the individual who was trampled upon by social injustice, insulted, and injured. He defends the human dignity of even those who do not recognize their rights to happiness and equality, and his writings ring with a fiery protest against treating the mass of humanity only as a means to an end. He makes a cult of the personal against the encroachments of the historical process. The theme of the inviolability of the human personality which, Grossman states, is in all his early stories,

later runs through *Notes from the House of the Dead* in his urging of humanitarianism, cuts through his *Notes from the Underground* as arrogantly defiant self-will and through his central novel *Crime and Punishment* as the demonic claim of superman morality, until, in Dostoyevski's last work, *The Brothers Karamazov*, all these motifs of humanitarian individualism and titanic arbitrariness are combined in a symphonic whole of a single, profound, and passionate defense of the personality striving for its loftiest manifestation.[1]

At the same time Dostoyevski was acutely aware of the danger of extreme individualism. In Raskol'nikov, split off from society, hatred, bitterness, and criminal instincts reach full growth, and his best spiritual qualities and human relationships wither.

Dostoyevski saw a preventive of degeneration from such individualism only in the unity of people, in overcoming their divisions and separateness. In Western Europe, in his opinion, all the forces working toward unity had been disrupted, and there were clear signs that society was disintegrating into small rival factions warring among themselves.

All his life, his thoughts were of a coming golden age, of universal brotherhood. From his first to his last writings, the issue is that of the universal unity of peoples, whether his char-

acters debate in terms of Christianity versus socialism or bread
versus spiritual food. The solution of many problems according
to the Gospel clearly shows the influence of his early interest in
utopian socialism. Yet even at the end of his life, in "The Legend
of the Grand Inquisitor" and the Pushkin speech, in which he
gave the final full expression to his longing for universal
harmony, Dostoyevski made no final answer to the problems
which had tormented him all his life. As before, the "two powerful forces," the earthly and the spiritual, continued to struggle
for supremacy in his philosophy. And in Dostoyevski's inability to put his faith finally in either principle, Grossman saw
the tragedy of all his work.

For Grossman, however, the vagueness of Dostoyevski's final
will and testament did not diminish the significance of his work:

> The great master of the novel is an extraordinary example of spiritual
> influence and moral teaching. His greatness was apparent not so much
> in those truths which he stated as in the anxiety with which he put
> these truths, often relative and disputable, into the fire of dialectics,
> and tried to resolve them. Not one of his predecessors, investigating
> these same age-old questions, raised them with such agonizing sharp-
> ness or went closer to the uttermost limits of despair in his deliberations.
> He is one of the greatest of those who awaken and kindle the soul, and
> there is, it seems, no other writer who can touch our conscience with
> the same power and force it to apply itself steadfastly to the unsolved
> problems of history and the universe.

> But although he raised these burning, sore, and urgent questions with
> such unprecedented sharpness, Dostoyevski did not give decisive answers
> to them. His statements have the character merely of great presentiments
> —as if he did not find for himself nor leave to us a firm doctrine of
> life.

> But perhaps the deepest wisdom lies not in final truths, but in arousing
> new, searching anxieties. And in this, without a doubt, lies the moral
> significance of Dostoyevski. His dark, arid, and burning soul loves to
> intoxicate itself with the greatest ideas of mankind, invariably lending
> them in his perception new depth, sharpness, and perturbation. Of the

writers of his century, his is the most tragic fate in life, and his spirit probably the most tormented. He is one of those sorrowful, stern, and frightening seekers after the absolute whom mankind never approaches during times of peaceful well-being but to whose pages it inevitably turns in moments of catastrophe and upheavals. It is as difficult to love him with reverential and even love as it is impossible not to turn to him in those moments of great paroxysms when the deep tragedy of an individual being or of the entire epoch makes us sudden sharers in his despair.

And without imparting to us new, comforting truths or precepts to guide us to salvation, he left us his own image, that of a searcher and zealot, seized with such infectious alarm over all the open wounds of life in the world and of the individual conscience that his name will forever remain one of the few greatest names in the spiritual culture of mankind.[2]

A decade later Grossman wrote on Dostoyevski in an entirely different vein. His study "Dostoyevski and Government Circles in the 1870s," written in 1933 and published in 1934, was a sharp attack on Dostoyevski's ideology—in the nature of a repudiation of his own earlier views and at the same time an attempt to refute those of Dolinin.

Dolinin held to the view that Dostoyevski's ideology had evolved through several stages. Until his imprisonment he had followed the socialistic and atheistic views of Vissarion Belinski. During the Siberian period he moved somewhat to the right, but at the same time the views of Herzen, in addition to those of Belinski, exerted an influence upon him. Then during his residence abroad, from 1867 to 1871, affected by his impressions of the Geneva émigrés, by the circumstances of his life, and by the opinions of A. N. Maikov, N. N. Strakhov, and others, he took his most conservative position. Between 1874 and 1876 he swung again to the left and once more came close to the ideals of his youth, as indicated by the writing of A Raw Youth. During his final synthesizing period The Brothers Kara-

mazov and the Pushkin speech reflected the idea of the Russian revolution with all its contradictions. This was Dolinin's basic scheme.

In 1934, Grossman, without naming Dolinin, decried his thesis and dismissed as unfounded all talk of Dostoyevski's secret revolutionism and the evolution of his philosophy:

Dostoyevski experienced no such inner crisis during the 1870s. Openly setting out at the beginning of the decade to combat "Europeanizing" tendencies in Russian thought, he never laid down his weapons until the end, yielded no position, and had no thought of returning to the political and social beliefs of his Fourierist youth.[3]

Dolinin drew his conclusions principally on the basis of Dostoyevski's portrayal of the Russian scene of the time, and, following Lenin's example in his articles on Tolstoi, called Dostoyevski, too, a mirror of the Russian revolution by virtue of his reflection of the period that prepared the revolution.

Grossman, on the other hand, based his conclusions mainly on Dostoyevski's own statements in *Diary of a Writer*, on various notes and letters, and on his personal relations with government circles in the 1870s. He cited Dostoyevski's references in the last period to socialism as a "visionary evil," devising "darkness and terror, under the guise of revitalizing and resurrecting"[4] mankind, and argued that in *The Brothers Karamazov* Christian socialism was represented as even more terrible than atheistic socialism; the object of Dostoyevski's idolatry in the 1840s had thus become to him a fatal illusion, lulling the mind with the usual humanistic ideals and actually leading to godlessness and bloodshed.

Dostoyevski's story "The Dream of a Ridiculous Man," published in the April number of *Diary of a Writer* for 1877, Grossman regarded as a satire on utopian socialism. The main thought of the story is that mankind can be united only on the basis of the ethics of the Gospel. Unity is possible not through equality or science, but only in the church and Christianity. The progressive Petersburg citizen, according to Grossman, debauched the sinless and happy people of the "golden age" by tainting them with knowledge, falsity, sensuality, and blood spilling. Dolinin, on the other hand, interpreted the story as a tribute by Dostoyevski to his youthful visions of a well-ordered world based on social justice.

The Brothers Karamazov, in Grossman's opinion of 1934, signified the complete triumph of Dostoyevski's theocratic ideal over his early utopian philosophy, and as evidence he quoted Zosima's formula: "The church should include in itself the entire state." It is true, Grossman admitted, that Dostoyevski, refusing to be turned into an editor of a government mouth-piece, preserved a semblance of literary independence and thus maintained his popularity among the young people of his time. Nevertheless, representatives and zealots of the imperial court, especially the Procurator of the Holy Synod, Konstantin Pobedonostsev, brought every possible influence to bear on Dostoyevski to elicit from his pen favorable words toward Russian tsarism. Therefore, Grossman concluded, while Dostoyevski did not become a court writer, some of his pages reflected opinions inspired by official governmental circles, and he was a reactionary publicist.

Grossman found pro-governmental attitudes in The Brothers Karamazov, "a new strong thrust at the 'demoniac hosts' of the revolution." [5] The influence of Dostoyevski's conversations with Pobedonostsev seemed to Grossman to manifest itself in The Brothers Karamazov in mockery of the progressive press and public courts, and hatred for those of different faith, atheists, and the revolutionary raznochintsy. Throughout he found traces of the dour teachings of Pobedonostsev. In the final analysis,

Grossman maintained, the novel gave voice to the retrograde program of the Russian autocracy, in advocating theocracy as the highest form of statehood for Russia.

The concluding words of the prosecutor, in which he pictures the wildly rolling Russian troika and the loathing and horror of the bystander nations, are an appeal to Russia to abandon the revolutionary movement.

And as if speaking directly to Dolinin, Grossman asserted: "Dostoyevski the victim and Dostoyevski the conspirator should be given up once and for all in depicting the last decade of his life." [6] Whatever evolution may have occurred in Dostoyevski's political outlook, it was only in the direction of further acceptance of the reactionary, autocratic ideology of Pobedonostsev and the court. Had not Dostoyevski personally presented a copy of *The Brothers Karamazov* inscribed in his own handwriting to the tsarevich in Anichkov Palace, on December 16, 1880? And had not Pobedonostsev expressed sorrow on the death of Dostoyevski? The Russian monarchy, Grossman concluded, "made a very great ideological gain when it won the pen of Dostoyevski to its cause." [7]

To the credit of Leonid Grossman it must be recognized that, although the ideological climate of the early 1930s forced him to accentuate certain aspects of the life and work of Dostoyevski, he succeeded in remaining on a serious scholarly plane. The factual side of his study was not open to doubt. It offered new facts from Dostoyevski's biography and made available unknown documents and letters dating from the last, "monarchical" period of Dostoyevski's life. Nor did Grossman resort to direct abuse or ideological caviling. Nevertheless, the change in Leonid Grossman's approach is an instructive example of the effect of Soviet literary policy at the beginning of the 1930s even upon seasoned scholars who had established a reputation for objective work.

. 14 .

ANATOLI VASIL'YEVICH LUNACHARSKI (1875– 1933): THE OLD-GUARD PARTY INTELLECTUAL

Lunacharski is one of the very few Party critics and scholars of the old generation who succeeded in maintaining their positions of authority to the end of their lives. Although many Bolsheviks looked askance at his devotion to the culture of the past, Lenin had great respect for Lunacharski and entrusted him with broad powers in the field of art. Lunacharski held the office of People's Commissar of Education of the RSFSR for the first twelve years after the revolution. He was chairman of the Learned Committee of the Central Executive Committee of the USSR, member of the Academy of Sciences, director of the Research Institute of Literature and Art of the Communist Academy, and editor-in-chief of the Soviet *Literary Encyclopedia*. Even among the old-guard Party intellectuals he was distinguished by his enormous erudition, great personal charm, and talent as a philosopher, writer, dramatist, critic, orator, and publicist.

Lunacharski began to write articles on Dostoyevski as early as the beginning of the century.[1] Soon after the revolution he appraised Dostoyevski from the point of view of the new ideology in an essay entitled "Dostoyevski as Artist and Thinker."[2]

In 1931, in connection with the fiftieth anniversary of Dostoyevski's death, Lunacharski published "Dostoyevski as Thinker and Artist,"[3] "On Dostoyevski,"[4] and "Dostoyevski and Writers."[5] In the same year the volume of the *Large Soviet Encyclopedia* containing the entry on Dostoyevski written by Lunacharski was published.[6]

The resemblance between the 1921 article "Dostoyevski as Artist and Thinker" and the 1931 "Dostoyevski as Thinker and

Artist" is more than one of title. There is no great change in Lunacharski's position, although the tone is utterly different. In 1921 he wrote rhapsodically:

Dostoyevski loves without limit the heavenly reaches above the stars, and they are open to him. . . . He can understand and feel the harmony of being. And thus the striving for a harmonious life and expiation possesses him. It forces him to go to the Petrashevtsy. It forces him to feel the fascination of utopian socialism. To the highest degree he was imbued with the idea that people should build for themselves a new kingdom on earth. And with this ideal of paradise on earth, of a harmonious life in the full sense of the word, Dostoyevski is also thoroughly imbued. Therefore Dostoyevski could not but feel upon himself the yoke of autocracy and all the terrors of evil, sin, and crime, which were closely connected with it. And Dostoyevski knew that there was only one way to overcome autocracy—the revolutionary way.[7]

In conclusion Lunacharski drew an analogy between Dostoyevski and Blok's Christ in *The Twelve*, going before the Red Army detachment on its bloody revolutionary march:

Russia goes forward on an agonizing but glorious path, and behind her, blessing her on this path, stand the figures of her great prophets, and among them the one of most compelling fascination and beauty may be the figure of Fyodor Dostoyevski.[8]

In 1931 Lunacharski's lyricism was discarded in favor of a quasi-scientific approach. Although the Pereverzev school as such was completely destroyed in this year, the sociological method remained firmly entrenched in Marxist literary scholarship, and for the time being only the extreme form of its application by Pereverzev and his followers was censured. As indication of the new line, Lenin's articles on Tolstoi began to be reprinted in the literary journals. Lenin maintained that the writing of a great artist, in spite of his class prejudices, sympathies, origin, and position, inevitably reflected aspects of reality beyond the life of his own social milieu and pointed out that

Tolstoi had gone over to the position of the peasantry. In 1931 Lunacharski, while essentially in agreement with Pereverzev's definition of Dostoyevski as the voice of the city *meshchanstvo*, aimed at some semblance of conformity with Lenin's views.

He began by citing Lenin's thesis that Tolstoi reflected the forces at work in an agricultural country during the crisis in the natural economy, the fall of the aristocratic manor and the peasant hut, and the process by which the new, rising bourgeoisie was everywhere drawn into the remaking of society. In an attempt to preserve the old moral virtues Tolstoi took a stand with the peasantry and criticized the social order on their behalf. Tolstoi depicted the crisis as a landowner taking it upon himself to represent the countryside. In Dostoyevski, on the other hand, Lunacharski wrote, "in this ambitious and ailing man, the *meshchanstvo* (especially the *meshchanstvo* intellectuals), shaking in convulsions, found their great voice." [9]

Lunacharski pointed out that the *meshchanstvo* had three possible courses in dealing with the ruthless competition they faced. The first, for the strong and predatory, who accepted competition as in the nature of things and were ready to make their way with their teeth, nails, and heels, led through cynicism, amorality, and violence. "And in Dostoyevski himself there was a *meshchanin* of this type, a conquistador and a sadist," [10] asserted Lunacharski. The second path, taken by those who foresaw the possibility of human happiness based on reason, and an escape from the suffering of the *meshchanstvo* through a union with the people, was the path of utopian socialism, of the progressive Dobrolyubov and Chernyshevski. All his life Dostoyevski was strongly tempted by this second path. Penal servitude and exile, however, had forced him to take the third path, of religion. But he was always drawn to all three paths.

Lunacharski argued that by means of his singular concept

of the church—as an organization opposed to the state and destined to be victorious over it through love and brotherhood, to build that community of souls prophesied by the Elder Zosima, and thus to replace the ideal of socialism which the writer had rejected—by means of this purely ethical concept, Dostoyevski maintained his belief in the essential truth of socialism, as distinct from materialistic, earthly socialism, which he cursed. This manner of thinking allowed Dostoyevski to be a loyal subject of the tsarist regime and at the same time to call for protest and rebellion through the mouths of his characters. Lunacharski defined Dostoyevski's orthodoxy as at once conservatism and political extremism. It was his own "cunningly contrived self-pacifier."

Dostoyevski again and again challenged his enemies to battle, and not only philistinism, not only every kind of vice, but first of all and mainly this accursed and self-assured materialism. In his soul he killed it, he buried it, he piled up huge stones on the grave. But under these stones there was no dead man. Someone keeps stirring all the time, there is a heart beating loudly there, and it gives Dostoyevski no rest. Dostoyevski continues to feel that it is not only socialism outside him, not only the developing Russian revolutionary movement—Chernyshevski and his theories—and the proletariat in the West, etc., that will not let him rest; it is mainly materialist socialism within himself that troubles him, which under no circumstances must be allowed above ground, which must be spat upon, trampled upon, besmirched, degraded, and made insignificant and ludicrous in his own eyes. Dostoyevski does this. Not once and not twice. In this respect he goes to frenzied lengths in *The Devils*. And then? A little time goes by, the smoke of objections and the mud of insinuations are gone, and then again the implacable disc of real truth begins to shine.[11]

The complexity and the polyphony of Dostoyevski's novels arose from his internal struggle. Dostoyevski had only to feel misgivings over his repudiation of his earlier ideals, and at once the agonizing realization that his new ideological structure stood on shaky ground fissioned his whole consciousness. Lunacharski likened Dostoyevski's attacks on socialism to a court trial arranged by the author himself in which the most damaging conditions are deliberately created for his opponents (as in *The Devils*). At the trial the characters speak with their own voices, and each is free to present his own case. In his creative laboratory Dostoyevski tries to control and manipulate the world of the characters he has called to life, but, because of the unlimited freedom to speak for themselves which his characters enjoy, his power over them is often very slight. His heroes, once put on the stage, begin to live an independent life and to enter into relationships contrary to the design of the writer. The confused drama of his characters engenders confusion in the author himself. Dostoyevski's secret sympathy with the revolutionary cause, a sympathy for which he hated himself and which he tried to uproot, laid claim upon him in the form of obsession:

The disintegration of his personality, its cleavage, the fact that he wished to believe in ideas and feelings which inspired no real faith in him and wished to refute that which persistently troubled him and seemed to be the truth—this made him subjectively fitted to be the painful but necessary voice of the confusion of his time.[12]

In concluding his discussion of Dostoyevski as a thinker, Lunacharski considered his belief in the messianic role of Russia. From its sufferings and its chains, Dostoyevski foresaw the Russian people emerging with lofty spiritual qualities which would enable it to perform a great and shining deed for the sake of universal happiness, a deed of which the West was not capable. In his article of 1921 Lunacharski had declared that there should no longer be any skepticism about Dostoyevski as prophet: Russia was leading the proletariat of the West and the East, and although the mission was being discharged at the price of terrible sufferings and sacrifices, Dostoyevski had not expected Russia's service to the world to be rendered without sin and torments.

In 1931 Lunacharski was chary of his panegyrics to Dostoyevski, remarking laconically that the Soviet leadership of the oppressed of the world had come about "not as Dostoyevski had thought [but] in a completely different sense and in a completely different manner." [13]

Lunacharski paid almost no attention to Dostoyevski's personality and disregarded many aspects of his work, in the manner of Lenin's articles on Tolstoi, viewing the writer only from the social and economic point of view. As an exception he dealt with Dostoyevski's epilepsy and outdid his fellow Marxists in searching for a sociological explanation. On the basis of the author's own statement that the first attack took place in prison and began with a radiance from above, which followed a stormy dispute on the theme of religion and faith in God, Lunacharski concluded that both social and biological factors were operative. His raw nerves and sufferings, his loathing of his surroundings, in contrast to an access of feelings of harmony and peace in an epileptic attack, made manifest his dreams of reconciling all social conflicts. Cruelty and ecstasy are two aspects of the same phenomenon. Social factors conducive to sickness found in the physiological structure a suitable medium for themselves and produced not only his philosophy of life and his literary style but also his disease. The extraordinary talent of Dostoyevski found in his sickness a greater power of expression and became genius as it was used to reveal the turmoil within the *meshchanin*-writer.

Lunacharski treated Dostoyevski as artist not in terms of his literary technique or form, but solely from the point of view of the inner meaning of his writings. He tried to reveal the peculiar philosophy or psychology of Dostoyevski's creative process. The critic was concerned to define what type of artist this writer was, to investigate the process by which, in the crucible of his writings, the internal contradictions of his thought were fused with the figurative language of concrete characters and plot patterns.

First of all, Dostoyevski was, according to Lunacharski, a lyric artist:

All his stories and novels are one fiery river of his own life experiences. They are pure confession of his inmost soul. They are a passionate attempt to make profession of his own inner truth. This is the first and basic element in his work. The second is the continuous attempt to infect, convince, shake the reader, in confessing his faith to him. Both these qualities of Dostoyevski's writing are present in him to a higher degree than in any other lyric writer, if by lyricism is meant the appeal of a shaken soul.[14]

Dostoyevski as a lyricist gives expression to his own emotional experiences and his confession in a pseudo-narrative form, in the form of stories and novels about external occurrences. In them he does not strive to individualize the language. Nor is he concerned with the purely artistic finish of his writings—in them there are no fine descriptions of nature, of external beauty. In Dostoyevski there is almost no thoroughly thought-out architectonics such as one finds in Dante, for instance, whose works were constructed, from the total mountain mass down to every small detail, in accordance with a general architectural plan, subject to the firm will of the author. However, the reader is always astounded by the quality of genius in the content of Dostoyevski's writings, by the power of expression in his confessions. And above all in Dostoyevski is the thirst for life:

Dostoyevski is closely connected with all his heroes. His blood courses through their veins. His heart beats in all the characters which he created. Dostoyevski gives birth to his characters in pain, with quickened heartbeat and heavy choked breathing. He resorts to crime together with his heroes. He lives a titanically intense life with them. He repents with them. With them, in his thoughts, he shakes heaven and earth. And out of this endless compulsion of his to live through every new adventure with terrible concreteness, he shakes us as does no one else.

But in addition to the fact that Dostoyevski himself experiences everything that happens together with his heroes, himself suffers from their sufferings, he still relishes these experiences. He constantly notices every detail in order to make concrete to the point of hallucination the life he leads in his imagination. He needs them, these details, for savoring as genuine, inner reality.[15]

Despite the fact that in emphasizing the indivisibility of Dostoyevski and his characters, Lunacharski was speaking not of social determinism but of the purely subjective psychological processes of the writer, his thought nonetheless showed the influence of Pereverzev's theory of the autogenous character whose psychology alone the writer can portray.

Dostoyevski, according to Lunacharski, is not only a lover of life, but also a great poet of the lust for life; his novels are one gigantic act of sensuality. Even the failures and ruin of life he experiences and describes as enjoyment—the newly discovered chapters of *The Devils* containing Stavrogin's confession are a striking illustration. In Lunacharski's opinion, however, Dostoyevski did not justify the filth of life—he suffered from it, and he often returned to the thought that the sole meaning of suffering is that it expiates this filth. And inasmuch as all are guilty of every sin and crime, all must suffer greatly in order to be purified.

Despite Dostoyevski's ability to draw the reader into the stream of consciousness of his characters, Lunacharski did not consider him a psychologist:

It is more correct . . . to say that in his writings an extraordinarily large amount of material for psychology may be found, for we understand a psychologist to be a person who is able not only to analyze the human soul but also to deduce psychological laws from this analysis. This Dostoyevski was unable to do.[16]

In conclusion Lunacharski undertook an ideological re-evaluation of Dostoyevski's writings from the point of view of the tasks of building a Communist order. In representing Dostoyevski, in contrast to the positive figure of Chernyshevski, as so tainted by traits of the *meshchanstvo* that he was unable to go beyond this social group, Lunacharski was in fact, if not explicitly, in accord with Pereverzev's interpretation. Because of Dostoyevski's ideological duality, his contemporaries felt ambivalence toward him; his friends and defenders distrusted him, and radical circles, fundamentally hostile to him, felt also some sympathy. Lunacharski's attitude was equally ambivalent. He acknowledged that Dostoyevski as an artist was unsurpassed in the history of mankind. His writing had been of colossal significance in the West after the First World War, which had revealed the chaos and instability of the external world and caused social and philosophical thought to falter. The appearance in Germany of writers like Hermann Hesse was evidence of the spread of Dostoyevskiism. As the dismay of the city-dweller increased, the fame of Dostoyevski grew throughout the world.

Soviet society also felt his power, Lunacharski stated, not only because he plucked the strings of revolutionism but also because Dostoyevskiism itself still existed:

But have we ourselves been saved from Dostoyevskiism? Of course not! We Communist proletarians and all people [engaged in] socialist construction must live in a petit-bourgeois environment. Under the conditions of our difficult and heroic building, this environment wavers and disintegrates in the most fantastic manner. In wrecking, which we are beginning to investigate to the bottom, is there not a good deal of very genuine Dostoyevskiism?

We cannot even assert that we ourselves, that is, the group which is building consciously and selflessly, are completely safe from Dostoyevskiism. For the struggle for socialism occurs not only outside man, but also inside, and, as Lenin said, there are many of the old bourgeois prejudices in the proletariat and even sometimes in Communists. The whole psychology of doubts and hesitations, of personal resentment, of fractionalism, everything that complicates relationships in political and everyday life, to our great shame, is akin to Dostoyevskiism.

For this reason Dostoyevski is for us also a living and vivid exponent of these negative forces in consciousness and behavior, and we must study them in him for our own purposes, for to know in people the weaknesses they have not yet overcome is now an important task for every organizer and for every builder.[17]

At the beginning of the thirties Lunacharski had begun to muddy his literary criticism with Party propaganda of the day. In another article he explicitly identified Ramzinism (Ramzin was an engineer accused in 1930 of wrecking and sabotage as a member of the so-called "Industrial Party") as a variety of Dostoyevskiism.[18]

To the credit of Lunacharski, however, it must be noted that he modified his earlier views only slightly in 1931. In all his articles of this year Lunacharski reiterated that Dostoyevski was entirely permissible under the new Soviet conditions, that he was a "contemporary" and in a sense even a teacher. The new reader must read Dostoyevski, with a critical attitude of course, in order to appraise him and temper himself. If armed with class consciousness, the reader would enrich his knowledge of life and learn to recognize and struggle against his class enemies. In the article "Dostoyevski and Writers" Lunacharski recommended that writers familiarize themselves with Dostoyevski, if only in order to know the mind of the enemy. For a study of the duality and the class differentiation among people, of the process by which some become counterrevolutionaries while others enthusiastically accept the socialist order, "Dostoyevski can serve as a better guide than our contemporaries." [19] Nonetheless, Lunacharski felt constrained to warn progressive proletarian writers of the danger involved:

To be carried away by Dostoyevski means to put a millstone around your neck, which forces you, once you have dived into the slough, to remain there. To study Dostoyevski, however, and to understand him— this means to be able to reach to the very bottom of the slough and then to pull yourself out of it, having enriched your own experience and the experience of society.[20]

In the case of people belonging psychologically to the past or wavering between the past and the present, to be carried away by Dostoyevski would signalize the hopelessness of their bourgeois disease, of duality, torments, mysticism, and hatred for the revolution, whereas study and understanding of Dostoyevski would aid the positive processes in their consciousness and hasten their recovery for socialist society:

In his mirror they see their own sickness and its monstrousness and the depressing weakness of this great genius in his attempts to find a cure within this sickness or to glorify some aspects of it at the expense of others. All this pushes them away from the old order and causes them to clutch convulsively at the life preservers which we throw them from the shore. But for those whose recovery is still a long way off, the study and understanding of Dostoyevski turn into a passion, which they may perhaps deplore and which may be half mixed with a curse, but nevertheless a passion which only deepens either their insanely haughty belief that their sickness is health or their vain hope of finding a cure for this sickness in mysticism, patriotism, self-analysis, self-exaltation, or self-degradation.[21]

For the Soviet public and its writers it was necessary to learn through Dostoyevski but not from Dostoyevski as teacher, to approach his work as a means, not as an end. Thus the most authoritative Soviet critic and interpreter of the classics expressed the revolutionary dialectic. Lunacharski's concluding words in "Dostoyevski as Thinker and Artist" are perhaps the clearest and most succinct formulation of the contradictoriness and duality of all Soviet criticism of Dostoyevski: "For the new man born of the revolution and aiding its victory it seems nothing short of impropriety not to be acquainted with such a giant as Dostoyevski, but it would be completely shameful and, so to speak, socially unhealthy, to fall under his influence." [22]

Lunacharski's attempt to find a compromise between recognition of the world significance of Dostoyevski and Communist intolerance of opposing ideologies was more or less continued in Soviet criticism until the beginning of the "Zhdanov period" after the Second World War. Dostoyevski's writings, at least in part, remained in the schools and libraries of the Soviet Union, and from time to time individual works of his were republished.

. 15 .

M. M. BAKHTIN ON
DOSTOYEVSKI'S POLYPHONIC NOVEL

M. M. Bakhtin's book *Problems of Dostoyevski's Writing* [1]
(1929) is the most significant contribution of Soviet scholarship to the stylistic study of Dostoyevski. Bakhtin was strongly
influenced by the theories of the "Opoyaz" (Society for the
Study of the Theory of Poetic Language), a group of formalists
who in their publications during the early years after the revolution enormously enriched the theory of poetry and of literature
in general.

Bakhtin was concerned with the formalist and structural
aspects of Dostoyevski's fiction, mainly from the theoretical
point of view. For the sake of the utmost possible clarity, he
deliberately avoided all the sociological and literary-historical
problems which might have complicated his exposition with a
great deal of inadequately studied material. No doubt to guard
himself from accusations of formalism and disregard of materialistic causality, Bakhtin acknowledged in his preface, however, that the omission was undesirable, that every theoretical
problem should be historically oriented, and that the various
factors involved in a work of literature were, of course, directly
related and mutually dependent. Out of purely technical considerations he had been obliged to study the theoretical problem
independently, but he had always had in mind the determining
historical factors although, as background, they did not appear
in the book. To deflect charges that he had ignored the social
element, he stated explicitly:

Even a purely formalistic analysis should take every element of artistic
structure as a point of refraction of living social forces, as an artificial

crystal, the facets of which are constructed and polished so as to refract certain rays of social opinions and to refract them at a certain angle.[2]

He rejected both the exclusively ideological and the exclusively formalist interpretation:

The narrow formalistic approach is unable to proceed beyond the periphery of this form [of Dostoyevski's novels]. Narrow ideologism, on the other hand, seeking first of all purely philosophical comprehension and insights, does not grasp that very element in Dostoyevski's writing which survived his philosophical and socio-political ideology— his revolutionary innovation in the field of the novel as an art form.[3]

It was impossible, Bakhtin thought, to apply to Dostoyevski any of the criteria developed during the history of the European novel. His book was devoted to the elucidation of the new type of novel which Dostoyevski created, the polyphonic novel.

The distinctive characteristic of this novel is the presence of a multiplicity of independent and discrete consciousnesses, a polyphony of voices, each given its full value. Each consciousness has equal rights, each its own separate world. The characters are not only objects in respect to the author but also subjects, independent voices, bearers of their own word. The word of a character is not limited to the usual functions of characterization or of advancing the plot; it does not directly express the ideology of the author. It is given as the expression of the consciousness of another, not simply the object of the author's consciousness. The voice of a character, like the voice of the author himself, has weight, meaningfulness, and independence. The word of the character lies alongside the author's word, not in the same line with it, and never combines with it for the usual pragmatic plot purposes.

The unity of the world of a Dostoyevski novel is based on the laws of the style of the polyphonic novel. A world of independent subjects, and not objects, requires a different handling of the

narrative and a new orientation. Dostoyevski performs the
historic task in art of destroying the established forms of the
monologic (homophonic) novel and constructing a new polyphonic novel.

Before proceeding to his analysis of Dostoyevski's style,
Bakhtin traced the course of earlier stylistic analyses which
came close to the basic traits of Dostoyevski as he understood
them.

Almost all critics of Dostoyevski, Bakhtin found, had been
unable to perceive the principles on which his novels are constructed because they were concerned merely with the ideology
of the characters and, furthermore, even reduced their various
ideologies to a systematic, monologic unity, that is, to a composite philosophizing of author and characters. Out of inertia
they approached Dostoyevski's novels, with their radically new
artistic intention, as they would approach the traditional monologic novel, ignoring the author's design of a multiplicity of
independent voices and consciousnesses. Other critics, able to
resist the immediate ideological fascination of individual characters, made them into objectified psyches—perceived by the
author as objects, not subjects—in other words, went along the
lines of the usual analysis of the socio-psychological realistic
novel. Instead of the philosophical monologue of the first group
of critics, there was now a monologically perceived objective
world, correlated with the single consciousness of the author.
Both approaches obscured the architectonics of Dostoyevski's
novels.

In Bakhtin's opinion, Rozanov, Volynski, Merezhkovski, and
Shestov were among the critics of the first group. They squeezed
all the diverse voices of Dostoyevski's characters into the framework of a single philosophy, substituted for the interaction of
several independent consciousnesses the ideas of one conscious-

ness, and constructed a dialectical series with the theses abstracted from individual voices and Dostoyevski's own voice or set these theses off against one another like absolute antinomies which could not be resolved. In criticism of this type the ideas in Dostoyevski's novels—wrenched away from their personal bearers and no longer seen in their interaction during the course of events, but squeezed into the context of a monologic system— became exercises in logic, philosophical syllogisms.

Vyacheslav Ivanov in *Dostoyevski and the Tragedy-Novel* was, according to Bakhtin, the first to discover a new approach to Dostoyevski's art as a whole. Ivanov's definition of Dostoyevski's realism as based on "penetration" and the affirmation of the "I" of another not as object but as another subject was of great assistance in groping toward the new principle of Dostoyevski's method. Yet Ivanov, too, had made a monologic formulation of Dostoyevski's relation to the world of his fiction. Furthermore, Ivanov had added to it a number of ethical and religious principles on an abstract metaphysical plane, and as a result had failed to find the essence of Dostoyevski's innovation.

Askol'dov, in many respects a follower of Ivanov, also treated Dostoyevski's novels as monologic, although he called attention to the inner freedom of the characters and their complete independence of the outside world.[4] But Dostoyevski's originality does not lie in the proclamation of the lofty value of the individual, as Askol'dov thought, but in the ability to portray the personality of another without mingling his own voice with that of the other. The freedom of the characters consists in the fact that they are not predetermined by the author. And it is their freedom and independence which shape the author's design. Askol'dov, explaining Dostoyevski's new vision of the inner world of man in terms of the philosophy of the author and the psychology of the characters, was farther from an understanding of Dostoyevski's method than Ivanov.

Leonid Grossman, in his book *Dostoyevski's Style*, had regarded as the distinctive features of Dostoyevski's novels the violation of the conventional unity of content, the combination of the most diverse elements in a unified composition, and the departure from the single, integrated style of narration, and had given a splendid description of Dostoyevski's composition. "This," wrote Grossman, "is the basic principle of his composition of the novel":

to subordinate the incompatible, polar-opposite elements of the narrative to the unity of the philosophical concept and the whirlwind movement of events. To combine in one artistic creation professions of philosophy with criminal acts, to bring religious drama into a thriller, to lead, through all the twists and turns of a detective story, to revelations of a new [religious] mystery—these were the artistic problems which challenged Dostoyevski. . . . Going counter to age-old aesthetic traditions which require correspondence between the material and its treatment and presuppose unity or, in any case, homogeneity and kinship among the structural elements of a work of art, Dostoyevski blends opposites. He openly defies the basic canon of the theory of art. His task is to overcome the greatest difficulty for the artist, to create out of diverse materials—materials with differing values attached to them and extremely incompatible—a single and integrated work of art. For this reason the Book of Job, the Revelation of St. John, gospel texts, the Epistle of Peter in the New Testament—everything on which he draws in the pages of his novels and which imparts the tone to various chapters— are here combined, in the manner peculiar to him, with the newspaper, the anecdote, the parody, the street scene, the grotesque, or even the lampoon. He daringly throws into his melting pots more and more new elements, knowing and believing that in the climax of his creative work the raw scraps of everyday reality, the sensations of the cheap thrillers, and the pages of the God-inspired holy books will fuse, blend into a new amalgam and bear the deep imprint of his personal style and tone.[5]

Despite such a thorough understanding of Dostoyevski's style, Grossman was, in Bakhtin's opinion, still far from a complete comprehension of the process by which Dostoyevski distributed heterogeneous elements among several worlds and several independent consciousnesses in the form of several different philosophies, and by which these worlds were fused into the higher unity of the polyphonic novel.

In another book, *The Path of Dostoyevski*, Grossman spoke of the significance for Dostoyevski of the forms of conversation and dispute, in which different points of view can "dominate in turn and reflect various shades of meaning of opposing creeds," and the dialogue

especially approaches the embodiment of this eternally forming and never crystallized philosophy. This form of philosophizing, in which every opinion is as a living being and is stated in an agitated human voice, inevitably suggested itself to such an artist and thinker in images as Dostoyevski when he was deep in his deliberating on the meaning of phenomena and the mystery of the world.[6]

Again, however, Grossman failed to appreciate dialogism as the essential characteristic of Dostoyevski's style, but tended to view it as a vestige of the unresolved contradictions in Dostoyevski's philosophy of life, a result of the conflict in him between humanistic faith and skepticism.

On one hand, Grossman was aware of the multiplicity of discrete consciousnesses and observed that every voice or opinion is endowed with traits of a living being and is indivisible from the human personality, and, on the other hand, he saw the structural principle of uniting unrelated and incompatible elements; but he did not connect these two discoveries and thus did not reach a full understanding of Dostoyevski's polyphony.

For confirmation of his own thesis concerning the multiplicity of ideological centers of consciousness and the mutually ex-

clusive concepts and opinions found in Dostoyevski's novels,
Bakhtin quotes the German scholar Otto Kaus. In his book
Dostojewski und sein Schicksal [7] Kaus had explained the many
sides and many planes of Dostoyevski's novels as produced by
the very spirit of capitalism, which had pushed together and
interwoven previously separate worlds into a contradictory
unity. No longer able to exist independently, these worlds nevertheless did not lose their individual identity. Their ideological
disregard of one another came to an end and their interrelation-
ship was discovered. But their unity, as before, was contradictory
and uneasy; it reflected the spirit of the incipient capitalist
world. And this was the world reflected in the work of Dostoyevski. Bakhtin agrees:

Otto Kaus's interpretation is correct in many respects. The polyphonic
novel could, in fact, have been written only in the period of capitalism.
Moreover, the most favorable soil for it was in Russia itself, where
capitalism came almost like a sudden catastrophe and caught a pristine
variety of social worlds and groups which had not begun to end their
individual isolation, as in the West, in the process of the gradual advance
of capitalism. Here the contradictory essence of the social life in the
making, which does not fit into a confident and serenely contemplative
monologic consciousness, necessarily manifested itself with particular
sharpness, and at the same time the individuality of the worlds that
had been thrown off their ideological balance and had collided was
necessarily especially full and clear. Thus were created the objective
premises for the essential multiplicity of planes and voices in the
polyphonic novel. [8]

To Bakhtin's mind, however, Kaus had erred in attempting to
explain the polyphony of Dostoyevski's novels by direct reference to the realities of capitalism without taking enough account
of the specific language of art.

    V. L. Komarovich, in "The Novel *A Raw Youth* as an Artistic

Unity," [9] had tried to explain the unity of the separate and heterogeneous plots in the novel on the basis of the dynamic unity of the act of the will (the impulses of the individual will of the characters toward the suprapersonal) or in teleological co-ordination. Komarovich likened Dostoyevski to the ensemble in polyphonic music, and the variety of voices in the novel to five voices of a fugue, entering successively and developing in contrapuntal harmony. In his attempts to find the unity of the novel in the laws of teleological activity, of the individual act of the will, Komarovich was distracted, in Bakhtin's opinion, by elements of reality and the series of plots, and dropped the main problem—the combination of independent consciousnesses and their worlds. He substituted the unity of the individual will for the unity of events. He reduced the polyphony of independent voices and their higher combination to homophony. In Komarovich's treatment, the plot unities of *A Raw Youth* emerge as primarily a lyric or monologic joining of emotions and wills. Nevertheless, Komarovich's metaphorical use of the terms polyphony and counterpoint had led Bakhtin himself to define Dostoyevski's novels as polyphonic.

B. M. Engel'gardt in his article "Dostoyevski's Ideological Novel" had come very close to grasping the distinctive features of his work. Engel'gardt considered Dostoyevski's *raznochintsy* characters, who have broken with cultural and family traditions, to illustrate most clearly the principles of Dostoyevski's ideological novel. Defenseless against ideas, they become obsessed by their idea. The idea leads an independent life in the man, completely dominating his will and desires. Dostoyevski did not depict a character's life but the history of the idea in him; he became the "historiographer" of the idea. The dominant factor in fictional characterization, biography, is superseded by the

idea. The novel becomes in the full sense of the word an "ideological novel," but by no means, Engel'gardt warned, a "special-
purpose" novel:

Dostoyevski portrayed the life of an idea in the consciousness of the
individual and of society, for he considered it the determining factor
of an intellectual milieu. But this should not be understood to mean
that he wrote purpose novels and slanted stories or that he was a
tendentious artist, more of a philosopher than poet. He wrote not purpose novels, nor philosophical novels in the taste of the eighteenth
century, but novels about an idea. Just as adventure, anecdote, a
psychological type, a genre painting, or a historical picture might serve
as central subject for other novelists, for him an "idea" served this
purpose. He cultivated and raised to an unparalleled height a very
special type of novel, which, in contrast to the detective, sentimental,
psychological, or historical novel, may be called ideological. In this
sense, his writing, despite its inherent polemicism, was not inferior in
objectivity to that of other great literary artists. He himself was a great
artist, and first and foremost in his novels he posed and resolved purely
artistic problems. Only his material was very original; his heroine was
an idea.[10]

The complex of idea-forces ruling a character engenders in
him a certain ideological attitude toward the world, which, in
turn, becomes the decisive principle in the artistic orientation
of the character. The dominant factor in the depiction of the
world of surrounding reality is the individual point of view of
the character, which controls his perception and representation
of reality. Dostoyevski is therefore not given to objective description, in his own name, of the external world, of the day-to-
day mode of life, or of nature, but concerns himself with his
characters' view of their environment, their land, and the world.
This method results in the many planes of his work and the
division of the world he portrays into the worlds of the characters in accordance with their ideas. Engel'gardt divides the
basic themes of Dostoyevski's novels according to the three

planes of the environment, the country, and the world, constituting the most profound concept of the higher reality in which the earthly life of the spirit which has attained a state of true freedom is lived. All three planes, according to Engel'-gardt, represent separate stages of the dialectical development of the spirit and the only path toward the unconditional affirmation of being.

For Bakhtin, the core of truth in Engel'gardt's discussion is the statement that ideas play the central role in Dostoyevski's novels, not as the principles guiding the portrayal, not as conclusions, but as the very thing being portrayed. These ideas are only those of Raskol'nikov, Ivan or Alyosha Karamazov, Prince Myshkin, Stavrogin, or the Grand Inquisitor, determining their perception of the world, and by no means the principles of the writer in the construction of the novels. Their monologic structure, therefore, in no way determines the construction of the novel as a whole. Dostoyevski's novels are not philosophically tendentious and single-stressed in the obvious sense, for the ideas of the characters do not form the architectonics of the novels.

In considering the method by which the disjoined worlds of the characters are united in the world of the author and the novels, Engel'gardt, in Bakhtin's opinion, also lost from sight the polyphony of Dostoyevski's novels. Engel'gardt's hypothesis that the three planes—the environment, the country, and the world—were stages of a single dialectical series did away with the polyphony. Logically vitiating Engel'gardt's theses, the last step in this series was inevitably the author's synthesis, surmounting the previous abstract stages and thus turning the novel into definite philosophizing on the part of the author, making it philosophical in the usual sense of the word. Bakhtin insisted that in Dostoyevski's novels the opposition of the many consciousnesses of the characters was not resolved dialectically, just as the spirits and souls in the world of Dante's *Divine Comedy* were not blended. In the world of Dostoyevski's characters Bakhtin attributed to the author only the role of outside observer. The relationships of the characters in the plot could by no means be reduced to the abstract terms of thesis, antithesis, and synthesis, and the entire work could not be understood as a dialectical proposition or an expression of the author's mind. A mind functioning dialectically could express only a monologic philosophy. Monistic idealism in no way fitted in with the multiplicity of discrete consciousnesses and the extreme pluralism of Dostoyevski's world. Bakhtin wrote:

The time itself made the polyphonic novel possible. Dostoyevski was subjectively involved in the contradictory multiplanar existence of his time. He changed camps, went from one to another, and in this respect the planes coexistent in actual social life were stages of his life's path and spiritual formation. This personal experience was profound, but Dostoyevski did not give it direct monologic expression in his writings. This experience only helped him to understand more deeply the coexistent, very widespread conflicts, conflicts between people but not between ideas in one consciousness. Thus the objective conflicts of the period determined the writings of Dostoyevski not on the plane on which he personally suffered through them in the history of his spirit, but on the plane on which he saw them objectively as forces existing simultaneously (his vision, it is true, was deepened by personal experience).[11]

Taking issue with Engel'gardt, Bakhtin argued that Dostoyevski's artistic vision focused mainly on coexistence and interaction, not on the process of formation. Dostoyevski saw the world in space and not in time. There was much dramatism of form in his fiction, but without a monologic premise. He perceived the world as simultaneous phenomena, and dramatically compared and contrasted these phenomena, but did not arrange them in a consecutive sequence in time. His mind dealt with the separate links of this world in their simultaneity; he saw them in the cross section of one moment, as coexisting in space. The conversations of the characters with their doubles were to Bakhtin a dramatization of the internal contradictions in man and their development in space:

Out of every contradiction within one person, Dostoyevski strives to make two persons, in order to dramatize the contradiction and to develop it extensively. This characteristic finds its external expression in Dostoyevski's predilection for mass scenes, in his attempt to concentrate in one place and at one time, often in contradiction to pragmatic verisimilitude, as many people as possible and as many themes as possible, that is, to concentrate in one instant the greatest possible qualitative diversity. Hence also Dostoyevski's attempt to observe in the novel the dramatic principle of unity of time. Hence the catastrophic swiftness of action, "the whirlwind movement," the dynamics of Dostoyevski. Dynamics and swiftness here (as everywhere) do not represent the victory of time, but the conquest of it, for swiftness is the only way to conquer time in time.[12]

Bakhtin went to the extreme of asserting that the world of Dostoyevski comprises only that which can be comprehended and combined at one time and that he will admit only such simultaneous phenomena into that eternity in which everything coexists in categories of simultaneity. For Dostoyevski, all elements of reality and all characters who find their justification in the past or set their hopes on the future are on principle unacceptable. His heroes, according to Bakhtin, do not remember anything; they have no biographies. The only thing in the past which has substance for them is that which is felt and experienced as the present (sin, twinges of conscience for the sins they have committed, resentments, and the like).

Dostoyevski's method of depicting the world in terms of coexistence also explains the fact that the behavior of his characters is represented as free, exempt from causality and motivation of daily life; their behavior is not explained by their past, their environment, nor their upbringing. Dostoyevski always railed against the error of law and legal practice in justifying everything by environment. He treated all the questions which troubled him from the point of view of the moment, and for this reason was addicted to newspapers and the current news. Also attributable to this trait is his extraordinary faculty of foreseeing the future as already existent in the present.

Although it involved a certain limitation of scope, this faculty of seeing everything as coexistent and interrelated sharpened Dostoyevski's vision and enabled him to see complexities and contradictions not visible to the ordinary observer. Each of the many components of his world took on many meanings. He gave his readers the full spectrum of human feelings and thoughts, every nuance, an unceasing chorus of disputing voices, separate and distinct.

In Bakhtin's opinion Engel'gardt had underestimated the deep personalism of Dostoyevski. The ideas in man are not the heroes of his novels; the hero is man himself in man, whom the idea—instead of the usual environment and circumstances of fiction—reveals and expresses. The consciousnesses of his heroes interact with other consciousnesses, struggle with them, are sharply aware of their opponents. They are internally dialogic, polemical and always open to the consciousness of another. As artist, Dostoyevski here "rises to an objective vision of the life of consciousnesses and the forms in which they coexist in life," [13]—his own sociology of consciousnesses. For Bakhtin, Engel'gardt's term "ideological novel" was not in accord with Dostoyevski's artistic function; the term suggested the traditional interpretation of the homophonic development of one consciousness. In Bakhtin's opinion, that which in the European and Russian novel before Dostoyevski was the final whole—the monologic, single world of the author's creation—in Dostoyevski's novel becomes a part, an element of the whole; that which was reality now becomes one of the aspects of reality; that which bound together the whole—the pragmatic plot line and the personal style and tone—becomes a subordinate element. New principles of the artistic combination of elements and of the construction of the whole appear; speaking metaphorically, the counterpoint of the novel appears.[14]

With an eye on Soviet conditions, Bakhtin declared that the ideological content of Dostoyevski's artistic world was "strange and unacceptable (and it is not new), just as the ideological content of a poem of Byron's or of Dante's cosmos is unacceptable." [15] He then added:

The structure of this world, which was achieved, it is true, in indissoluble connection with that ideology which fills it and the time which gave rise to it, nevertheless remains, after the time with its ideologies has already passed. It remains, as the monuments of art surrounding us remain—not only as document, but also as model.[16]

Dostoyevski's great innovations in the art of the novel had influenced contemporary prose throughout the whole world, whatever the ideology and sympathies of the writer, but critics, in Bakhtin's opinion, were still arrested by the ideology of individual voices and had failed to grasp Dostoyevski's artistic credo in its entirety:

Each one interprets in his own way the final word of Dostoyevski, but all alike interpret him as *one word, one voice, one accent,* and right here there is a mistake that goes to the very root. The supraverbal, supravocal, supra-accentual unity of the polyphonic novel remains unrevealed.[17]

Bakhtin then developed his own thesis of Dostoyevski's polyphonic novel, concentrating attention mainly on the freedom of the hero, his idea, and the principles which bind the entire novel together.

Dostoyevski, Bakhtin asserted, was not interested in his hero as typification of a way of life, as an object of reality, but only as "a special point of view on the world and himself, as a man's conception of meaning and value in respect to himself and in respect to surrounding reality." [18]

All the elements in Dostoyevski's characterization become elements in the self-knowledge and self-characterization of the hero, and the function of this self-knowledge becomes the object of the author's portrayal. All the other elements of characterization and reality are the property of the hero himself. Whereas before Dostoyevski the self-knowledge of the characters was only an element of their reality, a fraction of the image, in his novels all reality is only an element of the characters' self-knowledge. Gogol's poor civil servant is replaced by the self-knowledge of Devushkin, Golyadkin, or Prokharchin. Dostoyevski's civil-servant heroes contemplate and interpret themselves. The main factor in their portrayal is not reality but only the process by which they realize their own existence. Existence is only the material of their self-knowledge. Dostoyevski, at first still using Gogol's material, takes the reader into the mind of the characters, and the characters themselves perform the functions of the author. They cast light upon themselves from various points of view. What remains of the author's vision serves only as a second reality. The objective world of reality, however, is transferred from the horizon of the author to the horizon of the hero, whose entire life has the sole function of cognition of self and of world. He is the dreamer, the underground man, not a man of life, but only the subject of consciousness and dreaming, ad infinitum.

The self-consciousness of a Dostoyevski character, the dominant factor in his portrayal, obviates any monologic unity of the novel. Every opportunity for monologue is given to the characters themselves. The underground man himself knows very well everything about himself and in advance renders useless any comment by an outsider, the author. What is dominant in a character's representation of a thing is exactly what is dominant in the thing represented. He himself thinks most of all of what others think or may think of him, reaches into the consciousness and thought of another, anticipates the opinions of others concerning himself, guesses their meaning and shade of meaning, formulates the words of others, punctuates his own speech with the remarks of others. But, looking into the mirror of the consciousness of another and discovering his own reflection there, he still reserves for himself the final word on himself and on his world. And it is this word, the pure voice of conscience, heard by the reader, too, which was in Dostoyevski's mind the crux of the novel. Everything else is absorbed in the word as its material. The entire structure of the novel is designed for the revelation of this word. Everything tangible and objective is dissolved in the pure self-expression, self-interpretation, self-revelation of the hero. Verisimilitude in Dostoyevski is the verisimilitude of the hero's inner word about himself. And for the expression of the final word of the hero about himself, confession is the most suitable form.

Dostoyevski faces a difficult problem in bringing the word of the characters into the narrative. In Tolstoi, for example, the word of the characters is enveloped in the author's words. The self-awareness of his characters is entirely a question of content and does not involve the necessity of a new form. There is no free, independent voice of a character sounding with the author's voice. For Tolstoi the problem of combining voices and setting forth the author's ideas of the characters does not arise, for his

monologic point of view penetrates every pore and levels everything to one Tolstoian unity.

Dostoyevski sets the word of the hero against the word of the
author. The problem is therefore not to be solved simply by
eliminating or attenuating the author's word. In view of the fact
that in Dostoyevski the character himself is the bearer of an
independent word, what the author says of it is, in Bakhtin's
definition, a word on a word; it is oriented toward the word,
dialogically directed toward the character. The conversation is
not about the character, but with the character. And only skill
in keeping his distance enables Dostoyevski to make an objective
portrayal. Through his objectivism he creates an atmosphere in
which the word of the character may be spoken and may be
self-explanatory:

> Not one element of this atmosphere can be neutral; everything must cut
> the character to the quick, provoke him, put questions to him, even enter
> into controversy and revile him; everything must be addressed to the
> character himself, turned toward him, everything must be felt as the
> *word of one who is present* and not as the word of one who is absent,
> as the word of the "second" person and not of the "third." The inter-
> pretive point of view of the "third" person, with a fixed image of the
> character formed in that view, would destroy this atmosphere. There-
> fore it is not part of Dostoyevski's creative world.[19]

The method of continuous dialogue necessitates the most
subtle deliberation over each tone, accent, and turn of events.
Underneath the apparent nervousness and restlessness of Dostoyevski there is usually hidden great virtuosity in the construction of the novel.

In regard to the "idea" of a Dostoyevski character, Bakhtin
saw a complete blending of the personality and world-view. The
ideology of the characters is intimately personal, colored by
their own experiences and emotions. The merging of the char-

acter's personal word and his ideological word increases the intensity of his self-expression, and the idea makes it possible for his consciousness to define itself and assert its independence.

Dostoyevski succeeds in representing the idea of another in all its connotation without mixing in his own idea as author, in the first place, by means of scrupulous observance of the self-awareness of the character as bearer of his own valid idea and, in the second place, by virtue of the fact that it is his creative principle not to work out in advance a separate, concrete, unified system of thought for a character. Each thought of a character derives from the total personality. The author himself does not think in isolated thoughts, but in points of view, in terms of the voices of his characters, in which the whole man is heard, "his entire world-view from alpha to omega." [20] He perceives every thought in the continuum of personality, and develops it dialogically through individualized voices. As a rule, Dostoyevski avoids exposition and only arranges the voices and sets ideologies to clashing in the form of dialogue, both in his fiction and in his publicist articles. His own thought is concealed in the ensemble of voices, words, and actions of others. He never argues his own views but merely juxtaposes various ideologies among which it is not easy to detect his. His is a world of

consciousnesses illuminating one another, a world of concomitant formulations of the meaning of man. Among them he seeks the loftiest formulation, the one most deserving of faith, and he perceives it not as his own true thought, but as another true man and his word. In the image of the ideal man or in the image of Christ there is offered to him a solution to his ideological searches. This image or this loftiest voice is to crown the world of voices, organize, and subject it. It was the image of man, with his voice that is not the author's voice, which was the final ideological criterion for Dostoyevski—not to remain true to his own convictions and not the truth of his own convictions taken in the abstract, but to remain true to the faith-commanding image of man.[21]

From this quest for truth in the authoritative image of ideal man, man other than himself, is derived Dostoyevski's orientation toward the voice of another and the word of another, which is the most important principle of his creative process. His own ideas do not enter his writings with the function of interpretation, but only as one view among other views, the word of one among the words of others, and do not give a personal coloration to the work.

The author does not touch upon material relations in the world, but transfers them completely to the vision and understanding of the characters; he merely serves to give direct expression to them and their ideas, and he himself is concerned only with the pure voice of man. The core of his design is not the relationship of the conscious and judging author to the world, but the interrelationships among the conscious and judging characters.

Bakhtin clarified the function of the adventure plot in Dostoyevski by comparing the hero of the adventure story with the heroes of the usual biographical and socio-psychological novel. Between Dostoyevski's heroes and the heroes of adventure stories in world literature Bakhtin found an essential formal resemblance. In his opinion, the hero of the conventional adventure tale lacked the typical social traits which would identify him as member of a specific social group, for to make him a fixed social type would limit the possibilities of adventure— and to engage in adventures is the sole plot function of the hero. Dostoyevski's heroes also lack all biographical data; it is impossible to say who they are:

With no biographical story, they are freer to become the bearers of a detective-story plot. With them nothing is brought about, but instead everything happens to them by chance. The circle of those ties which can bind the heroes and of those events in which they can participate is not predetermined and not limited either by their character or by that social world in which they would in reality be embodied. Therefore Dostoyevski could, with no scruples, use the most extreme and regular devices not only of the great adventure novel, but also of the cheap thriller. His hero excludes nothing from his life except one thing—the social seemliness of the completely embodied hero of the biographical-plot novel.[22]

Although he named no names, it is clear that Bakhtin was arguing against the theory of the Pereverzev school that all the characteristics of Dostoyevski's writing, including form and structure, were socially predetermined.

Dostoyevski's predilection for detective-story plots was not a new discovery. Several years earlier Leonid Grossman had written in his book *Dostoyevski's Style:*

Primarily he reproduced—the only time in the entire history of the classical Russian novel—typical plots of adventure literature. The traditional patterns of the European adventure novel more than once served Dostoyevski as outlines for construction of his intrigue.[23]

. . . . .

He even utilized the stereotypes of his literary genre. In the frenzy of hurried work he was tempted by the common types of adventure plot which had been vulgarized by the thriller novelists and the *feuilleton* writers.[24]

. . . . .

No, it seems there was not one attribute of the old adventure novel which was not used by Dostoyevski; in addition to the mysterious crimes and mass catastrophes, titles and unexpected fortunes, we find here the most typical feature of melodrama—aristocrats knocking about in the slums and their comradely fraternization with the social dregs. Of Dostoyevski's heroes, it is not Stavrogin alone who has this trait; it is equally characteristic of Prince Valkovski, Prince Sokol'ski, and even partly of Prince Myshkin.[25]

Grossman had concluded that Dostoyevski used elements of
the detective story in order to grip the reader's interest, to
arouse sympathy for the insulted and injured, and to bring the
extraordinary into the everyday, to merge the lofty with the
grotesque, to carry the commonplace to the verge of the fantastic.

Bakhtin disagreed with Grossman's explanation. In Bakhtin's
opinion, to create reader interest was never an end in itself for
Dostoyevski, nor was the romantic principle of combining the
elevated and the extraordinary with the everyday and the
grotesque. And almost never had Dostoyevski used as a model
the socio-psychological or biographical novel or the novel of
manners. The very plot construction in the family novel, the
biographical novel, or the novel of manners made these types
entirely unsuitable for Dostoyevski's purposes. In these novels
the plot is indivisible from the hero; it is not only his outer
garment, but his body and soul. Even the personal relationships
among the characters are based not on abstract human qualities,
but on social and class relations, firmly established and all-
determining. There is no place for chance happenings, for the
individual appears already wearing the unchangeable garb of
class, family, or social position. All the traits of his character
are strictly localized and determined by definite circumstances
which cannot be changed. The plot is placed in the firm framework of the relationships of the hero, and extra-plot relationships are eliminated.

In the detective story, on the contrary, there is boundless
scope for the expression of the "humanness" of the hero as
such, without reference to his place in society. "The adventure
plot," wrote Bakhtin,

is clothing that fits the hero, clothing which he can change as often as
he likes. The adventure plot is based not on what the hero is or on what
place he occupies in life, but rather on what he is not and on what,

from the point of view of all actuality already in evidence, is not ordained and is unexpected. The adventure plot is not based on existing and established positions—family, social, biographical; it is developed in spite of them. The adventure situation is a situation in which any man, as a man, may find himself. Moreover, the adventure plot always uses every established social position not as a final form of life, but as a "situation." Thus the aristocrat of the thriller has nothing in common with the aristocrat of the social or family novel. The aristocrat of the thriller is a situation in which a man has found himself. The man acts in the costume of an aristocrat like a man. He shoots, commits crimes, flees from his enemies, overcomes obstacles, and so forth. The adventure plot in this sense is deeply human. All social and cultural institutions, regulations, strata, classes, and family relations are only situations in which the eternal man, as man himself, finds himself. The needs dictated by his eternal human nature—by self-preservation, the thirst for conquest and triumph, the thirst for possessions, sensual love—determine the adventure plot.[26]

Thus the adventure plot with its eternal man was eminently suited to Dostoyevski's purposes. He needed to throw together his characters in all sorts of situations which would serve to reveal their humanness. The detective story enabled him to go far beyond the bounds of a conventional plot and to find extra-plot relationships and principles of combining voices, in Dostoyevski's words "with complete realism to find man in man" and to depict "all the depths of the human soul."

In the concluding part of his book Bakhtin considered the principles by which Dostoyevski combines the various voices and binds together the novel as a whole.

Among the astonishing diversity of types, Bakhtin found the largest number of characters speaking a word composed of two voices, at cross purposes. The combination of the inner dialogue between these two voices with the word of an outsider brings the inner polemics and confession of the character to their most forceful expression. The word of the characters lacks objectivity in the usual sense of the word; it is subjective and constantly fluctuating from parody to suppressed dialogue, then to tones of worldly sophistication and again to parody, or to open, tense dialogue. The dry, protocol language which breaks into the narrative also often bears the equivocal character of two-voiced, inner dialogue. In every particular it is Dostoyevski's purpose to sharpen to the utmost the opposing accents of a two-voiced word, thus contributing still further to the final effect of a multiplicity of voices. The tense communication between independent centers of meaning and of speech in the polyphonic design is the main stylistic unifying device.

The apparent monologue of Dostoyevski's underground man is in fact a three-way communication in which his two inner voices address each other and also address themselves to the outsider. The inner speech of the characters unfolds like a philosophical drama, in which embodied attitudes toward life are the actors. Bakhtin offered many examples of dramatized inner speech to illustrate how the word of the character searches for itself, is revealed, and orients itself toward the word of others. Sometimes the word of another is involved directly in the inner dialogue of the character, sometimes only potentially, with the possibility of mastering the consciousness of the hero.

Dostoyevski gives no final, concluding word of his own.

There is therefore no hard and fast image of the character answering the question, "Who is he?" There are only the questions, "Who am I?" and, "Who are you?" But it is in the continuous and inconclusive inner dialogue that even these questions are heard. The word of the character and the word about the character are defined by the unclosed dialogic relationship to himself and to the other. The author's word cannot enfold the hero and his word from all sides, supply the last link in the chain and bring him to completion from outside. It may only be addressed to him. All definitions and all points of view are made part of the dialogue, are brought into it as it develops. The word at a remove which, without entering into the inner dialogue of the character, would neutrally and objectively draw up his final image is unknown to Dostoyevski. The word "at a remove," which would add up the grand total of the personality, is not part of his design. That which is fixed, dead, finished, unable to speak back, which has said its final word, does not exist in the world of Dostoyevski.[27]

In his novels the dialogue is indivisibly united with the action. It is not a means, but an end. Man is revealed in dialogue. All the action is reduced to the dialogic opposition of the "I" and "the other." The dialogue often moves outside time, as the conversation of man with man, and outside the plot, although it is prepared for by the plot (for example, the dialogue of Myshkin with Rogozhin, or of Ivan Karamazov with Alyosha).

The power of the dialogue in Dostoyevski results from the complex intermingling of voices, from the interaction of the internal and external dialogue. Two characters are always intimately related to the inner voice of each other. Ivan Karamazov in conversation with Alyosha hears Alyosha's answer to questions which Ivan puts to himself in his own inner dialogue. He hears his own secret words in Alyosha's answers. In the dialogue between Ivan and the Devil, the latter introduces accents of censure and mockery into Ivan's internal dialogue. Alyosha, on the other hand, introduces words of love and reconciliation. Each reinforces one side of Ivan's inner dialogue, their open remarks being a response to his unvoiced remarks.

In *The Idiot* Nastas'ya Filippovna also has two voices. Rogozhin responds to her inner voice which acknowledges that she is a "fallen woman," and Prince Myshkin replies to the inner voice which justifies her. The alternation of these voices parallels the alternation in the plot of her relationship with Rogozhin and Myshkin.

In the conversation of Ivan Karamazov with Smerdyakov,

Dostoyevski, in Bakhtin's opinion, reaches the height of his dialogic art. Smerdyakov catches the hidden wish for the death of his father in Ivan's inner dialogue; he hears one voice increased in intensity by the interference of the other, without noticing the seriousness of the voice which resists the criminal impulse. Alyosha hears both voices in Ivan perfectly. Ivan's inner dialogues after the murder gradually lead him to the consciousness of his own responsibility and the recognition of his own secret desire acting in another man. Likewise, Stavrogin in *The Devils* hears in the voices of Shatov, Kirilov, and Pyotr Verkhovenski his own voices, which in the others, however, have become more nearly monologic.

A word free of inner struggle and duality is seldom encountered in a Dostoyevski character. The most cogent speeches are often made when one of the voices of the inner dialogue breaks through in an effort to overpower the voice speaking aloud. The inspector Porfiri in *Crime and Punishment* constantly addresses innuendoes to the suppressed voice of Raskol'nikov in order to force it to break out into the open and interrupt Raskol'nikov's carefully calculated remarks. Stavrogin's confession is also based on the same intermittent sounding of two voices and at its culmination transcends the plot, carrying to the heights of pure human relations.

"Everywhere," Bakhtin wrote,

a certain aggregate of ideas, thoughts, and words is conveyed through several independent voices, sounding differently in each one. The object of the author's intentions is not at all this aggregate of ideas in itself, as something neutral and homologous. No, the object of his intentions is precisely the execution of the theme in many different voices, an unceasing polyphony and diversity of voices on principle, so to speak. The very arrangement of the voices and their interaction are the important thing for Dostoyevski.[28]

In Dostoyevski the characters' ideological views, too, even when expressed in what is apparently a monologue directed outward, are combined with an inner dialogue. Thus "The Legend of the Grand Inquisitor," in the form of an exchange between the Inquisitor and Christ, is in fact the internal dialogue of Ivan with himself, and the ambiguity of its ending is the duality of Ivan himself.

Bakhtin insisted that Dostoyevski's dialogues were not dialectical and denied that the terms thesis, antithesis, and synthesis were applicable. In his opinion the dialogue between Ivan and Alyosha is less a dispute between two opponents than a dispute of Ivan with himself, accompanied by Alyosha's attempts to intervene in Ivan's inner dialogue in order to reinforce in him the voice of Christian love and forgiveness. There can be no merging, no unity, but only the triumph of one of the two inner voices or their external combination. The moving force and the final factor is the occurrence of the interaction of voices.

The nature of Bakhtin's conclusions, and, for that matter, of his entire approach to Dostoyevski displayed a daring independence of thought for a book published in 1929, when his methods of literary analysis were already under attack. In the teeth of the increasing claims of Marxist critics to hegemony in the study of Dostoyevski's writing, Bakhtin withdrew at the end his earlier acknowledgment that art is socially determined and denied that social and class factors govern the formation of Dostoyevski's images; the dialogue "of man with man" and the awareness of self and of the self of others were, in Bakhtin's view, free of the influence of concrete social factors—family or class:

Man has a somehow immediate awareness of himself in the world as a whole, with nothing intermediary, apart from any social collective to which he may belong. And this contact of the "I" with another and with others occurs directly on the basis of the ultimate questions, skipping over all the next intermediary forms.[29]

Bakhtin attributed the absolute humanness of Dostoyevski's characters to the fact that they are nonsocial, being members of the socially disoriented intelligentsia, *raznochintsy*, feeling themselves outside any coherent group, isolated in the world and therefore oriented toward their own solitary individuality. All of them belong to "chance families and chance collectives," without real relationship to a normal social milieu. Lacking such a relationship, they yearn toward it. Prince Myshkin, Alyosha, and the hero of "The Dream of a Ridiculous Man" dream of the utopian commonalties of the future. The Elder Zosima is possessed by the idea of a universal church, and Versilov dreams of the Golden Age. Myshkin tries to unite in a bond of love the rivals Aglaya and Nastas'ya Filippovna. The lack of opportunity for social activity and contact is compensated for in purely human affairs. And it is this very circumstance which gives universal significance to Dostoyevski's writing and at the same time accounts for its basic style. Without material possessions and background, in a state of conflict between their external and inner selves, Dostoyevski's characters are not to be put into the usual monologic structure of the novel. Their conflicting voices require the author to sharpen and intensify the clash of their interchange, to combine them without fusing them, and, in the final instance, to break with the convention of a single voice and a single idea:

> To the self-awareness of each character individually the author contrasts not his own consciousness of him, unifying and completing him from outside, but the multiplicity of other consciousnesses, revealed in the tense interaction with him and with one another.
> Such is Dostoyevski's polyphonic novel.[30]

As might be expected, Bakhtin's book evoked much unfavorable criticism, not always, it is true, for purely ideological reasons. N. Berkovski, for example, simply disagreed with Bakhtin's main thesis, asserting that in his own opinion, Dostoyevski's novels are permeated by the mind and thought of the author, who judges the "voices" of his characters and their behavior. For Berkovski, Bakhtin's notion of polyphony had vitiated his entire argument and only the linguistic and stylistic analysis in the second part of the book was of value.[31]

On the other hand, in an unsigned review in the journal *Oktyabr'* [October] Bakhtin's book was sharply criticized for ignoring the class character of Dostoyevski's ideology: "What social groups, then, are the 'bearers' in Dostoyevski's writing? We learn nothing about this from Bakhtin!"[32] The reviewer reproached Bakhtin for ignoring the peculiar mixture of questionable dialectics and unquestionably hostile sophistries in Dostoyevski and for failing to reveal the genesis of Dostoyevski's writing in respect to its social nature. In his opinion, Bakhtin had tried to direct the study of Dostoyevski to a false "idealistic and anti-class path." "In truth the devil led Bakhtin astray. . . . M. M. Bakhtin's book is a step backward. The author obviously drags us into the morass of idealism."[33]

A similar position was taken by I. Grossman-Roshchin, writing in the leading literary journal *Na literaturnom postu* [On Literary Guard], the organ of RAPP (Russian Association of Proletarian Writers). The reviewer accuses Bakhtin of attacking the positions of dialectical materialism under a smoke screen of strained metaphors about "crystals," "grains," and the refraction of social forces.[34]

Thus Bakhtin's attempt to depart from the narrow ideological approach to Dostoyevski and also from the narrow formalist study of the mere periphery of art, to combine detailed stylistic analysis with interpretation of the fundamental polyphonic principle of Dostoyevski's novels and of their universal significance, was irreconcilably opposed and rejected by Party critics and their followers.

Lunacharski, however, was able to make a genuinely scholarly appraisal of Bakhtin's book. In his lengthy article "On the Polyphony of Dostoyevski" [35] he spoke favorably of Bakhtin's basic theses:

M. M. Bakhtin has succeeded not only in establishing with greater clarity than anyone else has done the enormous significance of polyphony in Dostoyevski's novels, the role of this polyphony as the quintessential feature of his novels, but also in defining correctly that extraordinary autonomy and fullness of each "voice" which were amazingly developed in Dostoyevski and which were completely inconceivable in the great majority of other writers.

I consider it necessary to emphasize also the correctness of another thesis. M. M. Bakhtin points out that all the voices which play a truly vital role in the novels represent "convictions" or "points of view toward the world." These, of course, are not simply theories; they are theories originating, as it were, in the very "composition of the blood" of the character, indissolubly connected with him, constituting his basic nature. In addition, these theories are activating ideas. They force the characters to definite actions; definite individual and social standards of behavior are derived from them—in a word, they have a deeply ethical and social character. . . .

Under these conditions, the extreme independence of the individual voices becomes, so to speak, especially piquant. We must assume that it was Dostoyevski's intention to raise various vital questions for deliberation by these individual "voices," which shake with passion and blaze with the fire of fanaticism, while he himself has the air of merely being present at these convulsive disputes and of watching with curiosity to see how it will end and what turn the matter will take. To a considerable degree this is so.[36]

Lunacharski also agreed with Bakhtin's assertion that, at least in the initial conception of a novel and during most of the process of writing it, if not at the final stage as well, Dostoyevski had no structural plan fixed in advance, for absolutely free personalities are in action in his novels—that is, the polyphony of voices asserted itself. True, Lunacharski confessed that he found it hard to understand what Bakhtin meant in his reference to an artistic unity of a higher order in a Dostoyevski novel and what he saw as welding it into a cohesive whole.

Although Lunacharski accepted most of Bakhtin's central theses, the doctrine binding upon him as a Marxist compelled him to call Bakhtin's attention to the presence of polyphony in other writers, for instance, Shakespeare, and to the fact that all great writers inevitably reflected the ideological tendencies of their times. The influence of Bakhtin's book on Lunacharski was apparent, however, even in Lunacharski's subsequent criticism of Dostoyevski. Thus in the article "Dostoyevski as Thinker and Artist," Lunacharski, speaking of the polyphony of Dostoyevski's novels and of his characters, wrote:

Set free from the inner world of Dostoyevski, the types which are engendered there—stretching in a long chain from revolutionaries to obscurantists—at once begin to speak with their own voices, break loose from his hands, and each one propounds his own thesis.[37]

And although Lunacharski as a Soviet Marxist hastened to curb this "unprecedented freedom of voices" and ascribed to Dostoyevski "manipulation of the process" and the role of "director" in restraining and controlling the chorus, he nevertheless acknowledged the fact that "in essence, Dostoyevski's power over the beings he has conjured up is limited":

Behind the scenes there will be no way of telling what is going on. Out there the actors can completely stop obeying; out there they can continue farther those contradictory lines which they have drawn on the visible horizon and begin really to lacerate the soul of Dostoyevski.[38]

Bakhtin's interpretation was so persuasive that the responsive and lively mind of Lunacharski could not resist it, despite his Marxism. Bakhtin's completely new and original theses would undoubtedly have stimulated further study of Dostoyevski's novels along similar lines, had his book not appeared, unfortunately, in 1929, at the turning point between two periods in Soviet life. In the following years literature and criticism were brought more and more under Party jurisdiction, and purely scholarly functions became impermissible. Bakhtin's book was soon relegated to oblivion and prevented from playing in Dostoyevski scholarship the role for which it was eminently qualified.

. 16 .

THE TWO TRENDS OF THE 1930S

The censure and dissolution of Pereverzev's "sociological" school left Soviet students of Dostoyevski in a quandary. Marxist critics were vociferously active in exposing Dostoyevski's reactionary ideology but displayed less energy and ability in positive research work. One of the first attempts to satisfy the new demands, still not clearly formulated or understood, was M. Polyakova's paper "The Social Nature of Dostoyevski's Heroes," published in 1931.[1] The main intention of this article was obviously to find social determinants of Dostoyevski's work other than that offered by Pereverzev—the social origin of the writer.

Polyakova rejected not only Pereverzev's general methodological principles but also his definition of Dostoyevski as a writer of the crumbling *meshchanstvo*, and attempted a radically different interpretation of the phenomenon of Dostoyevskiism as the sum of the psychological qualities of his characters. Polyakova defined Dostoyevskiism not as a mere portrayal of stress, suffering, and disharmony but as an affirmation and idealization of disharmony and stress as the higher life worthy of representation in art. Such an apotheosis of suffering and humility, of renunciation of vain strife, Polyakova states, was characteristic of the *déclassé* nobility. Members of this group, who had broken with their class and family traditions at the very beginning of their lives, did not, when they found themselves in the capitalist city, accept the spirit of competition but remained complete outsiders. From a rural, feudal way of life, they entered the ranks of the urban government personnel—civil servants, army officers, and intelligentsia. Cut off from their own

class and ceasing to be nobility in this strict sense, they nevertheless retained a feeling of repugnance for the entrepreneurial
spirit and for amassing wealth. To Polyakova the rebellion of
Dostoyevski's characters was an expression of their opposition
to capitalist reality. Sonya Marmeladova, Prince Myshkin, and
Alyosha Karamazov represent an idealization of those who reject both the feudal world and bourgeois money-grubbing. Their
metaphysical refusal to recognize harsh reality is akin to the
attitude of the *déclassé* nobility toward the kulak speculators
who bought up the property of the ruined landowners after the
emancipation of the serfs in 1861. Prince Myshkin, according
to Polyakova, is the exact antithesis of "noisy manufacturing"
humanity: "In affirming his own detachment and renunciation,
he finds a very convenient formula for the existence of his
group." [2] Thus, although Polyakova appeared to discard Pereverzev's thesis, in fact she only modified it somewhat by offer-
ing the plight of another social group without a future. Like
Pereverzev, Polyakova reduced such phenomena as the religion
of suffering in Dostoyevski's characters to a result of their social
position and thus diminished their substance and universality.

Polyakova's discussion of the "reactionary revolutionism"
and "revolutionary reactionism" of Dostoyevski was reminiscent
of the theses of Gorbachov and other Marxist predecessors. Her
article was a pseudoscholarly reiteration, on the pretext of
interpreting Dostoyevski, of RAPP arguments for the dialectical-
materialist method in art, and simply served to draw attention
away from the essential questions.

With the dissolution of RAPP by the April, 1932, decree of
the Central Committee of the Communist Party and the proclamation of socialist realism as the method of Soviet literature,
attention was redirected to the realism of the classical literature

of the past. In this atmosphere of relative tolerance, several volumes of Dostoyevski materials which had been prepared earlier were published. In 1934 the third volume of Dostoyevski's letters, under the editorship of A. S. Dolinin, appeared, and in 1935, the collection *F. M. Dostoyevski: Materials and Studies,* also edited by Dolinin. The bifurcation of Soviet critical opinion and policy concerning Dostoyevski, which became so conspicuous during the second half of the 1930s following Gorki's ambivalent speech at the First Congress of Soviet Writers in 1934, had a paradoxical effect on the publication of other materials and texts. The fourth and final volume of the letters failed to appear. And although Dostoyevski's notebooks for *The Devils* were published in their entirety in 1935, the new edition of the novel itself, which had been announced for publication during 1934, has never come out.

In a foreword to the materials for *The Devils,* published under the title *F. M. Dostoyevski's Notebooks,*[3] the publishers took a middle-of-the-road course by calling Dostoyevski an enemy of the Russian revolutionary movement and at the same time warning the reader that it was an oversimplification to consider him an outright ideologist of the landowners and bourgeoisie, a supporter of the autocratic regime. The publishers noted his powerful treatment of the internal contradictions in Russian psychology of the time, of the illusions of the *meshchanstvo,* and of the helpless efforts to find an escape other than revolution during the time when the Russian revolution was brewing. His own feeling of involvement in the coming revolution, it was stated, persisted despite all his misgivings, his slanders against the leaders of the revolution, and his hope that the Russian city *meshchantsvo* might serve as bulwark.

By the end of the 1930s two well defined and antagonistic

trends in Dostoyevski criticism were again flourishing, both
finding sanction in Gorki's re-evaluation at the First Congress
of Soviet Writers.

One faction, slavishly following Gorki's denunciation of Dostoyevski's ideology, strove, in the words of the Futurist manifesto of 1912, "to throw . . . Dostoyevski . . . overboard
from the steamship of modernity." [4] The other, justifying itself
by Gorki's unstinting praise of Dostoyevski's artistry, employed
all its resources to reinstate him in Soviet favor.

Of the arguments offered by the first group, V. V. Yermilov's
"Gorki and Dostoyevski" was a quasi-official statement of the
Communist Party view of these two writers.[5] Yermilov drew a
sharp contrast between the great humanistic traditions of Russian classical literature, embodied in Gorki's writing, and the
antihumanism of Dostoyevski.

Dostoyevski, Yermilov asserted, discarded Pushkin's bright,
optimistic, unwavering faith in man and his limitless possibilities, in human reason, aspirations for a better life, and
hatred of suffering. He distorted the Russian dream of a free and
integrated human being, whereas Maxim Gorki, combating
such retrograde tendencies, upheld the great humanistic traditions of Russian culture. Yermilov dismissed the obvious legacy
which Gorki inherited from Dostoyevski—the themes of city
life, the interest in psychological complexities, even the frequent
sounding of the author's voice amid the polyphony of the characters' voices. To characterize Dostoyevski's style, the critic
artificially applied to it the words of Klim Samgin, hero of
Gorki's novel *The Life of Klim Samgin*, who defines his life as
a monologue expressed in his thoughts as a dialogue: Dostoyevski's entire writing becomes a "monologue in the form of
dialogue." [6]

According to Yermilov, in Dostoyevski the subjective is extended until it swallows up objective reality. The thoughts of Dostoyevski's characters are not controlled by actuality, whereas in Gorki the correspondence is always maintained.

Yermilov maintained that only one voice was heard in Dostoyevski's writing and denied that it was characterized by polyphony. His method is "subjectively experimental"; reality is built up in his novels by "putting material into shape for experiment." [7] Yermilov displayed no understanding of the structural traits and the "aggressiveness" of the plot in Dostoyevski's novels when he compared them to the results of an experiment performed under laboratory conditions in which the objective movement of reality is lost. While Tolstoi primarily portrayed in his novels the course of reality itself, which shapes people and their characters and changes their relationships, Dostoyevski, the critic asserted, was primarily and excessively concerned with the course of the processes of consciousness, with the result that his characters are insufficiently objectivized, are not far enough separated from the author's consciousness to become independent and "material." "All this," concluded Yermilov, "signified a tendency to end the epic line of Russian prose. The line of decadence was observable here." [8]

For this reason, the critic asserted, Gorki, as a writer of the rising class, always took issue with Dostoyevski by bringing Dostoyevski's characters down to earth. Dostoyevski usually removed his heroes from the milieu of ordinary existence into a lofty realm of unaccustomed emotions and tense ideological struggle; Gorki placed his heroes in a real environment, killing two birds with one stone—he countered Dostoyevski, revealing the true significance of his reactionary heroes and their "elevating fraud" and, on the other hand, achieved realism.

Yermilov explained away all indications of Dostoyevski's influence on Gorki and the similarities between the two writers as a manifestation of Gorki's attack upon his ideological and artistic antithesis. Despite the fact that Dostoyevski's and Gorki's characters often share the same ideas about freedom and happiness, and also about quietude and passivity, Yermilov read into these characterizations completely different attitudes on the part of the authors. Dostoyevski he placed in the camp of the extreme reactionaries who desired to "freeze" Russia and to stop the course of life. He spoke for philistinism, while Gorki implacably exposed its bestial countenance. In *The Life of Klim Samgin* Gorki shows Dostoyevskiism for what it is—an apotheosis of philistinism—by transferring the ideas of Raskol'nikov and Ivan Karamazov to their proper real-life milieu, that of bourgeois counterrevolution, and by stripping away the mystification with which Dostoyevski had enshrouded them.

Both authors dealt with the combination of good and evil, the two infinities in man, the capacity for love and noble feelings together with the proclivity for vileness, the mixture of rebellion and humility—Karamazovism in Dostoyevski and Okurovism [9] in Gorki—but from diametrically opposed positions. Dostoyevski would overcome Karamazovism by "narrowing" the human being; Gorki would end Okurovism by broadening the inherently good elements in man. Yermilov gave entirely different interpretations to the two writers' portrayal of the disintegration of the individual. Both Smerdyakov in *The Brothers Karamazov* and Klim Samgin are characterized by complete inner devastation and parasitism. Yet Dostoyevski's characterization bespeaks his reactionary philosophy, whereas Gorki's Klim Samgin is "a figure of broad social significance, a composite of many varieties of the parasitic bourgeois man." [10]

In the characters of *The Devils* Yermilov saw the fathers of the Soviet bourgeois "spies" and "conspirators," "the predecessors of the fascist, Trotskyite-Bukharinist provocateurs and murderers." "This kinship is accounted for by the social environment they have in common—the environment of counterrevolutionary traitors and renegades, 'capable of anything.'" [11]

Resorting to the stereotypes of Party hacks and borrowing the views of Mikhailovski and of Gorki in his publicist writing, Yermilov reduced Dostoyevski's final philosophy to a repudiation of his early sympathy for the insulted and injured, to "an idealization of suffering, a worship of it which involved sanctioning it in actuality, a sanctification of all the ugliness of reality," to an idealization of the lie of religion, "the morality of the masters" [12] and slave psychology. In the last analysis Dostoyevski's writing conveyed "the inhumanity of a society of property owners, the perversion of all relationships between people, the terror of the human soul which knows no reality which might be upheld against the wolfish laws of the world of property." [13]

The split personality of the doubles, Yermilov concluded, was a result of their ambivalence toward the Western bourgeois world, which not only allured but frightened them, and of their wavering between "master-and-slave morality" and fear of revolution. His tendentious laudation of Gorki's *Life of Klim Samgin* as the objective truth which invalidated Dostoyevski's preaching of the religious lie and slave psychology is an eloquent example of the lengths to which the sacrifice of independent thought led Dostoyevski scholars.

In the same year, 1939, the more liberal climate which had set in after the fall of the head of the NKVD, Nikolai Yezhov, and the ebbing of the wave of terror permitted the publication of the important book *How Dostoyevski Worked* by Georgi Ivanovich Chulkov (1879–1939).[14] Chulkov made another marked attempt to emphasize the aspects of Dostoyevski which would rehabilitate him in Soviet eyes. Like Dolinin, Chulkov stressed Dostoyevski's warm feelings toward his radical past, as expressed in the article entitled "Old Times in the Petrashevski Circle," which the censor had banned for publication in *Diary of a Writer* for 1877.

Little or nothing was said of Dostoyevski's monarchic views in his last years, and his relationship with Pobedonostsev was described as a guarded and distrustful one. Chulkov considered Dostoyevski a religious democrat. He was inclined to attribute Dostoyevski's duality to his restlessness and hostility toward the psychology of the *meshchanstvo*. Chulkov's favorable attitude toward Dostoyevski was especially apparent in his tribute to the humility and wisdom of Prince Myshkin.

In a long discussion of Dostoyevski's Christianity, Chulkov with surprising boldness characterized him as a devout believer. Many of Dostoyevski's own admissions, however, challenge Chulkov's conclusions. Dostoyevski himself did not hide his religious doubts. In a letter to Natal'ya Dmitriyevna Fon-Vizina on February 20, 1854, Dostoyevski said of himself: "I am a child of the age, a child of disbelief and doubts up to this time and even (I know it) to the very grave." [15] And in a letter to A. N. Maikov on March 25, 1870, he stated: "The main question which will be developed throughout [the planned novel *Life of a Great Sinner*] is the same one which has tortured me, consciously or unconsciously, all my life—the existence of God." [16]

Speaking of the radicals who accused him of being a fanatic adherent of religious dogmatism, he wrote in a notebook:

The rotters have taunted me for my unenlightenment and retrograde faith in God. These numskulls have never dreamed of such a powerful denial of God as is formulated in the "Inquisitor" and in the preceding chapter, to which the whole novel serves as answer. My belief in God is not that of a fool (a fanatic). And they tried to teach me and laughed at my failure to develop! While their stupid natures have never dreamed of such a powerful negation as I have gone through. It is up to them to teach me! [17]

He also states that the force of his "Legend of the Grand Inquisitor" as the "argument of atheism" has no precedent in Europe and acknowledges that he himself had gone through "a great furnace of doubt" to achieve his faith.[18]

In his analysis of the formal characteristics of Dostoyevski's novels, Chulkov developed the theses of Vyacheslav Ivanov, his teacher, concerning the "tragedy-novel," and in certain respects carried them to extremes. In Chulkov's opinion, all the elements of Dostoyevski's writing were those of drama and the theater, despite Dostoyevski's own view that the theatrical possibilities of his works were limited. The fact that his concern is with psychological analysis rather than with external action militates against the effective interpretation of his characters on the stage. Vyacheslav Ivanov's conception of the "tragedy-novel," valid in his philosophical context, is no longer applicable when the word "tragedy" is construed in the narrower sense of the theater.

Chulkov regarded Dostoyevski's style as a manifestation not of reaction but of rebellion and daring:

Dostoyevski, like Columbus, did not know himself what he had discovered. He sailed for India and caught sight of the New World. Dostoyevski, too, was always preparing for some creative exploit, without realizing that the exploit had already been performed, that his creations had already radically changed the "face of this world," that he had initiated a tremendous cultural revolution.[19]

Although certain of Chulkov's theses may be disputed, the scrupulous accuracy of the abundant factual material offered by this non-Party scholar of the old generation makes his book of lasting value to students able to disregard the charges by

Marxist circles that Georgi Chulkov was an anarchistic aesthete
of the decadent-symbolist persuasion.

The publication of a selection of Dostoyevski's longer stories
in 1940 [20] and the tone of the commentary by the Marxist editor,
O. V. Tsekhnovitser, unmistakably signalized a reversal of
Soviet policy toward Dostoyevski. On the eve of the war it was
found expedient to bring to an end the obloquy which had been
visited upon him for many years. Tsekhnovitser's success in
formulating an interpretation which might be labeled genuinely
Marxist, free of the earlier "vulgar sociology" and oversimplification, was soon rewarded by the grant of a state stipend for
the preparation and defense of a doctoral dissertation on the
theme "The Writing of F. M. Dostoyevski."

Tsekhnovitser attempted to reinterpret the significance of the
Hoffmannesque tradition in Dostoyevski, the problem of the
double, and the theme of the conflict of the individual with
society.

In contrast to the frequent objections of Soviet critics to the
duality of Dostoyevski's characters, Tsekhnovitser considered
the treatment of this theme legitimate and fruitful for Russian
literature. To support his argument he turned to Marx and
Engels and quoted passages from the *Communist Manifesto* concerning the conversion of personal worth into exchange value
and the ruin of the personality in a society in which money is
the ruling force determining all relations between people, as
well as passages from Marx in which he spoke of the corrupting
power of money which turns loyalty into treachery, love into
hate, virtue into vice, intellect into imbecility, and so on. Under
such conditions, man's nobility is suppressed by his "double,"
who must try to make his way in life. This development gave
rise to the Hoffmannesque method of taking the reader into the
realm of the subconscious, of removing the masks from human

beings and revealing the depths of the personality. Tsekhnovitser saw the use of the split personality in fiction as a device for censuring a world based on callous "cash payment." He defined the central theme of *Crime and Punishment, The Gambler, A Raw Youth,* and *The Idiot* as that of the impact of money on capitalist society.

In Tsekhnovitser's opinion, Dostoyevski was a single personality, who throughout his entire career dealt consistently with the most vital social, political and philosophical problems of his time; and if, at different periods, he offered different solutions, they were dictated by the changing social and political situation:

It is time to put an end to the widespread opinion that there were two Dostoyevskis, one before and one after prison. Questions of morality, humanity, good and evil, ideas of Christianity and socialism, ideas of the people and of populism—all these questions were raised by Dostoyevski from 1845 to 1881 inclusively.[21]

Tsekhnovitser called attention to the influence of Belinski on the young writer and to the echoes of Dostoyevski's early socialism in his later writings, glossing over the repudiation of Belinski's views. Although, according to Tsekhnovitser, Dostoyevski gave evidence again and again of the vitality of his belief in socialism, as in "Dream of a Ridiculous Man," he never found the final correct answer to the great questions of the day but remained entangled in the contradictions between good and evil, compassion and cruelty, reaction and revolution. Nonetheless, the portrayal of these contradictions is one of extraordinary power, especially in *The Brothers Karamazov,* and its profundity should not be underestimated:

Mankind at a most crucial moment of its development, on the threshold between the old world and the new, found its clearest portrayal in that magnificent symphony which unfolds in the writing of this Russian genius. The struggle between the dark and the light, between reaction and progress, Christianity and atheism, capitalism and socialist teaching—all this is recorded with extraordinary power and clarity by Dostoyevski. He knew how to embody current philosophical ideas in the concrete, living personalities which came to full life on the pages of his novels, books which are entertaining in plot and tragic in their plethora of conflicts.[22]

Like Yermilov, Tsekhnovitser found it expedient to bolster his argument by reference to Gorki, whose divided opinion of Dostoyevski offered abundant support for both critics. Tsekhnovitser seized upon the passage in *History of Russian Literature*, quoted earlier, in which Gorki described Dostoyevski as the writer destined to embody and express the memory of all human tortures. In essence, Tsekhnovitser urged disregard of Dostoyevski's ideological defects from the Soviet point of view and recognition of the bold realism of his art, which revealed the contradictions of life "with astounding, truly Rembrandtesque severity and Shakespearean power":

Despite all the mistakes, all the failures which were characteristic of Dostoyevski, despite the fact that the "voice of evil" was often stronger in him than the "voice of good," our socialist epoch cannot but give this writer of genius his due.[23]

To clinch his argument, Tsekhnovitser harked back to the fact that in 1918 Dostoyevski's name stood in second place on the list of Russian writers in whose memory Lenin authorized the erection of monuments.

With war imminent, the party had embarked upon a policy of stimulating patriotism, and Soviet citizens were again invited to take pride in the great Russian writers of the past.

. 17 .

THE SECOND WORLD WAR AND
THE REHABILITATION OF DOSTOYEVSKI

From the beginning of the 1940s to the end of the war, Dostoyevski was treated with high esteem by Soviet critics. In any enumeration of the great patriotic writers of Russia, Fyodor Dostoyevski was mentioned along with Pushkin, Lermontov, Gogol, Turgenev, Chernyshevski, Nekrasov, Saltykov-Shchedrin, Tolstoi, Chekhov, and Gorki.

Bolshevik propaganda is, of course, guided by purely strategic considerations of the moment. As the war advanced, the Bolsheviks found themselves in acute need of new ideological tactics to arouse patriotism and hatred of the enemy. When the Party slogans calling for defense of the achievements of socialism proved a failure in the early stage of the war, the Bolsheviks swiftly regarbed themselves as protectors of the national interests of the peoples of the USSR, their territories, culture, languages, literature, and even religion, and closed their eyes to much that they had formerly castigated as reactionary. They seized upon the idea of Slavic community and revived the old belief in the messianic role of the Russian people, which was now represented as destined to free mankind from the terrors of fascism.

The great names of Russian culture of the past appeared in a new light, as the classics of Russian literature were turned into anti-German propaganda. The abundance of Dostoyevski's unflattering references to the Germans made his writing especially suitable; such quotations had been used during the First World War for the same purpose.[1]

In August, 1942, in *Bol'shevik*, theoretical organ of the

Party, Yemel'yan Mikhailovich Yaroslavski (1878–1943), member of the Central Committee of the Party and a high functionary of the Agitation and Propaganda Section, director of prewar antireligious campaigns, granted official amnesty to Dostoyevski and summoned him to the battle with the Germans.[2] In defense of Dostoyevski against the attempts of Nazis, such as Rosenberg, to use his name in the struggle against Russia, Yaroslavski traced Dostoyevski's career from the 1840s and aligned him with the "best representatives of Russian democracy of that time," such as Belinski and Nekrasov. Speaking of Dostoyevski's activity in the Petrashevski circle, Yaroslavski pointed out that, in addition to their general interest in the utopian socialism of Saint-Simon, several members (the Speshnyov group) were acquainted even with *The Communist Manifesto* of Marx and Engels. As evidence of Dostoyevski's democratic political outlook, the favorable reception of *Poor Folk* by progressives and Dostoyevski's reading of Belinski's letter to Gogol in his revolutionary circle were cited. Dostoyevski was to be regarded as in sympathy with both utopian socialism and the democratic movement of his time. As a result of his physical and spiritual breakdown in prison and exile, he had lost his faith in revolution, had searched in anguish for other remedies for the plight of the insulted and injured, and, in the futility of his quest, had become a tragic and unhappy figure. Although he had repudiated everything in which he believed as a youth, he nevertheless heeded the inner voice which remained with him until the end of his life. Despite criticism by progressive Russians for his ideological defection, he was always acknowledged as a writer of genius. "With all his faults," Yaroslavski wrote, "Dostoyevski was and remains a deeply Russian writer who loved his people,"[3] "a profound Russian patriot."[4]

Dostoyevski loved the Russian people and dreamed of their happiness in his own way, although he went toward this happiness by false paths, although his voice was often false. This Russian has nothing in common with the infamous hangmen of the Hitlerite band. Dostoyevski is full of compassion, full of love for the people, while the Hitlerites are enemies of the people, enemies of mankind.[5]

Yaroslavski then quoted angry words from Dostoyevski to prove his hatred of the Germans for their aspiration to dominate the world.

The same number of *Bol'shevik* carried an article by Ilya Ehrenburg entitled "Maturity," in which, with his characteristic cynicism and opportunism, Ehrenburg expatiated upon the universal scope, the humanism and compassion of the classics of Russian literature—qualities not usually mentioned on the pages of the Party press—and assigned Dostoyevski a high place among the great Russian writers of the past:

The broad humanity of the old Russian intelligentsia, their ties with the West, their conscientiousness precluded chauvinism. Against the cruelty of Nietzsche and the soulless power of Wagner, the Russian intelligentsia of the past century put humanism, conscience, the sufferings of Garshin, the pity of Dostoyevski, the "I cannot be silent" of Tolstoi.[6]

Once *Bol'shevik* had given the signal, V. V. Yermilov, long practiced in retaining his rank as a leading Party critic by swift adaptation to the successive zigzags of Communist literary policy, completely reversed the views on Dostoyevski which he had expressed in 1939. A critic without formal higher education in literature, a product of Komsomol journalism and of the RAPP school, Yermilov, although he had displayed a certain independence of thought as one of the formulators of the "living man" theory,[7] had distinguished himself after the dissolution of

RAPP in 1932 chiefly by his alacrity in pioneering every new
Party-sponsored literary cause. Until 1932 a close associate and
supporter of Leopol'd Averbakh in the leadership of RAPP,
Yermilov at once confessed his errors and went on to become
an official of the Union of Soviet Writers, a leading literary
critic, and editor of *Literaturnaya gazeta* [Literary Gazette],
always ready to serve the Party campaign of the hour—against
formalism, Pereverzevism, the survivals of RAPPism, bourgeois
liberalism, cosmopolitanism, or any other "deviation" in Soviet
literature.

When in September, 1942, Yermilov's long article entitled
"The Great Russian Writer F. M. Dostoyevski" [8] was published
in the newspaper *Literatura i iskusstvo* [Literature and Art],
it was clear that the Bolsheviks had gone as far as it was possible for them to go in the direction of reconciliation with Dostoyevski.

The very title of Yermilov's article, pointing simultaneously
to Dostoyevski's greatness and to his Russian nationality, epitomized the new trend. In 1939 Yermilov had scourged Dostoyevski for idealization of slave mentality and humility, for
portraying the disintegration of the human being in the in-
humane conditions of a society of private enterprise and at the
same time teaching that mankind is powerless to change those
conditions.

In 1942, noting that during wartime it was necessary to regard Russian literature in a new light, Yermilov still considered
Dostoyevski's vision a terrible one, but one redeemed by his
obsession with the idea of freeing mankind from this nightmare.
Dostoyevski's prophetic characterization of the Stavrogins and
Smerdyakovs had helped mankind to perceive the threatened
loss of human values. Although he did not know from what
quarter the threat actually came (that is, he did not foresee the

concrete forms of twentieth-century fascism), and although he confused social terms, he was nevertheless aware of the danger. Moreover, he opposed the division of mankind into the masters, to whom everything was permitted, and their submissive slaves. Dostoyevski the seer had prefigured the superman philosophy of Nietzsche. Yermilov angrily assailed Lev Shestov for asserting in his book *Dostoyevski and Nietzsche* that the core of the work of both writers is the doctrine of the amoral superman. The Yermilov of 1942 made a sharp distinction between the author and his characters: "In Dostoyevski's eyes those views which were later designated as Nietzschean are actually *crime*, calling for ruthless *punishment*." [9]

In an interesting interpretation of Dostoyevski's method of characterization, Yermilov commented that, unlike Nietzsche, Dostoyevski did not portray a beast in human form. He took man himself in all his humanness and added to him, as a gauge, antihuman ideas. As the idea is developed in the behavior of the characters, its unsoundness, perniciousness and falsity are displayed. Entertaining the idea, the character has lost his human aspect, has turned into a loathsome biting insect, into a spider sucking the "vital juices out of mankind," or, realizing the full horror of isolation and delusion, has become a human being again. The sufferings of Raskol'nikov, the torments of Ivan Karamazov, the frenzies of the hero of *A Raw Youth* demonstrate that in Dostoyevski's mind "superman" morality is incompatible with real men. The feeling of being cut off and separated from humanity is such torture to Raskol'nikov that it forces him to give himself up in order to rid himself of a burden of sin beyond human endurance.

Yermilov saw in Dostoyevski's Smerdyakov a foreshadowing of Nietzsche's and Spengler's heroes who pride themselves on having nothing in common with human society, and offered such characterization as evidence of Dostoyevski's antifascist attitude.

Yermilov retreated from the implacable hostility of earlier Soviet criticism toward *The Devils* and even appeared to be seeking a pretext to clear it of the charge of antisocialism. For one thing, Yermilov was able to say, in the character of Pyotr Verkhovenski, Dostoyevski unmasks the political charlatan and adventurist Nechayev. Applying current Soviet publicist terminology to the conspirators and calling them "renegades," "political gangsters," "adventurers," "murderers," and "blackmailers," referring to Shigalyov as "the theorist of Smerdyakovism," and laying stress on the disavowals of socialism by characters in the novel, Yermilov little by little suggested that there was no attempt in *The Devils* to attack socialists—for the plotters of the novel had no relation to the genuine socialist movement of the time—but that Dostoyevski was simply setting forth his eternal theme that one small part of mankind cannot rule over all the others. Making good use of Dostoyevski's many gibes at German smugness, boastfulness, arrogance, swaggering, banality, and chauvinism, Yermilov strained to relate the intention in *The Devils* to the Soviet war effort against the Germans.

All his life, Yermilov announced in 1942, Dostoyevski's goal was the happiness of all mankind, even if he quarreled with the progressive thinkers of his time over the paths to be taken. In disputing with them he disputed with himself, with his past and present, and for this reason the quarrel was an extremely bitter one. Furthermore, Dostoyevski's quarrel was with vulgar socialism—for he knew no other—and with its theories "of heroes and the mob," of masters and slaves. In the final analysis, through his fictional characters, he involuntarily repudiated his own ideological errors and overcame his contradictions. As an illustration Yermilov offered Ivan Karamazov's conquest of his Napoleonic tendencies, which yield to progressive thoughts unacceptable to both author and character but nonetheless passionately enunciated. Another example is the rejection by Ivan of future divine harmony in the name of atonement for the tears of the tormented child and revenge for the insulted and injured. That is, Yermilov argued, in Dostoyevski's mind not everything is permitted, since Ivan Karamazov will not abjure violence against the violators and since the gentle novice Alyosha is so infected with his brother's rebellion and protest that he agrees that the landowner who hunts a child with dogs must be punished.

Unable to deny the contradictions in Dostoyevski, Yermilov justified them by pointing out that in nature nothing exists in a pure state, without contradictions. They were not the important thing in Dostoyevski.

The important thing in Dostoyevski is his frenzied and violent protest against insult and injury to man, against turning man into a slave, his rebellious spirit, his call for swift vengeance, today, for every tear shed by a child. No matter how Dostoyevski tried—also violently!—to smother this protest, it sounds more loudly than anything else in his writings. And it sounds with particular power in our days, filled as they are with the thirst to take vengeance on the present enslavers who dream of becoming the "masters" of all mankind, to take vengeance swiftly and mercilessly, with full Russian "unrestraint," to use Dostoyevski's expression, to take vengeance every hour, every minute for the tears of the tortured children, the unprecedented wrongs, to kill, to shoot the monsters who hunt our children with dogs and burn them in bonfires. The great friend of children, the great fighter against insult and injury to man, the Russian writer Dostoyevski is with *us* in this holy battle! Perhaps he was against all violence. But still he said, or his favorite hero, Alyosha Karamazov, said, "Shoot [him]!" This whisper is louder than any shout.

Thus we have perceived more clearly during the Fatherland War the main thing in Dostoyevski—the Russian nature of his writing, which cannot reconcile itself to insult and injury. And is it possible that we should not take pride in the fact that our literature, through the lips of Dostoyevski, warned of the terrible menace to all mankind, remaining true to its humanistic, noble traditions? It is said that "nothing is given free; fate requires sacrifices in repayment." Dostoyevski's delusions, which brought so much harm, were a sacrifice—a heavy sacrifice! But Dostoyevski's *truth*—this is our truth, Russian truth.[10]

Thus, in the wartime effort to stress unity and solidarity, social and class criteria disappeared, and Dostoyevski became a writer speaking for all Russians and all mankind, maintaining and deepening the great humanist traditions of Russian literature. Even his predilection for the theme of the split personality Yermilov interpreted as arising from his longing for single-heartedness and from his struggle against rapaciousness and violence in man; his "cruel talent" itself has the virtue of inculcating "cruel ruthlessness toward ourselves, teaches us 'not to indulge' ourselves in anything and to seek out the most deeply buried reasons for our actions, words and thoughts." [11] This "cruelty" which teaches the reader honesty with self is, Yermilov proclaimed, essentially a striving for final, pure truth and an aversion for compromises with conscience; it is one of the typical traits of the Russian character, and Dostoyevski is its great representative.

This about-face, from which the Party critic emerged the standard-bearer of "Russian truth," Yermilov performed with the consummate skill and the tactical flexibility of those chosen by the Party to execute its literary policy.

In the course of the war many others joined in the rehabilitation of Dostoyevski. In 1943 L. Dmitriyev, for instance, berating Mikhail Zoshchenko for portraying only the dark sides of Soviet life, upheld Dostoyevski, in company with Saltykov-Schchedrin, as a writer who had combated the negative aspects of Russian life in the past and who was worthy of emulation. The two nineteenth-century writers, previously contrasted as a revolutionary and a reactionary, were brought into wartime alliance for the sake of glorifying the love they shared for their own people and their opposition to its malicious representation:

And when Saltykov-Shchedrin and Dostoyevski depicted with unsurpassed power the ulcers of human psychology and social life, was this not dictated by the same active aspiration to cleanse the world of vileness, and was it not for the benefit of their own people that they touched its wounds? [12]

. 18 .

THE 125TH ANNIVERSARY
OF DOSTOYEVSKI'S BIRTH

From the end of the Second World War until late 1947, Soviet critics of Dostoyevski took their cue from the mood prevailing during the celebration in November, 1946, of the 125th anniversary of Dostoyevski's birth. During this time, in universities, theaters, clubhouses, and elsewhere, speeches were made, readings from his works were given, and stage adaptations produced. The press reported these activities and carried new tributes to Dostoyevski by orthodox spokesmen of the Party. From 1946 to 1948 the publishing houses released several new books of criticism and various new editions of Dostoyevski's works, including *Selected Writings* in 1946; *Poor Folk, The Insulted and Injured, A Raw Youth,* and *The Boys* in 1947; and *Crime and Punishment* in 1948.

The articles which appeared in the press during the anniversary days continued the wartime practice of ranking Dostoyevski among the great precursors of the Soviet epoch in art. The patriotic fervor of the war had passed, however, and with it the need to burn incense before the idols of the past. The tone of the articles published in November, 1946, by the Party war horses Zaslavski and Aleksandrov was far less rhapsodic than had been Yermilov's during the war. The sober moderation and the commonsense attitude toward Dostoyevski of the immediate postwar period promised a sound basis for future study.

D. I. Zaslavski, well-known contributor to the newspaper *Pravda* and mouthpiece of Soviet literary policy, who, after the death of Yemel'yan Yaroslavski, set the pace in ideological campaigns, served notice in his article in *Literaturnaya gazeta* of November 16, 1946, that the wartime amnesty for Dostoyevski had been extended. He speaks sympathetically of the young Dostoyevski as an admirer of Belinski, a progressive, a champion of the downtrodden, and in his writing a continuator of the traditions of Russian realism deriving from Pushkin's *Stationmaster* and Gogol's *Overcoat*. Like Tolstoi, Dostoyevski gave no quarter to false people or false ideas. Despite the change that occurred during his years in prison, Dostoyevski's writing continued to engender rebellion against social injustice in Russian youth. His rebellious characters were more forceful and clearer than his God-fearing heroes.

Zaslavski declined to put Dostoyevski in the camp of revolution or of "democracy" because of the very self-contradictoriness which accounts for the power of his portrayal of the contradictions in man and for his universal significance.

To explain these contradictions, Zaslavski again resorted to Lenin's articles on Tolstoi and reiterated that Dostoyevski, like Tolstoi, portrayed the period of the Russian peasant revolution, when old concepts and ideas were being smashed and the new had not yet been established.

Although in Zaslavski's eyes Dostoyevski's answers were often wrong, the fact was that he posed the most important questions of the life of his time. In *Crime and Punishment* he raised the question of the place and rights of Raskol'nikov in contemporary society. In the accusations of Ivan Karamazov he bared the fraud of idealistic religion. He questioned the justification of social and class strata, but answered incorrectly, advocating submission. He propounded the question of the future role of Russia and the leadership of the Russian people toward world unity of nations. As a loyal supporter of the postwar Soviet policy of imperialistic expansion, Zaslavski stressed Dostoyevski's prophetic power in the very posing of this question, although, because Dostoyevski was unable to predict the concrete forms of later developments, his answers were unsound. Still, because of the stirring force with which he raised the cardinal questions of his time, Dostoyevski's writing was vital not only within the Soviet Union but also abroad, as a merciless censure of social inequality.

In a question of literary relationships, Zaslavski's opinion flatly contradicted the prewar opinion of his fellow mouthpiece for the Party, Yermilov. Zaslavski stated that Maxim Gorki's tramps were descended from Fyodor Dostoyevski's convicts in "a straight line, with that difference which separates the *raznochinets* democrat of the 1860s from the proletarian democrat of the 1890s." [1] In 1939 Yermilov had been at considerable pains to demonstrate precisely the opposite in his study "Gorki and Dostoyevski." Zaslavski's own views on Dostoyevski's love of young people and the warmth of his treatment of them were also strikingly at variance with those he later felt constrained to air. In 1946 he wrote: "The children in Dostoyevski are almost always wonderful. No one has portrayed the Russian boy better than he. What Dostoyevski wrote of Kolya Krasotkin and his companions is full of the truth of life." [2]

V. Aleksandrov's article of the same time [3] followed the same general line, repeating, point after weary point, the opinions of earlier critics which served to substantiate the author's position of the moment. For Aleksandrov also there were two Dostoyevskis: one stanch, courageous and noble, the youth; the other, darkened by reactionary illusions after prison, the author of the vile caricature *The Devils*. Like Dolinin, however, Aleksandrov saw some of the aspirations and faith of his youth surviving in the later Dostoyevski. Side by side with the submissiveness of Zosima and Alyosha, he had put the rebellion of Ivan Karamazov; he had rhapsodized on the need for heroic deeds; he had written Versilov's dream in *A Raw Youth;* he had believed in the future of the Russian people, in a free and just society, in the brotherly unity of all nations.

Like Yermilov, and citing the opinions expressed by the latter in 1942 in "The Great Russian Writer F. M. Dostoyevski," Aleksandrov did honor to Dostoyevski for the service rendered in the prophetic warning against the future antisocial, aggressive, imperialistic "superman" theories of Nietzsche. And like Dolinin, Zaslavski, and many others, Aleksandrov once more fell back on Lenin's interpretation of Tolstoi as guide to the appraisal of Dostoyevski. So once more, by virtue of his portrayal of the contradictions of his era, of his penetrating insight into the psychology produced by the opposition between individual aims and social aims, and his passionate search for a way to justice and harmony, Dostoyevski was accorded a primary place in world literature. Like all the other Soviet Marxist critics, Aleksandrov concluded by pointing out that the problems raised by Dostoyevski could have been, and had been, solved only by the workers' movement, and that only from the summits of Marxist-Leninist thought was it possible to comprehend the strong and weak aspects of Dostoyevski's work and to evaluate it correctly.

The pronunciamentos of Zaslavski and Aleksandrov evidently encouraged others to speak more freely of Dostoyevski and to publish the findings of their research. The old Marxist scholar Vasili Alekseyevich Desnitski (1878–) in an article which appeared in 1947, "M. Gorki and the National Traditions of Russian Literature," wrote:

Such a bond, even an outright apprenticeship in the narrow sense of the word, may be found in M. Gorki in respect also to Dostoyevski, who was a writer of city themes, a portrayer of city life, as was Gorki. This may be said, for example, of Gorki's first long story, "Goremyka Pavel" [The Poor Wretch Pavel], published in 1894 in the Nizhni Novgorod newspaper *Volgar'*. This tie with Dostoyevski, which, it is true, subsequently turned into a sharper and sharper struggle against the general trend of the writings of the author of *The Brothers Karamazov*, always remained with Gorki and is shown in the similarity of themes [resulting] from their common interest in posing and solving complex psychological problems, etc. This kinship, one may say, is also evident in the placing of the author's "I" among the characters by means of including the author's voice in the complex symphony of attitudes toward reality which are expressed by the characters.[4]

In Desnitski's last sentence the influence of Bakhtin's theory of the polyphonic novel is unmistakable. The cropping up at this time of Bakhtin's ideas and even of phrases used in his 1929 book is indication of the continued influence of genuine Dostoyevski scholarship despite the condemnation of Bakhtin's work as formalistic. In 1931 Lunacharski's interpretation of Dostoyevski had obviously been affected by Bakhtin's views; at the end of the Second World War, when Soviet critics seized their brief opportunity to speak out freely, even the old confirmed Marxist, Desnitski, once a student of Plekhanov, again demonstrated the community of scholars behind the ideological barriers.

Dramatic critics, too, aided in rehabilitating Dostoyevski in 1946–47. One of the most prominent, Yu. Yuzovski, completely disregarding Party dogma, protested against "the inertia of a negative attitude toward Dostoyevski":

Dostoyevski is not only love for suffering, for the underground of the soul, for Christian humility. Dostoyevski is also the gigantic emotional inspiration of the Russian soul, the gigantic passion that throws off the fetters of life, with which it cannot be reconciled. . . .

This feature is present even in such seemingly contradictory writers as Gorki and Dostoyevski.[5]

Another critic even ventured to take Gorki to task for his article on Karamazovism. On the occasion of the production of

Gorki's play *Starik* [The Old Man] by the Moscow *Kamernyi* Theater, B. Yemel'yanov wrote:

Surprisingly, Gorki's *Old Man* as played by Gaideburov looks as though Dostoyevski had written [the role]. This very close union of baseness and greatness, of intellect and debauchery, is extremely characteristic of the "Karamazov soul." Gorki, censuring Dostoyevski for his excessive interest in this "morbidly evil, very perverted soul," himself portrays in no less detail all its innermost twists and turns. The performance at the *Kamernyi* Theater confirms the idea that it was not Dostoyevski's "cruel talent" which is the reason for the appearance of the Karamazovs, Svidrigailovs, and Stavrogins. These people existed in the actual life toward which the attention of the artist was directed. Gorki, who depicts completely different aspects of life, uses, without intending to, the same artistic devices as Dostoyevski when he chooses the same subject as the latter.[6]

Thus, during the discussions of Dostoyevski in 1946–47, an open attack was made upon that long trend in Dostoyevski scholarship which had its source in the views of Mikhailovski and was later stimulated by Gorki. The wartime acceptance of Dostoyevski by the Soviet dictatorship and the somewhat freer expression permitted scholars in the immediate postwar period culminated in the publication in 1947 of three major studies which for many years have remained the last really scholarly treatment of Dostoyevski: Dolinin's *In Dostoyevski's Creative Laboratory* and the two books by Kirpotin entitled *The Young Dostoyevski* and *F. M. Dostoyevski.*

Dolinin's purpose in his 1947 book was to show the complexity of Dostoyevski's method of work on *A Raw Youth*, which resulted from contradictions in his ideology. Since the notebooks and manuscript materials for this novel had never been published in the USSR, Dolinin's book took on especial value in that it made many of Dostoyevski's original pages generally accessible. All the manuscript materials were available to Dolinin, and he was therefore able to trace the creative work step by step.

Dolinin regarded *A Raw Youth* as a compendium of Dostoyevski's writing, in which the author gives the impression of looking back on the whole path that he has traveled and of reevaluating all his own works. "On the ideological plane," wrote Dolinin,

these are the same thoughts which had occupied Dostoyevski all his life: the great destiny of the Russian people, its historical mission, the future fate of mankind in Europe, [the question of] the East and the West, the relationship between the individual and society in the decaying bourgeois order of the time, and the future order of mankind.[7]

As in his earlier studies, Dolinin, arguing that Dostoyevski's convictions had moved close to the revolutionary democratic program of Nekrasov and Saltykov-Shchedrin, the ideas of the progressive *raznochintsy*, made much of the fact that *A Raw Youth* was published in their journal *Otechestvennye Zapiski* [Notes of the Fatherland], rather than in Katkov's *Russkii Vestnik* [The Russian Courier] or in Stasyulevich's *Vestnik Yevropy* [Courier of Europe].

Using the comparative historical method, Dolinin traced the development of the main characters in the novel and found their real-life prototypes. The Fyodor Fyodorovich of the original notes, a socialist fanatic and advocate of atheistic communism, gradually underwent a radical change until he finally emerged as the character of Makar Dolgoruki. The prototype for the raw youth, Arkadi Dolgoruki, was the young Nekrasov. The portrait of Nekrasov as a youth which Dostoyevski drew in his obituary resembled the portrayal of Arkadi in the fifth chapter of the novel. Young Nekrasov and Arkadi Dolgoruki, offspring of "chance families," were both obsessed by the dream of riches and independence. In Dostoyevski's characterization Nekrasov fought this demon in himself and became a martyr to the cause of the people. Dolinin pointed out, however, that the personality of the Nekrasov described by Dostoyevski was far from that of the real man.

Much of Dostoyevski's intention in *A Raw Youth* Dolinin found by no means at variance with the editorial views of Nekrasov and Saltykov-Shchedrin. He cited as evidence the portrayal of the moral and intellectual decay on the higher levels of society as represented by the young and old Princes Sokol'ski and their circle, the contrast between them and the truth of the people as represented by Makar Dolgoruki, and Versilov's dream about the happy future of mankind and the role of the Russian people in its realization. On the other hand, Dolinin perceived a hidden criticism of revolutionary democracy in the aspect of Makar Dolgoruki. Although in general he was likened to Nekrasov's Vlas in the poem *Komu na Rusi zhit' khorosho* [Who Can Live Well in Russia], Dolinin saw a meaningful difference in Makar's broader perception of "the living life," his love for all things living. He compared the significance of the character of Makar to that of Platon Karatayev in Tolstoi's *War and Peace*, both embodying the spirit of passivism and nonresistance to evil. When the raw youth comes to a comprehension of the "seemliness" embodied in Makar Dolgoruki, with his joyous perception of life and his acceptance of it in its entirety with a "wise heart," he recognizes his own personal motives, which have so long tormented him, as narrow and false. Even the ideas of the Russian European Versilov are affected by the encounter with Makar.

On the basis of Dostoyevski's initial notes and later drafts, Dolinin demonstrated that in planning the form of the novel he went through painful doubts and changes of mind, and finally resolved to write in the Pushkin manner, that is, to follow the

Pushkin method of putting the hero in the center of the stage, holding to chronological order in developing the action, exercising restraint in the plot, and striving for terseness. For this reason he decided to relate the story in the first person from the point of view of the hero himself. And although Dostoyevski did not succeed in following Pushkin's example and limiting himself to a small number of scenes and characters, nevertheless in many respects Pushkin had a beneficial effect on the form of *A Raw Youth*.

Dolinin skillfully maintained that ideas of changing the world on the basis of social law and justice are implicit throughout *A Raw Youth*. This interpretation by Dolinin in 1946–47 was nothing new; he was merely developing, on the basis of *A Raw Youth*, ideas which he had clearly stated as early as 1934 in his introduction to the third volume of Dostoyevski's letters and in 1935 in his introduction to the manuscript materials for *The Brothers Karamazov*.[8] The new book set forth the same thesis, namely, that Dostoyevski had never freed himself completely from the radicalism of his youth and that *A Raw Youth* represented a return to liberalism. When later Dolinin's *In Dostoyevski's Creative Laboratory* was severely censured, the reason was by no means that Dolinin had "whitewashed" to a greater extent than in his earlier studies.

In the publishing program of 1947 Dolinin represented the non-Party Dostoyevski scholars, and Valeri Yakovlevich Kirpotin (1900–) the official Communist critics. A member of the Bolshevik Party since 1918, Kirpotin for a number of years held the post of assistant director of the Leningrad branch of the Communist Academy, was editor of the journal *Problemy marksizma* [Problems of Marxism], wrote extensively on Soviet literature, and published a number of studies on Pisarev and other *raznochintsy* critics, interpreting their work from "the class viewpoint of the proletariat." Even before the war, however, Kirpotin attempted to discard narrow class criteria in evaluating the literature of the past, notably in his study of Pushkin, in which he deplored tirades against the harmful, aristocratic ideology of the poet and acknowledged the legacy contemporary Soviet culture had received from Pushkin.

After the Second World War, Kirpotin attempted a similar reinterpretation of Dostoyevski. The time seemed propitious. At the beginning of 1946, in connection with the 100th anniversary of the publication of Dostoyevski's first novel, Kirpotin published an essay on *Poor Folk*,[9] which was later incorporated in his book *The Young Dostoyevski*.[10] During the anniversary celebration in November, 1946, Kirpotin delivered an address on Dostoyevski at a special session of the Academy of Sciences. First published in the journal *Zvezda* [Star] under the title "Fyodor Mikhailovich Dostoyevski," [11] the address was issued in the following year (1947) in book form.[12] *The Young Dostoyevski* was a detailed analysis of the early stories, and the second book a survey of all his writing.

Various opinions expressed in these studies were new for a Party writer and represented the heartiest reception into the revolutionary fold which had ever been accorded Dostoyevski in the long postrevolutionary debate on his acceptability.

Kirpotin's method was that of the ideologist and publicist, with excursions into psychological characterizations. Treating material rife with "ideological deviations," Kirpotin was, of course, obliged to arm himself carefully with quotations from Marx and Engels, Belinski, Dobrolyubov, and Chernyshevski. He began his article "Fyodor Mikhailovich Dostoyevski" with an exposition of the Marxist concern for the individual, quoting Marx on the necessity of creating a humane world order in which man may recognize the genuinely human and foster human qualities in himself. Thus immediately it was possible to set a high valuation on Dostoyevski: "In the center of Fyodor Mikhailovich Dostoyevski's searchings stood man," [13] Kirpotin asserted on the first page of the study.

The young Dostoyevski's concern for man arose both spontaneously and as a result of the widespread discussions of the nature of man and utopian socialism at the time. Under the strong influence of Belinski, who maintained that man's instincts are noble, that evil resides not in man, but in society, Dostoyevski in *Poor Folk* echoed Belinski's convictions; an appeal for the brotherhood of man through a reformation of the social structure which prevents it was the central idea of his first novel. There was no preaching of humility, self-perfection, and repentance. In *Poor Folk* the author was in company with Belinski, Dobrolyubov, and Chernyshevski.

Even in the 1840s, however, Kirpotin pointed out, Dostoyevski's humanist views were coupled with misgivings in regard to man. Now and then Dostoyevski joined in the feudal-clerical judgment, and, like Hoffmann, cast a shadow on man in *The Double*. Without abandoning the ideas of *Poor Folk*, Dostoyevski nevertheless was unable to stifle his misgivings, and his dreamer-heroes who followed (in *The Landlady* and *White Nights*) were again "superfluous men," helpless in society. In *Netochka Nezvanova*, however, he once more demonstrated that man, driven by circumstances, can develop an active attitude toward life and thus find happiness. Dostoyevski's participation in the Petrashevski movement was therefore, Kirpotin reasoned, the logical outcome of his convictions during the early period. Disenchantment in the revolution, which began in prison, was then joined to his belief in freedom, equality, and social harmony. The resultant conflict determined the nature of all his later writings.

Kirpotin's argument was distinguished from that of earlier Party critics by his insistence that the social protest in Dostoyevski the artist was always stronger than the reactionary views of Dostoyevski the thinker. This conclusion flatly contradicted not only the prewar official attitude but even the more lenient treatment of Dostoyevski by Zaslavski and Aleksandrov during the anniversary celebration. Kirpotin essentially denied that Dostoyevski underwent a radical change in prison. Although he admitted a loss of fighting spirit there, he saw Dostoyevski's humanism emerging reinforced and more mature from the prison ordeal. The cruelty and evil he saw made him probe deeper into the nature of man, but his faith in the latter was not shaken. The ideal of the brotherhood of man remained; he merely rejected the use of force for its establishment, as a crime against the free will of man. *The Insulted and Injured* and *Notes from the House of the Dead*, like his earlier writings, were permeated with a passionate defense of man, desire for brotherhood, deep alarm, and consciousness of moral responsibility for the social order of the world. And although Dostoyevski wanted to arouse pity, humility, and love as healing agents, his novels aroused anger in the reader. The muse of grief was understood as the muse of vengeance and grief. Suffering was interpreted by the reader as the expression of compassion for the sufferers and a protest against the wrongs which produced it. The progressive critics such as Dobrolyubov read Dostoyevski in this light. And only in *Notes from the Underground*, according to Kirpotin, did Dostoyevski take the side against Chernyshevski and lose his faith in man.

Crime and Punishment was intended to demonstrate that it is inadmissible to resort to violence and bloodshed in deciding social questions. But the novel itself as a work of art, contrary to the will of the author, actually demonstrates that the blame

for all offenses lies in the social order and not in the nature of
man, and thereby prompts the reader to the conclusion that
deliverance lies only in activity which will affect social development, that personal happiness is inseparable from general happiness. Raskol'nikov escapes only by joining his protest to the
protest of the fighting masses, in other words, through revolutionary struggle: "Revolution, driven out the door, came in by
the window." [14]

In *The Idiot* the positive hero Prince Myshkin, who has
achieved complete moral and spiritual balance, is unable to
overcome evil by humane, religious teaching alone. The moral?
According to Kirpotin, again obviously that meekness and humility will not change the old world; battle must be done.

Seeing that *Crime and Punishment* and *The Idiot* were being
interpreted by radical critics as arguments in favor of revolution, Dostoyevski decided on a frontal attack on the revolutionary underground in *The Devils*. Unlike Yermilov in 1942,
Kirpotin made no attempt to justify this novel as Dostoyevski's
attack on the predecessors of fascism; Kirpotin saw it as a
furious onslaught on the revolutionaries, "a malicious slander
against the revolution." But the assault did not still the inner
discord in Dostoyevski. The unceasing conflict led him to publish *A Raw Youth* in Nekrasov's and Saltykov-Shchedrin's
journal, and manifested itself again in the simultaneous existence of mutually exclusive ideas in *The Brothers Karamazov*.
Kirpotin, like Yermilov in 1942, quoted with great satisfaction
Alyosha's reply when Ivan asked him how he would punish the
landowner who hunted down the child before his mother's eyes.
Kirpotin contrived to make this passage sound like the final
message of the entire novel:

And in this "Shoot [him]" how much faith there is in justice, in the
selflessness of man, in his righteous anger, in his ability, battling the

opposition of evil and socially dangerous enemies, to assert the free brotherhood of those who earlier were oppressed, insulted, and annihilated! [15]

With the same penchant for wrenching Dostoyevski's words out of context and applying them to the contemporary Soviet situation as Soviet authorities represented it, Kirpotin wrote of Dostoyevski's Pushkin speech:

The reasoned part of Dostoyevski's prophecy restates Belinski's prophecy and is a vague presentiment of the fact that the center of gravity in the struggle for socialism would be transferred to our country, a vague foresight of the fact that Russia would lead other peoples on the path of both social and national brotherhood.[16]

Dostoyevski's prophecy that the Russian people would play a liberating and enlightening role throughout the world, Kirpotin exulted, had been fulfilled in the course of the Second World War and the victory over fascism. The Kremlin had become a universal symbol.

Although Kirpotin did not gloss over the doubts in man which continued to trouble Dostoyevski in his "Legend of the Grand Inquisitor," he again disagreed with earlier Communist critics by reiterating that the belief in universal brotherhood and social harmony still remained stronger. True, Dostoyevski admitted that man is weak, that the rebellious still fall down before idols, and that the readiness of rebels to become slaves again and to bow before miracle, mystery and authority makes all attempts to transform the world futile. Yet Dostoyevski also offered arguments which shattered the faith of others in the religious path to freedom and caused Leont'yev and Pobedonostsev to distrust him.

Also in contradiction to the earlier Soviet position, Kirpotin asserted that "Dostoyevski remained a realist to the end of his life," [17] and as such revealed the inner world of man with unprecedented subtlety. His gift lay wholly in the faculty of seeing into the psychological life of others; the plastic perfection of external portrayal in Tolstoi's writing was therefore lacking in Dostoyevski's. Based on introspection and observation of people, as well as on intense study of literature, Dostoyevski's psychologism, Kirpotin argued, is not subjective in character, as Yermilov had asserted in 1939. It affirms the dignity and worth of man in the world:

In contrast to degenerate decadent psychologism such as that of Proust and Joyce, which signifies the decline and ruin of bourgeois literature, Dostoyevski's psychologism in his positive works is not subjective, but realistic. His psychologism is a special artistic method of penetrating into the objective essence of a contradictory human collective, into the very core of the social relations which troubled him, and a special artistic method of reproducing them in the art of the word. With the full force of his restless, impatient temperament, Dostoyevski shared the sufferings of his contemporaries in their ideological searchings, but as an artist he reinterpreted them in psychologically colored characters. Dostoyevski thought in images worked out in psychological terms, but his thought was social thought.[18]

Thus from the point of view of Marxism, Dostoyevski became doubly acceptable. Not only did he make the problem of man the central one in his work, but his psychological thought was of undying significance. Kirpotin points out that in materialist philosophy man has always been held to be a cell of the social world and psychology has been regarded as the science leading to the objective cognition of society.

The social significance of Dostoyevski's psychologism lay in the fact that he portrayed the psychological world of those who are injured by their degraded position on the social ladder and are striving to raise themselves and to establish their individuality in social opinion. Such psychologism aided in freeing the individual from feudal dependence and in the last analysis contributed to the general struggle for the liberation of mankind.

Even in the stanch Party writer Kirpotin there is evidence of the deep roots which Bakhtin's theories of Dostoyevski's polyphonic novel had struck in Soviet criticism despite their condemnation as formalistic seventeen years before (1929). Kirpotin wrote:

Whether the narration in Dostoyevski is in the first person, in the form of a confession, or from the person of author-narrator, it does not matter —we see that the writer proceeds from the premise of equality of rights among simultaneously existing people, simultaneously undergoing emotional experiences. His world is a world of a multiplicity of objectively existent psychologies affecting each other, which precludes the subjectivism, or even solipsism, in treating psychological processes which is so typical of bourgeois decadence.[19]

As might be expected, Kirpotin still retained certain Party prejudices toward Dostoyevski. Labeling *The Devils* a counterrevolutionary slander, he at the same time denied its artistic value and accused Dostoyevski of waiving his psychological objectivism in this novel, of tailoring life to fit his reactionary political motives, of turning into a "pamphleteer . . . in defiance of the truth." [20]

Out of the same ideological considerations Kirpotin inveighed against *Notes from the Underground* and *Crocodile*. Of the characters in them he wrote: "Marionettes, mere semblances of people, they move in a void, and no efforts of the genius can conceal the white strings with which he sets them in motion." [21]

In repeating the Communist stereotype that a reactionary thesis vitiates a work of art Kirpotin apparently lost sight of the dictum of Lenin, in his articles on Tolstoi, that a great artist, despite his reactionary philosophy, involuntarily reflects his epoch because of his special flair for the truth of life and the faculty of reproducing reality in images. In singling out a few ideologically unacceptable pieces from the body of Dostoyevski's works and in evaluating them on an entirely different basis, Kirpotin was guilty of misrepresentation.

Nonetheless, Kirpotin upheld Dostoyevski's psychological realism, his revelation of the inner riches of man, as a model for Soviet literature, against the non-psychologism of bourgeois literature, which allegedly scorned man, viewing him as the object of statistics or as labor force, and paying no attention to his feelings, thoughts, pain, and joys. This attitude toward man, which in Kirpotin's opinion, stemmed from Nietzsche and the practice of imperialistic and fascist writers, had no place in a "free literature."

When he approached the question of the social nature of Dostoyevski's writing, Kirpotin based himself on Lenin's appraisal of Tolstoi, making the usual contrast between Tolstoi and Dostoyevski and adding a few touches of his own. For one thing, Kirpotin made the point that, although the "transitional" period had already begun, the social conflicts during much of Dostoyevski's time were less sharp than in the later nineteenth century and at the beginning of the twentieth century when Tolstoi was describing the peasant masses who had not yet freed themselves completely from feudal servitude and its survivals. At the earlier stage of the transitional period, when the petit-bourgeois city dwellers and the *raznochintsy* of whom Dostoyevski wrote were being ruined by the accelerating pace of capitalism, these groups were divided between two ideological poles—the views of Chernyshevski and Dobrolyubov on one hand, and philistine inertia on the other. From this opposition arose the contradictoriness of his writing. In Kirpotin's opinion, before the proletarian movement revolutionism was stronger in the peasantry than in the city people, who were captive to age-old prejudices and who had not yet shown an inclination toward a mass movement. Dostoyevski therefore viewed a revolutionary as a lone intellectual, a failure lacking the support of the people and doomed to defeat. Dostoyevski's solitary hero, ignorant of the laws of social development, feeling himself a grain of sand in a world of disunited individuals, and unable to struggle alone, merely pushes away his own kind and retreats more deeply into himself. The writer, too, staggered by the ineffable sufferings of mankind and seeing no escape from them, continues to protest against inequality and oppression, calling for help the while. His works ring with the tocsin of disaster. Repeating Lenin, Kirpotin declared that neither Tolstoi nor Dostoyevski understood the historical role of social classes, but, holding to the ideology of the old feudal order, which, in Lenin's terminology, had been turned upside down, made abstract judgments in terms of eternal principles of morality and eternal truths of religion.

By likening Dostoyevski's compassion for his characters struggling against the fetters of capitalism to the "proletarian humanism" shown in Soviet sympathy for the peoples of the non-Soviet world, allegedly still suffering under the conditions Dostoyevski described, Kirpotin contrived to find still another basis for Soviet reconciliation with Dostoyevski. Through all the overlay of discreet reservations and numerous quotations from Marxist doctrine, Kirpotin's own sincere respect was evident:

For Dostoyevski the verdict of posterity has long since been rendered. "The mystery of man," which troubled him all his life, has been solved. The reasons for the sufferings about which he shouted to the whole world have been determined. Dostoyevski was not a prophet, not a teacher of life, not the interpreter of the "Russian soul," as has frequently been written. But to this day we read with the greatest sympathy and the greatest agitation his brilliant books, from the pages of which resounds the plea of one gone astray to be led on the right road. Dostoyevski's heroes hurled themselves from side to side, searching for legitimate happiness, and clutched only air, only a mirage, in their hands. But their sufferings were not invented sufferings. So they suffered, so they struggled in the snares of "fate," the insulted and injured, until the working class, come to maturity, called to them and led them. But our sympathy with Dostoyevski is sympathy for the sufferings of the masses, in misfortune and misery seeking the path to the bright future, to real happiness on earth.[22]

Kirpotin was exceedingly wary in tracing the line of descent from Dostoyevski to the "socialist" present. To avoid difficulties he resorted to the ingenious device of substituting for Dostoyevski himself the Soviet-canonized teachers of his youth in the direct line of succession:

The banner of the first teachers of Dostoyevski, the banner of the preceptors of his youth, was handed down to the Russian working class, serving as evidence of the line of succession between the ideals of scientific socialism and Dobrolyubov, whose significance Dostoyevski did not understand.[23]

That the last words in the quotation were nothing but camouflage was indicated by Kirpotin himself, in his book *The Young Dostoyevski,* in which he argued that the 1840s, when Dostoyevski was attracted to Belinski and the ideas of the Petrashevski circle, were the determining factor in his philosophy: "In both the ideological and the artistic respect the foundation for Dostoyevski's world-view was laid in the 1840s, and in these same years the character of his artistry was determined." [24]

Kirpotin's main purpose in his writings on Dostoyevski in the immediate postwar period was evidently to restore Dostoyevski in his entirety to Soviet readers, to clear away the ideological misrepresentations current for many years. Kirpotin's criticism, almost exclusively publicist in character, contained little strictly literary analysis and contributed no new interpretation of the psychological content. His work does not bear comparison with many studies of the form of Dostoyevski's novels, his art of psychological analysis, and his biography which have been written by early Soviet and prerevolutionary Russian critics, Western European and American scholars. Only the special circumstances surrounding the publication of his articles and books on Dostoyevski in 1946–47 justify the attention that has been devoted to them.

Every Soviet critic of Dostoyevski is under the constant necessity of bringing the expression of his personal views into conformity with Marxist methodology and the current Party line. This condition being understood by Soviet readers, the appearance of the postwar books by Kirpotin and Dolinin must have been interpreted only as presaging a new official treatment of Dostoyevski. The book of the non-Party Dolinin, of genuine scholarly interest, itself would have conveyed this meaning. Kirpotin, however, standard-bearer of the Party, commanded much wider attention. His publications seemed to invest Dostoyevski with the authority of Marx, Engels, and Lenin and to set the official seal of approval on his writings for Soviet readers in general.

With such expectation Kirpotin's books were received by the first critics. R. Uralov, reviewing *The Young Dostoyevski* in *Literaturnaya gazeta* in November, 1947, commented on the many merits of the book, including knowledge of the facts, ability to interpret them, telling argumentation and a well-considered conception, love and respect for the writer, and even a conscientious observance of "Bolshevik principles." "All this," wrote R. Uralov, "makes V. Kirpotin's book *The Young Dostoyevski* a valuable contribution to Soviet literary scholarship." [25]

F. Yevnin, in a lengthy review in *Novyi mir* [New World], expressed a similarly favorable opinion of Kirpotin's book *F. M. Dostoyevski*. At the same time the critic availed himself of the

opportunity to set forth his own views on Dostoyevski. He began
with Gorki's statements, singling out those in which he referred
to the greatness of Dostoyevski and compared him with Shakespeare. Yevnin himself recognized Dostoyevski's penetrating
insight into the life of the society in which he lived and worked.
At times, in the critic's opinion, he attempted to subordinate his
vision of the world to subjective reactionary tendencies, but in
his writings life was victorious over dogma. Dostoyevski's characters say more than the author wanted to express and often
fail to say what he intended to express. Even as a thinker, however, Dostoyevski was to Yevnin far from a monolithic reactionary. Dostoyevski, he asserted, retained his faith in the future
rebirth of mankind to the end of his life, however out of harmony
with this belief were his ideas of humility and his attack on
revolutionary democracy in the 1860s.

Yevnin noted with approval that Kirpotin in his book had not
concealed the reactionary aspects of the writer's philosophy but
throughout had conducted "an uninterrupted ideological dispute
with Dostoyevski." [26] Kirpotin's attempt to focus on the significant and valuable features of Dostoyevski was also praise-
worthy. The reviewer agreed with Kirpotin's thesis in general
and accepted his evidence, arguments, and conclusions as in-
disputable. True, Kirpotin's concentration on the main problem
of man in Dostoyevski's work, of necessity and with justification,
involved limited treatment of other problems such as various
philosophical and socio-political views and the journalistic
polemics of the 1860s.

Yevnin inveighed as forcefully as Kirpotin against the claims
of the so-called "decadents" to be the spiritual heirs of Dostoyevski. In Dostoyevski the base, the amoral, and the antisocial
produced disgust and indignation, whereas the "decadents," in
Yevnin's opinion, placed these phenomena on a pedestal.

Yevnin was prepared to make even greater ideological concessions to Dostoyevski than had Kirpotin, and suggested to the latter that a comparison of Dostoyevski's views with reactionary fascist ideology would more clearly define the boundaries of Dostoyevski's alleged disbelief in man. Although he may have believed in the sinfulness of man's nature, Yevnin pointed out, Dostoyevski was always sharply repelled by amoral individualists and egocentrics, such as Stavrogin, Svidrigailov, and old Karamazov.

Furthermore, Yevnin was in favor of complete rehabilitation of several of Dostoyevski's stories toward which Kirpotin had expressed the usual censorious Soviet attitude. In *The Double*, for instance, Kirpotin saw Dostoyevski's characteristic doubts of the worth of man. To Yevnin, however, Golyadkin by no means personified base and abominable traits. On the contrary, in this character the critic saw the world of external forces, of careerism, opportunism, and meanness, overpowering the weak, anxiety-ridden and maladjusted, but morally decent, Golyadkin. Yevnin also found the significance of duality as an artistic device in this thrusting out of the positive man from all the positions of life. Thus the humanistic significance of *The Double*, frequently obscured by tendentious critics, was clarified. Yevnin, too, saw signs of a re-evaluation of man in Dostoyevski, but he found them first in Foma Fomich Opiskin in *The Village of Stepanchikovo*, who began the series of characters conventionally lumped together in the category of Dostoyevski's "negative man."

Thus at the end of November, 1947, the reviewer of Kirpotin's book was going beyond even Kirpotin himself in the effort to rehabilitate Dostoyevski. There was apparently no portent of the storm which was soon to break over the heads of Soviet scholars.

. 19 .

ZHDANOVISM AND THE
COLLAPSE OF DOSTOYEVSKI SCHOLARSHIP

The campaign which has come to be known as Zhdanovism, after A. A. Zhdanov, the chief instigator—a campaign against "bourgeois objectivity," liberalism, and an apolitical approach in art and scholarship—began in 1946 with the directive of the Central Committee of the All-Union Communist Party (Bolsheviks) "On the Journals *Zvezda* [Star] and *Leningrad*," of August 14,[1] and with the speeches of Zhdanov to meetings of active Party members and writers in Leningrad in the same month.[2] Other measures intended to curb the "Western bourgeois influence" which had spread during and after the war and to impose "Party spirit" upon all Soviet culture followed. A Communist directive on the theatrical repertoire and measures for "improving" it was issued on August 26, 1946, a directive on films on September 4, 1946, and a directive concerning music on February 10, 1948.[3]

In December, 1947, the wave of ideological purges reached the field of Dostoyevski scholarship, in the form of abusive attacks on the recent books of Dolinin and Kirpotin.

The campaign was begun by the same D. I. Zaslavski who had led off in the postwar accolades to Dostoyevski. On December 20, 1947, the newspaper *Kul'tura i zhizn'* [Culture and Life], organ of the Propaganda and Agitation Section of the Central Committee of the Communist Party, published Zaslavski's article entitled "Against Idealization of the Reactionary Views of Dostoyevski."[4] In it there was no reference to his own article of the preceding year.

Four days later, in *Literaturnaya gazeta* [Literary Gazette], V. V. Yermilov, editor of the paper, joined in the attack.[5]

Zaslavski, long practiced in journalistic abuse on the pages of *Pravda*, reviled Dolinin and Kirpotin for the same "errors" which he himself had recently committed, but which he now failed to acknowledge. In November, 1946, Zaslavski had described Dostoyevski as a devoted adherent of Belinski, pronounced the latter basically correct when he foresaw in Dostoyevski the outstanding representative of Russian realistic literature, established a straight line of descent from Dostoyevski's convicts to Gorki's tramps, considered Dostoyevski's pages on children the best in Russian literature, objected to cataloguing Dostoyevski as a counterrevolutionary, and recognized his skill in clearly portraying the contradictions in man.

In 1947 Zaslavski's views had undergone a radical, if tacit, reappraisal. He now condemned attempts to represent Dostoyevski as a socialist and labeled as a falsification the frequent division of Dostoyevski's career into three ideological phases, the last of which constituted a return to the socialist and revolutionary ideas of his youth. Even in the 1840s, Zaslavski argues, Dostoyevski had gone counter to Belinski. As early as 1846, in *The Double*, he had portrayed the split personality which he later exalted as a law of human nature. The character of Golyadkin was at odds with the world-view of all progressive literature, the seed of the philosophy of double-dealing, treachery and provocation which later flowered luxuriantly in *The Devils*. The fact that Dostoyevski had embraced utopian socialism and had read Belinski's letter to Gogol at meetings of the Petrashevtsy merely indicated that he himself had not yet gained an understanding of his own contradictions. And no better understanding, Zaslavski charged, had been displayed by Kirpotin in studying Dostoyevski's early years. In Zaslavski's opinion, Dostoyevski had gone to prison with Golyadkin in his mind; the character was still in his thoughts when he returned from exile; and Dostoyevski had always considered Golyadkin one of his most important artistic achievements. "In rank and social standing," wrote Zaslavski,

Golyadkin cannot be compared with Stavrogin. But in essence this is the same combination in man of beauty with ugliness, of belief with disbelief, of dreams of communism and some kind of "harmony" with the crime of cruelty. And in conclusion, the unavoidable bankruptcy of man: Golyadkin went mad, Stavrogin hanged himself.[6]

To Zaslavski at this time the distinctive feature of *The Devils* was the extreme "vulgarity and baseness" of its slander of the revolution. In all Dostoyevski's other writing, especially in *Crime and Punishment*, there is the same opposition to the revolution. Raskol'nikov is evidently required by Dostoyevski's philosophy to become a murderer in order to demonstrate that without faith in God man cannot escape his inner conflicts and will succumb to evil, that the closer he is to materialism and socialism, the stronger the criminal principle in him. If in his thoughts Dostoyevski at times strays back to his early enthusiasm, it is the return of an enemy and traitor, trying to take vengeance on future generations of revolutionaries for the sins of his youth. For this purpose he sometimes chooses to deal with democratic ideas as a decoy. Then, deceiving even progressive literary circles, as in the case of *A Raw Youth*, he utilizes his great artistry and tremendous power to malign the progressives of Russia and to uphold his beloved Golyadkins: "As artist and publicist he served the rightist camp, becoming friendly with the extreme monarchists. To poison Russian youth with ideological venom was his direct aim." [7]

In the very form of the polyphonic novel Zaslavski saw a skillful device for confounding the revolutionists. Realizing the ineffectuality of dogmatic church ideology, Dostoyevski brings diametrically opposed ideas into his writing, and allows violent clashes and disputes to develop in the form of dialogue in order to lend sharpness to revolutionary ideology and then attempt to discredit it as morally base and utterly worthless. The atheist characters of *A Raw Youth*, torn by contradictions, suffer the collapse of their ideals and find no meaning in life. The progressives of the time are scoffed at in the character of Versilov. "The Legend of the Grand Inquisitor" Zaslavski called "The Legend of the Grand Agent-Provocateur." In *The Brothers Karamazov* he saw embodied the same double-dealing, treachery, and provocation as in *The Devils*, but with greater subtlety and power. Ivan Karamazov is a new Golyadkin, culmination of a long series.

The same aim of demolishing socialism and proving the duality of the Russian intelligentsia permeates Dostoyevski's Pushkin speech, according to Zaslavski; to the end he remains an enemy of the revolution and a defender of the monarchy and the church. Yet:

Dolinin and Kirpotin try to convince us that Dostoyevski became different, made friends with revolutionary and democratic circles, that his love for his ideals of the forties flared up again. And to what lengths they go in their effort to embellish Dostoyevski's reactionary outlook! Dolinin offers the opinion that Dostoyevski, had he lived until 1905, would have hailed the working class. Kirpotin goes still further. There is a monstrous sound in his words to the effect that Dostoyevski had a presentiment of the socialist revolution in Russia. . . . This is nonsense! Dostoyevski did in fact prophesy for Russia, for the Russian people, a great role in the future, prophesied that it would hold first place among the peoples of the world. But it happens that he saw this role consisting in the fact that the Russian people, with its "humility" and its Christian virtues, would save the whole world from the victory of socialism, a victory which to him, a terrified, conservative publicist, represented a universal catastrophe and the ruin of civilization.[8]

Kirpotin's remark that posterity had already rendered the verdict on Dostoyevski was interpreted by Zaslavski as a questioning of Gorki's judgment in 1913, when he had opposed the idealization of Dostoyevski and called him the "evil genius" of the Russian people. Zaslavski accused Kirpotin and Dolinin of deliberately ignoring these statements of Gorki, which destroyed their false hypothesis. Zaslavski even suspected Kirpotin of leaning toward the opinions of the liberal *Smenovekhovtsy* [9] and of disagreeing with Gorki.

During the war Soviet critics had sprung to Dostoyevski's defense against the attempts of Nazis to appropriate him for their own purposes; in 1947 Zaslavski classified him among "the enemies of the Soviet people and the working class." Branding him the "spiritual father" of "double-dealers and traitors," [10] Zaslavski implied that the Nazi effort to use Raskol'nikov in explanation of the "enigmatic Russian soul" was a stigma upon Dostoyevski. In his writings foreign reactionaries, "preachers of decadence, decay, political stagnation, all mystics of different slants, seek support and find justification." [11]

In behalf of the Soviet struggle against the rotten products of ideological and political decadence, Zaslavski declared war on all his preaching of amorality. The Soviet critics Dolinin and Kirpotin, who had observed Dostoyevski playing on "socialist" motifs in *A Raw Youth* and had then assumed a reversion to the revolutionary democratic ideas of Belinski, were guilty of false "objectivism," of defection from a Bolshevik attitude toward literature, of repeating the jabbering of liberal bourgeois critics.

Even in his tirade against the idealization of Dostoyevski, however, Zaslavski paused to deny statements in the foreign press that Dostoyevski's writings were well-nigh under a ban in the USSR:

This is a lie. His works are published and republished. But for this very reason the ideological and artistic outlook of Dostoyevski must be clear to the Soviet reader and to Soviet youth, without any embellishment. In the past the sophisms of Ivan Karamazov and of Dostoyevski himself have confused young people who were not steadfast; the reactionary playing on opposing passions attracted and bewildered them. *Narodnik* criticism was not able to withstand it. Liberal criticism went along in its leading strings. In the light of Marxism-Leninism all these literary trills and turns about faith and disbelief, about the ideal of Sodom and the ideal of the Madonna, about acceptance and rejection of the world, are cheap philosophical-theological chatter in bad taste. Gorki called it, trenchantly and correctly, "fornication of the word." [12]

Zaslavski did not close the doors to the study of Dostoyevski's writing, on certain conditions:

Dostoyevski is an outstanding Russian writer, a master of artistic image and word. But at the same time he is one of the most passionate opponents of socialism, revolution, and democracy. This has given bourgeois critics, publicists, and literary scholars an opportunity to surround Dostoyevski with a malicious tangle of confusion.

Every new work dispelling this confusion and promoting a better understanding of Dostoyevski's complex and contradictory writing without embellishing it and without depreciating its merits, without trying to justify the reactionary essence of the writer's philosophy of life by its lofty artistic form, will be welcomed. [13]

The situation in scholarship in the USSR is such that the slightest criticism in publications of the Central Committee of the Party may be taken as a Communist directive and produce unforeseen results. Although Zaslavski's article was not completely one-sided—in addition to what he labeled the reactionary aspects of Dostoyevski's work, he had spoken of the vivid and realistic pictures of Russian life, of the many true-to-life and artistically powerful characters, of "the excellent depiction of prerevolutionary Russian society" even in *The Devils,* of the "satirically poisonous" portrayal of the bourgeoisie, and of the sympathy aroused in the reader for the injury and suffering of the little people—it would certainly have alerted critics to the possible need to shift position and have caused confusion in the ranks of the Dostoyevski scholars.

When Yermilov's article followed four days afterwards in *Literaturnaya gazeta* and when somewhat later the *Pravda* publishing house issued in brochure form the transcript of a public lecture Yermilov had delivered at the central lecture hall of the All-Union Society for the Dissemination of Political and Scientific Knowledge, under the title *Against the Reactionary Ideas in Dostoyevski's Writing*,[14] uncertainty at least was removed. The propaganda machine had been set in motion against Dostoyevski and those engaged in the study or publication of his works. Thereafter no one raised a voice in his defense.

Yermilov's first article at this time, "F. M. Dostoyevski and Our Criticism," contained both sharp censure of Dolinin and Kirpotin and "self-criticism." He confessed that, as editor of *Literaturnaya gazeta*, he had been wrong in publishing R. Uralov's favorable review of Kirpotin's book *The Young Dostoyevski* in the November 26 issue, one month before. He also reproached A. Fadeyev, chairman of the Union of Soviet Writers, for overrating Kirpotin's books on Dostoyevski. Furthermore, Yermilov acknowledged mistakes in his own thinking in respect to Dostoyevski. In 1939 in "Gorki and Dostoyevski," he had exaggerated the objective reflection of reality in Dostoyevski's works, especially in his analysis of *A Raw Youth*. His article of 1942, "The Great Russian Writer F. M. Dostoyevski," had been basically erroneous, with its idealization of Dostoyevski's writings as a whole and of their humanistic content. The time had come, Yermilov now asserted, to review all the appraisals of Dostoyevski, to refrain from liberal idealization and to advance the Marxist-Leninist study of this great, complex, and contradictory writer, who drew attention to many important social problems but based his solutions on false and reactionary ideology.

In the pamphlet *Against the Reactionary Ideas in Dostoyevski's Writing*, Yermilov took it upon himself to reinterpret Dostoyevski from the point of view of the new Party campaign for ideological purity and irreconcilability with bourgeois ideology in any form. He began his argument by condemning the thesis that man is essentially base and corrupt, a thesis which he alleged is typical of Western literature, notably in the writing of Henry Miller, Jean-Paul Sartre, and Louis Ferdinand Céline. The main idea of all foreign "reactionary" literature is, Yermilov alleged, that man, being vile and criminal, must be restrained by all possible means. The critic then approached the question of Dostoyevski from the point of view of the dispute over man which he represented as occurring between progressive Soviet-led forces in literature and reactionary forces, under the control of American imperialism. The efforts ascribed to foreign writers, agents of Wall Street in literature, to corrupt human beings and to poison them with moral and political defeatism in order to break their will to fight and thereby justify the use of force against them, were contrasted to the glowing faith of Soviet literature in man which had found expression in Gorki's cry: "Man—this has a proud ring!"

Without hesitation Yermilov placed Dostoyevski "in the vanguard of reaction." During the war Yermilov had lashed out at Nazi propagandists exploiting Dostoyevski for their own cause; in 1947 Yermilov agreed with Zaslavski and saw in such use of Dostoyevski's name evidence of the similarity of his ideology to that of "the ideological lackeys of Wall Street": "And this is completely understandable, because he squandered the whole power of his talent in proving the weakness, sinfulness, and criminality of human nature." [15]

Resting on Gorki's authority but citing only one side of Gorki's divided opinion, Yermilov berated Dostoyevski for portraying man as too weak to resist vice, crime, and violence. In depreciating human intelligence and representing duality as an eternal law of human nature, which is torn between good and evil, the beautiful and the ugly, and is invariably anarchistic and destructive, Dostoyevski had, Yermilov charged, devoted most of his work to proving that freedom only unleashes in man the tendencies of an evil insect, given to ridicule, insult, and cruel torture. Therefore, in Dostoyevski's eyes, man must be restrained through religion, submission, humility, and the cleansing power of suffering. Like Gorki, Yermilov repeated the comparison made by Mikhailovski between Dostoyevski and his Inquisitor. Regarding man as pitiful and weak when unrestrained, Dostoyevski advocated both religious and political restraint—the church, the tsar-father, and the coercive police apparatus. It was not accidental that Dostoyevski became a personal friend of Pobedonostsev, arch-obscurantist and reactionary, a cynical and sanctimonious hypocrite, a cruel "restrainer" and executioner, and a mortal enemy of Russian culture and freedom.

To illustrate Dostoyevski's fundamental view of human nature, Yermilov quoted from *Diary of a Writer:*

It is self-evident . . . that evil lies deeper in humanity than the socialist physicians suppose, that in no order of society can evil be avoided, that the human soul remains the same, that abnormality and sin are derived from it itself.[16]

This opinion, according to Yermilov, caused Dostoyevski to depart from the main principle of realism and to disregard the requirement of the "natural" school that a social explanation be made of human traits. His creative method, which Yermilov defined as subjectively psychological and metaphysical, manifested itself primarily in the fact that he portrayed cruelty and perversion as unrelated to social reality, to the factors which corrupt the best qualities in man. Emphasizing that human nature is eternal and unchangeable and concentrating on the portrayal of cruel and villainous characters, Dostoyevski strayed farther and farther from realism and paved the way for the decadence which later, in his name, battled against "democratic" and "progressive" trends in literature. He broke with the best national traditions of humanist, freedom-loving Russian literature and social thought. Appealing to the insulted and injured to find salvation and purification through humility and resignation to suffering, Dostoyevski betrayed them and falsified the national character of the Russian people. For this purpose he resorted to devious devices. In Mitya Karamazov, for example, Yermilov recognized an element of rebellion in his reaction to his dream of the baby blue with cold, the woman's grief, and the destitute villages, but accused the author of nullifying this element by an appeal to be humble and suffer for the sake of the child, for the children of all the world, to be dissolved in universal suffering: "It is Dostoyevski's usual method to allow the motif of rebellion and revolution, which was repugnant to him, to ring out strongly, only in order to stifle it, to overthrow it, to prove its injustice and harmfulness." [17]

The main tenet of Dostoyevski's philosophy, that all are guilty for all, Yermilov dismissed as a "trite, sanctimoniously witless crotchet of lifeless Christian morality," [18] a justification of suffering and the social order which engenders it. In Dostoyevski's treatment of the problem of suffering—for example, in Mitya's acceptance of punishment and suffering as expiation for the injuries to the child and mankind, regardless of his innocence of the actual killing of his father—the author, Yermilov protested, eliminates the responsibility of man for social injustice, exonerates the offenders, and betrays his characters.

Yermilov had assiduously scanned the criticism of Belinski and Dobrolyubov for support of his contention that Dostoyevski lacked faith in man, and contrasted their opinions to that of N. N. Strakhov, who admired Dostoyevski for never treating his characters, even the least laudable, as "unpersons" and for perceiving and depicting human traits in all of them. Yermilov himself disapproved the warmth manifested in the portrayal of "parasites and scoundrels like Svidrigailov." [19] For the Bolshevik critic, the Party criteria for the ideal Soviet character precluded tolerance of Dostoyevski's principle of portraying every man so that he is "both repulsive and appealing" at the same time. Repeating the long-since hackneyed opinion of Mikhailovski and Gorki, Yermilov served notice that the new Party requirements would no longer permit of such equivocation as Dostoyevski's: "[In him] every martyr is capable of becoming a torturer and, conversely, every torturer is capable of turning into a martyr, atoning for all his sins through suffering; consequently, in the torturer there is also 'appeal.' " [20]

In Dostoyevski's compassion Yermilov detected no signs of Gorki's positively humanist attitude toward man, but rather an antihumanistic tendency, an endless poetization of suffering and the seductiveness of cruelty, horror, degradation, and human insignificance in order to intimidate and to preach humility.

Like Zaslavski, Yermilov took Kirpotin and Dolinin to task for disregarding the opinions of the *raznochintsy* critics and of Gorki himself, for including Dostoyevski among the great Russian realists of the nineteenth century, and for representing him as favoring socialism to the end of his life. Such idealization ignored the basic law of realism—the social explanation of the phenomena of life—and, Yermilov warned, was incompatible with Marxist-Leninist methods.

The strong aspect of Dostoyevski's writings is inseparable from their basic ideology, which is not only anticapitalistic, but also antiproletarian, antisocialistic, antirevolutionary, and antidemocratic. His heroes know only two paths, that of the executioner or the victim, of the slave-owner or the slave. The third path, that of battling the laws of the capitalist world, they do not know.

Truth and lies are entangled in his writing, Yermilov asserted. He portrays the revolutionary camp, but slanderously, peopling it with all kinds of "devils," from Raskol'nikov to Ivan Karamazov. He depicts bourgeois rapaciousness, self-will, and cruelty, mixed with touches of depravity, corruption, crime, and treachery, but in such a fashion that these qualities not only provoke fear but are also irresistibly tempting. Instability or lack of moral standards makes Dostoyevski's heroes more susceptible to the allurements of evil. However great his indignation at the idea in 1942, in 1947 Yermilov regarded it as in the nature of things that Nietzsche had taken lessons from the author of *Crime and Punishment* and its hero Raskol'nikov. At this point Yermilov came perilously near the position of the discredited "Menshevik critic" Pereverzev, who identified the heroes of the novels with the personality of Dostoyevski himself and whom Yermilov himself had once censured. Yermilov wrote:

> The horror of evil and an irresistible pull toward it, a duality of the psyche, creating the basis for a defense of treachery—this is one of the main traits of the personality of both Dostoyevski and his heroes.
>
> Beginning his literary career with an enthusiasm for utopian socialism, a participant in the revolutionary Petrashevski circle, Dostoyevski turned into the most active ideologist of reaction.[21]

Yermilov regarded *Notes from the Underground* as a declaration of Dostoyevski's transfer to the camp of reaction. According to Yermilov, the writer saw the salvation of Russia from both the horrors of capitalism and the coming proletarian revolution in the unity of the people with the tsar, and advocated this course in the Pushkin speech in appealing to the revolutionary intelligentsia to humble themselves. Dolinin and Kirpotin had idealized Dostoyevski unconscionably when they identified his reactionary utopian dream of the Russian people saving the world from the misery of socialism with Belinski's hopes for a revolutionary, socialist, and democratic Russia, and when they had practically equated the views of Belinski, Herzen and Dostoyevski in the 1840s. Belinski's appraisal of *The Double*, according to Yermilov, had effectively invalidated this version, and features of all Dostoyevski's subsequent works proved him an outright renegade. Kirpotin, however, had "fenced off the young Dostoyevski with a blank wall from the Dostoyevski of the second and third periods." [22]

In his book *In Dostoyevski's Creative Laboratory* Dolinin, according to Yermilov, had carried his myth-spinning about Dostoyevski as revolutionary and socialist to greater lengths than in his earlier works, characterizing him as more revolutionary than Tolstoi and even as a supporter of the Paris Commune. Yermilov scoffed at Dolinin's sympathetic commentaries on the notes for *A Raw Youth*, in which the editor found a prediction by Dostoyevski of the revolution and the triumph of the proletariat:

Dolinin does not understand or does not want to understand that Dostoyevski uses the prospect of the proletarian revolution to frighten the reader, is malicious, derides the instability of capitalist society which is incapable of opposing the proletarian revolution, and contrasts to this unstable society his own ideal of a "quiet," patriarchal Russia, avoiding both capitalism and revolution, with a fatherly tsar, an Orthodox Church, with Pobedonostsev and all his other favorite accouterments! And the Soviet scholar Dolinin ascribes to Dostoyevski the revolutionary "language of class struggle" and tries to convince us that "one more step" and Dostoyevski would have taken the stand of the very most progressive Russian social thought of that time.[23]

Dolinin's evidence, found in Dostoyevski's notes for *A Raw Youth*, of a parallel between the attitude of Herzen and that of Dostoyevski, Yermilov did not examine. It was enough for his purposes to cite Lenin's opinion that the collapse of Herzen's illusions of bourgeois democratism signified his acceptance of the necessity of the class struggle of the proletariat and to declare that, in the light of the sole truth enunciated by Lenin, there is no possible similarity between the reactionary political views of Dostoyevski and those of Belinski or Herzen.

The articles of Zaslavski and Yermilov, in effect announcing that no deviation would be tolerated from canonized "Marxist-Leninist truth," served to halt all genuine Dostoyevski scholarship in the USSR. The followers of these leading Bolshevik critics soon joined in the cry against the books and publications brought out in commemoration of the Dostoyevski anniversary in 1946.

In a brutal review of Dolinin's book published early in 1948 under the title "A Crude Falsification," I. Al'tman wrote: "A. Dolinin's book is harmful to Soviet literary scholarship and to the cause of the socialist education of the reader." [24]

Beginning with Yermilov's article, *Literaturnaya gazeta* conducted a systematic attack on the anniversary publications of Dostoyevski's works, accusing the editors and commentators of bourgeois objectivism, liberalism, and of forgetting the principle of "Party spirit" in literature. N. Burov, in an article entitled "Apologists for the Reactionary Ideas of Dostoyevski," [25]

sharply criticized the editor of the 1926–30 edition of Dostoyevski's complete works, B. V. Tomashevski, for his editorial
comments in the one-volume *Selected Works* of Dostoyevski which had been published late in 1946.[26] Tomashevski was
accused by the reviewer of dodging all prickly questions of
Dostoyevski's ideology, fearing to state his own opinion, and
writing in the vein of obsolescent academic objectivity, in basic
contradiction to Party spirit.

Burov also censured a collection of excerpts for children
published in 1947 under the title *The Boys* (*From the Novel
The Brothers Karamazov*).[27] The decision to issue such a book
may well have been taken in response to Zaslavski's 1946
article "Concerning Dostoyevski," in which he wrote of Dostoyevski's warm love for youth, of the wonderful children in his
works and of the fine portrayal of the Russian boy in the characters of Kolya Krasotkin and his friends in *The Brothers
Karamazov*. A little over a year later, however, *Literaturnaya
gazeta* regarded it as damaging to give young readers an excerpt
from the novel. The editor of the text, A. Slonimski, had written
in the foreword to *The Boys:*

> The character of Alyosha is one of the cheerful characters created
> by Dostoyevski. In him Dostoyevski expressed his cherished convictions
> —faith in the victory of truth in human relations. Alyosha appears at the
> beginning in the garb of a novice, that is, a future monk, since he planned
> to enter a monastery. But later he discards this intention.
>
> The meaning of the story of Ilyusha is revealed in Alyosha's speech
> at the rock. How good life is when you do something good and honest! [28]

In this passage Burov saw an idealization of the monk Alyosha
and a misrepresentation of the young characters and their
author as proponents of an optimistic and life-affirming philosophy, calling for social action. In short the publication of
the excerpt for children was "ideologically harmful." [29]

During 1948 the authors of the "objectionable" books on Dostoyevski were criticized at public gatherings in higher educational and scientific research institutes. At a tragicomic session of the Learned Council of the Philological Faculty of Leningrad University on April 1, 1948, Dolinin was forced under pressure to acknowledge his mistaken views on Dostoyevski and, despite his long and devoted work in the field of Dostoyevski study, to announce that he would thereafter transfer his attention to the revolutionary *raznochintsy*. In his public "self-criticism" Dolinin said: "I must confess that in my long-lasting attraction to this theme [Dostoyevski] I in fact took an incorrect position; I in fact spoke of his reactionary ideology in tones that were too mild." [30] After acknowledging that he had distorted the truth in his 1935 work on *The Brothers Karamazov* and in the last book on *A Raw Youth*, he also repented his grievous error in misapplying Lenin's words on Tolstoi to Dostoyevski. Professor Dolinin said:

A chronic disease apparently is not cured so quickly. . . . This book, too, was in error. . . . The consciousness of one's own mistakes puts one under great obligation. Recently I have been concentrating my scholarly interests on the theme of the revolutionary democrats, especially the work of Belinski and Herzen.[31]

The well-known philologist and Academy Member V. V. Vinogradov, who in 1929 had published *The Evolution of Russian Naturalism: Gogol and Dostoyevski*, was in the same unhappy situation in 1948. At a session of the Learned Council of the Institute of Russian Literature and the Moscow Section of the Institute of Language and Thought of the USSR Academy of Sciences, Professor Vinogradov also beat his breast in confession of his philological mistakes, acknowledged the justice of the criticism, and promised to master the Marxist method of linguistic analysis as bodied forth in the works of his opponents,

N. Ya. Marr and I. I. Meshchaninov.[32] His 1929 book concerning Dostoyevski was not mentioned during the discussion,
however, and after Stalin's articles on linguistics and the censure
of Marr's theories, Professor Vinogradov came out on top.

Dolinin and Kirpotin were less fortunate. Criticism of Dostoyevski's ideology continued. Publication of objective, scholarly
studies of Dostoyevski was ended, and his very name was mentioned only for the sake of making invidious comparisons between him and more acceptable writers. The "optimistic"
Maxim Gorki was contrasted to Dostoyevski in B. Byalik's
articles "Gorky and Dostoyevski," [33] 1948 (in English), and
"The Struggle of Gorki the Artist against the Reactionary Ideas
of Dostoyevski," 1951.[34] A completely tendentious contrast of
the "revolutionary democrat" and the "retrograde *pochvennik*"
is drawn in S. Borshchevski's 1948 article "[Saltykov-] Shchedrin and Dostoyevski." [35]

After 1948 even the scholarly periodicals of the USSR
Academy of Sciences were unable to avoid extreme tendentiousness. In the only treatment of Dostoyevski that appeared for
several years in the Literature and Language Section of the
News of the USSR Academy of Sciences, U. A. Gural'nik in
1950 extolled the fight of the journal *Sovremennik* [The Con-
temporary] with Dostoyevski's journals *Vremya* [Time],
published 1861–63, and *Epokha* [The Epoch], published
1864–65.[36] In the harsh, intolerant polemical writings of
Saltykov-Shchedrin, Antonovich, and other essayists of *Sovremennik* against the *pochvenniki* and the aesthetic views of Dostoyevski, Grigor'yev, and Strakhov, there was a sacrifice of
objective truth and literary principles to current political aims
which furnished clear precedent for the Soviet Communist
Party approach to art. Gural'nik, of course, represents the
Sovremennik critics as courageous fighters for Russian realism,

who aided in neutralizing the pernicious influence of the ideas of the *pochvenniki* and in revealing, under the cover of abstract aesthetic principles, Dostoyevski's noxious doctrine of restraint and humility for the Russian people. The question of the controversy over *pochvennichestvo* in Dostoyevski's journals and *Sovremennik* still awaits scholarly Soviet study.

Somewhat more objective treatment was accorded Dostoyevski in the unsigned article in the fifteenth volume of the second edition of the *Large Soviet Encyclopedia*, which appeared in 1952. It may have been a prudent precaution on the part of the editors to omit the name of the writer of the article, which is marked by relative moderation and objectivity for its time. Dostoyevski is described as a pupil of Gogol during the period of *Poor Folk* and a continuator of the traditions of democratic realism in the spirit of Belinski: "Truthfully portraying the sufferings of these people, revealing their human dignity, spiritual purity and nobility, the writer evokes profound sympathy for them on the part of the reader." [37]

Despite his departure from the realistic tradition of Gogol, the development of his reactionary philosophy during the Siberian period, and his subsequent apostasy from the liberation movement, stated the article, his writings reflect the unique historical features of a period of crisis in the life of Russia and the painful and tragic social situation. His awareness of the moral strength in the people resulted in powerful characterizations of types from the broad lower strata of society in *Notes from the House of the Dead*. The serious social accusations which Dostoyevski made in his fictional writing refuted his own reactionary views. As a great artist thinking in images, Dostoyevski was unable to depart completely from the truth of life and the traditions of realism in Russian literature. The article in the *Large Soviet Encyclopedia* is a symptom of the search for escape from the blind alley in which Soviet scholars of Dostoyevski found themselves after 1947.

The most elementary literary, and political, amenities forbade the omission of Dostoyevski from the Soviet encyclopedia. No such considerations prevailed in the case of a collection of articles for children and young people entitled *Classics of Russian Literature* which was published in 1952.[38] In it the name of Dostoyevski is missing.

. 20 .

CONCLUSION

For six and one half years after the taboo was imposed in December, 1947, the genuine Dostoyevski scholars of the Soviet Union held their silence. Malenkov's pronouncements at the Nineteenth Party Congress late in 1952 that Soviet Gogols and Shchedrins were needed,[1] despite the ostensible promise of a relaxation of ideological pressure, brought forth no new studies of Dostoyevski. By mid-1954 the situation apparently had become irksome and undesirable to those in command. *Literaturnaya gazeta* [Literary Gazette] of May 6, 1954, carried a long article by the editor-in-chief, B. Ryurikov, in which he expressed alarm at the paralysis of Soviet Dostoyevski scholarship, scoffed at the fear of Soviet scholars that they might fall into "error," and deplored the harmful consequences of their timidity:

This applies not only to the study of Gorki's work. . . . In recent years not one scholar has given his attention to the work of such a great Russian writer as Dostoyevski. In the collection of articles entitled *Classics of Russian Literature*, which was published by Detgiz (State Publishing House of Juvenile Literature), there are no articles on this writer. Soviet public opinion has been justly critical of the works on Dostoyevski by V. Kirpotin and A. Dolinin, which contained an idealization of Dostoyevski's writing and toned down his reactionary views.

But the Party press, in pointing to the necessity of criticizing mistakes made by Soviet scholars and of exposing the malicious tangle of confusion caused by reactionary writers, also pointed out: "Every new work dispelling this confusion and promoting a better understanding of Dostoyevski's complex and contradictory writing without embellishing it and without depreciating its merits, without trying to justify the reactionary essence of the writer's philosophy of life by its lofty artistic form, will be welcomed" (*Kul'tura i zhizn'* [Culture and Life] . . . December 20, 1947).[2]

Thus Ryurikov renewed Zaslavski's 1947 invitation, but on the same conditions.

In April, 1955, the publication of an excerpt from Vladimir Bonch-Bruyevich's memoirs further particularized the terms of the invitation, serving notice that scholars and critics were once more to look directly to Lenin for authority in expressing views on Dostoyevski. Acknowledging that Lenin had seconded Gorki's opposition to the production of *The Devils* by the Moscow Art Theater and that he had once condemned a "reactionary" novelist as "an ultra-bad imitation of the ultra-bad Dostoyevski," Bonch-Bruyevich also called attention to the more favorable opinion of Dostoyevski that Lenin had entertained at other times:

> Vladimir Il'ich said more than once that Dostoyevski was a truly great writer who scrutinized the morbid aspects of the society of his time, that there were many contradictions and breakdowns [in Dostoyevski's work], but also vivid pictures of reality.
>
> He roundly condemned *The Devils*, but said that in reading this novel one should not forget that it dealt with events connected with the activities not only of S. Nechayev but also of M. Bakunin. At the very time that *The Devils* was being written, K. Marx and F. Engels were carrying on a fierce fight against Bakunin. It is the critics' job to sort out what refers to Nechayev in the novel, and what to Bakunin.
>
> On the whole, Vladimir Il'ich esteemed Dostoyevski's talent. [He once said:] "Don't forget that Dostoyevski had been sentenced to death . . . and then it was announced that Nicholas I had 'pardoned' him, and exiled him to penal servitude."
>
> *Notes from the House of the Dead*, Vladimir Il'ich observed, is a work unsurpassed in Russian and world literature, a marvelous picture not only of penal servitude but also of the "house of the dead" in which the Russian people lived under the Romanov tsars.[3]

Bonch-Bruyevich's opportunely timed disclosure of Lenin's views sounded the keynote for the commemorative ceremonies in

February, 1956, when the seventy-fifth anniversary of the death of Dostoyevski was observed with great fanfare.

For the occasion the State Publishing House announced the forthcoming publication of a new ten-volume edition of Dostoyevski's works, under the august editorship of Grossman, Dolinin, Yermilov, Kirpotin, Nechayeva, and Ryurikov. The first volume appeared in February, 1956,[4] and the final volume was scheduled for 1958. In addition, two volumes of selected stories and short novels were published in time for the anniversary celebration.[5] New editions of *Poor Folk, The Village of Stepanchikovo and Its Residents, The Insulted and Injured, Crime and Punishment, The Idiot,* and *A Raw Youth* had been published in 1954 and 1955.

The first works of research on Dostoyevski after the eight-year drought appeared in connection with the anniversary: Yermilov's *F. M. Dostoyevski,*[6] S. Borshchevski's *Shchedrin and Dostoyevski,*[7] and Zaslavski's *F. M. Dostoyevski: A Critical and Biographical Sketch.*[8] A collective volume of critical essays entitled *F. M. Dostoyevski in Russian Criticism* was also announced at the time and published later in the year.[9]

The most significant scholarly work is the Dostoyevski volume now in preparation in the *Literaturnoye nasledstvo* [Literary Heritage] series. I. Zil'bershtein, assistant to the editor-in-chief of the series, has stated that the volume will contain "hitherto unknown texts of fictional, critical, and publicist pieces by Dostoyevski, as well as new documentary materials which shed light on various stages of the writer's biography."[10] For instance, V. Nechayeva is editing thirteen fragments of the manuscript of *Crime and Punishment,* representing various stages of work on the novel and differing substantially from the final text. At long last the copious manuscript materials for *A Raw Youth*

will become available in the original Russian in this collection;
they have been edited by A. Dolinin. These manuscripts show
how the characters in *A Raw Youth* were derived from Dostoyevski's plans for the two unwritten novels Zhitiye velikovo
greshnika [The Life of a Great Sinner] and Ateizm [Atheism]
and how he developed his plots, incorporating actual happenings
and using newspaper crime reports. His notes will disclose the
relation of *A Raw Youth* to earlier works and to his last novel
The Brothers Karamazov. L. Grossman, in his contribution to
the volume, reconstructs, on the basis of unpublished manuscript materials, the major steps in Dostoyevski's work on *The
Brothers Karamazov*. V. Vinogradov establishes, through analysis of style and subject matter, that a number of unsigned
articles, *feuilletons*, and stories published in the periodical
Grazhdanin [The Citizen] belong to Dostoyevski. Seven of
Dostoyevski's notebooks, dating from the early 1860s to his
death, are being published for the first time. They contain outlines and rough drafts of articles, outlines of novels (including
detailed sketches of the unwritten "Fathers and Children" and
"The Dreamer," both of 1876), a detailed plan of an unfinished
article "Socialism and Christianity," drafts of articles on the
"positive" hero in literature, on Russian satire, Turgenev, and
Zola's novels, notes on architecture and painting, outlines of
literary reminiscences, notes concerned with his work on language and on improving his writing, and much else. The volume
will contain also an annotated bibliography, "Dostoyevski in the
Reminiscences of His Contemporaries." Numerous other scholars have supplied commentaries on the material being published. The previously unknown texts prepared for inclusion in
this volume amount to about fifty signatures.[11]

The publication schedule which was promised was only part
of the anniversary program arranged by a large committee

comprising representatives of the Union of Soviet Writers, the USSR Ministry of Culture, the Soviet Peace Committee, the RSFSR Ministry of Education, VOKS (All-Union Society for Cultural Relations with Foreign Countries), publishing houses, Moscow museums, and theaters. Conferences of scholars on problems of Dostoyevski's writing took place at the Gorki Institute of World Literature and at various other higher educational institutions; lectures and exhibitions were held in clubs and "houses of culture" throughout the country. To lend the celebration an international character, foreign writers were invited to participate.[12]

Exhibitions of materials illustrating the life and work of Dostoyevski were arranged by the All-Union Lenin State Library in Moscow, by the Saltykov-Shchedrin State Public Library in Leningrad, and by republic, krai and oblast libraries. The Executive Committee of the Moscow Soviet passed a resolution to refurbish and expand the Dostoyevski Museum in a wing of the former Mariinskaya Hospital in Moscow, where the writer's father served as doctor and where Fyodor Mikhailovich spent his childhood and boyhood years. The street on which the museum is located was renamed for Dostoyevski.[13]

Preparations for the anniversary affected even fields in which little attention had been paid to Dostoyevski in the past. The Central Studio of Documentary Films announced that it would produce a film dealing with his life and work. Mosfil'm planned to film *The Idiot* from a scenario written by I. Pyr'yev, a well-known director. A revival of the film *Petersburg Night*, based on Dostoyevski's *Netochka Nezvanova* and *White Nights* and released in 1934, was promised for the occasion.[14] Censorship difficulties had attended its production in the 1930s.[15]

Many theaters announced plans for the production of plays based on Dostoyevski's novels during 1956. *The Brothers Kara-*

mazov, in a stage adaptation by B. Livanov and Ye. Surkov, was offered by the Moscow Art Theater; *The Village of Stepanchikovo*, in an adaptation by N. Erdman, by the Malyi Theater in Moscow; *The Idiot*, adapted by Yuri Olesha, by the Moscow Vakhtangov Theater; *The Gambler*, adapted by Yuri German, by the Pushkin Drama Theater in Leningrad; *The Insulted and Injured*, in a stage version by L. Rakhmanov, by the Leningrad Komsomol Theater; and *Uncle's Dream*, adapted by N. Gorchakov, by the Moscow Cine-Theater and the Leningrad Comedy Theater. At the Central State Theatrical Museum in Moscow and the Leningrad Theatrical Museum, materials pertaining to all productions of Dostoyevski's works during the Soviet period were exhibited, and conferences, lectures and readings from Dostoyevski were held at the Moscow and Leningrad Theatrical Libraries.[16]

Even more astonishing than the scope of these activities was the announcement that Yuri Olesha had been engaged to write the stage adaptation of *The Idiot*. Olesha, one of the most talented of Soviet writers, had been the victim of frequent and severe "administrative procedures," and for many years had disappeared from the Soviet literary scene. N. Erdman and Yuri German also had suffered from official Soviet disfavor. The singling out of these writers for a share in the honors accorded the long-suspect Dostoyevski must be regarded as a gesture carefully calculated to convey the impression that the moment of "universal forgiveness" had come.

As always in shifts of literary policy, the motive behind this new phase in the Soviet treatment of Dostoyevski lends itself to various interpretations. Only in the context of Soviet criticism as a whole, however, can the significance of the most recent move be accurately read. All the foregoing survey of this criticism demonstrates that the one approach to Dostoyevski which has been consistently approved by the Soviet regime has been the critical attempt to "use" his writings to further the interests of the regime. In the eyes of Party critics the degree of usefulness has varied with changing political circumstances, but the main criterion has remained the same. It was aptly phrased by L'vov-Rogachevski when he acknowledged in 1927 that "the question is still put too tendentiously and in too publicist a manner: whether or not Dostoyevski was on the same road with Soviet Russia."

The shifting trends in the effort to relate Dostoyevski to the revolution have been traced in some detail in the present book. In summary, the words of the stanch Marxist Gorbachov may serve as keynote to the use envisaged for Dostoyevski in the 1920s: "The young people of the revolution" would do well "to harden their teeth by gnawing through Dostoyevski until they understand" the warning against individualism which his writings constitute. At the beginning of the 1930s the Party literary arbiter, Lunacharski, recommended the reading of Dostoyevski, who, if accepted merely as a means and not as an end, might "serve as a better guide than our contemporaries" to the mind of the enemy, to the duality in human beings and to class differentiations. Then, as Soviet scholarship took on its Stalinist aspect during the 1930s, it became increasingly difficult to find acceptable "uses" for Dostoyevski under the guise of which the reading and study of his work as a whole might be condoned. The Second World War, however, converted Dostoyevski into a highly esteemed ally, and a close rapprochement was encouraged between the Soviet public and the Russian writer who had disliked the Germans, warned against the appearance of Nietzsche's amoral superman and the danger of the contempt for man embodied in Nazi philosophy, and prophesied the glorious future role of the Russian people.

Throughout the course of these developments, up to the time of "Zhdanovism," Dostoyevski scholars had been able, by various ingenious maneuvers, to accommodate their findings, at least in part, to the rigid utilitarian framework, and to publish studies which were often illuminating and original. It still remains to be seen whether their energies, insights, and resourcefulness have survived the many years of tension and alarm. The materials so far published in connection with the 1956 anniversary observances indicate that, in the field of Dostoyevski study, crippling restrictions are still imposed upon scholars. It is noteworthy that the only book-length studies offered in the anniversary fare were those by Yermilov, Zaslavski, and Borshchevski, who distinguished themselves by their tendentious pieces during the Zhdanov period. The potential importance of the Dostoyevski volume in the *Literaturnoye nasledstvo* series cannot be gainsaid; the documentary materials it comprises will be of interest and value, regardless of the slanted commentaries which may accompany them.

That the new criticism of Dostoyevski is subject to dictation from above is plain in the flurry of newspaper and magazine articles during the anniversary. They all rested on Lenin's evaluation of Dostoyevski as recently made public through the article by Bonch-Bruyevich. Every one of the writers praised *Notes from the House of the Dead* as "a vivid picture of reality," approved of the early Dostoyevski—the writer of *Poor Folk* and member of the Petrashevski circle—and denounced the "reactionary tendencies" of *The Devils* and *Notes from the Underground*. Many of the articles even had the same title: "A Great Russian Writer" or "A Russian Writer of Genius." [17]

The February, 1956, issue of *Communist*, the policy organ of the Party's Central Committee, carried an article by B. Ryurikov, "The Great Russian Writer F. M. Dostoyevski," placing

Dostoyevski among "the most outstanding names in Russian and world literature." [18] *Pravda* of February 6, 1956, spoke of "the powerful realism of Dostoyevski's creative genius which has brought him universal recognition" and proclaimed his writing a repository of "the idea of humanism." [19] Almost every article printed during the commemoration argued that Dostoyevski's work is essentially anticapitalist, and underscored his protest against the persecution of man by man, the power of wealth, and social inequality. To be sure, every writer mentioned also the "reactionary tendencies," but many added that these were neutralized by the power of realistic art.

Party policy of the mid-1950s—that of courting worldwide approval of Soviet cultural advances and readiness for "peaceful coexistence"—forced literary arbiters to be mindful of Lunacharski's opinion: "It seems nothing short of impropriety not to be acquainted with such a giant as Dostoyevski." But that Lunacharski's accompanying qualification—"It would be completely shameful and, so to speak, socially unhealthy, to fall under his influence"—was not ignored is evident from the precautions taken against such an eventuality in issuing new editions of Dostoyevski's writings.

Although the new ten-volume collected works now being published will include *The Devils*, from *Diary of a Writer* the publishers promise only the stories "Dream of a Ridiculous Man," "Bobok," "A Gentle Spirit," "A Little Boy at Christ's Christmas Tree," "The Peasant Marei," "A Centenarian," and Dostoyevski's speech on Pushkin; the publicist and philosophical parts of *Diary of a Writer* have been discarded.

Lenin's injunction to critics in regard to *The Devils*, that they "sort out what refers to Nechayev . . . and what to Bakunin," has, as it were, justified the republication of the novel. Soviet readers are protected from its dangers by suitable admonitions in Yermilov's introduction to the new edition.[20] The 1955 edition of *Crime and Punishment* also contains a commentary by B. Ryurikov, in which he painstakingly enumerates for Soviet readers the pitfalls of the book and lays across them a sturdy plank of Soviet ideology so that the readers may proceed in safety.[21]

Apparently *Notes from the Underground* has now become the chief bête noire. There is even strong indication that its omission from the new edition of Dostoyevski's works was contemplated but that it was later decided to forgo this safeguard.[22] The thesis that evil is inherent in man, carried in this story to its ultimate conclusion, makes it possible to interpret *Notes from the Underground* as a rebuttal of Chernyshevski's ideas and to discover in it an antirevolutionary spirit. Being ideologically obnoxious, the story may then, in the eyes of Party critics such as V. Yermilov, be unceremoniously branded as an artistic failure as well. Yermilov writes in his new monograph on Dostoyevski:

The fanaticism of an apostle of reaction so blinded and deafened Dostoyevski the artist that it apparently made it difficult for him to sense the falseness of the wooden or porcelain-angel dolls he occasionally turned out in his artistic workshop. More than that, he was sometimes capable of consciously sacrificing the requirements of his craft to [his] reactionary tendencies.[23]

"We, the Soviet people," concludes Yermilov,

however highly we may value Dostoyevski as an artist, cannot "forget," cannot "forgive" him his blinding, black hatred of the best democratic forces of his time, which finds expression in his more reactionary works. Nor can we forget that even at the present time [the forces of] reaction, the churchmen and other obscurantists attempt to use his works for their dark purposes.[24]

The anniversary observances of 1956 were not designed to encourage independent study of Dostoyevski. Dostoyevski is still not permitted to speak for himself to the peoples of the Soviet Union, nor are they permitted to speak freely of him. Concerning the effort to "use" Dostoyevski for ulterior motives, however, the prerevolutionary critic Merezhkovski may fittingly be given the concluding word, originally spoken in another connection: "[They] stood before the mysterious phenomenon of poetry . . . like people with bare hands, without a ladder, before a sheer granite cliff. They did not even suspect whom they were up against."

Soviet literary policy in relation to Dostoyevski has manifestly entered a new phase with the elaborate ceremonies of 1956 and with the decision to publish the valuable factual materials forthcoming. Yet the old duality of the official attitude still persists.

Dostoyevski's philosophy and Soviet ideology are fundamentally incompatible. No matter to what dimensions works of research and criticism may swell, there will be little opportunity for an objective, open-minded approach to Dostoyevski in the Soviet Union so long as the present regime exists. Cogent evidence is found in the tendentiously selected critical fare provided the general reader—in the 1956 volume *F. M. Dostoyevski in Russian Criticism*,[25] for example—at the very time when the official "rehabilitation" of Dostoyevski was in full progress. And for the few individuals specialized in the field and still able to carry on free-ranging inquiry, publication of their interpretive insights remains problematical.

NOTES

1: THE EARLY "RADICAL" CRITICS

[1] V. G. Belinski, "Peterburgskii sbornik," *Otechestvennye zapiski* [National Notes] (St. Petersburg), XLV, No. 3 (1846), 1–30; republished in Belinski, *Sobraniye sochinenii* [Collected Works] (Moscow, OGIZ), III (1948), 61–86.

[2] See G. I. Chulkov's commentaries on *Poor Folk*, in F. M. Dostoyevski, *Sochineniya* [Works], ed. A. V. Lunacharski (Moscow and Leningrad, GIKhL, 1931), p. 689.

[3] Belinski, "Peterburgskii sbornik," in *Sobraniye sochinenii*, III, 69.

[4] *Ibid.*, pp. 68–69.   [5] *Ibid.*, p. 70.   [6] *Ibid.*, pp. 71–72.

[7] *Ibid.*, p. 72.   [8] *Ibid.*, p. 85.   [9] *Ibid.*, p. 72.

[10] *Ibid.*, p. 82–83.   [11] *Ibid.*, p. 83.

[12] Belinski, "Vzglyad na russkuyu literaturu 1846 goda" [Review of Russian Literature in 1846], *ibid.*, p. 675.

[13] Belinski, "Vzglyad na russkuyu literaturu 1847 goda" [Review of Russian Literature in 1847], *ibid.*, p. 837.

[14] In a letter to his brother Mikhail, written October 10, 1859, in Tver'; see F. M. Dostoyevski, *Pis'ma* [Letters], ed. A. S. Dolinin (Moscow and Leningrad), I (Gosizdat, 1928), 257.

[15] Belinski, "Vzglyad na russkuyu literaturu 1847 goda," in *Sobraniye sochinenii*, III, 837.

[16] See P. V. Annenkov, "Zametki o russkoi literature proshlovo goda" [Remarks on Russian Literature of the Past Year], *Sovremennik* [Contemporary] (St. Petersburg), No. 13 (1849), pp. 1–2, 5.

[17] See A. V. Druzhinin, "Sovremennye zametki: Pis'ma inogorodnovo podpischika v redaktsiyu 'Sovremennik' o russkoi zhurnalistike [Contemporary Notes: Letters of an Out-of-Town Subscriber to the Editors of *The Contemporary* concerning Russian Journalistic Practices], *Sovremennik*, No. 14 (1849), p. 67.

[18] See A. V. Nikitenko, "Peterburgskii sbornik izdannyi N. Nekrasovym" [The *Petersburg Miscellany* Published by N. Nekrasov], *Biblioteka dlya chteniya* [Library for Reading] (St. Petersburg), No. 75 (1846), pp. 23, 30, 34.

[19] The word *raznochintsy* (singular *raznochinets*) means literally "men of various stations in life." Educated scions of the clergy, urban petit bourgeoisie, and peasantry, they had ceased to be members of their former class by virtue of their education and constituted a socially anomalous segment of the intelligentsia.

[20] V. N. Maikov, "Nechto o russkoi literature v 1846 godu" [Something on Russian Literature in 1846], in his *Kriticheskiye opyty* [Essays in Criticism] (St. Petersburg, Panteon literatury, 1889), p. 325. The essay was first published in *Otechestvennye zapiski* [National Notes] (St. Petersburg), No. 50 (1847).

[21] Maikov, "Nechto," in *Kriticheskiye opyty*, p. 326.

[22] *Ibid.*, pp. 327–28.   [23] *Ibid.*, p. 328.

[24] See N. A. Dobrolyubov, "Zabitye lyudi," in *Sochineniya* [Works] (4th ed.; St. Petersburg, L. F. Panteleyev, 1885), III, 486–532. The article was first published in *Sovremennik* (St. Petersburg), No. 9 (1861).

[25] Dobrolyubov, "Zabitye lyudi," in *Sochineniya*, III, 513.

[26] *Ibid.*, p. 518.   [27] *Ibid.*, p. 524.   [28] *Ibid.*, p. 503.

[29] *Ibid.*, p. 508.   [30] *Ibid.*, p. 507.   [31] *Ibid.*, pp. 506–7.

[32] *Ibid.*, p. 513.   [33] *Ibid.*   [34] *Ibid.*, pp. 531–32.

[35] *Ibid.*, p. 532.   [36] *Ibid.*

[37] See D. I. Pisarev, "Pogibshiye i pogibayushchiye," in *Polnoye sobraniye sochinenii v shesti tomakh* [Complete Works in Six Volumes] (St. Petersburg, F. Pavlenkov, 1897), V, 254–314.

[38] Pisarev, "Bor'ba za zhizn'," in *Polnoye sobraniye*, VI, 283–344. The first part of this article was first published in the magazine *Delo* [The Cause] in 1867 under the title "Budnichnye storony zhizni" [The Everyday Sides of Life]. The second part appeared after the death of the author in the same magazine in 1868, under the title "Bor'ba za sushchestvovaniye" [Struggle for Existence]. In the manuscript, however, the article bore the title "Bor'ba za zhizn'," which was also used in the 1897 edition of Pisarev's complete works and in the many reprintings of the article.

[39] "Bor'ba za zhizn'," in *Polnoye sobraniye*, VI, 283–84.

[40] *Ibid.*, p. 288.   [41] *Ibid.*, p. 332.   [42] *Ibid.*, pp. 310–11.

[43] *Ibid.*, p. 301.   [44] *Ibid.*, pp. 301–2.   [45] *Ibid.*, p. 314.

[46] *Ibid.*, p. 323.   [47] *Ibid.*, p. 328.

⁴⁸ "Populists"—members of that part of the radical intelligentsia which looked to the peasantry as the main force in the inevitable socialist revolution and saw the basis for agrarian socialism already existing in traditional Russian peasant institutions such as communal land tenure.

⁴⁹ See P. N. Tkachov, "Bol'nye lyudi. 'Besy' Dostoyevskovo" [Sick People: Dostoyevski's *The Devils*], *Delo* (St. Petersburg), Nos. 3 and 4 (1873); and M. Vovchek (pseudonym of Tkachov), "Literaturnoye popuri" [Literary Potpourri], *Delo*, Nos. 4, 5, 6, and 8 (1876).

⁵⁰ N. K. Mikhailovski, "Kommentarii k *Besam*" (part of "Iz literaturnykh i zhurnal'nykh zametok 1873 goda" [From Literary and Journalistic Remarks of 1873]), *Otechestvennye zapiski* (February, 1873); included in Mikhailovski, *Sochineniya* [Works] (St. Petersburg, "Russkoye bogatstvo"), I (1896), 840–72.

⁵¹ Mikhailovski, "Zhestokii talant," *Otechestvennye zapiski*, September-October, 1882; included in his *Sochineniya*, V (1897), 1–78.

⁵² Mikhailovski, "O Pisemskom i Dostoyevskom," *Otechestvennye zapiski*, February, 1881; included in his *Sochineniya*, V, 410–31.

⁵³ Mikhailovski, "Pis'ma postoronnevo v redaktsiyu 'Otechestvennykh zapisok,'" *Otechestvennye zapiski*, February, 1881; included in his *Sochineniya*, V, 874–901.

⁵⁴ See, for instance, M. A. Protopopov (articles under his pseudonym "Aleksandr Gorshkov"), "Novyi roman g. Dostoyevskovo 'Brat'ya Karamazovy'" [Mr. Dostoyevski's New Novel *The Brothers Karamazov*], *Russkaya pravda* [Russian Truth] (St. Petersburg), No. 51 (1879); and "Propovednik novovo slova: 'Dnevnik pisatelya'" [Preacher of a New Word: *Diary of a Writer*], *Russkoye bogatstvo* [Russian Wealth] (St. Petersburg), No. 8 (August, 1880), pp. 6–20.

⁵⁵ See, for instance, the following articles by Skabichevski, all signed *Zauryadnyi chitatel'* (Ordinary Reader) and all under the general heading "Mysli po povodu tekushchei literatury" [Thoughts on Current Literature]: "O g. Dostoyevskom voobshche i yevo romane 'Podrostok'" [Concerning Mr. Dostoyevski in General and concerning His Novel *A Raw Youth*], *Birzhevye vedomosti* [Stock Exchange News] (St. Petersburg), No. 8 (1876); "'Dnevnik pisatelya' g. Dostoyevskovo" [Mr. Dostoyevski's *Diary of a Writer*], *ibid.*, No. 36 (1876); No. 70 (1876); and No. 239 (1877); "Nechto o predskazaniyakh g. Dostoyevskovo, o

tom, pochemu oni ne mogut sbyt'sya, i chto bylo by, yesli by oni sbylis' "
[Something on Mr. Dostoyevski's Predictions, on Why They Cannot
Come True, and What Would Be If They Were to Come True], *ibid.*,
No. 267 (1877); " 'Brat'ya Karamazovy.' Novyi roman g. Dostoyev-
skovo" [*The Brothers Karamazov:* Mr. Dostoyevski's New Novel],
Molva [Report] (St. Petersburg), No. 45 (1879); and "Sravneniye
cheloveka s sharmankoi. Sharmanka g. Dostoyevskovo zavedennaya na
luchshuyu i naiboleye simpatichnuyu yeyo ariyu" [Comparison of Man
to a Hurdy-Gurdy: Mr. Dostoyevski's Hurdy-Gurdy Wound up to Its
Best and Most Sympathetic Aria], *ibid.*, No. 141 (1879).

[56] Mikhailovski, "Zhestokii talant," *Sochineniya*, p. 78.

[57] Mikhailovski, "O Pisemskom i Dostoyevskom," *ibid.*, p. 419.

[58] *Ibid.*, p. 420.   [59] Mikhailovski, "Zhestokii talant," *ibid.*, pp. 6–7.

[60] *Ibid.*, p. 7.   [61] *Ibid.*   [62] *Ibid.*, p. 72.

[63] *Ibid.*, p. 70.   [64] *Ibid.*, p. 7.   [65] *Ibid.*, p. 11.

[66] *Ibid.*, p. 56.   [67] *Ibid.*, p. 57.   [68] *Ibid.*, p. 58.

[69] V. F. Pereverzev, "Dostoyevskii v kritike" [Dostoyevski in Criti-
cism], in F. M. Dostoyevski, *Sochineniya* [Works], ed. A. V. Lunacharski (Moscow and Leningrad, GIKhL, 1931), pp. xxv–xxvi.

[70] Mikhailovski, "O Pisemskom i Dostoyevskom," *Sochineniya*, p.
425.

[71] Mikhailovski, "Zhestokii talant," *ibid.*, p. 36.

[72] Mikhailovski, "Kommentarii k Besam," *ibid.*, p. 844.

[73] *Ibid.*, p. 845.   [74] *Ibid.*, p. 849.   [75] *Ibid.*, p. 851.

[76] *Ibid.*, p. 863.   [77] *Ibid.*, p. 855.   [78] *Ibid.*, p. 853.

[79] *Ibid.*, p. 872.

2: DECADENTS, SYMBOLISTS, AND MYSTICS

[1] Solov'yov was himself influenced by Dostoyevski in developing his
mystical philosophical system. In his twelve "Lectures on Godmanhood"
in 1877 to 1881, he spoke of the God-man toward whom the whole
history of mankind has been directed. In 1878 Solov'yov and Dostoyevski took a trip together to Optina Pustyn' to visit Father Amvrosi,
who was the prototype for Father Zosima in *The Brothers Karamazov*.
After Dostoyevski's death at the beginning of 1881, Solov'yov made three
speeches (1881–83) in his memory which were a continuation of the

earlier "Lectures on Godmanhood." Strictly speaking, Solov'yov used Dostoyevski for justification of his own philosophical views on the purity, holiness, and beauty of matter—instinct with the divine principle of Sophia [the Divine Wisdom]—on the necessity of national self-renunciation, of submersion in the universal, and finally of a universal theocracy. See "Chteniya o Bogochelovechestve" [Lectures on God-manhood], in *Sobraniye sochinenii* [Collected Works] (2d ed.; St. Petersburg, Obshchestvennaya pol'za), III (1912), 1–168; and "Tri rechi v pamyat' Dostoyevskovo" [Three Speeches in Memory of Dos-toyevski], *ibid.*, pp. 186–223. For a detailed exposition of the philosophy of Solov'yov, see V. V. Zenkovsky, *A History of Russian Philosophy*, trans. from the Russian by George L. Kline (New York, Columbia University Press, 1953), II, 469–531; and for a discussion of Dostoyevski's influence on Solov'yov, *ibid.*, I, 425–26.

² D. S. Merezhkovski, "O prichinakh upadka i o novykh techeniyakh sovremennoi russkoi literatury," in *Polnoye sobraniye sochinenii* [Complete Works] (Moscow, Sytin), XVIII (1914), 226. The essay was first published in a book of the same title, St. Petersburg, 1893.

³ "O prichinakh upadka," in *Polnoye sobraniye sochinenii*, XVIII, 224.

⁴ *Ibid.*, p. 225.　　　　　　　　⁵ *Ibid.*, p. 226.

⁶ Merezhkovski, "O 'Prestuplenii i nakazanii' Dostoyevskovo," *Russkoye obozreniye* [Russian Review] (St. Petersburg), II, No. 3 (1890), 155–86.

⁷ Merezhkovski, "Dostoyevskii," in *Polnoye sobraniye sochinenii*, XVIII, 5–32.

⁸ Merezhkovski, *L. Tolstoi i Dostoyevskii* (St. Petersburg, Mir iskusstva, 1901–2); Vol. I: *Zhizn' i tvorchestvo* [Life and Writings]; Vol. II: *Religiya* [Religion]. An English translation has been published under the title *Tolstoy as Man and Artist, with an Essay on Dostoyevski*, New York, 1902.

⁹ Merezhkovski, "Prorok russkoi revolyutsii," *Vesy* [The Scales] (Moscow), No. 3–4 (1906), pp. 19–47; reprinted in *Polnoye sobraniye sochinenii* (St. Petersburg and Moscow, Vol'f), XI (1911), 173–224.

¹⁰ Merezhkovski, "Gor'kii i Dostoyevskii," in his *Bylo i budet* [Past and Future] (Petrograd, 1915), pp. 269–83.

¹¹ Merezhkovski, *Vechnye sputniki* (St. Petersburg, Pirozhkov,

1897); republished in Vol. XVIII of *Polnoye sobraniye sochinenii* (Moscow, Sytin, 1914), and as Vol. XIII of *Polnoye sobraniye sochinenii* (St. Petersburg and Moscow, Vol'f, 1911).

[12] Merezhkovski, "Dostoyevski," p. 6.   [13] *Ibid.*
[14] *Ibid.*, pp. 10–11.   [15] *Ibid.*, p. 25.   [16] *Ibid.*, pp. 26–27.
[17] *Ibid.*, p. 30.   [18] *Ibid.*, p. 31.   [19] *Ibid.*, p. 32.   [20] *Ibid.*
[21] Lev Shestov, *Dostoyevskii i Nitsshe: Filosofiya tragedii* (St. Petersburg, 1903; 2d ed., St. Petersburg, Stasyulevich, 1909).

[22] V. V. Rozanov, *Legenda o Velikom Inkvizitore F. M. Dostoyevskovo: Opyt kriticheskovo kommentariya* (Berlin, "Razum," 1924); first published in *Russkii vestnik* [Russian Courier] (Moscow, 1890), then in book form (St. Petersburg, 1894; 3d ed., St. Petersburg, Pirozhkov, 1906).

[23] Rozanov, *Legenda* (Berlin, 1924), p. 59.

[24] *Ibid.*, p. 211.

[25] A. L. Volynski, *F. M. Dostoyevskii. Kriticheskiye stat'i* (St. Petersburg, Energiya, 1906).

[26] Yuli Aikhenval'd, *Spor o Belinskom* [Dispute over Belinski] (Moscow, 1914), p. 100.

[27] Aikhenval'd, "Dostoyevskii," in *Siluety russkikh pisatelei* [Silhouettes of Russian Writers] (2d ed.; Moscow, Izdaniye Nauchnovo slova), II (1908), 90–108; republished under the title "Noch' russkoi literatury" [The Night of Russian Literature], in the anthology *F. M. Dostoyevskii: Zhizn' i tvorchestvo* [F. M. Dostoyevski: Life and Work] (St. Petersburg and Warsaw, "Oros" [1912?]), pp. 200–220 (Vol. XII of the series *Korifei russkovo slova* [Coryphaei of the Russian Word], comp. N. G. Priluko-Prilutski).

[28] Aikhenval'd, "Noch' russkoi literatury," in *F. M. Dostoyevskii: Zhizn' i tvorchestvo*, p. 205.

[29] *Ibid.*, p. 207.   [30] *Ibid.*, p. 208.   [31] *Ibid.*, pp. 210–11.
[32] *Ibid.*, p. 211.   [33] *Ibid.*, p. 214.   [34] *Ibid.*, p. 217.
[35] *Ibid.*, p. 215.   [36] *Ibid.*, p. 216.   [37] *Ibid.*, p. 220.   [38] *Ibid.*

[39] V. Ivanov, "Dostoyevskii i roman-tragediya," *Russkaya mysl'* [Russian Thought] (Moscow), No. 5–6 (1911); reprinted in Ivanov, *Borozdy i mezhi* [Furrows and Boundaries] (Moscow, Musaget, 1916), pp. 5–60; published, in slightly expanded form, in English translation, under the title *Freedom and the Tragic Life*, trans. Norman

Cameron and ed. S. Konovalov (New York, Noonday Press, 1952).

[40] *Sobornost'* is the term applied, notably in the interpretation of Aleksei Khomyakov (Khomiakov), to the principle of the Orthodox Church that the Church is constituted by all its members, lay and clerical, bound together by love, that it is in this united body that truth and freedom reside, and that this body as a whole bears responsibility for the doctrine and teaching of the Church. See Zenkovsky, *A History of Russian Philosophy*, pp. 186–88; and Sir John Maynard, *Russia in Flux*, ed. and abridged by S. Haden Guest (New York, Macmillan, 1948), pp. 58–59.

[41] Ivanov, "Dostoyevskii i roman-tragediya," *Borozdy i mezhi,* p. 21.

[42] *Ibid.,* p. 23.   [43] *Ibid.,* p. 24.   [44] *Ibid.,* p. 29.

[45] *Ibid.,* p. 36.   [46] *Ibid.,* p. 42.

3: THE EARLY MARXIST CRITICS

[1] Ye. A. Solov'yov (Andreyevich, pseud.), *F. Dostoyevskii. Yevo zhizn' i literaturnaya deyatel'nost'* (St. Petersburg, 1891; 2d ed., 1898; and Kazan', Molodye sily, 1922). The study was included in abridged form under the title "F. M. Dostoyevskii, kak khudozhnik i publitsist" [F. M. Dostoyevski as Artist and Publicist] in the author's *Ocherki po istorii russkoi literatury XIX veka* [Studies in the History of Russian Literature in the Nineteenth Century] (St. Petersburg, 1902); in the anthology *F. M. Dostoyevskii: Zhizn' i tvorchestvo* [F. M. Dostoyevski: Life and Work] (St. Petersburg and Warsaw, "Oros" [1912?]), pp. 221–43 (Vol. XII of the series *Korifei russkovo slova* [Coryphaei of the Russian Word], comp. N. G. Priluko-Prilutski); and, under the title "F. M. Dostoyevskii," in a collection of articles entitled *F. M. Dostoyevskii* (Moscow, "Nikitinskiye subbotniki," 1928) (Vol. III of *Klassiki v marksistskom osveshchenii* [The Classics in the Light of Marxism], in the series *Biblioteka pisatelei dlya shkoly i yunoshestva* [Library of Writers for Schools and Young People], ed. Ye. F. Nikitina).

[2] Solov'yov, "F. M. Dostoyevskii," in *F. M. Dostoyevskii* (1928), pp. 131–32.

[3] *Ibid.,* p. 133.   [4] *Ibid.,* p. 139.   [5] *Ibid.,* p. 142.

[6] *Ibid.,* pp. 149–50.   [7] *Ibid.,* p. 152.   [8] *Ibid.,* p. 168.

⁹ See Plekhanov, "Proletarskoye dvizheniye i burzhuaznoye iskus-stvo," in *Sobraniye sochinenii* [Collected Works], ed. D. Ryazanov (Moscow, GIZ), XIV (1922), 74–94; first published in *Pravda* [Truth] (Moscow), No. 11, 1905.

¹⁰ L. Aksel'rod, "Ob otnoshenii G. V. Plekhanova k iskusstvu, po lichnym vospominaniyam" [On G. V. Plekhanov's Attitude toward Art, from Personal Recollections], *Pod znamenem marksizma* [Under the Banner of Marxism] (Moscow), No. 5–6 (1922), p. 17.

¹¹ G. V. Plekhanov, *Russkii rabochii v revolyutsionnom dvizhenii* (Geneva, 1892), pp. 25–26.

¹² N. Valentinov, *Vstrechi s Leninym* [Meetings with Lenin] (New York, Chekhov Publishing House, 1953), p. 85.

¹³ V. I. Lenin, "Pis'mo Inesse Armand" [Letter to Inessa Armand], June 5, 1914, in *Sochineniya* [Works] (4th ed.; Moscow, Gospolit-izdat), XXXV (1950), 107.

¹⁴ Sergei Bulgakov, "Geroizm i podvizhnichestvo" [Heroism and Asceticism], in *Vekhi* (3d ed.; Moscow, Kushnerov, 1909), p. 68.

¹⁵ V. V. Veresayev, "Chelovek proklyat," *Sovremennyi mir* [Con-temporary World] (St. Petersburg), Nos. 1 and 2 (1910).

¹⁶ Veresayev, *Zhivaya zhizn'* (Moscow, Popova, 1911; 3d ed., Mos-cow, Knigoizdatel'stvo Pisatelei, 1922).

¹⁷ See N. I. Korobka, "Merezhkovskii o Tolstom i Dostoyevskom" [Merezhkovski on Tolstoi and Dostoyevski], *Obrazovaniye* [Educa-tion] (St. Petersburg), No. 11, 1901; *Opyt obzora istorii russkoi literatury dlya shkol i samoobrazovaniya* [Attempt at a Survey of the History of Russian Literature for Schools and Self-Education] (St. Petersburg, 1907), Part 3 (*Epokha realisticheskovo romana* [The Pe-riod of the Realistic Novel]).

¹⁸ See N. Rozhkov, "Eticheskiye i esteticheskiye kharaktery" [Ethical and Aesthetic Qualities], *Obrazovaniye*, No. 10–11 (1900).

¹⁹ See V. M. Shulyatikov, "Kriticheskiye etudy: Nazad k Dosto-yevskomu" [Critical Studies: Back to Dostoyevski], *Kur'yer* [Courier] (St. Petersburg), No. 287 (1903).

²⁰ V. B. Kranikhfel'd, "Preodoleniye Dostoyevskovo," *Teatr i iskus-stvo* [Theater and Art] (St. Petersburg), Nos. 14 and 16 (1911); re-printed in the anthology *V mire idei i obrazov* [In the World of Ideas and Images] (St. Petersburg, "Zhizn' i znaniye," 1917), Vol. III.

4: CRITICISM ON THE EVE OF THE REVOLUTION

[1] See Ch. Vetrinski (pseudonym of Vasili Yevgrafovich Cheshikhin), "Ocherk istorii zhurnalistiki za vtoruyu polovinu XIX veka" [Outline of the History of Journalism during the Second Half of the Nineteenth Century], in *Istoriya russkoi literatury XIX v.* [History of Nineteenth-Century Russian Literature], ed. D. N. Ovsyaniko-Kulikovski (Moscow, "Mir"), V (1911), 417. See also V. V. Zenkovsky, *A History of Russian Philosophy*, trans. George L. Kline (New York, Columbia University Press, 1953), I, 400–406, 428; D. S. Mirsky, *A History of Russian Literature*, ed. and abridged by Francis J. Whitfield (New York, Knopf, 1949), p. 207; and "Grigor'yev, Apollon Aleksandrovich," *Literaturnaya entsiklopediya* [Literary Encyclopedia] (Moscow), Vol. III (1930), cols. 4–10.

[2] See A. A. Grigor'yev, "Russkaya literatura v 1851 g." [Russian Literature in 1851], in *Sochineniya* [Works] (St. Petersburg, 1876), I, 15, 32, 50, 55–56 (first published in *Moskvityanin* [The Muscovite] [Moscow], Nos. 1–4 [1852]); "O komediyakh Ostrovskovo i ikh znachenii v literature i na stsene" [Concerning the Comedies of Ostrovski and Their Significance in Literature and on the Stage], in *Sochineniya*, I, 109 (first published in *Moskvityanin*, No. 8 [1855]); and "I. S. Turgenev i yevo deyatel'nost' (po povodu romana 'Dvoryanskoye gnezdo')" [I. S. Turgenev and His Work: In Connection with the Novel *Nest of Noblemen*], in *Sochineniya*, I, 350 (first published in *Russkoye slovo* [The Russian Word] [St. Petersburg], Nos. 4–6 and 8 [1859]).

[3] One of Antonovich's early attacks on *pochvennichestvo* is "O pochve (ne v agronomicheskom smysle, a v dukhe 'Vremeni')" [Concerning the Soil (Not in the Agricultural Sense but in the Spirit of *Vremya* [Time])], *Sovremennik* [The Contemporary] (St. Petersburg), No. 90 (December, 1861), pp. 171–88. See also his "Mistiko-asketicheskii roman: 'Brat'ya Karamazovy'" [A Mystically Ascetic Novel: *The Brothers Karamazov*], *Novoye obozreniye* [New Review] (St. Petersburg), No. 3 (March, 1881), pp. 190–239.

[4] N. N. Strakhov, "Vospominaniya o Dostoyevskom" [Reminiscences of Dostoyevski], in O. F. Miller and N. N. Strakhov, *Biografiya, pis'ma, zametki iz zapisnoi knizhki F. M. Dostoyevskovo* [Biography of F. M.

Dostoyevski, Letters, and Notes from His Notebook] (St. Petersburg, 1883). Miller's article in the book, "Materialy dlya zhizneopisaniya F. M. Dostoyevskovo" [Materials for a Biography of F. M. Dostoyevski], covers the period from Dostoyevski's birth to the establishment of the journal *Vremya*, and Strakhov's article the remaining period. The contents of the book had been published previously in Dostoyevski, *Polnoye sobraniye sochinenii* [Complete Works] (St. Petersburg, A. G. Dostoyevskaya), Vol. I (1882).

[5] See, for instance, Strakhov, " 'Prestupleniye i nakazaniye' F. M. Dostoyevskovo" [F. M. Dostoyevski's *Crime and Punishment*], *Otechestvennye zapiski* [National Notes] (St. Petersburg), Vol. CXXI, Nos. 3 and 4 (1867).

[6] O. F. Miller, *Russkiye pisateli posle Gogolya* (St. Petersburg, Vol'f, 1886), and in several later editions.

[7] A. P. Milyukov (1817–1897), "Vospominaniya o F. Dostoyevskom" [Reminiscences of F. Dostoyevski], in *Literaturnye vstrechi i znakomstva* [Literary Encounters and Acquaintances] (St. Petersburg, 1890).

[8] Vsevolod Solov'yov, "Vospominaniya o F. M. Dostoyevskom" [Reminiscences of F. M. Dostoyevski], *Istoricheskii vestnik* [Historical Courier] (St. Petersburg), No. 3 (1881), pp. 602–16; and No. 4 (1881), pp. 839–53.

[9] Anatoli Fyodorovich Koni, *Ocherki i vospominaniya* [Sketches and Memoirs] (St. Petersburg, 1906), pp. 73–90; and Koni, *Na zhiznennom puti* [On Life's Way], Vol. II (St. Petersburg, "Trud," 1912).

[10] Ch. Vetrinski, *Dostoyevskii v vospominaniyakh sovremennikov, v pis'makh i zametkakh* [Dostoyevski in Reminiscences of His Contemporaries and in Letters and Notes] (Moscow, Svetin, Vol. I, 1912, and Vol. II, 1914) ; 2d ed. revised and enlarged under the title *F. M. Dostoyevskii v vospominaniyakh sovremennikov i v yevo pis'makh* [F. M. Dostoyevski in Reminiscences of His Contemporaries and in His Letters] (Moscow, Dumnov, Vol. I, 1923, and Vol. II, 1924).

[11] V. F. Chizh, "Dostoyevskii kak psikhopatolog" [Dostoyevski as a Psychopathologist], *Russkii vestnik* [Russian Courier] (Moscow), No. 5–6 (1884); published in book form, Moscow, Universitetskaya tipografiya, 1885.

[12] L. N. Voitolovski, "F. M. Dostoyevskii. K tridtsatiletiyu so dnya konchiny" [F. M. Dostoyevski: On the Thirtieth Anniversary of His

Death], *Kiyevskaya mysl'* [Kievan Thought] (Kiev), No. 28 (1911).

[13] L. P. Grossman, "Bal'zak i Dostoyevskii," *Russkaya mysl'* [Russian Thought] (Moscow), No. 1 (1914), pp. 44–55.

[14] Grossman, "Gofman, Bal'zak i Dostoyevskii," *Sofiya* [Sophia] (Moscow), No. 5 (1914), pp. 87–96.

[15] Grossman, "Russkii *Kandit* (k voprosu o vliyanii Vol'tera na Dostoyevskovo)," *Vestnik Yevropy* [Courier of Europe] (St. Petersburg), No. 5 (1914), pp. 192–203.

[16] Grossman, "Dostoyevskii i Yevropa," *Russkaya mysl'*, No. 11 (1915), pp. 54–93.

[17] Grossman, "Kompozitsiya v romane Dostoyevskovo," *Vestnik Yevropy* (Petrograd), No. 9 (1916), pp. 121–56.

[18] Grossman, "Problema realizma u Dostoyevskovo," *ibid.*, No. 2 (February, 1917), pp. 65–100.

[19] V. L. Komarovich, "Dostoyevskii i Geine," *Sovremennyi mir* [The Contemporary World] (Petrograd), No. 10 (1916), pp. 97–107.

[20] Komarovich, "Dostoyevskii i shestidesyatniki," *ibid.*, No. 1 (1917), pp. 129–39.

[21] S. I. Rodzevich, "K istorii russkovo romantizma (Gofman v 30–40 g.g. v nashei literature)," *Russkii Filologicheskii Vestnik* [Russian Philological Courier] (Petrograd), LVII, No. 1–2 (1917), 223–30.

[22] See, for instance, V. L. Komarovich, *Dostoyevskii: Sovremennye problemy istoriko-literaturnovo izucheniya* [Dostoyevski: Contemporary Problems in the Study of Literary History] (Leningrad, "Obrazovaniye," 1925), p. 64.

5: MAXIM GORKI

[1] Maxim Gorki, *Istoriya russkoi literatury* (Moscow, Goslitizdat, 1939).

[2] See V. I. Lenin, "Pis'mo Gor'komu" [Letter to Gorki], June 18–20, 1913, in *Sobraniye sochinenii* [Collected Works] (2d ed.; Moscow, Goslitizdat), XXIX (1932), 37; and *Lenin o literature* [Lenin on Literature] (Moscow, GIKhL, 1941), pp. 153–233.

[3] Gorki, *Istoriya russkoi literatury*, p. 250.   [4] *Ibid.*, p. 251.
[5] *Ibid.*, p. 252.   [6] *Ibid.*
[7] Gorki, "Zametki o meshchanstve," in *Stat'i 1905–1916 gg.* [Articles

of 1905–16] (2d ed.; Petrograd, "Parus," 1918); republished in Gorki's *Literaturno-kriticheskiye stat'i* [Articles of Literary Criticism] (Moscow, Goslitizdat, 1937), pp. 7–9. The article was first published in the newspaper *Novaya zhizn'* [New Life] (St. Petersburg), in 1905.

[8] Gorki, "Zametki o meshchanstve," in *Literaturno-kriticheskiye stat'i,* pp. 7–8.

[9] "O karamazovshchine" [On Karamazovism], *ibid.*, p. 146; first published in *Russkoye slovo* [Russian Word] (St. Petersburg), September 22, 1913.

[10] "O karamazovshchine," *Literaturno-kriticheskiye stat'i,* p. 146.

[11] See, for instance, "O vypade g. Gor'kovo protiv Dostoyevskovo" [On Mr. Gorki's Attack on Dostoyevski], *Birzhevye vedomosti* [Stock Exchange News] (St. Petersburg), October 8 and 9, 1913. This protest was signed by the writers A. Kuprin, A. Budishchev, I. Yasinski, I. Potapenko, D. Merezhkovski, F. Sologub, A. Remizov, S. Vengerov, F. Batyushkov, and Ivanov-Razumnik.

[12] See, for instance, the following articles which appeared in the newspaper *Za pravdu* [For the Truth] (St. Petersburg): A. Vitminski (M. S. Ol'minski), "Pokhod protiv M. Gor'kovo" [The Campaign against M. Gorki], October 4, 1913; "Otkrytoye pis'mo M. Gor'komu" [An Open Letter to M. Gorki], signed by a group of workers, October 30, 1913; "Po povodu karamazovshchiny" [On the Subject of Karamazovism], November 15, 1913; and an article under the anonym Rabochii (A Worker), "K pokhodu protiv Gor'kovo" [On the Campaign against Gorki], December 3, 1913.

[13] "Yeshcho o karamazovshchine" [More on Karamazovism], in *Literaturno-kriticheskiye stat'i,* p. 153; first published in *Russkoye slovo,* October 27, 1913.

[14] "Yeshcho o karamazovshchine," in *Literaturno-kriticheskiye stat'i,* p. 152.

[15] *Ibid.*   [16] *Ibid.*, p. 153.

[17] Gorki, "Besedy o remesle" [Shop Talks], in *O literature. Stat'i i rechi, 1928–1935* [On Literature: Articles and Speeches] (Moscow, GIKhL, 1935), p. 263; first published in *Literaturnaya uchoba* [Literary Studies] (Moscow), No. 6 (June, 1930).

[18] Gorki, "O tom, kak ya uchilsya pisat' " [On the Way I Learned to Write], in *O literature,* p. 198; first published as a brochure under the

title *Rabsel'koram i voyenkoram o tom, kak ya uchilsya pisat'* [To the Industrial and Rural Correspondents and the Military Correspondents on the Way I Learned to Write] (Moscow, Gosizdat, 1928).

[19] "Besedy o remesle," in *O literature*, p. 263.

[20] "Doklad na s"yezde sovetskikh pisatelei" [Speech at the Congress of Soviet Writers], *ibid.*, p. 377.

[21] *Ibid.*   [22] *Ibid.*, p. 378.

6: SURVEY OF SOVIET STUDIES OF DOSTOYEVSKI

[1] See A. Lunacharski, "Lenin ob iskusstve" [Lenin on Art], in his *Lenin i literaturovedeniye* [Lenin and Literary Scholarship] (Moscow, Sovetskaya literatura, 1934), p. 107.

[2] V. I. Lenin, "Pis'mo k A. M. Gor'komu" [Letter to A. M. Gorki], mid-November, 1913, in *Lenin o literature* [Lenin on Literature] (Moscow, GIKhL, 1941), p. 153.

[3] A. L. Bêm, ed., *O Dostoyevskom* [On Dostoyevski] (Prague, Vol. I, 1929; Vol. II, 1933; Vol. III, 1936).

[4] V. I. Lenin, "Partiinaya organizatsiya i partiinaya literatura," *Novaya zhizn'* [New Life] (St. Petersburg), No. 12 (November 13, 1905).

[5] *F. M. Dostoyevskii* (Moscow, Izdatel'stvo Pisatelei "Nikitinskiye subbotniki," 1928) (Vol. III of *Klassiki v marksistskom osveshchenii* [The Classics in the Light of Marxism], in the series *Biblioteka pisatelei dlya shkoly i yunoshestva* [Library of Writers for Schools and Young People], ed. Ye. F. Nikitina).

[6] B. Engel'gardt, "Ideologicheskii roman Dostoyevskovo" [Dostoyevski's Ideological Novel], in A. S. Dolinin, ed., *Dostoyevskii. Stat'i i materialy* [Dostoyevski: Articles and Materials] II (Leningrad and Moscow, "Mysl'," 1925), 71.

[7] A. S. Dolinin (pseud. of Arkadii Semyonovich Iskoz), ed., *Dostoyevskii: Stat'i i materialy* Vol. I (Petrograd, "Mysl'," 1922); Vol. II (Leningrad and Moscow, "Mysl'," 1925); and Dolinin, ed., *F. M. Dostoyevski: Materialy i issledovaniya* [F. M. Dostoyevski: Materials and Studies] (Leningrad, Izd. Akademii Nauk SSSR, 1935).

[8] N. L. Brodski, ed., *Tvorcheskii put' Dostoyevskovo* [The Creative Path of Dostoyevski] (Leningrad, "Seyatel'," 1924),

[9] L. Grossman, ed., *Tvorchestvo Dostoyevskovo* [Dostoyevski's Writing] (Odessa, Vseukrainskoye gosudarstvennoye izdatel'stvo, 1921).

[10] *Dostoyevskii* (Moscow, 1928), Issue No. 3 of *Trudy Gosudarstvennoi Akademii Khudozhestvennykh Nauk, Literaturnaya Sektsiya* [Papers of the State Academy of the Arts, Literature Section].

[11] "Dostoyevskii i o Dostoyevskom" [Dostoyevski and on Dostoyevski], in *Zven'ya* [Links] (Moscow and Leningrad, "Academia"), Issue No. 6 (1936), pp. 413–600.

[12] Georgi I. Chulkov, *Kak rabotal Dostoyevskii* (Moscow, Sovetskii pisatel', 1939).

[13] V. Ya. Kirpotin, *F. M. Dostoyevskii* (Moscow, Sovetskii pisatel', 1947).

[14] Kirpotin, *Molodoi Dostoyevskii* (Moscow, GIKhL, 1947).

[15] A. S. Dolinin, *V tvorcheskoi laboratorii Dostoyevskovo* (Moscow, Sovetskii pisatel', 1947).

7: DOCUMENTARY RESEARCH AND PUBLICATION OF THE MATERIALS

[1] Leonid Grossman, *Put' Dostoyevskovo* (Leningrad, Brockhaus-Efron, 1924; 2d ed., Moscow, "Sovremennye problemy," 1928—Vol. II, Part One, of Grossman's *Sobraniye sochinenii* [Collected Works]). *Put' Dostoyevskovo* is an expansion and reworking of Grossman's article "Put' Dostoyevskovo," in Grossman, ed., *Tvorchestvo Dostoyevskovo* [Dostoyevski's Writings] (Odessa, vseukrainskoye gosudarstvennoye Izdatel'stvo, 1921), pp. 83–110.

[2] L. Grossman, comp. and ed., *Dostoyevskii na zhiznennom puti* (Moscow, "Nikitinskiye subbotniki," 1928).

[3] Grossman, "Dostoyevskii i pravitel'stvennye krugi 1870-kh godov" [Dostoyevski and Government Circles in the 1870s], in *Literaturnoye nasledstvo* [Literary Heritage] (Moscow, Izdaniye zhurnal'no-gazetnovo ob"yedineniya), Issue No. 15 (1934), pp. 83–162.

[4] Grossman, "Grazhdanskaya smert' F. M. Dostoyevskovo" [The Civil Death of F. M. Dostoyevski], *ibid.*, Issue No. 22–24 (1935), pp. 683–736.

[5] Grossman, *Zhizn' i trudy F. M. Dostoyevskovo: Biografiya v datakh i dokumentakh* (Moscow and Leningrad, Academia, 1935).

[6] Grossman, *Kazn' Dostoyevskovo* [Dostoyevski's Punishment] (Moscow, "Ogonyok," 1928); and *Ruletenburg: Povest' o Dostoyevskom* [Roulettenburg: A Story of Dostoyevski] (Moscow, GIKhL, 1932).

[7] V. L. Komarovich, "Yunost' Dostoyevskovo," *Byloye* [The Past] (Leningrad), No. 23 (1924), pp. 3–42.

[8] Komarovich, "Mirovaya garmoniya," *Atenei* [Athenaeum] (Leningrad), No. 1–2 (1924), pp. 112–42.

[9] See A. S. Dolinin, "Dostoyevskii i Gertsen" [Dostoyevski and Herzen], in Dolinin, ed., *Dostoyevskii: Stat'i i materialy* [Dostoyevski: Articles and Materials], I (Petrograd, "Mysl'," 1922), 275–326.

[10] Dolinin, "Dostoyevskii i Suslova," in *Dostoyevskii: Stat'i i materialy*, II (Moscow and Leningrad, "Mysl'," 1925), 153–283.

[11] Dolinin, "Dostoyevskii sredi petrashevtsev," *Zven'ya* [Links] (Moscow and Leningrad, "Academia"), Issue No. 6 (1936), pp. 512–45.

[12] M. P. Alekseyev, *Rannii drug F. M. Dostoyevskovo* (Odessa, Vseukrainskoye gosudarstvennoye izdatel'stvo, 1921).

[13] K. K. Istomin, "Iz zhizni i tvorchestva Dostoyevskovo v molodosti," in N. L. Brodski, ed., *Tvorcheskii put' Dostoyevskovo* [The Creative Path of Dostoyevski] (Leningrad, "Seyatel'," 1924), pp. 3–48.

[14] L. K. Il'inski, "F. M. Dostoyevskii i Gl. Iv. Uspenskii" [F. M. Dostoyevski and Gleb Ivanovich Uspenski], in Dolinin, ed., *Dostoyevskii: Stat'i i materialy*, I, 327–53.

[15] Ye. Pokrovskaya, "Dostoyevskii i petrashevtsy" [Dostoyevski and the Petrashevtsy], *ibid.*, pp. 257–73.

[16] N. F. Bel'chikov, "Dostoyevskii i Pobedonostsev" [Dostoyevski and Pobedonostsev], in *Krasnyi Arkhiv* [Red Archive] (Moscow), No. 2 (1922), pp. 240–55; "Chernyshevskii i Dostoyevskii" [Chernyshevski and Dostoyevski], *Pechat' i revolyutsiya* [Press and Revolution] (Moscow), No. 5 (1928), pp. 35–53; and "Kak pisal romany Dostoyevskii" [How Dostoyevski Wrote Novels], *ibid.*, No. 2 (1928), pp. 88–93.

[17] Bel'chikov, ed., "Pokazaniya F. M. Dostoyevskovo po delu petrashevtsev" [Testimony of F. M. Dostoyevski in the Petrashevtsy Case], *Krasnyi Arkhiv* No. 45 (1931), pp. 130–46, and No. 46, pp. 160–78.

[18] See P. N. Sakulin, *Russkaya literatura i sotsializm* [Russian Literature and Socialism] (Moscow, Gosizdat, 1922), Part I (Rannii russkii sotsializm [Early Russian Socialism]), pp. 352–53, 357–58.

[19] Bel'chikov, "Pokazaniya," *Krasnyi Arkhiv*, No. 45 (1931), p. 134.

²⁰ *Ibid.*, No. 46 (1931), pp. 166–67.   ²¹ *Ibid.*, p. 165.

²² *Ibid.*, No. 45 (1931), p. 132.   ²³ *Ibid.*, No. 46 (1931), p. 163.

²⁴ *Ibid.*, No. 45 (1931), p. 132.

²⁵ K. Chukovski, "Dostoyevskii i pleyada Belinskovo," in *Nekrasov: Stat'i i materialy* [Nekrasov: Articles and Materials] (Leningrad, Kubuch, 1926), pp. 326–49. The article was written in 1915 but not published at the time.

²⁶ G. I. Chulkov, "Dostoyevskii i utopicheskii sotsializm," *Katorga i ssylka* [Penal Servitude and Exile] (Moscow, 1929), No. 2, pp. 9–36; No. 3, pp. 134–51.

²⁷ S. N. Kulikov, "K biografii F. M. Dostoyevskovo" [More on F. M. Dostoyevski's Biography], *Katorga i ssylka*, No. 112 (1934), pp. 108–14.

²⁸ "Iz vospominanii A. G. Dostoyevskoi" [From the Reminiscences of A. G. Dostoyevskaya], *Krasnyi Arkhiv*, No. 3 (1923), pp. 251–90; *Vospominaniya A. G. Dostoyevskoi* [Reminiscences of A. G. Dostoyevskaya], ed. L. Grossman (Moscow, Gosizdat, 1925); A. G. Dostoyevskaya, "Vospominaniya" [Reminiscences], in Dolinin, ed., *Dostoyevskii: Stat'i i materialy*, I, 477–504, and II, 285–301; *Dnevnik A. G. Dostoyevskoi, 1867 g.* [Diary of A. G. Dostoyevskaya, 1867] (Moscow, Novaya Moskva, 1923). In large part, these materials are available in English translation: *Dostoyevsky: Letters and Reminiscences*, trans. S. S. Koteliansky and J. M. Murry (New York, 1923); and *Dostoyevsky Portrayed by His Wife: The Diary and Reminiscences of Mme Dostoyevsky*, trans. and ed. S. S. Koteliansky (New York, 1926).

²⁹ L. Dostoyevskaya, *Dostoyevskii v izobrazhenii yevo docheri L. Dostoyevskoi* [Dostoyevski As Portrayed by His Daughter L. Dostoyevskaya], trans. from the German by L. Ya. Krukovskaya, ed. and with a foreword by A. G. Gornfel'd (Moscow and Petrograd, Gosizdat, 1922); this is a somewhat abridged translation of *Dostojewski, geschildert von seiner Tochter A. Dostojewski* (Munich, Reinhardt, 1920); the latter was published in English translation: Aimée [Lyubov'] Dostoyevsky, *Fyodor Dostoyevsky: A Study* (London, Heinemann, 1921).

³⁰ A. M. Dostoyevski, *Vospominaniya Andreya Mikhailovicha Dostoyevskovo* [Reminiscences of Andrei Mikhailovich Dostoyevski] (Leningrad, Izdatel'stvo pisatelei, 1930).

³¹ A. P. Suslova, *Gody blizosti s Dostoyevskim* [Years of Intimacy

with Dostoyevski], with an introduction and commentaries by A. S. Dolinin (Moscow, Sabashnikovy, 1928).

[32] S. Lyubimov, "F. M. Dostoyevskii (Vopros ob yevo proiskhozhdenii)" [F. M. Dostoyevski: The Question of His Origin], *Literaturnaya mysl'* [Literary Thought] (Petrograd), No. 1 (1923), pp. 208–10.

[33] Lyubimov, "K voprosu o genealogii Dostoyevskovo" [More on the Question of Dostoyevski's Genealogy], in Dolinin, ed., *Dostoyevskii: Stat'i i materialy*, II, 303–6.

[34] M. V. Volotskoi, *Khronika roda Dostoyevskovo, 1506–1933* [Chronicle of the Dostoyevski Family, 1506–1933] (Moscow, Sever, 1933).

[35] See Note 29 above.

[36] See Leo Okinshevich, *The Law of the Grand Duchy of Lithuania: Background and Bibliography* (New York, Research Program on the U.S.S.R., 1953), pp. 3, 51; mimeographed. The error of Lyubov' Dostoyevskaya is further explained by the influence of the strongly nationalistic book by the Lithuanian journalist W. St. Vidunas, *La Lituanie dans le passé et dans le présent* (Paris, 1920), which she had read.

[37] Peregrinus (pseud. of Vatslaŭ Lastoŭski), "Todar Dastaeŭski i Adam Mitskevich, syny kryvitskaha narodnaha heniya" [Fyodor Dostoyevski and Adam Mickiewicz, Sons of the Kryvichian National Genius], *Kryvich* (Kaunus), No. 1(11) (1926), pp. 79–81.

[38] N. F. Bel'chikov, *Dostoyevskii v protsesse petrashevtsev* (Leningrad, Izdaniye Akademii Nauk SSSR, Institut Russkoi literatury, 1936).

[39] Georgi I. Chulkov, *Kak rabotal Dostoyevskii* (Moscow, Sovetskii pisatel', 1939).

[40] V. S. Nechayeva, *V sem'ye i usad'be Dostoyevskikh* (Moscow, Gosudarstvennoye sotsial'no-ekonomicheskoye izdatel'stvo, 1939).

[41] N. K. Piksanov, ed., *Shestidesyatye gody* (Moscow, Izdaniye Akademii Nauk SSSR, 1940).

[42] O. F. Miller and N. N. Strakhov, *Biografiya, pis'ma, zametki iz zapisnoi knigi F. M. Dostoyevskovo* (St. Petersburg, Suvorin, 1883); previously published in Dostoyevski, *Sobraniye sochinenii* [Collected Works] (St. Petersburg, A. G. Dostoyevskaya, Vol. I, 1882).

[43] S. Sharapov, ed., *Moskovskii sbornik* (Moscow, 1887).

[44] *Severnyi vestnik* (St. Petersburg), Nos. 10 and 11 (1891).

[45] Ch. Vetrinski (pseudonym of Vasili Yevgrafovich Cheshikhin), *Dostoyevskii v vospominaniyakh sovremennikov, v pis'makh i zametkakh* (Moscow, Svetin, Vol. I, 1912, and Vol. II, 1914; 2d ed., revised and enlarged, under the title *F. M. Dostoyevskii v vospominaniyakh sovremennikov i v yevo pis'makh* [F. M. Dostoyevski in Reminiscences of His Contemporaries and in His Letters], Moscow, Dumnov, Vol. I, 1923, and Vol. II, 1924).

[46] "Pis'ma Dostoyevskovo k Pobedonostsevu" [Letters of Dostoyevski to Pobedonostsev], *Krasnyi Arkhiv*, No. 2 (1922), pp. 240–55.

[47] *Pis'ma F. M. Dostoyevskovo k zhene* [Letters of F. M. Dostoyevski to His Wife], ed. V. F. Pereverzev, with a foreword and notes by N. F. Bel'chikov (Moscow and Leningrad, Gosizdat, 1926).

[48] *F. M. Dostoyevskii i I. S. Turgenev: Perepiska* [F. M. Dostoyevski and I. S. Turgenev: Correspondence], ed. and with commentaries by I. S. Zil'bershtein, and with an introduction by N. F. Bel'chikov (Moscow and Leningrad, "Academia," 1928).

[49] Yu. Nikol'ski, *Turgenev i Dostoyevskii: Istoriya odnoi vrazhdy* [Turgenev and Dostoyevski: The Story of an Enmity] (Sofia, Ross.-Bolg. Knigoizdatel'stvo, 1921).

[50] See *Pervoye Sobraniye pisem I. S. Turgeneva* [First Collection of Letters of I. S. Turgenev] (St. Petersburg, Izdaniye Obshchestva dlya posobiya nuzhdayushchimsya literatoram i uchonam, 1884), pp. 96–123, *passim;* 314–15.

[51] See André Mazon, "Quelques Lettres de Dostoevsky à Turgenev," *Revue des Etudes Slaves* (Paris), No. 1 (1921), pp. 117–37; the letters of Dostoyevski, in the original Russian, constitute pp. 121–37 of the article.

[52] Dolinin, ed., *Dostoyevskii: Stat'i i materialy*, II, 309–20.

[53] *Iz arkhiva F. M. Dostoyevskovo: Pis'ma russkikh pisatelei* [From the F. M. Dostoyevski Archive: Letters of Russian Writers], ed. and with introduction by N. K. Piksanov, commentaries by N. F. Bel'chikov and N. K. Piksanov (Moscow, GIZ, 1923).

[54] D. I. Abramovich, ed., *Pis'ma russkikh pisatelei k A. S. Suvorinu* (Leningrad, Gosudarstvennaya Publichnaya Biblioteka, 1927).

[55] F. M. Dostoyevski, *Pis'ma* [Letters], ed. A. S. Dolinin (Moscow and Leningrad, Vol. I [for the period 1832–67], Gosizdat, 1928; Vol.

II [for the period 1867–71], Gosizdat, 1930; Vol. III [for the period 1872–77], "Academia," 1934).

⁵⁶ V. L. Komarovich, "Literaturnoye nasledstvo Dostoyevskovo za gody revolyutsii: Obzor publikatsii 1917–1933" [Literary Heritage of Dostoyevski in the Years of the Revolution: A Survey of the Publications of 1917–1933], in *Literaturnoye nasledstvo* [Literary Heritage] (Moscow, Izdaniye zhurnal'no-gazetnovo ob"yedineniya), Issue No. 15 (1934), p. 271. ,

⁵⁷ Dolinin, "Predisloviye" [Foreword], in F. M. Dostoyevski, *Pis'ma*, III, 5–6.

⁵⁸ *Ibid.*, p. 11.   ⁵⁹ *Ibid.*   ⁶⁰ *Ibid.*, p. 13.   ⁶¹ Quoted *ibid.*

⁶² "Ot izdatel'stva" [From the Publishers], *ibid.*, p. 3.

⁶³ *Ibid.*, p. 2.   ⁶⁴ *Ibid.*   ⁶⁵ *Ibid.*   ⁶⁶ *Ibid.*, p. 3.

⁶⁷ *Ibid.*   ⁶⁸ *Ibid.*, p. 2.   ⁶⁹ *Ibid.*, p. 3.

⁷⁰ F. M. Dostoyevski, *Polnoye sobraniye sochinenii* [Complete Works] (14 vols.; St. Petersburg, A. G. Dostoyevskaya, 1882–83). The most important of the other prerevolutionary editions were: *Polnoye sobraniye sochinenii*, with a biographical sketch by D. V. Averkiyev (6 vols.; St. Petersburg, Suvorin, 1885–86); *Polnoye sobraniye sochinenii*, with a biographical sketch by K. K. Sluchevski (St. Petersburg, Tipografiya brat'yev Panteleyevykh, 1889); *Sochineniya* [Works], with a biographical and critical sketch by V. V. Rozanov (12 vols.; St. Petersburg, Marks, 1894–95); *Polnoye sobraniye sochinenii*, with a biographical sketch by S. N. Bulgakov (6th [Jubilee] ed., 14 vols.; St. Petersburg, Tipografiya P. F. Panteleyeva, 1904–6; 7th ed., 12 vols.; St. Petersburg, Tipografiya P. F. Panteleyeva, 1906–7); *Polnoye sobraniye sochinenii* (23 vols.; St. Petersburg, "Prosveshcheniye"): Vols. I–XXI (1911–14), and Vols. XXII–XXIII, ed. L. P. Grossman under the subtitle *Zabytye stranitsy Dostoyevskovo* [Forgotten Pages of Dostoyevski] (critical articles, early writings, variants, etc.) (1916).

⁷¹ F. M. Dostoyevski, *Polnoye sobraniye khudozhestvennykh proizvedenii* [Complete Literary Works], ed. B. V. Tomashevski and K. I. Khalabayev (Moscow and Leningrad, Gosizdat): Vols. I–X (1926–27); Vols. XI–XII, *Dnevnik pisatelya* [Diary of a Writer] (1929); Vol. XIII, *Stat'i za 1845–1878 gody* [Articles of 1845–1878] (1930).

⁷² "Ispoved' Stavrogina," in *Dokumenty po istorii russkoi literatury i*

obshchestvennosti [Documents on the History of Russian Literature and Social Thought] (Moscow), Vol. I (1922). A variant was published in the journal *Byloye*, No. 18 (1923), pp. 227–52.

[73] See R. I. Avanesov, "Dostoyevskii v rabote nad 'Dvoinikom' " [Dostoyevski at Work on *The Double*], in the collection *Tvorcheskaya istoriya* [Creative History], ed. N. K. Piksanov (Moscow, Nikitinskiye subbotniki, 1927), pp. 154–91.

[74] "Rukopisi 'Netochki Nezvanovoi' " [Manuscripts of *Netochka Nezvanova*], ed. N. F. Bel'chikov, *Pechat' i revolyutsiya*, No. 2 (1928), pp. 88–93.

[75] *Iz arkhiva F. M. Dostoyevskovo: "Prestupleniye i nakazaniye,"* Neizdannyi material [From the F. M. Dostoyevski Archive: *Crime and Punishment*, Unpublished Material], ed. I. M. Glivenko (Moscow, GIKhL, 1931). Materials for the novel had been published earlier in *Krasnyi Arkhiv*, No. 6 (1924), pp. 146–200.

[76] *Iz arkhiva F. M. Dostoyevskovo: 'Idiot,'* Neizdannye materialy [From the F. M. Dostoyevski Archive: *The Idiot*, Unpublished Materials], ed. P. N. Sakulin and N. F. Bel'chikov (Moscow, GIKhL, 1931).

[77] See Bel'chikov, "Neizvestnyi rasskaz 'Domovoi' " [An Unknown Story "House Demon"], *Zvezda* [Star] (Leningrad), No. 6 (1930), pp. 257–59.

[78] See Bel'chikov, "Turgenev i Dostoyevskii" [Turgenev and Dostoyevski] (a critique of *Dym* [Smoke]), *Literatura i marksizm* [Literature and Marxism] (Moscow), No. 1 (1928), pp. 63–94; "Turgenev i Dostoyevskii," *Krasnyi Arkhiv*, No. 2 (21) (1927), pp. 241–44.

[79] "Krotkaya," ed. A. S. Dolinin, in *Dostoyevskii: Stat'i i materialy*, II, 439–507.

[80] "Nenapechatannye stranitsy iz 'Zapisok iz myortvovo doma' " [Unpublished Pages from *Notes from the House of the Dead*], *ibid.*, I, 359–67.

[81] "Teksty chernovykh zapisei k 'Brat'yam Karamazovym' " [Texts of the Draft Materials for *The Brothers Karamazov*], in Dolinin, ed., *F. M. Dostoyevskii: Materialy i issledovaniya* [F. M. Dostoyevski: Materials and Studies] (Leningrad, Izd. Akademii Nauk SSSR, 1935), pp. 81–346.

[82] Komarovich, "Langschriftliche Aufzeichnungen, Varianten und Briefe zu dem roman der 'Jüngling,' " in *Der unbekannte Dostojewski*,

ed. René L. Fülop-Miller and Friedrich Eckstein (Munich, R. Piper, 1926), pp. 445–519.

[83] Komarovich, *Die Urgestalt der Brüder Karamasoff*, in *Dostojewskis Quellen, Entwürfe und Fragmente*, ed. René L. Fülop-Miller and Friedrich Eckstein (Munich, R. Piper, 1928).

[84] *Zapisnye tetradi F. M. Dostoyevskovo* [F. M. Dostoyevski's Notebooks], ed. Ye. N. Konshina, with commentaries by N. I. Ignatova and Ye. N. Konshina (Moscow, Academia, 1935). Several chapters were also published in Dolinin, ed., *F. M. Dostoyevskii: Materialy i issledovaniya*, pp. 405–28.

[85] "Zhitiye velikovo greshnika," in Grossman, ed., *Tvorchestvo Dostoyevskovo*.

[86] In regard to *The Idiot*, see Sakulin's analysis of the notes and drafts published in 1931: "K tvorcheskoi istorii romana" [On the Creative History of the Novel], in *Iz arkhiva F. M. Dostoyevskovo: Idiot*. A summary of Dostoyevski's creative process in writing *Crime and Punishment* and *The Idiot*, as revealed in the materials published in 1931, is given in Ernest J. Simmons, *Dostoyevsky: The Making of a Novelist* (London, John Lehmann, 1950), pp. 115–18, and 159–69.

[87] Dolinin, *V tvorcheskoi laboratorii Dostoyevskovo* (Moscow and Leningrad, Sovetskii pisatel', 1947).

[88] In 1956, however, publication of these materials was promised in a volume of *Literaturnoye nasledstvo*; see pp. 297–98.

8: STYLISTIC AND HISTORICAL STUDIES

[1] L. P. Grossman, "Bal'zak i Dostoyevskii," *Russkaya mysl'* [Russian Thought] (Moscow), No. 1 (1914), pp. 44–55.

[2] Grossman, *Biblioteka Dostoyevskovo: Po neizdannym materialam* (Odessa, Ivasenko, 1919).

[3] Grossman, *Poetika Dostoyevskovo* (Moscow, Gosudarstvennaya Akademiya Khudozhestvennykh Nauk, 1925). The collection contained "Kompozitsiya v romane Dostoyevskovo" [Composition of Dostoyevski's Novels], first published in *Vestnik Yevropy* [Courier of Europe] (Petrograd), No. 9 (1916), pp. 121–56; "Dostoyevskii i Bal'zak" [Dostoyevski and Balzac]; "Zhivopis' u Dostoyevskovo" [The Pictorial in Dostoyevski]; "Stilistika Stavrogina" [The Stylistics of Stavrogin]; and

"Iskusstvo romana u Dostoyevskovo" [The Art of the Novel in Dos-
toyevski], first published in the collection *Svitok* [The Scroll] (Moscow,
Nikitinskiye subbotniki, 1922), pp. 73–83.

[4] A. S. Dolinin, "Bluzhdayushchiye obrazy" [Vagrant Characters],
Vestnik literatury [Literary Courier] (Petrograd), No. 2 (26) (1921),
p. 71.

[5] Grossman, "Put' Dostoyevskovo," in *Tvorchestvo Dostoyevskovo*
(Odessa, Vseukrainskoye izdatel'stvo, 1921), pp. 83–110.

[6] Grossman, *Put' Dostoyevskovo* (Leningrad, Brockhaus-Efron,
1924).

[7] "Zametki o yazyke Dostoyevskovo" [Remarks on Dostoyevski's
Language], in *Seminarii po Dostoyevskomu: Materialy, bibliografiya i
kommentarii* [Seminar on Dostoyevski: Materials, Bibliography and
Commentaries] (Moscow, Gosizdat, 1923).

[8] Yuri N. Tynyanov, *Dostoyevskii i Gogol'. K teorii parodii* (Petrograd, "Opoyaz," 1921) (reprinted in his collection of articles *Arkhaisty
i novatory* [Archaists and Innovators] [Leningrad, "Priboi," 1929],
pp. 412–56).

[9] M. P. Alekseyev, "O dramaticheskikh opytakh Dostoyevskovo" [On
Dostoyevski's Experiments in Drama], in Grossman, ed., *Tvorchestvo
Dostoyevskovo*, p. 56.

[10] *Ibid.*, pp. 58–59.

[11] Not to be confused with Western European "naturalism" of the
second half of the nineteenth century. The Russian term "natural
school" is often used interchangeably with "literature of the Gogol
period," and is now used to designate the trend in the 1840s away from
"rhetoric" and prettification toward realistic treatment accompanied by
a growing concern with social problems.

[12] A. I. Beletski, "Dostoyevskii i natural'naya shkola v 1846 g.,"
Nauka na Ukraine [Scholarship in the Ukraine] (Kharkov), No. 4
(1922), pp. 332–42.

[13] N. L. Brodski, ed., *Tvorcheskii put' Dostoyevskovo* (Leningrad,
"Seyatel'," 1924).

[14] V. V. Vinogradov, "Syuzhet i arkhitektonika romana Dostoyevskovo *Bednye lyudi* v svyazi s voprosom o poetike natural'noi shkoly"
[Plot and Architectonics of Dostoyevski's Novel *Poor Folk* in Connec-

tion with the Question of the Style of the Natural School], *ibid.*, pp. 49–103.

[15] V. V. Vinogradov, *Evolyutsiya russkovo naturalizma: Gogol' i Dostoyevskii* (Moscow, "Academia," 1929) ; see especially pp. 291–389.

[16] A. P. Skaftymov, "Tematicheskaya kompozitsiya romana 'Idiot,' " in Brodski, ed., *Tvorcheskii put' Dostoyevskovo*, pp. 131–85.

[17] K. K. Istomin, "Iz zhizni i tvorchestva Dostoyevskovo v molodosti" [From the Life and Work of Dostoyevski in His Youth], *ibid.*, pp. 3–48.

[18] A. Gizetti, "Gordye yazychnitsy," *ibid.*, pp. 186–97.

[19] M. G. Davidovich, "Problema zanimatel'nosti v romanakh Dostoyevskovo," *ibid.*, pp. 104–30.

[20] D. Darski, "Dostoyevskii—myslitel'," *ibid.*, pp. 198–215.

[21] A. G. Tseitlin, *Povesti o bednom chinovnike Dostoyevskovo (K istorii odnovo syuzheta)* (Moscow, Gosizdat, 1923).

[22] Tseitlin, " 'Prestupleniye i nakazaniye' i 'Les Misérables': Sotsiologicheskiye parallely," *Literatura i marksizm* [Literature and Marxism] (Moscow), No. 5 (1928), pp. 20–58.

[23] Tseitlin, "Vremya v romanakh Dostoyevskovo," *Rodnoi yazyk v shkole* [Native Language in the School] (Moscow), No. 2 (1929), pp. 9–36; No. 3, pp. 134–51.

[24] I. Lapshin, "Estetika Dostoyevskovo," in A. S. Dolinin, ed., *Dostoyevskii: Stat'i i materialy*, I (Petrograd, "Mysl'," 1922), 93–152.

[25] V. L. Komarovich, "Nenapisannaya poema Dostoyevskovo," *ibid.*, pp. 177–210.

[26] V. V. Vinogradov, "Stil' peterburgskoi poemy 'Dvoinik,' " *ibid.*, pp. 211–56.

[27] S. Askol'dov, "Psikhologiya kharakterov u Dostoyevskovo," in A. S. Dolinin, ed., *Dostoyevskii: Stat'i i materialy*, II (Leningrad and Moscow, "Mysl'," 1925), 5–30.

[28] B. Engel'gardt, "Ideologicheskii roman Dostoyevskovo" [Dostoyevski's Ideological Novel], *ibid.*, pp. 71–108.

[29] V. L. Komarovich, "Roman 'Podrostok' kak khudozhestvennoye yedinstvo," *ibid.*, pp. 31–70.

[30] V. Sidorov, "O 'Dnevnike pisatelya' " [On *The Diary of a Writer*], *ibid.*, pp. 109–18.

[31] L. P. Grossman, "Stilistika Stavrogina," *ibid.*, pp. 139–48.

³² The following are important in this respect: Ye. Pokrovskaya, "Dostoyevskii i petrashevtsy" [Dostoyevski and the Petrashevtsy], *ibid.*, I, 257–73; A. S. Dolinin, "Dostoyevskii i Gertsen" [Dostoyevski and Herzen], *ibid.*, pp. 275–326; L. K. Il'inski, "F. M. Dostoyevskii i Gl. Iv. Uspenskii" [F. M. Dostoyevski and Gleb Ivanovich Uspenski], *ibid.*, pp. 327–53; "Pis'ma i vospominaniya" [Letters and Reminiscences], *ibid.*, pp. 379–516; Dolinin, "Turgenev v 'Besakh'" [Turgenev in *The Devils*], *ibid.*, II, 119–38, and "Dostoyevskii i Suslova" [Dostoyevski and Suslova], *ibid.*, pp. 153–283; A. G. Dostoyevskaya, "Vospominaniya" [Reminiscences], *ibid.*, pp. 285–301; S. Lyubimov, "K voprosu o genealogii Dostoyevskovo" [On the Question of Dostoyevski's Genealogy], *ibid.*, pp. 303–6; and a number of articles on literary history and of the character of memoirs in the fourth section and in the appendices.

³³ V. S. Nechayeva, "Sravneniya v rannikh povestyakh Dostoyevskovo," in *Dostoyevskii* (Moscow, 1928), pp. 83–114 (Issue No. 3 of *Trudy Gosudarstvennoi Akademii Khudozhestvennykh Nauk, Literaturnaya Sektsiya* [Papers of the State Academy of the Arts, Literature Section]).

³⁴ M. A. Petrovski, "Kompozitsiya 'Vechnovo muzha,'" *ibid.*, pp. 115–62.

³⁵ S. N. Durylin, "Ob odnom simvole u Dostoyevskovo," *ibid.*, pp. 163–98.

³⁶ V. S. Dorovatovskaya-Lyubimova, "Dostoyevskii i shestidesyatniki," *ibid.*, pp. 5–60.

³⁷ F. F. Berezhkov, "Dostoyevskii na Zapade," *ibid.*, pp. 277–326.

³⁸ P. S. Popov, "'Ya' i 'Ono' v tvorchestve Dostoyevskovo," *ibid.*, pp. 217–75.

³⁹ Georgi I. Chulkov, "Posledneye slovo Dostoyevskovo o Belinskom," *ibid.*, pp. 61–81.

⁴⁰ M. M. Bakhtin, *Problemy tvorchestva Dostoyevskovo* (Leningrad, "Priboi," 1929).

⁴¹ For a detailed account of developments on the Soviet literary scene during the period 1928–32, see Edward J. Brown, *The Proletarian Episode in Russian Literature 1928–1932* (New York, Columbia University Press, 1953).

[42] L. Pogozheva, "Kompozitsiya romana 'Prestupleniye i nakazaniye,' " *Literaturnaya uchoba* [Literary Studies] (Moscow), No. 8–9 (August-September, 1939), pp. 110–20.

[43] Pogozheva, "Masterstvo kolorita u Dostoyevskovo," *ibid.*, No. 4 (1939), pp. 51–61.

[44] B. G. Reizov, "K istorii zamysla 'Brat'yev Karamazovykh,' " in *Zven'ya* [Links] (Moscow and Leningrad, "Academia"), Issue No. 6 (1936), pp. 545–73.

9: THE QUESTION OF DOSTOYEVSKI AND REVOLUTION

[1] D. S. Merezhkovski, "Prorok russkoi revolyutsii," in *Polnoye sobraniye sochinenii* [Complete Works] (St. Petersburg and Moscow, Vol' f), IX (1911), 175.

[2] *Ibid.*, p. 223.   [3] *Ibid.*

[4] V. F. Pereverzev, "Dostoyevskii i revolyutsiya (k stoletiyu so dnya rozhdeniya)" [Dostoyevski and Revolution (on the One-hundredth Anniversary of His Birth)], *Pechat' i revolyutsiya* [Press and Revolution] (Moscow), No. 3 (1921), pp. 3–10; reprinted in lieu of foreword to Pereverzev's book *Tvorchestvo Dostoyevskovo* [Dostoyevski's Writing] (2d ed.; Moscow, Gosizdat, 1922), pp. 3–14.

[5] Pereverzev, "Dostoyevskii i revolyutsiya," *Tvorchestvo Dostoyevskovo*, p. 4.

[6] *Ibid.*, p. 6.   [7] *Ibid.*, p. 8.   [8] *Ibid.*

[9] *Ibid.*   [10] *Ibid.*, p. 13.   [11] *Ibid.*

[12] S. Shchukin, *Dve kritiki: Plekhanov i Pereverzev* (Moscow, Gosizdat RSFSR, 1930); see especially Chapter 10, "Dostoyevskii, Pereverzev i revolyutsiya" [Dostoyevski, Pereverzev and Revolution].

[13] See *Literaturnaya gazeta* [Literary Gazette] (Moscow), February 9, 1931.

[14] A. G. Tseitlin, "Dostoyevskii i revolyutsiya" [Dostoyevski and Revolution], *ibid.*

[15] Terrorist bands organized by monarchist sympathizers after the 1905 revolution to carry out pogroms against Jews and also against intellectuals and workers suspected of revolutionary tendencies.

[16] Tseitlin, "Dostoyevskii i revolyutsiya."

[17] *Ibid.*   [18] *Ibid.*

[19] N. L. Brodski, "Neizdannye materialy F. M. Dostoyevskovo" [Unpublished Materials of F. M. Dostoyevski], *ibid.*

[20] Editorial note, *ibid.*

[21] Levidov, "Mif o Dostoyevskom: Razroznennye mysli," *ibid.*

[22] *Ibid.*

[23] The letter was published under the heading "O nekotorykh voprosakh istorii bolshevizma" [Concerning Certain Questions in the History of Bolshevism], in *Proletarskaya revolyutsiya* (Moscow), No. 6 (113) (1931), pp. 3–12.

[24] "Ot redaktsii" [From the Editors], *Literaturnaya gazeta*, February 9, 1931. The "oncoming revolution" referred to is the industrialization of the USSR and the collectivization of agriculture during the first Five-Year Plan.

[25] V. I. Lenin, "Lev Tolstoi kak zerkalo russkoi revolyutsii," *Proletarii* [The Proletarian] (Geneva, September 11, 1908); reprinted in Lenin, *Sochineniya* [Works] (4th ed.; Moscow, Gospolitizdat), XV (1947), 179–86.

[26] A. S. Dolinin, "Brat'ya Karamazovy (k istorii sozdaniya 'Brat'yev Karamazovykh')" [*The Brothers Karamazov:* More on the Story of the Creation of *The Brothers Karamazov*], in Dolinin, ed., *F. M. Dostoyevskii: Materialy i issledovaniya* [F. M. Dostoyevski: Materials and Studies] (Leningrad, Izdaniye Akademii Nauk SSSR, 1935), p. 80.

[27] *Ibid.*, p. 32.

10: V. F. PEREVERZEV: THEORIST OF THE SOCIOLOGICAL SCHOOL

[1] *Rossiiskaya Assotsiatsiya nauchno-issledovatel'skikh institutov obshchestvennykh nauk* (Russian Association of Scientific Research Institutes of the Social Sciences).

[2] V. F. Pereverzev, ed., *Literaturovedeniye* (Moscow, GAKhN, 1928).

[3] A. Mikhailov, "Pereverzev," in *Literaturnaya entsiklopediya* [Literary Encyclopedia] (Moscow, OGIZ RSFSR), VIII (1934), col. 503.

[4] V. F. Pereverzev, "Neobkhodimye predposylki marksistskovo literaturovedeniya," in *Literaturovedeniye*, pp. 3–18.

[5] Pereverzev, "Problemy marksistskovo literaturovedeniya," *Litera-*

tura i marksizm [Literature and Marxism] (Moscow), No. 2 (1929), pp. 20–34.

[6] Pereverzev, "Neobkhodimye predposylki," in *Literaturovedeniye*, pp. 14–15.

[7] *Ibid.*, p. 18.

[8] Pereverzev, "Problemy marksistskovo literaturovedeniya," *Literatura i marksizm*, No. 2 (1929), pp. 20–21.

[9] Pereverzev, *Tvorchestvo Dostoyevskovo: Kriticheskii ocherk* [Dostoyevski's Writing: A Critical Sketch], with a Foreword by P. N. Sakulin (Moscow, "Sovremennye problemy," 1912; 2d ed., Moscow, Gosizdat, 1922; 3d ed., Moscow, Gosizdat, 1928).

[10] Pereverzev, *F. M. Dostoyevskii* (Moscow and Leningrad, Gosizdat, 1925), in the series *Biograficheskaya biblioteka* [Biographical Library]; 3d ed., 1928.

[11] Pereverzev, "Dostoyevskii, Fyodor Mikhailovich," *Literaturnaya entsiklopediya*, III (1930), cols. 396–408.

[12] *Ibid.*, col. 401.   [13] Pereverzev, *F. M. Dostoyevski* (1925), p. 76.

[14] *Ibid.*, p. 78.   [15] *Ibid.*, p. 113.   [16] *Ibid.*, p. 118.   [17] *Ibid.*, p. 133.

[18] Quoted in A. S. Dolinin, *V tvorcheskoi laboratorii Dostoyevskovo* [In Dostoyevski's Creative Laboratory] (Moscow, "Sovetskii pisatel'," 1947), p. 137.

[19] *Ibid.*

[20] Pereverzev, "O teorii sotsial'novo zakaza" [On the Theory of the Social Command], *Pechat' i revolyutsiya* [Press and Revolution] (Moscow), No. 1 (1929), pp. 62–63 (quoted in A. Mikhailov, "Pereverzev," col. 508).

[21] Dostoyevski, "Pushkin," in "Dnevnik pisatelya" [Diary of a Writer] (1880), *Polnoye sobraniye sochinenii* (St. Petersburg, Suvorin), V (1886), 774.

[22] Quoted in Dolinin, *V tvorcheskoi laboratorii Dostoyevskovo*, p. 147.

[23] See O. F. Miller and N. N. Strakhov, *Biografiya, pis'ma i zametki iz zapisnoi knizhki F. M. Dostoyevskovo* [Biography of F. M. Dostoyevski, Letters, and Notes from His Notebook] (St. Petersburg, Suvorin, 1883), p. 378.

11: GEORGI YEFIMOVICH GORBACHOV: DOSTOYEVSKI
AS A WARNING AGAINST INDIVIDUALISM

[1] G. Ye. Gorbachov, *Kapitalizm i russkaya literatura* (Leningrad, GIZ, 1925), pp. 85–110. The section cited is reprinted under the title "Dostoyevskii i yevo reaktsionnyi demokratizm" [Dostoyevski and His Reactionary Democratism] in the volume *F. M. Dostoyevskii* (Moscow, "Nikitinskiye subbotniki," 1928), pp. 207–59 (Vol. III of *Klassiki v marksistskom osveshchenii* [The Classics in the Light of Marxism], in the series *Biblioteka pisatelei dlya shkoly i yunoshestva* [Library of Writers for Schools and Young People], ed. Ye. F. Nikitina).

[2] "Revolyutsiya i Dostoyevskii," *Zapiski Petrogradskovo im. Tolmachova Instruktorskovo Instituta* [Notes of the Tolmachov Teachers Institute of Petrograd] (Petrograd), No. 3 (1922), pp. 1–28.

[3] "Sotsial'nye korni propovedi Dostoyevskovo," *Bor'ba klassov* [The Class Struggle] (Leningrad), No. 1–2 (1924), pp. 172–207.

[4] *Ibid.*, p. 172.   [5] *Ibid.*   [6] *Ibid.*, p. 177.   [7] *Ibid.*, p. 178.

[8] Gorbachov, "Dostoyevskii i yevo reaktsionnyi demokratizm," in *F. M. Dostoyevskii*, p. 214.

[9] *Ibid.*, p. 224.   [10] *Ibid.*, pp. 255–56.

[11] V. F. Pereverzev, "Dostoyevskii v kritike" [Dostoyevski in Criticism], in F. M. Dostoyevski, *Sochineniya* [Works], ed. A. V. Lunacharski (Moscow and Leningrad, GIKhL, 1931), p. 34.

12: V. L'VOV-ROGACHEVSKI AND LEV VOITOLOVSKI:
DOSTOYEVSKI IN SURVEYS OF RUSSIAN LITERATURE

[1] V. L'vov-Rogachevski (pseudonym of Vasili L'vovich Rogachevski), *Noveishaya russkaya literatura* (6th ed., rev.; Moscow, "Mir," 1927).

[2] Yakov Antonovich Nazarenko, *Istoriya russkoi literatury XIX veka* (Leningrad, GIZ, 1925; 2d ed., rev., Moscow and Leningrad, GIZ, 1926; 3d ed., Moscow and Leningrad, GIZ, 1927).

[3] Oblomov is the hero of Goncharov's novel of the same name, Tentetnikov a character in Gogol's *Dead Souls*, and Lavretski the hero of Turgenev's *Nest of Gentlefolk*.

[4] L'vov-Rogachevski, p. 113.

[5] "Otryvok iz romana 'Shchedrodarov,'" *Epokha* [Epoch] (St. Petersburg), No. 5 (May, 1864).

[6] L'vov-Rogachevski, p. 114.

[7] "Hamlet of the Shchigrov District" is the title of a story by Turgenev.

[8] L'vov-Rogachevski, p. 116.   [9] *Ibid.*

[10] L. Dostoyevskaya, *Dostoyevskii v izobrazhenii yevo docheri L. Dostoyevskoi* [Dostoyevski As Portrayed by His Daughter L. Dostoyevskaya], trans. L. Ya. Krukovskaya, ed. and with a Foreword by A. G. Gornfel'd (Moscow and Petrograd, Gosizdat, 1922), p. 17.

[11] L'vov-Rogachevski, p. 118.

[12] *Ibid.*   [13] *Ibid.*   [14] *Ibid.*, p. 119.   [15] *Ibid.*, p. 121.

[16] *Ibid.*, pp. 121–22.   [17] *Ibid.*, p. 122.   [18] *Ibid.*, p. 123.

[19] *Ibid.*, p. 125.   [20] *Ibid.*, p. 129.

[21] See S. Lyubimov, "F. M. Dostoyevskii (Vopros ob yevo proiskhozhdenii)" [F. M. Dostoyevski: The Question of His Origin], *Literaturnaya mysl'* [Literary Thought] (Petrograd), No. 1 (1923), pp. 208–10.

[22] L'vov-Rogachevski, p. 129.   [23] *Ibid.*, p. 131.   [24] *Ibid.*, p. 113.

[25] *Ibid.*, p. 131.   [26] *Ibid.*, p. 134.   [27] *Ibid.*, p. 135.

[28] L. Novitskaya, "L'vov-Rogachevskii," *Literaturnaya entsiklopediya* [Literary Encyclopedia] (Moscow, OGIZ RSFSR), Vol. VI (1932), col. 645.

[29] L. N. Voitolovski, "F. M. Dostoyevskii: K tridtsatiletiyu so dnya konchiny" [F. M. Dostoyevski: On the Thirtieth Anniversary of His Death], *Kiyevskaya mysl'* [Kievan Thought] (Kiev), No. 28 (1911).

[30] Voitolovski, *Istoriya russkoi literatury XIX i XX vekov* (Moscow, GIZ), I (1926), 232–48.

[31] *F. M. Dostoyevskii* (Moscow, "Nikitinskiye subbotniki," 1928), pp. 169–204 (Vol. III of *Klassiki v marksistskom osveshchenii* [The Classics in the Light of Marxism], in the series *Biblioteka pisatelei dlya shkoly i yunoshestva* [Library of Writers for Schools and Young People], ed. Ye. F. Nikitina).

[32] *Ibid.*, p. 177.   [33] *Ibid.*, p. 182.   [34] *Ibid.*, p. 185.   [35] *Ibid.*, p. 186.

13: LEONID GROSSMAN: FROM APOLOGETICS TO
ACCUSATION

[1] L. Grossman, *Put' Dostoyevskovo* [The Path of Dostoyevski] (2d
ed.; Moscow, "Sovremennye problemy," 1928), p. 12 (Vol. II, Part
One, of Grossman's *Sobraniye sochinenii* [Collected Works]). The first
edition of the book, an expansion and reworking of a 1921 article of
the same title, was published in Leningrad in 1924.

[2] *Put' Dostoyevskovo*, 2d ed., pp. 207–8.

[3] Grossman, "Dostoyevskii i pravitel'stvennye krugi 1870–kh godov,"
Literaturnoye nasledstvo [Literary Heritage] (Moscow, Izdaniye
zhurnal'no-gazetnovo ob"yedineniya), Issue No. 15 (1934), pp. 92–93.

[4] *Ibid.*, p. 96. [5] *Ibid.*, p. 114. [6] *Ibid.*, p. 96. [7] *Ibid.*, p. 94.

14: ANATOLI LUNACHARSKI: THE OLD-GUARD
PARTY INTELLECTUAL

[1] See Lunacharski, "Russkii Faust" [The Russian Faust], *Voprosy
psikhologii i filosofii* [Questions of Psychology and Philosophy] (Moscow), No. 3 (May–June, 1902), pp. 783–95; and *Etyudi: Kriticheskiye
i polemicheskiye stat'i* [Studies: Critical and Polemical Articles] (St.
Petersburg, "Pravda," 1905).

[2] Lunacharski, "Dostoyevskii kak khudozhnik i myslitel'," *Krasnaya
nov'* [Red Virgin Soil] (Moscow), No. 4 (1921), pp. 204–12. The essay
was republished in Lunacharski, *Literaturnye siluety* [Literary Silhou-
ettes] (2d ed.; Leningrad, GIZ, 1925), pp. 155–69; and in *F. M. Dostoyevskii* (Moscow, "Nikitinskiye subbotniki," 1928), pp. 7–29 (Vol. III
of *Klassiki v marksistskom osveshchenii* [The Classics in the Light of
Marxism], in the series *Biblioteka pisatelei dlya shkol i yunoshestva*
[Library of Writers for Schools and Young People], ed. Ye. F. Nikitina).

[3] Lunacharski, "Dostoyevskii kak myslitel' i khudozhnik" [Dosto-
yevski as Thinker and Artist], in F. M. Dostoyevski, *Sochineniya*
[Works], ed. A. V. Lunacharski (Moscow and Leningrad, GIKhL,
1931), pp. v–xiv; republished in Lunacharski, *Klassiki russkoi literatury*
[Classics of Russian Literature], ed. and with commentaries by N. F.
Bel'chikov (Moscow, GIKhL, 1937), pp. 295–311.

[4] Lunacharski, "O Dostoyevskom," *Rost* [Growth] (Moscow), No. 4 (1931); reprinted in Lunacharski, *Russkaya literatura* [Russian Literature], ed. and with commentaries by N. F. Bel'chikov (Moscow, OGIZ, 1947), pp. 241–46.

[5] Lunacharski, "Dostoyevskii i pisateli," *Literaturnaya gazeta* [Literary Gazette] (Moscow), February 9, 1931.

[6] Lunacharski, "Dostoyevskii, F. M.," *Bol'shaya sovetskaya entsiklopediya*, Vol. XXIII (1931), cols. 332–45.

[7] Lunacharski, "Dostoyevskii kak khudozhnik i myslitel'," in *F. M. Dostoyevskii* (1928), p. 22.

[8] *Ibid.*, p. 29.

[9] Lunacharski, "Dostoyevskii kak myslitel' i khudozhnik," in *Dostoyevski, Sochineniya* (1931), p. vi.

[10] *Ibid.*   [11] *Ibid.*, p. ix.   [12] *Ibid.*, p. x.   [13] *Ibid.*, p. xi.

[14] *Ibid.*   [15] *Ibid.*, pp. xi–xii.   [16] *Ibid.*, p. xii.

[17] *Ibid.*, pp. xiii–xiv.   [18] Lunacharski, "Dostoyevskii i pisateli."

[19] *Ibid.*   [20] *Ibid.*   [21] *Ibid.*

[22] Lunacharski, "Dostoyevskii kak myslitel' i khudozhnik," in *Dostoyevski, Sochineniya* (1931), p. xiv.

15: M. M. BAKHTIN ON DOSTOYEVSKI'S POLYPHONIC NOVEL

[1] M. M. Bakhtin, *Problemy tvorchestva Dostoyevskovo* (Leningrad, "Priboi," 1929).

[2] *Ibid.*, p. 4.   [3] *Ibid.*

[4] See S. Askol'dov, "Religiozno-eticheskoye znacheniye Dostoyevskovo" [The Religious and Ethical Significance of Dostoyevski], in A. S. Dolinin, ed., *Dostoyevskii: Stat'i i materialy* [Dostoyevski: Articles and Materials], I (Petrograd, "Mysl'," 1922), 2 and 5.

[5] Leonid Grossman, *Poetika Dostoyevskovo* (Moscow, Gosudarstvennaya Akademiya Khudozhestvennykh Nauk, 1925), p. 175.

[6] Grossman, Leonid, *Put' Dostoyevskovo* (Leningrad, Brockhaus-Efron, 1924), p. 10.

[7] Otto Kaus, *Dostojewski und sein Schicksal* (Berlin, Laub, 1923).

[8] Bakhtin, p. 30.

[9] V. L. Komarovich, "Roman 'Podrostok' kak khudozhestvennoye

yedinstvo," in A. S. Dolinin, ed., *Dostoyevskii: Stat'i i materialy*, II (Leningrad and Moscow, "Mysl'," 1925), 31–70.

[10] B. M. Engel'gardt, "Ideologicheskii roman Dostoyevskovo" [Dostoyevski's Ideological Novel], *ibid.*, p. 91.

[11] Bakhtin, p. 43.   [12] *Ibid.*, p. 45.   [13] *Ibid.*, p. 51.

[14] *Ibid.*   [15] *Ibid.*   [16] *Ibid.*

[17] *Ibid.*, p. 52.   [18] *Ibid.*, p. 53.   [19] *Ibid.*, p. 70.

[20] *Ibid.*, p. 85.   [21] *Ibid.*, p. 88–89.   [22] *Ibid.*, p. 95.

[23] Grossman, *Poetika Dostoyevskovo*, p. 53.   [24] *Ibid.*, p. 56.

[25] *Ibid.*, p. 57.   [26] Bakhtin, p. 99.   [27] *Ibid.*, pp. 212–13.

[28] *Ibid.*, p. 238.   [29] *Ibid.*, pp. 240–41.   [30] *Ibid.*, p. 243.

[31] N. Berkovski, in *Zvezda* [Star] (Leningrad), No. 7 (1929), pp. 187–89.

[32] *Oktyabr'* (Moscow), No. 11 (1929), p. 196.   [33] *Ibid.*, p. 197.

[34] I. Grossman-Roshchin, "Dni nashei zhizni. O poznavayemosti khudozhestvennovo proshlovo: O sotsiologizme M. M. Bakhtina, avtora knigi 'Problemy tvorchestva Dostoyevskovo' " [Days of Our Life: On the Cognoscibility of the Artistic Past: On the Sociologism of M. M. Bakhtin, Author of the Book *Problems of Dostoyevski's Writing*], *Na literaturnom postu* (Moscow), No. 18 (1929), pp. 5–10.

[35] A. V. Lunacharski, "O mnogogolosnosti Dostoyevskovo (po povodu knigi M. M. Bakhtina 'Problemy tvorchestva Dostoyevskovo')" [On the Polyphony of Dostoyevski (in Connection with M. M. Bakhtin's Book *Problems of Dostoyevski's Writing*)], *Novyi mir* [New World] (Moscow), No. 10 (1929), pp. 195–209; reprinted in Lunacharski, *Klassiki russkoi literatury* [Classics of Russian Literature], ed. N. F. Bel'chikov (Moscow, GIKhL, 1937), pp. 312–34.

[36] Lunacharski, "O mnogogolosnosti Dostoyevskovo," *Klassiki russkoi literatury*, pp. 314–15.

[37] A. V. Lunacharski, "Dostoyevskii kak myslitel' i khudozhnik" [Dostoyevski as a Thinker and Artist], in F. M. Dostoyevski, *Sochineniya* [Works], ed. Lunacharski (Moscow and Leningrad, GIKhL, 1931), p. ix.

[38] *Ibid.*, pp. ix–x.

16: THE TWO TRENDS OF THE 1930S

[1] M. Polyakova, "Sotsial'naya priroda geroyev Dostoyevskovo," *Novyi mir* [New World] (Moscow), No. 4 (1931), pp. 145–54.

[2] *Ibid.*, p. 152.

[3] *Zapisnye tetradi F. M. Dostoyevskovo,* ed. Ye. N. Konshina, with commentaries by N. I. Ignatova and Ye. N. Konshina (Moscow, Academia, 1935).

[4] From *Poshchochina obshchestvennomu vkusu* [A Slap on the Face to Public Taste], quoted in "Lef," *Literaturnaya entsiklopediya* [Literary Encyclopedia] (Moscow, OGIZ), Vol. VI (1932), col. 344. For a partial English translation, see George Reavey and Marc Slonim, *Soviet Literature: An Anthology* (New York, Covici Friede, 1934), pp. 394–95.

[5] V. V. Yermilov, "Gor'kii i Dostoyevskii," *Krasnaya nov'* [Red Virgin Soil] (Moscow), No. 4 (April, 1939), pp. 157–77; No. 5–6 (May–June, 1939), pp. 240–72.

[6] *Ibid.*, No. 4, p. 159.   [7] *Ibid.*, p. 161.   [8] *Ibid.*

[9] From the name of the village described by Gorki in *Gorodok Okurov* [The Town of Okurov, 1909] and elsewhere as an example of the viciousness, ignorance, and stagnation of Russian provincial life, which only a few isolated individuals were striving to overcome.

[10] Yermilov, "Gor'kii i Dostoyevskii," No. 5–6, p. 254.

[11] *Ibid.*, p. 266.   [12] *Ibid.*   [13] *Ibid.*, p. 268.

[14] G. I. Chulkov, *Kak rabotal Dostoyevskii* (Moscow, Sovetskii pisatel', 1939).

[15] F. M. Dostoyevski, *Pis'ma* [Letters], ed. A. S. Dolinin (Moscow and Leningrad), I (Gosizdat, 1928), 142.

[16] *Ibid.*, II (1930), 263.

[17] F. M. Dostoyevski, "Iz zapisnoi knizhki F. M. Dostoyevskovo" [From the Notebook of F. M. Dostoyevski], in *Sobraniye sochinenii* [Collected Works] (St. Petersburg), I (1883), 368.

[18] *Ibid.*, p. 375.   [19] Chulkov, p. 335.

[20] F. M. Dostoyevski, *Povesti* [Short Novels], ed. O. V. Tsekhnovitser (Leningrad, GIKhL, 1940).

[21] Tsekhnovitser, "Povesti Dostoyevskovo" [Dostoyevski's Short Novels], *ibid.*, p. 479.

[22] *Ibid.*   [23] *Ibid.*, p. 480.

17: THE SECOND WORLD WAR AND THE REHABILITATION
OF DOSTOYEVSKI

[1] See, for example, N. L., "Dostoyevskii o Germanii i Nemtsakh" [Dostoyevski on Germany and the Germans], *Rech'* [Speech] (St. Petersburg), No. 290 (October 27, 1914), p. 3.

[2] Yem. Yaroslavski, "Fyodor Mikhailovich Dostoyevskii protiv nemtsev" [Fyodor Mikhailovich Dostoyevski against the Germans], *Bol'shevik* (Moscow), No. 16 (August, 1942), pp. 38–43.

[3] *Ibid.*, p. 40.   [4] *Ibid.*, p. 41.   [5] *Ibid.*, p. 43.

[6] Il'ya Ehrenburg, "Zrelost'," *ibid.*, p. 94.

[7] See Edward J. Brown, *The Proletarian Episode in Russian Literature, 1928–1932* (New York, Columbia University Press, 1953), *passim*.

[8] V. V. Yermilov, "Velikii russkii pisatel' F. M. Dostoyevskii," *Literatura i iskusstvo* (Moscow, September 5, 1942).

[9] *Ibid.*   [10] *Ibid.*   [11] *Ibid.*

[12] L. Dmitriyev, "O novoi povesti M. Zoshchenko" [About M. Zoshchenko's New Story], *Literatura i iskusstvo* (December 4, 1943).

18: THE 125TH ANNIVERSARY OF DOSTOYEVSKI'S BIRTH

[1] D. I. Zaslavski, "O Dostoyevskom: 125 let so dnya rozhdeniya" [Concerning Dostoyevski: The 125th Anniversary of His Birth], *Literaturnaya gazeta* [Literary Gazette] (Moscow, November 16, 1946).

[2] *Ibid.*

[3] V. Aleksandrov, "F. M. Dostoyevskii," *Ogonyok* [The Light] (Moscow), No. 46–47 (November, 1946), pp. 26–27.

[4] V. A. Desnitski, "M. Gor'kii i natsional'nye traditsii russkoi literatury," in *Uchonye zapiski Gosudarstvennovo Pedagogicheskovo Instituta im. Gertsena* [Scholarly Papers of the Herzen State Pedagogical Institute] (Leningrad), LVIII (1947), 18.

[5] Yu. Yuzovski, "Rostovskiye spektakli" [Rostov Plays], *Teatral'nyi al'manakh* [Theatrical Almanac] (Moscow), No. 1 (1946), p. 38.

[6] B. Yemel'yanov, "Dva gor'kovskikh spektaklya" [Two Gorki Plays], *Teatr* [Theater] (Moscow), No. 5–6 (1946), p. 33.

[7] A. S. Dolinin, *V tvorcheskoi laboratorii Dostoyevskovo: Istoriya sozdaniya romana "Podrostok"* [In Dostoyevski's Creative Laboratory:

The History of the Creation of the Novel *A Raw Youth*] (Moscow, "Sovetskii pisatel'," 1947), p. 6.

[8] See A. S. Dolinin, "Brat'ya Karamazovy (k istorii sozdaniya 'Brat'yev Karamazovykh')" [*The Brothers Karamazov*: More on the Story of the Creation of *The Brothers Karamazov*], in *F. M. Dostoyevskii: Materialy i issledovaniya* [F. M. Dostoyevski: Materials and Studies], ed. Dolinin (Leningrad, Izd. Akademii Nauk SSSR, 1935), pp. 9–80.

[9] V. Ya. Kirpotin, " 'Bednye lyudi'—pervyi roman F. M. Dostoyevskovo" [*Poor Folk*, F. M. Dostoyevski's First Novel], *Oktyabr'* [October] (Moscow), No. 1–2 (1946), pp. 160–70.

[10] Kirpotin, *Molodoi Dostoyevskii* (Moscow, GIKhL, 1947).

[11] Kirpotin, "Fyodor Mikhailovich Dostoyevskii (k 125-letiyu so dnya rozhdeniya)" [On the 125th Anniversary of His Birth], *Zvezda* (Leningrad), No. 11 (1946), pp. 173–88.

[12] Kirpotin, *F. M. Dostoyevskii* (Moscow, Sovetskii pisatel', 1947).

[13] Kirpotin, "Fyodor Mikhailovich Dostoyevskii," *Zvezda*, p. 173.

[14] *Ibid.*, p. 180.   [15] *Ibid.*, p. 182.   [16] *Ibid.*, p. 185.   [17] *Ibid.*

[18] *Ibid.*, pp. 185–86.   [19] *Ibid.*, p. 186.   [20] *Ibid.*, p. 185.

[21] *Ibid.*, p. 186.   [22] *Ibid.*, p. 188.   [23] *Ibid.*

[24] Kirpotin, *Molodoi Dostoyevskii*, p. 358.

[25] R. Uralov, "Pravda o Dostoyevskom (o knige V. Kirpotina 'Molodoi Dostoyevskii')" [The Truth About Dostoyevski: On V. Kirpotin's Book *The Young Dostoyevski*], *Literaturnaya gazeta* (Moscow, November 26, 1947).

[26] F. Yevnin, "Novaya kniga o Dostoyevskom (o knige V. Kirpotina 'F. M. Dostoyevskii')" [A New Book on Dostoyevski: On V. Kirpotin's Book *F. M. Dostoyevski*], *Novyi mir* [New World] (Moscow), No. 10 (October, 1947), p. 262.

19: ZHDANOVISM AND THE COLLAPSE OF DOSTOYEVSKI SCHOLARSHIP

[1] This directive and those referred to below are assembled in a pamphlet headed *O zhurnalakh "Zvezda" i "Leningrad": Iz postanov-leniya TsK VKP(b) ot 14 avgusta 1946 g.* [On the Journals *Zvezda* and *Leningrad:* From the Resolution of the Central Committee of the

All-Union Communist Party (Bolsheviks) of August 14, 1946] (Moscow, Gospolitizdat, 1952).

² "Doklad t. Zhdanova o zhurnalakh 'Zvezda' i 'Leningrad': Obobshchonnaya stenogramma dokladov na sobranii partiinovo aktiva i na sobranii pisatelei v Leningrade" [Report of Comrade Zhdanov on the Journals *Zvezda* and *Leningrad*: Composite and Condensed Stenographic Transcript of the Reports at the Meeting of the Leningrad Party *Aktiv* and the Meeting of Leningrad Writers], *Literaturnaya gazeta* [Literary Gazette] (Moscow, September 21, 1946).

³ See the pamphlet *O zhurnalakh*, cited above.

⁴ D. I. Zaslavski, "Protiv idealizatsii reaktsionnykh vzglyadov Dostoyevskovo," *Kul'tura i zhizn'* (Moscow, December 20, 1947).

⁵ See V. V. Yermilov, "F. M. Dostoyevskii i nasha kritika" [F. M. Dostoyevski and Our Criticism], *Literaturnaya gazeta* (December 24, 1947).

⁶ Zaslavski, "Protiv idealizatsii reaktsionnykh vzglyadov Dostoyevskovo."

⁷ *Ibid.*   ⁸ *Ibid.*

⁹ The *Smenovekhovtsy* (literally "change of landmarks group") were Russian *émigrés*, mainly of the intelligentsia, who had fled Russia after the revolution of November, 1917, but, upon the inauguration of the New Economic Policy, modified their political views in favor of the Soviet Union. The name derives from the title of a collection of essays published by such *émigrés* in Prague in 1921, *Smena vekh* [Changing of Landmarks], in contradistinction to the title *Vekhi* [Landmarks], used in 1909 for the manifesto of apostates from the revolutionary cause. See p. 72.

¹⁰ Zaslavski, "Protiv idealizatsii reaktsionnykh vzglyadov Dostoyevskovo."

¹¹ *Ibid.*   ¹² *Ibid.*   ¹³ *Ibid.*

¹⁴ V. V. Yermilov, *Protiv reaktsionnykh idei v tvorchestve Dostoyevskovo* (Moscow, Pravda, 1948).

¹⁵ *Ibid.*, p. 4.   ¹⁶ *Ibid.*, p. 7.   ¹⁷ *Ibid.*, p. 8.   ¹⁸ *Ibid.*
¹⁹ *Ibid.*, p. 10.   ²⁰ *Ibid.*   ²¹ *Ibid.*, p. 15.   ²² *Ibid.*, p. 16.
²³ *Ibid.*, p. 17.

²⁴ I. Al'tman, "Grubaya fal'sifikatsiya," *Znamya* [Banner] (Moscow), No. 3 (1948), p. 184.

[25] N. Burov, "Apologety reaktsionnykh idei Dostoyevskovo," *Literaturnaya gazeta* (January 3, 1948).

[26] F. M. Dostoyevskii, *Izbrannye sochineniya*, ed. B. V. Tomashevski (Moscow, GIKhL, 1946).

[27] F. M. Dostoyevskii, *Mal'chiki* (*iz romana "Brat'ya Karamazovy"*) (Moscow, Detgiz, 1947) (in the series *Biblioteka shkol'nika* [Library for the School Child]).

[28] Quoted from Burov, "Apologety reaktsionnykh idei Dostoyevskovo."

[29] *Ibid.*

[30] Quoted in an editorial entitled "Bol'shevistskaya partiinost'—osnova sovetskovo literaturovedeniya" [Bolshevik Party Spirit, the Basis of Soviet Literary Scholarship], *Literaturnaya gazeta* (November 13, 1948).

[31] *Ibid.*

[32] See the editorial "Protiv idealizma i nizkopoklonstva v yazykoznanii" [Against Idealism and Kowtowing in Linguistic Scholarship], *Literaturnaya gazeta* (November 17, 1948).

[33] B. Byalik, "Gorky and Dostoyevski," *Soviet Literature* (Moscow, 1948), No. 10, pp. 134–40.

[34] B. Byalik, "Bor'ba Gor'kovo-khudozhnika protiv reaktsionnykh idei Dostoyevskovo," in A. M. Yegolin, B. V. Mikhailovski, and S. M. Petrov, eds., *Gor'kovskiye chteniya, 1949–1950* [Gorki Lectures, 1949–1950] (Moscow, Izd. Akademii Nauk SSSR, 1951), pp. 418–65.

[35] S. Borshchevski, "Shchedrin i Dostoyevskii: Iz istorii ikh ideinoi bor'by" [Shchedrin and Dostoyevski: From the Story of Their Ideological Combat], *Novyi mir* [New World] (Moscow), No. 4 (1948), pp. 251–71.

[36] U. A. Gural'nik, "*Sovremennik* v bor'be s zhurnalami Dostoyevskovo" [*The Contemporary* in the Fight with Dostoyevski's Journals], *Izvestiya Akademii Nauk SSSR, Otdeleniye Literatury i yazyka* [News of the USSR Academy of Sciences, Literature and Language Section] (Moscow and Leningrad), IX, No. 4 (1950), 265–85.

[37] "Dostoyevskii, F. M.," in *Bol'shaya Sovetskaya Entsiklopediya* (2d ed., Moscow), XV (1952), 148.

[38] *Klassiki russkoi literatury* (Moscow, Detgiz, 1952; 2d ed., 1954).

20: CONCLUSION

[1] See "Otchotnyi doklad TsK VKP(b) XIX s"yezdu partii—Doklad sekretarya TsK VKP(b) tov. G. M. Malenkova" [Report on the Work of the Central Committee of the All-Union Communist Party (Bolsheviks) to the Nineteenth Party Congress—Report of the Secretary of the Central Committee of the All-Union Communist Party (Bolsheviks), Comrade G. M. Malenkov], *Pravda* (Moscow, October 6, 1952).

[2] B. Ryurikov, "Nekotorye voprosy izucheniya tvorchestva Gor'kovo" [Certain Questions concerning the Study of Gorki's Writing], *Literaturnaya gazeta* [Literary Gazette] (Moscow, May 6, 1954).

[3] Vlad. Bonch-Bruyevich, "Lenin o knigakh i pisatelyakh" [Lenin on Books and Writers], *Literaturnaya gazeta* (April 21, 1955).

[4] F. M. Dostoyevski, *Sobraniye sochinenii* [Collected Works], ed. L. P. Grossman *et al.* (Moscow, GIKhL), Vol. I (Writings of 1846–1848) (1956).

[5] Dostoyevski, *Povesti i rasskazy* [Short Novels and Stories] (2 vols.; Moscow, GIKhL, 1956).

[6] V. Yermilov, *F. M. Dostoyevskii* (Moscow, GIKhL, 1956).

[7] S. Borshchevski, *Shchedrin i Dostoyevskii: Istoriya ikh ideinoi bor'by* [Shchedrin and Dostoyevski: The Story of Their Ideological Combat] (Moscow, GIKhL, 1956).

[8] D. Zaslavski, *F. M. Dostoyevskii: Kritiko-biograficheskii ocherk* (Moscow, Goslitizdat, 1956).

[9] *F. M. Dostoyevskii v russkoi kritike: Sbornik statei* [F. M. Dostoyevski in Russian Criticism: A Collection of Essays] (Moscow, GIKhL, 1956).

[10] Quoted in "Neizdannyi Dostoyevskii' [Unpublished Dostoyevski], *Literaturnaya gazeta* (February 7, 1956).

[11] *Ibid.*

[12] "K 75-letiyu so dnya smerti F. M. Dostoyevskovo" [For the Seventy-fifth Anniversary of the Death of F. M. Dostoyevski], *Literaturnaya gazeta* (December 8, 1955).

[13] I. Bazarova, "V museye-kvartire F. M. Dostoyevskovo" [At the F. M. Dostoyevski Museum Quarters], *Literaturnaya gazeta* (September 8, 1955).

[14] "K 75-letiyu so dnya smerti F. M. Dostoyevskovo" [For the

Seventy-fifth Anniversary of the Death of F. M. Dostoyevski], *Sovet-skaya kul'tura* [Soviet Culture] (Moscow, December 8, 1955).

[15] See Paul Babitsky and John Rimberg, *The Soviet Film Industry* (New York, Praeger, 1955), pp. 170–71.

[16] "K 75-letiyu," *Sovetskaya kul'tura.*

[17] See the articles in *Pravda* (February 6, 1956); *Uchitel'skaya gazeta* [Teachers' Gazette] (Moscow, February 8, 1956); *Sovetskaya kul'tura, Izvestiya, Vechernyaya Moskva* [Evening Moscow], *Trud* [Labor], *Krasnaya zvezda* [Red Star], *Sel'skoye khozyaistvo* [Agriculture], *Gudok* [Whistle], and many provincial papers of February 9, 1956.

[18] B. Ryurikov, "Velikii russkii pisatel' F. M. Dostoyevskii" [The Great Russian Writer F. M. Dostoyevski], *Kommunist* (Moscow), No. 2 (1956), p. 89.

[19] "Velikii russkii pisatel' " [A Great Russian Writer], *Pravda* (February 6, 1956).

[20] V. Yermilov, "F. M. Dostoyevskii: Ocherk tvorchestva" [F. M. Dostoyevski: Outline of His Work], in Dostoyevski, *Sobraniye sochinenii,* I, 7–76.

[21] See B. S. Ryurikov, "O romane 'Prestupleniye i nakazaniye' " [Concerning the Novel *Crime and Punishment*], in Dostoyevski, *Prestupleniye i nakazaniye* [Crime and Punishment] (Moscow, GIKhL, 1955), pp. 525–51.

[22] The "Publisher's Note" at the beginning of the first volume lists the contents of each of the ten volumes. *The Devils* is to appear in Volume VII, but there is no mention of *Notes from the Underground;* the latter has nevertheless been included in Volume IV (1956).

[23] Yermilov, "F. M. Dostoyevskii" (chapters from his 1956 book of the same title), *Novyi mir* [New World] (Moscow), No. 12 (1955), p. 169.

[24] *Ibid.,* p. 222.

[25] See the listing of the contents of *F. M. Dostoyevskii v russkoi kritike: Sbornik statei* in the Bibliography.

BIBLIOGRAPHY

The following list contains (a) works mentioned in the text which concern Dostoyevski primarily or in large part, (b) other books and articles published in prerevolutionary Russia which are representative of main currents in Dostoyevski scholarship before 1917 or which exerted an influence on subsequent Dostoyevski study, and (c) all additional materials on the subject of Dostoyevski published in the Soviet Union through early 1956 which have been available for examination in present circumstances and also in the USSR in the past, with the exception of purely derivative works and repetitious journalistic pieces; a number of unavailable items which may be assumed, on the basis of secondary sources, to contribute new information or interpretation are also included.

A list of the systematic bibliographies of Dostoyevski's writings and of the critical literature about them published in Russia and in the USSR up to 1929, with a selective bibliography from 1923 to 1929, may be found in F. M. Dostoyevski, *Polnoye sobraniye khudozhestvennykh proizvedenii* [Complete Literary Works], edited by B. V. Tomashevski and K. I. Khalabayev (Moscow and Leningrad, Gosizdat), Volume XIII (1930).

Abramovich, D. I. "Varianty 'Rechi o Pushkine.'" *See* Dolinin, A. S., ed., Dostoyevskii: Stat'i i materialy, Vol. II.

Abramovich, D. I., ed. Pis'ma russkikh pisatelei k A. S. Suvorinu [Letters of Russian Writers to A. S. Suvorin]. Leningrad, Gosudarstvennaya Publichnaya Biblioteka, 1927.

—— "Rech' o Pushkine." *See* Dolinin, A. S., ed., Dostoyevskii: Stat'i i materialy, Vol. II.

Abramovich, N. Ya. Khristos Dostoyevskovo [Dostoyevski's Christ]. Moscow, 1914.

Aikhenval'd, Yuli I. "Noch' russkoi literatury." *See* Priluko-Prilutski, N. G., comp. F. M. Dostoyevskii: Zhizn' i tvorchestvo. This essay was previously published under the title "Dostoyevskii" in Aikhenval'd, *Siluety russkikh pisatelei* [Silhouettes of Russian Writers] (2d ed.; Moscow, Izdaniye Nauchnovo slova), II (1908), 90–108.

Aleksandrov, V. "F. M. Dostoyevskii," *Ognoyok* [The Light] (Moscow), No. 46–47 (November, 1946), pp. 26–27.

Alekseyev, L. "O 'Brat'yakh Karamazovykh'" [Concerning *The Brothers Karamazov*], *Russkoye bogatstvo* [Russian Wealth] (St. Petersburg, 1881), No. 11, pp. 1–42; No. 12, pp. 1–33.

Alekseyev, M. P. "O dramaticheskikh opytakh Dostoyevskovo." *See* Grossman, Leonid P., ed., Tvorchestvo Dostoyevskovo.

—— Rannii drug F. M. Dostoyevskovo [An Early Friend of F. M. Dostoyevski]. Odessa, Vseukrainskoye gosudarstvennoye izdatel'stvo, 1921.

Al'tman, I. "Grubaya fal'sifikatsiya" [A Crude Falsification], *Znamya* [Banner] (Moscow), No. 3 (1948), pp. 179–84.

Andreyevich, pseud. *See* Solov'yov, Yevgeni A.

Andreyevski, S. A. "Brat'ya Karamazovy" [The Brothers Karamazov], *Russkii vestnik* [Russian Courier] (Moscow), No. 202 (1889), pp. 123–63. Republished in his book *Literaturnye ocherki* [Literary Sketches] (St. Petersburg, 1913), pp. 30–100.

Anin, N. "Raznochinets Dostoyevskii" [The *Raznochinets* Dostoyevski], *Krasnaya nov'* [Red Virgin Soil] (Moscow), No. 2 (1941), pp. 152–72.

Anisimov, I. "Dostoyevskii i yevo 'issledovateli'" [Dostoyevski and His "Investigators"], *Literaturnaya gazeta* [Literary Gazette] (Moscow, February 9, 1956).

Annenkov, P. V. "Uspekh 'Bednykh lyudei.'" *See* Priluko-Prilutski, N. G., comp., F. M. Dostoyevskii: Zhizn' i tvorchestvo.

—— "Zamechatel'noye desyatiletiye (1838–1848)." *See* F. M. Dostoyevskii v russkoi kritike: Sbornik statei.

—— "Zametki o russkoi literature proshlovo goda" [Remarks on Russian Literature of the Past Year], *Sovremennik* [Contemporary] (St. Petersburg), No. 13 (1849).

Antonovich, M. A. "Mistiko-asketicheskii roman: 'Brat'ya Karamazovy'" [A Mystically Ascetic Novel: *The Brothers Karamazov*], *Novoye obozreniye* [New Review] (St. Petersburg), No. 3 (March, 1881), pp. 190–239. *See also* F. M. Dostoyevskii v russkoi kritike: Sbornik statei.

—— "O pochve (ne v agronomicheskom smysle, a v dukhe 'Vremeni')" [Concerning the Soil (Not in the Agricultural Sense but in the Spirit

of *Vremya* [Time])], *Sovremennik* [The Contemporary] (St. Petersburg), No. 90 (December, 1861), pp. 171–88.

Antsiferov, N. P. Peterburg Dostoyevskovo [Dostoyevski's Petersburg].
Petrograd, Brockhaus-Efron, 1923.

Askol'dov, S. "Psikhologiya kharakterov u Dostoyevskovo." *See* Dolinin, A. S., ed., Dostoyevskii: Stat'i i materialy, Vol. II.

—— "Religiozno-eticheskoye znacheniye Dostoyevskovo." *See* Dolinin,
A. S., ed., Dostoyevskii: Stat'i i materialy, Vol. I.

Astrov, V. A. Ne nashli puti: Iz istorii religioznovo krizisa: Stankevich-
Belinskii-Gertsen-Kireyevskii-Dostoyevskii [They Did Not Find the
Way: From the History of a Religious Crisis (Stankevich, Belinski,
Herzen, Kireyevski, and Dostoyevski)]. St. Petersburg, Stasyulevich,
1914.

Auezov, Mukhtar. "F. M. Dostoyevskii i Chokan Valikhanov" [F. M.
Dostoyevski and Chokan Valikhanov], *Druzhba narodov* [Friendship
of the Peoples] (Moscow), No. 3 (March, 1956), pp. 154–56.

Avanesov, R. I. "Dostoyevski v rabote nad 'Dvoinikom' " [Dostoyevski
at Work on *The Double*], in N. K. Piksanov, ed., Tvorcheskaya
istoriya [Creative History]. Moscow, Nikitinskiye subbotniki, 1927.
Pages 154–91.

Averkiyev, D. B. *See* Dostoyevski, F. M., Polnoye sobraniye sochinenii
(1885–86).

Bakhtin, M. M. Problemy tvorchestva Dostoyevskovo [Problems of
Dostoyevski's Writing]. Leningrad, "Priboi," 1929.

Batyushkov, F. D. "Fyodor Mikhailovich Dostoyevskii," in D. N.
Ovsyaniko-Kulikovskii, ed., Istoriya russkoi literatury XIX v. [History
of Russian Literature of the Nineteenth Century]. Moscow, "Mir."
Vol. IV (1910), pp. 284–334.

Bazarova, I. "V museye-kvartire F. M. Dostoyevskovo" [At the F. M.
Dostoyevski Museum Quarters], *Literaturnaya gazeta* [Literary Ga-
zette] (Moscow, September 8, 1955).

Bel'chikov, N. F. "Chernyshevskii i Dostoyevskii" [Chernyshevski and
Dostoyevski], *Pechat' i revolyutsiya* [Press and Revolution] (Moscow), No. 5 (1928), pp. 35–53.

—— "Dostoyevskii i Pobedonostsev" [Dostoyevski and Pobedonostsev],
Krasnyi Arkhiv [Red Archive] (Moscow), No. 2 (1922), pp. 240–
55.

—— "Dostoyevskii o Tyutcheve" [Dostoyevski on the Subject of Tyutchev], *Byloye* [The Past] (Leningrad), No. 5 (1928), pp. 155–62.

—— Dostoyevskii v protsesse petrashevtsev [Dostoyevski in the Trial of the Petrashevtsy]. Leningrad, Izd. Akademii Nauk SSSR, Institut Russkoi literatury, 1936.

—— "Kak pisal romany Dostoyevskii" [How Dostoyevski Wrote Novels], *Pechat' i revolyutsiya* [Press and Revolution] (Moscow), No. 2 (1928), pp. 88–93.

—— "Neizvestnyi rasskaz 'Domovoi'" [An Unknown Story "House Demon"], *Zvezda* [Star] (Leningrad), No. 6 (1930), pp. 257–59.

—— "Odin iz zamyslov F. M. Dostoyevskovo (plan rasskaza dlya zhurnala 'Zarya')" [One of F. M. Dostoyevski's Plans (Outline of a Story for the Journal *Dawn*], *Krasnyi Arkhiv* [Red Archive] (Moscow), No. 3 (1926), pp. 224–28.

—— "Turgenev i Dostoyevskii" [Turgenev and Dostoyevski], *Krasnyi Arkhiv* [Red Archive] (Moscow), No. 2 (21) (1927), pp. 241–44.

—— "Turgenev i Dostoyevskii" [Turgenev and Dostoyevski], *Literatura i marksizm* [Literature and Marxism] (Moscow), No. 1 (1928), pp. 63–94.

—— See also Dostoyevski, F. M., Iz arkhiva F. M. Dostoyevskovo: Pis'ma russkikh pisatelei and Pis'ma F. M. Dostoyevskovo k zhene; and Dostoyevski, F. M., and I. S. Turgenev, F. M. Dostoyevski i I. S. Turgenev: Perepiska.

Bel'chikov, N. F., ed. "Pokazaniya F. M. Dostoyevskovo po delu petrashevtsev" [Testimony of F. M. Dostoyevski in the Petrashevtsy Case], *Krasnyi Arkhiv* [Red Archive] (Moscow, 1931), No. 45, pp. 130–46; No. 46, pp. 160–78.

—— See also Dostoyevski, F. M., Iz arkhiva F. M. Dostoyevskovo: "Idiot": Neizdannye materialy and "Rukopisi 'Netochki Nezvanovoi.'"

Beletski, A. I. "Dostoyevskii i natural'naya shkola v 1846 g." [Dostoyevski and the Natural School in 1846], *Nauka na Ukraine* [Scholarship in the Ukraine] (Kharkov), No. 4 (1922), pp. 332–42.

Belinski, V. G. "Bednye lyudi." See Priluko-Prilutski, N. G., comp., F. M. Dostoyevskii: Zhizn' i tvorchestvo.

—— "Peterburgskii sbornik" [Petersburg Miscellany], *Otechestvennye zapiski* [National Notes] (St. Petersburg), XLV, No. 3 (1846), 1–30.

Republished in Belinski, *Sobraniye sochinenii* [Collected Works] (Moscow, OGIZ), III (1948), 61–86.

—— "Vzglyad na russkuyu literaturu 1846 goda" [Review of Russian Literature in 1846], in Sobraniye sochinenii [Collected Works]. Moscow, OGIZ. Vol. III, 1948.

—— "Vzglyad na russkuyu literaturu 1847 goda" [Review of Russian Literature in 1847], in Sobraniye sochinenii [Collected Works]. Moscow, OGIZ. Vol. III, 1948.

Belkin, A. A. "Dostoyevskii v otsenke russkoi kritiki." *See* F. M. Dostoyevskii v russkoi kritike: Sbornik statei.

Belyi, Andrei. "Dostoyevskii: Po povodu 25 letiya so dnya smerti" [Dostoyevski: On the Occasion of the Twenty-fifth Anniversary of His Death], *Zolotoye runo* [The Golden Fleece] (Moscow), No. 2 (1906), pp. 8–90.

Bém, A. L. (Boehm, Alfred L.), ed. O Dostoyevskom [On Dostoyevski]. Prague. Vol. I, 1929. Vol. II, 1933. Vol. III, 1936.

Berdyayev, N. A. "Velikii Inkvizitor" [The Grand Inquisitor], *Voprosy filosofii i psikhologii* [Questions of Philosophy and Psychology] (Moscow), No. 1 (1907), pp. 1–36.

Berezhkov, Fyodor F. "Dostoyevskii na Zapade." *See* Dostoyevskii (Moscow, 1928).

Berkovski, N. Review of M. M. Bakhtin's *Problemy tvorchestva Dostoyevskovo*, *Zvezda* [Star] (Leningrad), No. 7 (1929), pp. 187–89.

Berliner, G. N. G. Chernyshevskii i yevo literaturnye vragi [N. G. Chernyshevski and His Literary Enemies]. Moscow, GIZ, 1930. Pages 127–40, 200–205.

Bobrov, Ye. A. Zamechaniya na doklad B. G. Reizova "Mneniya Valishevskovo o Dostoyevskom" [Remarks on B. G. Reizov's Report "Valishevski's Opinions concerning Dostoyevski"]. Offprint from *Izvestiya Severo-Kavkazskovo Gosudarstvennovo Universiteta* [News of the North Caucasus State University] (Rostov-on-Don), No. 3 (16) (1928), pp. 11–13.

—— Zamechaniya na doklad B. G. Reizova "Odin iz literaturnykh istochnikov Alyoshi Karamazova" [Remarks on B. G. Reizov's Report "One of the Literary Sources of Alyosha Karamazov"]. Offprint from *Izvestiya Severo-Kavkazskovo Gosudarstvennovo Universiteta* [News

of the North Caucasus State University] (Rostov-on-Don), No. 3
(16) (1928), pp. 14–15.

Boehm, Alfred L. *See* Bėm, A. L.

"Bol'shevistskaya partiinost'—osnova sovetskovo literaturovedeniya"
[Bolshevik Party Spirit, the Basis of Soviet Literary Scholarship],
Literaturnaya gazeta [Literary Gazette] (Moscow, November 13,
1948).

Bonch-Bruyevich, Vladimir. "Lenin o knigakh i pisatelyakh: Iz vospominaniyakh" [Lenin on Books and Authors: From Reminiscences],
Literaturnaya gazeta [Literary Gazette] (Moscow, April 21, 1955).

Borisov, I. "F. M. Dostoyevskii: K semidesyatipyatiletiyu so dnya
smerti" [F. M. Dostoyevski: On the Seventy-fifth Anniversary of His
Death], *Pravda Ukrainy* [Ukrainian Pravda] (Kiev, February 9,
1956).

Borshchevski, S. "Novoye litso v 'Besakh' Dostoyevskovo" [A New
Person in Dostoyevski's *The Devils*], in Slovo o kul'ture [The Word
of Culture]. Moscow, 1918.

—— "Shchedrin i Dostoyevskii" [Shchedrin and Dostoyevski], *Literaturnyi kritik* [Literary Critic] (Moscow, 1939), No. 5–6, pp. 66–
102; No. 8–9, pp. 85–108.

—— Shchedrin i Dostoyevskii: Istoriya ikh ideologicheskoi bor'by
[Shchedrin and Dostoyevski: The Story of Their Ideological Com-
bat]. Moscow, GIKhL, 1956.

—— "Shchedrin i Dostoyevskii: Iz istorii ikh ideinoi bor'by" [Shchedrin
and Dostoyevski: From the Story of Their Ideological Combat],
Novyi mir [New World] (Moscow), No. 4 (1948), pp. 251–71.

Brodski, N. L. "Neizdannye materialy F. M. Dostoyevskovo" [Unpub-
lished Materials of F. M. Dostoyevski], *Literaturnaya gazeta* [Liter-
ary Gazette] (Moscow, February 9, 1931).

Brodski, N. L., ed. Tvorcheskii put' Dostoyevskovo [The Creative Path
of Dostoyevski]. Leningrad, "Seyatel'," 1924. *Contents:* K. K. Istomin,
"Iz zhizni i tvorchestva Dostoyevskovo v molodosti" [From the Life
and Work of Dostoyevski in His Youth], pp. 3–48; Viktor V. Vinogradov, "Syuzhet i arkhitektonika romana Dostoyevskovo 'Bednye
lyudi' v svyazi s voprosom o poetike natural'noi shkoly" [Plot and
Architectonics of Dostoyevski's Novel *Poor Folk* in Connection with

the Question of the Style of the Natural School], pp. 49–103; M. G. Davidovich, "Problema zanimatel'nosti v romanakh Dostoyevskovo" [The Problem of Interest in Dostoyevski's Novels], pp. 104–30; A. P. Skaftymov, "Tematicheskaya kompozitsiya romana 'Idiot' " [Thematic Composition of the Novel *The Idiot*], pp. 131–85; A. Gizetti, "Gordye yazychnitsy" [Proud Pagans], pp. 186–96; and D. Darski, "Dostoyevskii—myslitel' " [Dostoyevski as Thinker], pp. 197–215.

Bulgakov, Sergei N. "Geroizm i podvizhnichestvo" [Heroism and Asceticism], in Vekhi [Landmarks]. 3d ed. Moscow, Kushnerov, 1909. Pages 23–69.

—— "Ivan Karamazov," *Voprosy filosofii i psikhologii* [Questions of Philosophy and Psychology] (Moscow), No. 1 (1902), pp. 826–63.

—— Venets ternovyi (pamyati F. M. Dostoyevskovo) [Crown of Thorns: In Memory of F. M. Dostoyevski]. St. Petersburg, 1907.

Burenin, V. P. " 'Besy,' roman F. Dostoyevskovo" [*The Devils*, a Novel by F. Dostoyevski], *S.-Peterburgskiye vedomosti* [St. Petersburg News] (St. Petersburg), No. 6 (1873), pp. 1–2.

—— "Dva slova o romane g. Dostoyevskovo" [Two Words about Mr. Dostoyevski's Novel], *Novoye vremya* [New Times] (St. Petersburg), No. 1087 (1879).

—— "Koye-chto o 'Dnevnike pisatelya' g. Dostoyevskovo i o yevo avtore" [A Few Words on Mr. Dostoyevski's *Diary of a Writer* and on Its Author], *Novoye vremya* [New Times] (St. Petersburg), No. 681 (1878).

—— "Nachalo novovo romana g. Dostoyevskovo: Obshchiye zamechaniya o darovanii avtora" [The Beginning of a New Novel by Mr. Dostoyevski: General Comments on the Author's Gift], *Novoye vremya* [New Times] (St. Petersburg), No. 1060 (1879).

—— "Poyavleniye snova 'Besov' v 'Russkom vestnike' " [Another Appearance of "The Devils" in the *Russian Courier*], *S.-Peterburgskiye vedomosti* [St. Petersburg News] (St. Petersburg), No. 15 (1872).

—— "Roman g. Dostoyevskovo: Obvineniya avtora 'Velikovo inkvizitora' v fanatizme i nenavisti" [Mr. Dostoyevski's Novel: The Author of "The Grand Inquisitor" Accused of Fanaticism and Hatred], *Novoye vremya* [New Times] (St. Petersburg), No. 1203 (1879).

Burov, N. "Apologety reaktsionnykh idei Dostoyevskovo" [Apologists for the Reactionary Ideas of Dostoyevski], *Literaturnaya gazeta* [Literary Gazette] (Moscow, January 3, 1948).

Byalik, B. "Bor'ba Gor'kovo-khudozhnika protiv reaktsionnykh idei Dostoyevskovo" [The Struggle of Gorki the Artist against the Reactionary Ideas of Dostoyevski], in A. M. Yegolin, B. V. Mikhailovski, and S. M. Petrov, eds., Gor'kovskiye chteniya, 1949–1950 [Gorki Lectures, 1949–1950]. Moscow, Izd. Akademii Nauk SSSR, 1951. Pages 418–65.

—— "Gorky and Dostoyevski," *Soviet Literature* (Moscow), No. 10 (1948), pp. 134–40.

Chernyshevski, N. G. "Moi svidaniya s F. M. Dostoyevskim" [My Meetings with F. M. Dostoyevski], unpublished memoirs of Chernyshevski, ed. N. F. Bel'chikov, *Chitatel' i pisatel'* [Reader and Writer] (Leningrad), No. 29 (1928).

Cheshikhin, Vasili Yevgrafovich. *See* Vetrinski, Ch., pseud.

Chicherin, A. V. "Prestupleniye i nakazaniye" [Crime and Punishment], *Russkii yazyk v sovetskoi shkole* [Russian Language in the Soviet School] (Moscow), No. 6 (1929), pp. 72–87.

Chizh, Vladimir F. "Dostoyevskii kak psikhopatolog" [Dostoyevski as a Psychopathologist], *Russkii vestnik* [Russian Courier] (Moscow), No. 5–6 (1884). Published in book form, Moscow, Universitetskaya tipografiya, 1885; and included in Priluko-Prilutski, N. G., comp., *F. M. Dostoyevskii: Zhizn' i tvorchestvo* (*q.v.*).

Chukovski, K. "Dostoyevskii i pleyada Belinskovo" [Dostoyevski and the Pleiad of Belinski], in Nekrasov: Stat'i i materialy [Nekrasov: Articles and Materials]. Leningrad, Kubuch, 1926. Pages 326–49.

Chulkov, Georgi I. "Dostoyevskii," in F. M. Dostoyevski, Sochineniya [Works], ed. A. V. Lunacharski. Moscow, GIKhL, 1931. Pages xxv–xxxix.

—— "Dostoyevskii i utopicheskii sotsializm" [Dostoyevski and Utopian Socialism], *Katorga i ssylka* [Penal Servitude and Exile] (Moscow, 1929), No. 2, pp. 9–36; No. 3, pp. 134–51.

—— Kak rabotal Dostoyevskii [How Dostoyevski Worked]. Moscow, Sovetskii pisatel', 1939.

—— "Kak rabotal Dostoyevskii v sorokovykh godakh" [How Dostoyevski Worked in the Forties], *Literaturnaya uchoba* [Literary Studies] (Moscow), No. 4 (1938), pp. 46–76.

—— "Posledneye slovo Dostoyevskovo o Belinskom." *See* Dostoyevskii (Moscow, 1928).

Darski, D. "Dostoyevskii—myslitel'." *See* Brodski, N. L., ed., Tvorcheskii put' Dostoyevskovo.

Davidovich, M. G. "Problema zanimatel'nosti v romanakh Dostoyevskovo." *See* Brodski, N. L., ed., Tvorcheskii put' Dostoyevskovo.

Delous, Dr. "Voprosy psikhoterapii v proizvedeniyakh Dostoyevskovo" [Questions of Psychotherapy in Dostoyevski's Writings], *Sovremennaya psikhonevrologiya* [Contemporary Psychoneurology] (Moscow), No. 5 (1925).

Derzhavin, N. S. Myortvyi Dom v russkoi literature XIX veka [The House of the Dead in Russian Literature of the Nineteenth Century]. Petrograd, Nachatki znanii, 1924.

Dikii, A. D. "Dostoyevskii v Khudozhestvennom Teatre" [Dostoyevski in the Art Theater], *Teatr* [Theater] (Moscow), No. 2 (1956), pp. 103–20.

Dmitriyev, L. "O novoi povesti M. Zoshchenko" [About M. Zoshchenko's New Story], *Literatura i iskusstvo* [Literature and Art] (Moscow, December 4, 1943).

Dobrolyubov, N. A. "Makar Devushkin." *See* Priluko-Prilutski, N. G., comp., F. M. Dostoyevskii: Zhizn' i tvorchestvo.

—— "Zabitye lyudi" [Downtrodden People], *Sovremennik* [The Contemporary] (St. Petersburg), No. 9 (1861). Republished in his *Sochineniya* [Works] (4th ed.; St. Petersburg, Panteleyev, 1885), III, 486–532; in his *Polnoye sobraniye sochinenii* [Complete Works] (Moscow, OGIZ), Vol. II (1935); and in the anthology *F. M. Dostoyevskii v russkoi kritike: Sbornik statei* (*q.v.*).

Dolinin, A. S. (pseud. of Arkadi Semyonovich Iskoz). "Bluzhdayushchiye obrazy" [Vagrant Characters], *Vestnik literatury* [Literary Courier] (Petrograd), No. 2 (26) (1921).

—— "Dostoyevskii i Gertsen" [Dostoyevski and Herzen], *Letopis' Doma literatorov* [Annals of the House of Writers] (Petrograd), No. 2 (November 15, 1921).

—— "Dostoyevskii i Gertsen." *See* Dolinin, A. S., ed., Dostoyevskii: Stat'i i materialy, Vol. I.

—— "Dostoyevskii i Suslova." *See* Dolinin, A. S., ed., Dostoyevskii: Stat'i i materialy, Vol. II.

—— "Dostoyevskii sredi Petrashevtsev." *See* "Dostoyevskii i o Dosto-yevskom."

—— F. M. Dostoyevskii. St. Petersburg [*sic*], Kolos, 1921. In the series Biograficheskaya biblioteka [Biographical Library].

—— "F. M. Dostoyevskii i N. N. Strakhov" [F. M. Dostoyevski and N. N. Strakhov], in L. K. Piksanov, ed., Shestidesyatye gody [The Sixties]. Moscow, Izd. Akademii Nauk SSSR, 1940. Pages 238–54.

—— "K istorii sozdaniya 'Brat'yev Karamazovykh'." *See* Dolinin, A. S., ed., F. M. Dostoyevskii: Materialy i issledovaniya.

—— "Krotkaya." *See* Dolinin, A. S., ed., Dostoyevskii: Stat'i i ma-terialy, Vol. II.

—— "K tsenzurnoi istorii zhurnalov Dostoyevskovo." *See* Dolinin, A. S., ed., Dostoyevskii: Stat'i i materialy, Vol. II.

—— "Novoye o F. M. Dostoyevskom" [New Material concerning F. M. Dostoyevski], in Uchonye zapiski Leningradskovo pedagogicheskovo instituta imeni M. N. Pokrovskovo [Scholarly Papers of the Pokrovski Pedagogical Institute in Leningrad]. Leningrad. Vol. IV (1940), pp. 311–22.

—— "Pleshcheyev i Dostoyevskii." *See* Dolinin, A. S., ed., F. M. Dosto-yevskii: Materialy i issledovaniya.

—— "Stranitsy iz 'Besov.' " *See* Dolinin, A. S., ed., Dostoyevskii: Stat'i i materialy, Vol. II.

—— "Turgenev v 'Besakh.' " *See* Dolinin, A. S., ed., Dostoyevskii: Stat'i i materialy, Vol. II.

—— V tvorcheskoi laboratorii Dostoyevskovo: Istoriya sozdaniya romana "Podrostok" [In Dostoyevski's Creative Laboratory: History of the Creation of the Novel *A Raw Youth*]. Moscow, Sovetskii pisa-tel', 1947.

—— "Vyaliki pis'men'nik" [Great Writer], *Litaratura i mastatstva* [Literature and Art] (Minsk, February 11, 1956).

—— *See also* Suslova, A. P.

Dolinin, A. S., ed. Dostoyevskii: Stat'i i materialy [Dostoyevski: Arti-cles and Materials]. Vol I. St. Petersburg [*sic*], "Mysl'," 1922. *Con-tents:* "Ot redaktora" [From the Editor], pp. i–iv; S. Askol'dov, "Religiozno-eticheskoye znacheniye Dostoyevskovo" [The Religious and Ethical Significance of Dostoyevski], pp. 1–32; L. Karsavin, "Dostoyevskii i katolichestvo" [Dostoyevski and Catholicism], pp.

33–64; N. Losski, "O prirode sataninskoi (po Dostoyevskomu)" [On Satanic Nature (According to Dostoyevski)], pp. 65–92; I. Lapshin, "Estetika Dostoyevskovo" [Dostoyevski's Aesthetics], pp. 93–152; E. L. Radlov, "Solov'yov i Dostoyevskii" [Solov'yov and Dostoyevski], pp. 153–72; V. L. Komarovich, "Nenapisannaya poema Dostoyevskovo" [An Unwritten Poem of Dostoyevski], pp. 175–207; Viktor V. Vinogradov, "Stil' peterburgskoi poemy 'Dvoinik'" [The Style of the Petersburg Poem *The Double*], pp. 209–54; Ye. Pokrovskaya, "Dostoyevskii i petrashevtsy" [Dostoyevski and the Petrashevtsy], pp. 255–72; Dolinin, "Dostoyevskii i Gertsen" [Dostoyevski and Herzen], pp. 273–324; L. K. Il'inski, "F. M. Dostoyevskii i Gl. Iv. Uspenskii" [F. M. Dostoyevski and Gleb Ivanovich Uspenski], pp. 325–53; Dolinin, ed., "Nenapechatannye stranitsy iz 'Zapisok iz myortvovo doma'" [Unpublished Pages from *Notes from the House of the Dead*], pp. 359–68; S. Pereselenkov, "Starina o 'Petrashevtsakh'" [Old Times in the Petrashevski Circle], pp. 369–75; "Pis'ma k A. Maikovu i drugim" [Letters to A. Maikov and Others], pp. 379–452; "Iz snoshenii F. M. i M. M. Dostoyevskikh s Ya. P. Polonskim" [From the Relations of F. M. and M. M. Dostoyevski with Ya. P. Polonski], pp. 453–60; "Dva pis'ma F. M. Dostoyevskovo k P. Ye. Gusevu" [Two Letters of F. M. Dostoyevski to P. Ye. Gusev], pp. 461–66; "Pis'ma F. M. Dostoyevskovo k Valikhanovu i k Kachenovskomu" [Letters of F. M. Dostoyevski to Valikhanov and Kachenovski], pp. 467–71; "Dva pis'ma F. M. Dostoyevskovo k I. A. Goncharovu" [Two Letters of F. M. Dostoyevski to I. A. Goncharov], pp. 472–74; "Vospominaniya A. G. Dostoyevskoi" [Reminiscences of A. G. Dostoyevskaya], pp. 477–504; "Neizdannye pis'ma M. M. Dostoyevskovo k M. F. De-Pule i N. S. Miloshevichu: K istorii zhurnala 'Vremya'" [Unpublished Letters of M. M. Dostoyevski to M. F. De-Pule and N. S. Miloshevich: On the History of the Journal *Vremya* (Time)], pp. 507–16.

—— Dostoyevskii: Stat'i i materialy [Dostoyevski: Articles and Materials]. Vol. II. Moscow and Leningrad, "Mysl'," 1925. *Contents:* "Ot redaktora" [From the Editor], pp. 1–3; S. Askol'dov, "Psikhologiya kharakterov u Dostoyevskovo" [Psychology of the Characters in Dostoyevski], pp. 5–30; V. L. Komarovich, "Roman 'Podrostok' kak khudozhestvennoye yedinstvo" [The Novel *A Raw Youth* as an Artistic Unity], pp. 31–70; B. Engel'gardt, "Ideologicheskii roman Dostoyevskovo" [Dostoyevski's Ideological Novel], pp. 71–108; V. Sidorov, "O 'Dnevnike pisatelya' " [On *The Diary of a Writer*], pp. 109–18; Dolinin, "Turgenev v 'Besakh' " [Turgenev in *The Devils*], pp. 119–38; Leonid P. Grossman, "Stilistika Stavrogina" [The Stylistics of Stavrogin], pp. 139–48; Dolinin, "Dostoyevskii i Suslova" [Dostoyevski and Suslova], pp. 153–284; A. G. Dostoyevskaya, "Vospominaniya" [Reminiscences], pp. 285–302; S. Lyubimov, "K voprosu o genealogii Dostoyevskovo" [More on the Question of Dostoyevski's Genealogy], pp. 303–6; F. M. Dostoyevski, "Pis'ma" [Letters], pp. 309–20; Dolinin, "Krotkaya" [A Gentle Spirit], pp. 323–438; F. M. Dostoyevski, "Novyi variant 'Krotkoi' " [A New Variant of "A Gentle Spirit"], pp. 439–508; F. M. Dostoyevski, "Rech' o Pushkine" [Pushkin Speech], ed. D. I. Abramovich, pp. 509–36; D. I. Abramovich, "Varianty 'Rechi o Pushkine' " [Variants of the Pushkin Speech], pp. 537–43; Dolinin, "Stranitsy iz 'Besov' " [Pages from *The Devils*], pp. 544–56; Dolinin, "K tsenzurnoi istorii zhurnalov Dostoyevskovo" [On the History of the Censorship of Dostoyevski's Journals], pp. 559–77; M. Stoyunina, "Vospominaniya o A. G. Dostoyevskoi" [Reminiscences of A. G. Dostoyevskaya], pp. 578–82; Z. Kovrigina, "Posledniye mesyatsy zhizni A. G. Dostoyevskoi" [The Last Months of the Life of A. G. Dostoyevskaya], pp. 583–90; N. A. Sokolov, "Bibliografiya Dostoyevskovo" [Bibliography of Dostoyevski], pp. 1–122 (paginated separately).

—— F. M. Dostoyevskii: Materialy i issledovaniya [F. M. Dostoyevski: Materials and Studies]. Leningrad, Izdatel'stvo Akademii Nauk SSSR, 1935. *Contents:* "Predisloviye" [Foreword], pp. 1–6. "Brat'ya Karamazovy" [The Brothers Karamazov]: Dolinin, "K istorii sozdaniya 'Brat'yev Karamazovykh' " [More on the Story of the Creation of *The Brothers Karamazov*], pp. 9–80; "Teksty chernovykh zapisei k 'Brat'yam Karamazovym' " [Texts of the Rough Drafts of *The Brothers Karamazov*], pp. 81–346; Dolinin, "Kommentarii" [Commentaries], pp. 347–93. "Besy" [The Devils]: B. Tomashevski, "Besy," pp. 397–403; "Teksty" [Texts], pp. 405–28. "Pis'ma A. N. Pleshcheyeva k F. M. Dostoyevskomu" [Letters of A. N. Pleshcheyev to F. M. Dostoyevski]: Dolinin, "Pleshcheyev i Dostoyevskii" [Ple-

shcheyev and Dostoyevski], pp. 431–35; "Pis'ma" [Letters], pp. 437–
68; "Primechaniya" [Notes], pp. 469–502. "Pis'ma M. M. Dostoyevskovo k F. M. Dostoyevskomu" [Letters of M. M. Dostoyevski to
F. M. Dostoyevski]: Dolinin, "M. M. Dostoyevskii," pp. 505–7;
"Pis'ma" [Letters], pp. 509–54; "Primechaniya" [Notes], pp. 555–
79.

—— *See also* Dostoyevski, F. M., Pis'ma, and Sobraniye sochinenii
(1956).

Dorofeyev, V. "Velikii russkii pisatel'" [A Great Russian Writer], *Sovetskaya kul'tura* [Soviet Culture] (Moscow, February 9, 1956).

Dorovatovskaya-Lyubimova, V. S. "Dostoyevskii i shestidesyatniki."
See Dostoyevskii (Moscow, 1928).

—— "'Idiot' Dostoyevskovo i ugolovnaya khronika yevo vremeni"
[Dostoyevski's *The Idiot* and the Criminal Record of His Time],
Pechat' i revolyutsiya [Press and Revolution] (Moscow), No. 3
(1928), pp. 31–53.

Dostoyevskaya, A. G. Dnevnik A. G. Dostoyevskoi: 1867 g. [Diary of
A. G. Dostoyevskaya: 1867]. Moscow, Novaya Moskva, 1923.

—— Dostoyevsky Portrayed by His Wife: The Diary and Reminiscences
of Mme Dostoyevsky, trans. and ed. S. S. Koteliansky. New York,
Dutton, 1926.

—— "Iz vospominanii A. G. Dostoyevskoi" [From the Reminiscences
of A. G. Dostoyevskaya], *Krasnyi Arkhiv* [Red Archive] (Moscow),
No. 3 (1923), pp. 251–90.

—— "Primechaniya k sochineniyam Dostoyevskovo." *See* Grossman,
Leonid, ed., Tvorchestvo Dostoyevskovo.

—— "Vospominaniya." *See* Dolinin, A. S., ed., Dostoyevskii: Stat'i i
materialy, Vols. I and II.

—— Vospominaniya A. G. Dostoyevskoi [Reminiscences of A. G.
Dostoyevskaya], ed. L. Grossman. Moscow, Gosizdat, 1925.

Dostoyevskaya, Lyubov'. Dostoyevskii v izobrazhenii yevo docheri L.
Dostoyevskoi [Dostoyevski As Portrayed by His Daughter L. Dosto-
yevskaya], trans. from the German by L. Ya. Krukovskaya, ed. and
with a Foreword by A. G. Gornfel'd. Moscow and Petrograd, Gosizdat, 1922. A somewhat abridged translation of her *Dostojewski, geschildert von seiner Tochter A. Dostojewski* (Munich, Reinhardt,
1920).

—— (under the name Aimée Dostoyevsky). Fyodor Dostoyevsky: A Study. London, Heinemann, 1921. Translation of her *Dostojewski, geschildert von seiner Tochter A. Dostojewski* (Munich, Reinhardt, 1920).

Dostoyevski, A. M. Vospominaniya Andreya Mikhailovicha Dostoyevskovo [Reminiscences of Andrei Mikhailovich Dostoyevski]. Leningrad, Izd. pisatelei, 1930.

Dostoyevski, F. M. For titles not listed here, *see also under* F. M. Dostoyevskii.

Dostoyevski, F. M. Bednye lyudi [Poor Folk]. Moscow, GIKhL, 1955.

—— "Domovoi." *See* Bel'chikov, N. F., "Neizvestnyi rasskaz 'Domovoi.' "

—— "Epizod iz 'Podrostka.' " *See* Grossman, Leonid P., ed., Tvorchestvo Dostoyevskovo.

—— Idiot [The Idiot]. Moscow, GIKhL, 1955.

—— "Ispoved' Stavrogina" [Stavrogin's Confession], in Dokumenty po istorii russkoi literatury i obshchestvennosti [Documents on the History of Russian Literature and Social Thought]. Moscow. Vol. I, 1922. A variant appeared in *Byloye* [The Past] (Leningrad), No. 18 (1923), pp. 227–52.

—— Iz arkhiva F. M. Dostoyevskovo: "Idiot": Neizdannye materialy [From the F. M. Dostoyevski Archive: *The Idiot,* Unpublished Materials], ed. P. N. Sakulin and N. F. Bel'chikov. Moscow, GIKhL, 1931.

—— Iz arkhiva F. M. Dostoyevskovo: Pis'ma russkikh pisatelei [From the F. M. Dostoyevski Archive: Letters of Russian Writers], ed. and with an Introduction by N. K. Piksanov, and commentaries by N. F. Bel'chikov and N. K. Piksanov. Moscow, GIZ, 1923.

—— Iz arkhiva F. M. Dostoyevskovo: "Prestupleniye i nakazaniye": Neizdannyi material [From the F. M. Dostoyevski Archive: *Crime and Punishment,* Unpublished Material], ed. I. M. Glivenko. Moscow, GIKhL, 1931.

—— Izbrannye sochineniya [Selected Works], ed. B. V. Tomashevski. Moscow, GIKhL, 1946.

—— "Iz 'Zapisnykh knizhek.' " *See* Grossman, Leonid P., ed., Tvorchestvo Dostoyevskovo.

—— "Iz zateryannykh statei Dostoyevskovo: 'Ne tron' menya' (*Vremya,*

1861)." *See* Grossman, Leonid P., ed., Tvorchestvo Dostoyevskovo.

—— Mal'chiki (iz romana "Brat'ya Karamazovy") [The Boys (from the Novel *The Brothers Karamazov*)]. Moscow, Detgiz, 1947. In the series Biblioteka shkol'nika [Library for the School Child].

—— "Nenapechatannye stranitsy iz 'Zapisok iz myortvovo doma.'" *See* Dolinin, A. S., ed., Dostoyevskii: Stat'i i materialy, Vol. I.

—— "Novyi variant 'Krotkoi.'" *See* Dolinin, A. S., ed., Dostoyevskii: Stat'i i materialy, Vol. II.

—— "Otryvki iz raznykh rukopisei." *See* Grossman, Leonid P., ed., Tvorchestvo Dostoyevskovo.

—— "Otryvok iz romana 'Shchedrodarov'" [Fragment from the Novel "Shchedrodarov"], *Epokha* [Epoch] (St. Petersburg), No. 5 (May, 1864).

—— "Perepiska F. M. Dostoyevskovo s M. P. Pogodinym." *See* "Dostoyevskii i o Dostoyevskom."

—— "Pervaya zapisnaya knizhka—Sibirskaya tetrad'." *See* "Dostoyevskii i o Dostoyevskom."

—— Pis'ma [Letters], ed. A. S. Dolinin. Moscow and Leningrad. Vol. I, Gosizdat, 1928. Vol. II, Gosizdat, 1930. Vol. III, Academia, 1934.

—— "Pis'ma." *See* Dolinin, A. S., ed., Dostoyevskii: Stat'i i materialy, Vol. II.

—— "Pis'ma Dostoyevskovo k Pobedonostsevu" [Letters of Dostoyevski to Pobedonostsev], *Krasnyi Arkhiv* [Red Archive] (Moscow), No. 2 (1922), pp. 240–55.

—— Pis'ma F. M. Dostoyevskovo k zhene [Letters of F. M. Dostoyevski to His Wife], ed. V. F. Pereverzev, with a Foreword and notes by N. F. Bel'chikov. Moscow and Leningrad, Gosizdat, 1926.

—— "Pis'mo F. M. Dostoyevskovo" [Letter of F. M. Dostoyevski (to M. A. Polivanova)], *Ogonyok* [The Light] (Moscow), No. 6 (February, 1956), p. 20.

—— "Plan romana 'Zhitiye velikovo greshnika.'" *See* Grossman, Leonid P., ed., Tvorchestvo Dostoyevskovo.

—— Podrostok [A Raw Youth], Moscow, GIKhL, 1955.

—— Polnoye sobraniye khudozhestvennykh proizvedenii [Complete Literary Works], ed. B. V. Tomashevski and K. I. Khalabayev. Moscow and Leningrad, Gosizdat. Vols. I–X, 1926–27. Vols. XI–XII (Diary of a Writer), 1929. Vol. XIII (Articles of 1845–1878), 1930.

—— Polnoye sobraniye sochinenii [Complete Works]. 14 vols. St. Petersburg, A. G. Dostoyevskaya, 1882–83.

—— Polnoye sobraniye sochinenii [Complete Works], with a Biographical Sketch by D. B. Averkiyev. 6 vols. St. Petersburg, Suvorin, 1885–86.

—— Polnoye sobraniye sochinenii [Complete Works], with a Biographical Sketch by K. K. Sluchevski. 12 vols. St. Petersburg, Tipografiya brat'yev Panteleyevykh, 1889.

—— Polnoye sobraniye sochinenii [Complete Works], with a Biographical Sketch by S. N. Bulgakov. 6th (Jubilee) ed., 14 vols. Moscow, Tipografiya P. F. Panteleyeva, 1904–6.

—— Polnoye sobraniye sochinenii [Complete Works]. 7th ed., 12 vols. St. Petersburg, Tipografiya P. F. Panteleyeva, 1906–7.

—— Polnoye sobraniye sochinenii [Complete Works]. 23 vols. St. Petersburg, "Prosveshcheniye." Vols. I–XXI, 1911–14. Vols. XXII–XXXIII, ed. Leonid P. Grossman under the subtitle *Zabytye stranitsy Dostoyevskovo* [Forgotten Pages of Dostoyevski] (critical articles, early writings, variants, etc.), 1916.

—— Povesti [Short Novels], ed. O. V. Tsekhnovitser. Leningrad, GIKhL, 1940.

—— Povesti i rasskazy [Short Novels and Stories]. 2 vols. Moscow, GIKhL, 1956.

—— Prestupleniye i nakazaniye [Crime and Punishment], with an article by B. S. Ryurikov appended ("O romane 'Prestupleniye i nakazaniye'" [q.v.]). Moscow, GIKhL, 1955.

—— "Rech' o Pushkine." See Dolinin, A. S., ed., Dostoyevskii: Stat'i i materialy, Vol. II.

—— "Rukopisi 'Netochki Nezvanovoi'" [Manuscripts of *Netochka Nezvanova*], ed. N. F. Bel'chikov, *Pechat' i revolyutsiya* [Press and Revolution] (Moscow), No. 2 (1928), pp. 88–93.

—— Selo Stepanchikovo i yevo obitateli [The Village of Stepanchikovo and Its Residents]. Moscow, GIKhL, 1955.

—— Sobraniye sochinenii [Collected Works], ed. Leonid P. Grossman, A. S. Dolinin, V. V. Yermilov, V. Ya. Kirpotin, V. S. Nechayeva, and B. S. Ryurikov. Moscow, GIKhL. Vol. I (Proizvedeniya 1846–1848 [Writings of 1846–1848]), 1956; Vol. II (Proizvedeniya 1848–1859 [Writings of 1848–1859]), 1956; Vol. III (Unizhonnye i oskorblyon-

nye, Zapiski iz myortvovo doma [The Insulted and Injured, Notes
from the House of the Dead]), 1956; Vol. IV (Proizvedeniya 1862–
1869 [Writings of 1862–1869]), 1956.

—— Sochineniya [Works], with a Biographical and Critical Sketch by
V. V. Rozanov. 12 vols. St. Petersburg, Marks, 1894–95.

—— Sochineniya [Works], ed. A. V. Lunacharski. Moscow and Leningrad, GIKhL, 1931.

—— "Teksty chernovykh zapisei k 'Brat'yam Karamazovym.'" *See*
Dolinin, A. S., ed., F. M. Dostoyevskii: Materialy i issledovaniya.

—— Unizhonnye i oskorblyonnye [The Insulted and Injured], with an
Introduction by L. M. Rozenblyum. Moscow, GIKhL, 1955.

—— "Variant k otryvku iz 'Besov.'" *See* Grossman, Leonid P., ed.,
Tvorchestvo Dostoyevskovo.

—— Zapisnye tetradi F. M. Dostoyevskovo [F. M. Dostoyevski's Note-
books], ed. Ye. N. Konshina, with commentaries by N. I. Ignatova
and Ye. N. Konshina. Moscow, "Academia," 1935.

Dostoyevski, F. M., and I. S. Turgenev. F. M. Dostoyevskii i I. S. Turgenev: Perepiska [F. M. Dostoyevski and I. S. Turgenev: Correspond-
ence], ed. and with commentaries by I. S. Zil'bershtein, and with
an Introduction by N. F. Bel'chikov. Moscow and Leningrad, "Academia," 1928.

Dostoyevskii. Moscow, 1928. Issue No. 3 of Trudy Gosudarstvennoi
Akademii Khudozhestvennykh Nauk. Literaturnaya sektsiya [Papers
of the State Academy of the Arts, Literature Section]. *Contents:*
"Predisloviye" [Foreword], pp. 3–4; V. S. Dorovatovskaya-Lyubimova, "Dostoyevskii i shestidesyatniki" [Dostoyevski and the Men of
the Sixties], pp. 5–60; Georgi Chulkov, "Posledneye slovo Dostoyevskovo o Belinskom" [Dostoyevski's Last Word on Belinski], pp.
61–81; V. S. Nechayeva, "Sravneniya v rannikh povestyakh Dostoyevskovo" [Comparisons in Dostoyevski's Early Stories], pp. 83–114;
M. A. Petrovski, "Kompozitsiya 'Vechnovo muzha'" [Composition
of *The Eternal Husband*], pp. 115–62; S. N. Durylin, "Ob odnom
simvole u Dostoyevskovo" [On One Symbol in Dostoyevski], pp.
163–98; I. N. Kubikov, "Obraz Smerdyakova i yevo obobshchayushchii smysl" [The Character of Smerdaykov and the Sense in Which
It Is a Generalization], pp. 199–216; P. S. Popov, "'Ya' i 'Ono' v
tvorchestve Dostoyevskovo" [The Ego and the Id in Dostoyevski's

Writing], pp. 217–75; Fyodor F. Berezhkov, "Dostoyevskii na Zapade" [Dostoyevski in the West], pp. 277–326.

"Dostoyevskii, F. M.," in Bol'shaya sovetskaya entsiklopediya [Large
Soviet Encyclopedia]. 2d ed. Moscow. Vol. XV (1952), pp. 148–
50.

"Dostoyevskii i o Dostoyevskom" [Dostoyevski and on the Subject of
Dostoyevski], in Zven'ya [Links]. Moscow and Leningrad, "Acade-
mia." Issue No. 6 (1936), ed. Vladimir Bonch-Bruyevich, pp. 413–
600. *Contents:* "Pervaya zapisnaya knizhka—Sibirskaya tetrad' "
[First Notebook—Siberian Booklet], with an Introduction by Leonid
P. Grossman, pp. 413–38; "Perepiska F. M. Dostoyevskovo s M. P.
Pogodinym" [Correspondence of F. M. Dostoyevski with M. P.
Pogodin], with an Introduction and annotations by L. Barsukov, pp.
439–54; "Besedy s Dostoyevskim: Zapisi i pripominaniya Ye. N.
Opochinina" [Conversations with Dostoyevski: Records and Recollec-
tions of Ye. N. Opochinin], with a Foreword and annotations by Yu.
Verkhovski, pp. 454–94; Sh. Tokarzhevski, "F. M. Dostoyevskii v
Omskoi katorge" [F. M. Dostoyevski in Omsk Prison], trans. from
the Polish by V. B. Arendt, pp. 495–512; A. Dolinin, "Dostoyevskii
sredi Petrashevtsev" [Dostoyevski in the Petrashevski Circle], pp.
512–45; B. G. Reizov, "K istorii zamysla 'Brat'yev Karamazovykh' "
[More on the History of the Conception of *The Brothers Karamazov*],
pp. 545–73; S. Panov, " 'Literaturnaya kadril' ' v romane 'Besy' "
[The "Literary Quadrille" in the Novel *The Devils*], pp. 573–82;
"Nerazvernuvshiisya roman F. M. Dostoyevskovo (Pis'ma Marfy
Braun k F. M. Dostoyevskomu)" [An Unrealized Novel of F. M.
Dostoyevski (Letters of Marfa Braun to F. M. Dostoyevski)], with
an Introductory Note by G. Prokhorov, pp. 582–86.

Dostoyevsky, Aimée. *See* Dostoyevskaya, Lyubov'.

Dostoyevsky: Letters and Reminiscences, trans. S. S. Koteliansky and
J. Middleton Murry. New York, Knopf, 1923.

Druzhinin, A. V. "Sovremennye zametki. Pis'ma inogorodnovo podpischika v redaktsiyu 'Sovremennik' o russkoi zhurnalistike" [Con-
temporary Notes: Letters of an Out-of-Town Subscriber to the Editors of *The Contemporary* concerning Russian Journalistic Practices],
Sovremennik [The Contemporary] (St. Petersburg), No. 14 (1849),
p. 67.

Durylin, S. N. "Ob odnom simvole u Dostoyevskovo." *See* Dostoyevskii (Moscow, 1928).

Ehrenburg, Il'ya. "Zrelost' " [Maturity], *Bol'shevik* (Moscow), No. 16 (August, 1942).

Engel'gardt, B. "Ideologicheskii roman Dostoyevskovo." *See* Dolinin, A. S., ed., Dostoyevskii: Stat'i i materialy, Vol. II.

Flekser, A. L. *See* Volynski, A. L., pseud.

F. M. Dostoyevskii. Moscow, "Nikitinskiye subbotniki," 1928. Vol. III of Klassiki v marksistskom osveshchenii [The Classics in the Light of Marxism], in the series Biblioteka pisatelei dlya shkoly i yunoshestva [Library of Writers for Schools and Young People], ed. Ye. F. Nikitina. *Contents:* "Khronologicheskaya tablitsa zhizni i tvorchestva F. M. Dostoyevskovo" [Chronological Table of the Life and Work of F. M. Dostoyevski], pp. 5–6; A. V. Lunacharski, "Dostoyevskii kak khudozhnik i myslitel' " [Dostoyevski as Artist and Thinker], pp. 7–29; V. F. Pereverzev, "F. M. Dostoyevskii," pp. 31–70; Vyacheslav P. Polonski, "Nikolai Stavrogin i roman 'Besy' " [Nikolai Stavrogin and the Novel *The Devils*], pp. 71–126; Yevgeni A. Solov'yov (Andreyevich, pseud.), "F. M. Dostoyevskii," pp. 127–68; L. Voitolovski, "F. M. Dostoyevskii," pp. 169–204; G. Ye. Gorbachov, "Dostoyevskii i yevo reaktsionnyi demokratizm" [Dostoyevski and His Reactionary Democratism], pp. 205–59; V. L. L'vov-Rogachevski, "Novoye khudozhestvennoye slovo" [A New Word in Art], pp. 261–315.

F. M. Dostoyevskii v russkoi kritike: Sbornik statei [F. M. Dostoyevski in Russian Criticism: A Collection of Essays], with an Introduction and annotation by A. A. Belkin. Moscow, GIKhL, 1956. *Contents:* Belkin, "Dostoyevskii v otsenke russkoi kritiki" [Dostoyevski As Evaluated in Russian Criticism], pp. iii–xxxvi; V. G. Belinski, "Peterburgskii sbornik" [Petersburg Miscellany] (excerpt), pp. 3–30; Belinski, "Vzglyad na russkuyu literaturu 1846 goda" [Review of Russian Literature in 1846] (excerpt), pp. 31–34; Belinski, "Vzglyad na russkuyu literaturu 1847 goda" [Review of Russian Literature in 1847] (excerpt), pp. 34–35; P. V. Annenkov, "Zamechatel'noye desyatiletiye (1838–1848)" [A Remarkable Decade (1838–1848)] (excerpt), pp. 36–38; N. A. Dobrolyubov, "Zabitye lyudi" [Downtrodden People], pp. 39–95; D. I. Pisarev, "Pogibshiye i pogibayushchiye" [The Perished and the Perishing], pp. 96–161; Pisarev, "Bor'ba za zhizn' " [Struggle for Life], pp. 162–228; M. Ye. Saltykov-Shchedrin, "Svetlov, yevo vzglyady, kharakter i deyatel'nost' " [Svetlov, His Views, Character, and Activity] (excerpt), pp. 229–32; G. I. Uspenski, "Prazdnik Pushkina" [The Pushkin Celebration] (excerpt), pp. 233–41; Uspenski, "Sekret" [A Secret], pp. 241–54; M. A. Antonovich, "Mistiko-asketicheskii roman" [A Mystically Ascetic Novel], pp. 255–305; N. K. Mikhailovski, "Zhestokii talant" [A Cruel Talent], pp. 306–85; M. Gorki, "Zametki o meshchanstve" [Remarks on the Petit Bourgeoisie], pp. 386–89; Gorki, "O Karamazovshchine" [On Karamazovism], pp. 389–93; Gorki, "Yeshcho o 'Karamazovshchine' " [More on "Karamazovism"], pp. 393–99; Gorki, "Doklad na pervom vsesoyuznom s"yezde sovetskikh pisatelei" [Speech at the First All-Union Congress of Soviet Writers] (excerpt), pp. 400–2; A. V. Lunacharski, "O 'mnogogolosnosti' Dostoyevskovo" [On the 'Polphony' of Dostoyevski's Writing], pp. 403–29; Lunacharski, "O Dostoyevskom" [On Dostoyevski], pp. 429–34; Lunacharski, "Dostoyevskii kak myslitel' i khudozhnik" [Dostoyevski as Thinker and Artist], pp. 435–53; "Primechaniya" [Notes], pp. 454–70.

F. M. Dostoyevskii: Zhizn' i tvorchestvo. See Priluko-Prilutski, N. G., comp.

Fridlender, G. "Obrazy i temy Dostoyevskovo" [Dostoyevski's Characters and Themes], Zvezda [Star] (Leningrad), No. 2 (February, 1956), pp. 157–63.

—— "Roman F. M. Dostoyevskovo 'Idiot' " [F. M. Dostoyevski's Novel The Idiot], in F. M. Dostoyevski, Idiot. Moscow, GIKhL, 1955. Pages 3–18.

"Fyodor Dostoyevsky," Soviet Union (Moscow), No. 2 (February, 1956), p. 36.

Galkina, I. "Velikii russkii pisatel': K 75-letiyu so dnya smerti F. M. Dostoyevskovo" [A Great Russian Writer: On the Seventy-fifth Anniversary of the Death of F. M. Dostoyevski], Sel'skoye khozyaistvo [Agriculture] (Moscow, February 9, 1956).

Ganzhulevich, G. Ya. Dostoyevskii i Gertsen v istorii russkovo samosoznaniya [Dostoyevski and Herzen in the History of Russian Self-Awareness]. St. Petersburg, Tsentral'naya tipo-litografiya M. Ya. Minkova, 1907.

Gerasimov, B. "Dostoyevskii v Semipalatinske" [Dostoyevski in Semi-
palatinsk], *Sibirskiye ogni* [Siberian Fires] (Novosibirsk), No. 3
(1926), pp. 124–44.

—— "Gde zhe otbyval katorgu i ssylku F. M. Dostoyevskii" [Where Did
F. M. Dostoyevski Serve His Prison Term and Exile?], *Sibirskiye
ogni* [Siberian Fires] (Novosibirsk), No. 4 (1926), pp. 174–77.

Gizetti, A. "Gordye yazychnitzy." *See* Brodski, N. L., ed., Tvorcheskii
put' Dostoyevskovo.

Glivenko, I. M., ed. *See* Dostoyevski, F. M., Iz arkhiva F. M. Dostoyevskovo: "Prestupleniye i nakazaniye."

Gnedich, F. "Prorochestva Dostoyevskovo" [Dostoyevski's Prophecies],
supplement to *Niva* [Ploughland] (Petrograd), No. 1 (1915), pp.
5–15.

Golant, I. B. "Evroendokrinologiya velikikh russkikh pisatelei i poetov:
F. M. Dostoyevskii i drugiye" [Heuristic Endocrinology of Great
Russian Writers and Poets: F. M. Dostoyevski and Others], *Kliniche-
skii arkhiv genial'nosti i odaryonnosti* [Clinical Archive of Genius and
Talent] (Moscow), No. 3 (1927), pp. 203–42.

Golovashenko, Yu. "Geroi Dostoyevskovo na stsene: 'Dyadyushkin son'
v Leningradskom teatre komedii" [Dostoyevski's Characters on the
Stage: "Uncle's Dream" in the Leningrad Theater of Comedy],
Sovetskaya kul'tura [Soviet Culture] (Moscow, March 20, 1956).

Gorbachov, Georgi Ye. "Dostoyevskii i yevo reaktsionnyi demokratizm."
See Gorbachov, Kapitalizm i russkaya literatura, and the compilation
F. M. Dostoyevskii.

—— Kapitalizm i russkaya literatura [Capitalism and Russian Litera-
ture]. Leningrad, GIZ, 1925. Pages 85–110. This section was republished under the title "Dostoyevskii i yevo reaktsionnyi demokratism"
in the compilation *F. M. Dostoyevskii (q.v.)*.

—— "Revolyutsiya i Dostoyevskii" [The Revolution and Dostoyevski],
Zapiski Petrogradskovo im. Tolmachova Instruktorskovo Instituta
[Notes of the Tolmachov Teachers Institute of Petrograd] (Petro-
grad), No. 3 (1922), pp. 1–28.

—— "Sotsial'nye korni propovedi Dostoyevskovo" [The Social Roots of
Dostoyevski's Teaching], *Bor'ba klassov* [The Class Struggle] (Leningrad), No. 1–2 (1924), pp. 172–207.

Gorki, Maxim (pseud. of Aleksei Maksimovich Peshkov). "Besedy o remesle" [Shop Talks], in O literature: Stat'i i rechi, 1928–1935 [On Literature: Articles and Speeches, 1928–1935]. Moscow, GIKhL, 1935.

—— "Doklad na s"yezde sovetskikh pisatelei" [Speech at the Congress of Soviet Writers], in O literature: Stat'i i rechi, 1928–1935 [On Literature: Articles and Speeches, 1928–1935]. Moscow, GIKhL, 1935. *See also* F. M. Dostoyevskii v russkoi kritike: Sbornik statei.

—— Istoriya russkoi literatury [History of Russian Literature]. Moscow, Goslitizdat, 1939. Pages 247–57.

—— "O karamazovshchine" [On Karamazovism]. Republished in *Literaturno-kriticheskiye stat'i* [Articles of Literary Criticism] (Moscow, Goslitizdat, 1937), pp. 145–48; in *O literature: Literaturno-kriticheskiye stat'i* [On Literature: Articles of Literary Criticism] (Moscow, Sovetskii pisatel', 1953), pp. 151–54; and in the compilation *F. M. Dostoyevskii v russkoi kritike: Sbornik statei (q.v.)*. The article was first published, under the heading "Pis'mo v redaktsiyu" [Letter to the Editor], in *Russkoye slovo* [Russian Word] (St. Petersburg, September 22, 1913).

—— "O petrashevtsakh, I. Turgeneve, F. Dostoyevskom, L. Tolstom" [Concerning the Petrashevtsy, I. Turgenev, F. Dostoyevski, and L. Tolstoi], *Literaturnyi kritik* [Literary Critic] (Moscow), No. 6 (1938), pp. 41–81.

—— "O tom, kak ya uchilsya pisat' " [On the Way I Learned to Write], in O literature: Stat'i i rechi, 1928–1935 [On Literature: Articles and Speeches, 1928–1935]. Moscow, GIKhL, 1935.

—— "Yeshcho o karamazovshchine" [More on Karamazovism]. Republished in *Literaturno-kriticheskiye stat'i* [Articles of Literary Criticism] (Moscow, Goslitizdat, 1937), pp. 149–53; in *O literature: Literaturno-kriticheskiye stat'i* [On Literature: Articles of Literary Criticism] (Moscow, Sovetskii pisatel', 1953), pp. 155–60; and in the compilation *Dostoyevskii v russkoi kritike: Sbornik statei (q.v.)*. The article was first published, under the heading "Otkrytoye pis'mo" [Open Letter], in *Russkoye slovo* [Russian Word] (St. Petersburg, October 27, 1913).

—— "Zametki o meshchanstve" [Remarks on the Petit Bourgeoisie]. Republished in *Stat'i 1905–1916 gg.* [Articles of 1905–1916] (2d ed.; Petrograd, "Parus," 1918); in *Literaturno-kriticheskiye stat'i* [Arti-

cles of Literary Criticism] (Moscow, Goslitizdat, 1937), pp. 7–9; and
in the compilation *Dostoyevskii v russkoi kritike: Sbornik statei*
(*q.v.*). The article was first published in the newspaper *Novaya
zhizn'* [New Life] (St. Petersburg), in 1905.

Gornfel'd, A. G. "Iz novoi literatury o Dostoyevskom" [From the New
Literature on Dostoyevski], *Letopis' Doma literatorov* [Annals of
the House of Writers] (Petrograd), No. 2 (November 15, 1921),
p. 2.

Gornfel'd, A. G., ed. *See* Dostoyevskaya, Lyubov', Dostoyevskii v izobrazhenii yevo docheri L. Dostoyevskoi.

Gornfel'd, A. G., and A. M. Remizov. Dostoyevskii: Stat'i [Dostoyev-
ski: Articles]. St. Petersburg [*sic*], Izd. Doma literatorov, 1921.

Gorshkov, Aleksandr (pseud. of M. A. Protopopov). "Novyi roman g.
Dostoyevskovo 'Brat'ya Karamazovy' " [Mr. Dostoyevski's New
Novel *The Brothers Karamazov*], *Russkaya pravda* [Russian Truth]
(St. Petersburg), No. 51 (1879).

—— "Propovednik novovo slova. 'Dnevnik pisatelya' " [Preacher of a
New Word: *Diary of a Writer*], *Russkoye bogatstvo* [Russian
Wealth] (St. Petersburg), No. 8 (August, 1880), pp. 6–20.

Govorov, A. S. "O prebyvanii F. M. Dostoyevskovo v Omske" [Concern-
ing the Time F. M. Dostoyevski Spent in Omsk], *Omskaya oblast'*
[Omsk Oblast] (Omsk), No. 8 (1940), pp. 49–53.

Grigorovich, D. V. Literaturnye vospominaniya [Literary Reminis-
cences], ed. V. L. Komarovich. Leningrad, Academia, 1928.

Grossman, Leonid P. "Bal'zak i Dostoyevskii" [Balzac and Dostoyev-
ski], *Russkaya mysl'* [Russian Thought] (Moscow), No. 1 (1914),
pp. 44–55. *See also* Grossman, Dostoyevskii: Put', poetika, tvorchestvo, and Grossman, Poetika Dostoyevskovo.

—— Biblioteka Dostoyevskovo: Po neizdannym materialam [Dosto-
yevski's Library: From Unpublished Materials]. Odessa, Ivasenko,
1919.

—— "Dostoyevskii i pravitel'stvennye krugi 1870-kh godov" [Dosto-
yevski and Government Circles in the 1870s], in Literaturnoye
nasledstvo [Literary Heritage]. Moscow, Izdaniye zhurnal'no-gazetnovo ob"yedineniya. Issue No. 15 (1934), pp. 83–162.

—— "Dostoyevskii i teatralizatsiya romana" [Dostoyevski and the

Dramatization of the Novel], in Grossman, Bor'ba za stil' [Struggle for Style]. Moscow, 1927. Pages 147–68.

—— "Dostoyevskii i Yevropa" [Dostoyevski and Europe], *Russkaya mysl'* [Russian Thought] (Moscow), No. 11 (1915), pp. 54–93. *See also* Grossman, Dostoyevskii: Put', poetika, tvorchestvo.

—— Dostoyevskii na zhiznennom puti [Dostoyevski on Life's Way]. Moscow, Nikitinskiye subbotniki, 1928.

—— Dostoyevskii: Put', poetika, tvorchestvo [Dostoyevski: Path, Style and Writing]. Moscow, "Sovremennye problemy," 1928. Vol. II of Grossman, Sobraniye sochinenii [Collected Works]. Part One contains Put' Dostoyevskovo [Path of Dostoyevski]; Part Two (Tvorchestvo Dostoyevskovo [Dostoyevski's Writing]) contains: "Kompozitsiya v romane Dostoyevskovo" [Composition of Dostoyevski's Novels], pp. 9–59; "Bal'zak i Dostoyevskii" [Balzac and Dostoyevski], pp. 60–106; "Zhivopis' Dostoyevskovo" [The Pictorial in Dostoyevski], pp. 107–30; "Stilistika Stavrogina" [The Stylistics of Stavrogin], pp. 131–48; "Dostoyevskii i Yevropa" [Dostoyevski and Europe], pp. 151–213; "Bakunin i Dostoyevskii" [Bakunin and Dostoyevski], pp. 214–311; "Zaklyucheniye: Iskusstvo romana u Dostoyevskovo" [Conclusion: Art of the Novel in Dostoyevski], pp. 312–33.

—— "Gofman, Bal'zak i Dostoyevskii" [Hoffmann, Balzac and Dostoyevski], *Sofiya* [Sophia] (Moscow), No. 5 (1914), pp. 87–96.

—— "Grazhdanskaya smert' F. M. Dostoyevskovo" [The Civil Death of F. M. Dostoyevski], in Literaturnoye nasledstvo [Literary Heritage]. Moscow, Izdaniye zhurnal'no-gazetnovo ob"yedineniya. Issue No. 22-24 (1935), pp. 683–736.

—— "Iskusstvo romana u Dostoyevskovo" [The Art of the Novel in Dostoyevski], in Svitok [The Scroll]. Moscow, Nikitinskiye subbotniki. Issue No. 1 (1922), pp. 73–83. *See also* Grossman, Dostoyevskii: Put', poetika, tvorchestvo, and Grossman, Poetika Dostoyevskovo.

—— Kazn' Dostoyevskovo [Dostoyevski's Punishment]. Moscow, "Ogonyok," 1928.

—— "Kompozitsiya v romane Dostoyevskovo" [Composition of Dostoyevski's Novels], *Vestnik Yevropy* [Courier of Europe] (Petrograd), No. 9 (1916), pp. 121–56. See also Grossman, Dostoyevskii: Put', poetika, tvorchestvo, and Grossman, Poetika Dostoyevskovo.

—— "Novoye o Dostoyevskom" [New Material concerning Dostoyev-ski], *Ogonyok* [The Light] (Moscow), No. 4 (1941), p. 10.

—— Poetika Dostoyevskovo [Dostoyevski's Style]. Moscow, Gosudar-stvennaya Akademiya Khudozhestvennykh Nauk, 1925. *Contents:* "Vvedeniye" [Introduction], pp. 5–6; "Kompozitsiya v romane Dosto-yevskovo" [Composition of Dostoyevski's Novels], pp. 7–63; "Bal'zak i Dostoyevskii" [Balzac and Dostoyevski], pp. 64–115; "Zhivopis' Dostoyevskovo" [The Pictorial in Dostoyevski], pp. 116–43; "Stilis-tika Stavrogina" [The Stylistics of Stavrogin], pp. 144–62; "Iskus-stvo romana u Dostoyevskovo" [The Art of the Novel in Dostoyevski], pp. 163–81; and " 'Chelovecheskaya komediya' v Rossii (1830–1900)" [*The Human Comedy* in Russia (1830–1900)], Appendix to the article "Bal'zak i Dostoyevskii," pp. 182–87.

—— "Problema realizma u Dostoyevskovo" [The Problem of Realism in Dostoyevski], *Vestnik Yevropy* [Courier of Europe] (Petrograd), No. 2 (February, 1917), pp. 65–100.

—— "Put' Dostoyevskovo." *See* Grossman, ed., Tvorchestvo Dostoyev-skovo.

—— Put' Dostoyevskovo [The Path of Dostoyevski]. Leningrad, Brock-haus-Efron, 1924. *See also* Grossman, Dostoyevskii: Put', poetika, tvorchestvo.

——Ruletenburg: Povest' o Dostoyevskom [Roulettenburg: A Story of Dostoyevski]. Moscow, GIKhL, 1932.

—— "Russkii *Kandit* (k voprosu o vliyanii Vol'tera na Dostoyevskovo)" [The Russian *Candide:* On the Question of the Influence of Voltaire on Dostoyevski], *Vestnik Yevropy* [Courier of Europe] (St. Petersburg), No. 5 (1914), pp. 192–203.

—— Seminarii po Dostoyevskomu: Materialy, bibliografiya i kom-mentarii [Seminar on Dostoyevski: Materials, Bibliography and Com-mentaries]. Moscow, Gosizdat, 1923.

—— "Stilistika Stavrogina." *See* Grossman, Dostoyevskii: Put', poetika, tvorchestvo, and Grossman, Poetika Dostoyevskovo; and Dolinin, A. S., ed., Dostoyevskii: Stat'i i materialy, Vol. II.

—— Tri sovremennika: Tyutchev, Dostoyevskii, Apollon Grigor'yev [Three Contemporaries: Tyutchev, Dostoyevski and Apollon Grigor'-yev]. Moscow, Knigoizdatel'stvo pisatelei, 1922.

—— "Velikii russkii pisatel': K 75-letiyu so dnya smerti F. M. Dosto-

yevskovo" [A Great Russian Writer: On the Seventy-fifth Anniversary
of the Death of F. M. Dostoyevski], *Vechernyaya Moskva* [Evening
Moscow] (Moscow, February 9, 1956).
—— Zhizn' i trudy F. M. Dostoyevskovo: Biografiya v datakh i dokumentakh [Life and Work of F. M. Dostoyevski: A Biography in Dates
and Documents]. Moscow and Leningrad, Academia, 1935.
—— *See also* "Dostoyevskii i o Dostoyevskom."
Grossman, Leonid·P., ed. Tvorchestvo Dostoyevskovo [Dostoyevski's
Writing]. Odessa, Vseukrainskoye gosudarstvennoye izdatel'stvo,
1921. *Contents:* "Ot redaktora" [From the Editor], pp. v–xii. "Materialy" [Materials], including the following unpublished Dostoyevski
manuscripts edited by Grossman: "Plan romana 'Zhitiye velikovo
greshnika' " [Plan for the Novel "Life of a Great Sinner"], pp.
7–11; "Variant k otryvku iz 'Besov' " [Variant to a Passage from *The
Devils*], pp. 11–13; "Iz 'Zapisnykh knizhek' " [From the "Notebooks"], pp. 13–20; "Epizod iz 'Podrostka' " [An Episode from *A
Raw Youth*], pp. 20–24; "Otryvki iz raznykh rukopisei" [Passages
from Various Manuscripts], pp. 24–28; A. G. Dostoyevskaya, "Primechaniya k sochineniyam Dostoyevskovo" [Notes to Dostoyevski's Writ-
ings], ed. Leonid P. Grossman, pp. 29–35; "Sekretnye instruktsii o
Dostoyevskom (materialy Odesskovo Arkhivnovo fonda)" [Secret
Instructions concerning Dostoyevski (Materials from the Odessa Archive)], ed. Yu. G. Oksman, pp. 36–38. "Stat'i" [Articles]: M. P.
Alekseyev, "O dramaticheskikh opytakh Dostoyevskovo" [On Dostoyevski's Experiments in Drama], pp. 41–62; Yu. G. Oksman, "Dostoyevskii v redaktsii 'Grazhdanina' " [Dostoyevski on the Editorial Staff
of *The Citizen*], pp. 63–82; L. P. Grossman, "Put' Dostoyevskovo"
[The Path of Dostoyevski], pp. 83–110. "Prilozheniye" [Appendix]:
"Iz zateryannykh statei Dostoyevskovo: 'Ne tron' menya' (Vremya,
1861)" [From the Lost Articles of Dostoyevski: "Touch Me Not"
(*Time*, 1861)], pp. 111–20; "Khronika (Novye izdaniya i literatura o
Dostoyevskom)" [Listing (New Publications and Literature concerning Dostoyevski)], pp. 121–29; "Bibliografiya pisem Dostoyevskovo"
[Bibliography of Dostoyevski's Letters], comp. A. Leifer and M. Rapa-
port, pp. 130–37; "Bibliografiya vospominanii o Dostoyevskom"
[Bibliography of Reminiscences of Dostoyevski], comp. Ye. Raspu-
tova, F. Semyatitskaya, and A. Shain, pp. 138–48.

—— Zabytye stranitsy Dostoyevskovo. *See* Dostoyevski, F. M., Polnoye sobraniye sochinenii (1911–16).

—— *See also* Dostoyevskaya, A. G., Vospominaniya A. G. Dostoyevskoi; and Dostoyevski, F. M., Sobraniye sochinenii (1956).

Grossman, L. P., and Vyacheslav Polonski. Spor o Bakunine i Dostoyevskom [Dispute over Bakunin and Dostoyevski]. Moscow, Gosizdat, 1926.

Grossman-Roshchin, I. "Dni nashei zhizni: O poznavayemosti khudozhestvennovo proshlovo: O sotsiologizme M. M. Bakhtina, avtora knigi 'Problemy tvorchestva Dostoyevskovo' " [Days of Our Life: On the Cognoscibility of the Artistic Past: On the Sociologism of M. M. Bakhtin, Author of the Book *Problems of Dostoyevski's Writing*], *Na literaturnom postu* [On Literary Guard] (Moscow), No. 18 (1929), pp. 5–10.

Gural'nik, U. A. " 'Sovremennik' v bor'be s zhurnalami Dostoyevskovo" [*The Contemporary* in the Fight with Dostoyevski's Journals], *Izvestiya Akademii Nauk SSSR, Otdeleniye Literatury i yazyka* [News of the USSR Academy of Sciences, Literature and Language Section] (Moscow and Leningrad), IX, No. 4 (1950), 265–85.

—— "Velikii russkii pisatel': K 75-letiyu so dnya smerti F. M. Dostoyevskovo" [A Great Russian Writer: On the Seventy-fifth Anniversary of the Death of F. M. Dostoyevski], *Uchitel'skaya gazeta* [Teachers' Gazette] (Moscow, February 8, 1956).

G . . . v, V. "F. M. Dostoyevskii," *Sibirskiye ogni* [Siberian Fires] (Novonikolayevsk [now Novosibirsk]), No. 3 (1924), pp. 124–44; No. 4 (1926), pp. 141–50.

Ignatova, N. I. *See* Dostoyevski, F. M., Zapisnye tetradi F. M. Dostoyevskovo.

Il'inski, L. K. "F. M. Dostoyevskii i Gl. Iv. Uspenskii." *See* Dolinin, A. S., ed., Dostoyevskii: Stat'i i materialy, Vol. I.

Iskoz, Arkadi Semyonovich. *See* Dolinin, A. S., pseud.

Istomin, K. K. "Iz zhizni i tvorchestva Dostoyevskovo v molodosti." *See* Brodski, N. L., ed., Tvorcheskii put' Dostoyevskovo.

—— Nachala i kontsy tvorchestva Dostoyevskovo [Beginnings and Endings of Dostoyevski's Writing]. Moscow, 1922.

Ivanov, Vyacheslav. "Dostoyevskii i roman-tragediya" [Dostoyevski and the Tragedy-Novel], *Russkaya mysl'* [Russian Thought] (Moscow, 1911), No. 5, pp. 46–61, and No. 6, pp. 1–17. Reprinted in

Ivanov, *Borozdy i mezhi* [Furrows and Boundaries] (Moscow, Musaget, 1916), pp. 5–60. Published, in slightly expanded form, in English translation under the title *Freedom and the Tragic Life*, trans. Norman Cameron and ed. S. Konovalov (New York, Noonday Press, 1952).

Ivanov-Razumnik [R. V.]. Russkaya literatura: Ot semidesyatikh godov do nashykh dnei [Russian Literature: From the Seventies to Our Day]. 6th ed. Berlin, Skify, 1923. Vol. II of Istoriya russkoi obshchestvennoi mysli [History of Russian Social Thought]. St. Petersburg, 1906. See especially Chap. 4, "Tolstoi i Dostoyevskii' [Tolstoi and Dostoyevski], pp. 105–77.

"K 75-letiyu so dnya smerti F. M. Dostoyevskovo" [For the Seventy-fifth Anniversary of the Death of F. M. Dostoyevski], *Literaturnaya gazeta* [Literary Gazette] (Moscow, December 8, 1955).

"K 75-letiyu so dnya smerti F. M. Dostoyevskovo" [For the Seventy-fifth Anniversary of the Death of F. M. Dostoyevski], *Sovetskaya kul'tura* [Soviet Culture] (Moscow, December 8, 1955).

Karolitskii, M. S. "Na grani poluveka (K 50-letiyu poyavleniya v svet 'Brat'yev Karamazovykh')" [At the Half-Century Mark (On the Fiftieth Anniversary of the Publication of *The Brothers Karamazov*)], *Vestnik Znaniya* [Herald of Knowledge] (Leningrad), No. 4 (1929), pp. 169–72.

Kashina-Yevreinova, A. A. Podpol'ye geniya [The Underground Phase of a Genius]. Petrograd, Tret'ya strazha, 1923.

Kaus, Otto. Dostojewski und sein Schicksal. Berlin, E. Laub, 1923.

Khalabayev, K. I., ed. *See* Dostoyevski, F. M., Polnoye sobraniye khudozhestvennykh proizvedenii.

Kirpichnikov, A. "Fyodor Mikhailovich Dostoyevskii (Biograficheskii ocherk)." *See* Priluko-Prilutski, N. G., comp., F. M. Dostoyevskii: Zhizn' i tvorchestvo.

Kirpotin, V. Ya. " 'Bednye lyudi'—pervyi roman F. M. Dostoyevskovo" [*Poor Folk*, F. M. Dostoyevski's First Novel], *Oktyabr'* [October] (Moscow), No. 1–2 (1946), pp. 160–70.

—— "Dostoyevskii v Sibiri" [Dostoyevski in Siberia], *Literaturnaya gazeta* [Literary Gazette] (Moscow, February 9, 1956).

—— F. M. Dostoyevskii. Moscow, Sovetskii pisatel', 1947.

—— "Fyodor Mikhailovich Dostoyevskii (k 125-letiyu so dnya rozhdeniya)" [Fyodor Mikhailovich Dostoyevski: On the 125th Anniversary of His Birth], *Zvezda* [Star] (Leningrad), No. 11 (1946), pp. 173–88.

—— Molodoi Dostoyevskii [The Young Dostoyevski]. Moscow, GIKhL, 1947.

—— "Velikii pis'mennik: Do 75-richchya z dnya smerti F. M. Dos-toyevs'kogo" [A Great Writer: On the 75th Anniversary of the Death of F. M. Dostoyevski], *Literaturna gazeta* [Literary Gazette] (Kiev, February 9, 1956).

—— "Velikii russkii pisatel': K 75-letiyu so dnya smerti F. M. Dosto-yevskovo" [A Great Russian Writer: On the Seventy-fifth Anniversary of the Death of F. M. Dostoyevski], *Izvestiya* (Moscow, February 9, 1956).

Kirpotin, V. Ya., ed. *See* Dostoyevski, F. M., Sobraniye sochinenii (1956).

Knizhnik-Vetrov, I. "F. M. Dostoyevskii i A. V. Kovrin-Krukovskaya" [F. M. Dostoyevski and A. V. Kovrin-Krukovskaya] in Literaturno-khudozhestvennyi sbornik Krasnoi Panoramy [Literature and Art Miscellany of *Red Panorama*]. Moscow, Molodaya gvardiya, May, 1929. Pages 31–45.

Komarovich, V. L. Die Urgestalt der Brüder Karamasoff: Dostojewskis Quellen, Entwürfe und Fragmente, ed. René L. Fülop-Miller and Friedrich Eckstein. Munich, R. Piper, 1928.

—— "Die Weltanschauung Dostojewskijs in der russischen Forschung des letzten Jahrzehnts (1914–1924)," *Zeitschrift für slavische Phi-lologie* (Leipzig), Bd. 3 (1926), pp. 217–28.

—— "Dostoyevskii i Geine" [Dostoyevski and Heine], *Sovremennyi mir* [The Contemporary World] (Petrograd), No. 10 (1916), pp. 97–107.

—— "Dostoyevskii i shestidesyatniki" [Dostoyevski and the Men of the Sixties], *Sovremennyi mir* [The Contemporary World] (Petrograd), No. 1 (1917), pp. 129–39.

—— Dostoyevskii: Sovremennye problemy istoriko-literaturnovo izu-cheniya [Dostoyevski: Contemporary Problems in the Study of Liter-ary History]. Leningrad, "Obrazovaniye," 1925.

—— "Genezis romana 'Podrostok'" [Genesis of the Novel *A Raw Youth*], *Literaturnaya mysl'* [Literary Thought] (Leningrad), No. 4 (1925), pp. 366–86.

—— "Langschriftliche Aufzeichnungen, Varianten und Briefe zu dem roman der 'Jüngling,' " in Der unbekannte Dostojewski, ed. René L. Fülop-Miller and Friedrich Eckstein. Munich, R. Piper, 1926. Pages 445–519.

—— "Literaturnoye nasledstvo Dostoyevskovo za gody revolyutsii: Obzor publikatsii 1917–1933" [Literary Heritage of Dostoyevski in the Years of the Revolution: A Survey of the Publications of 1917–1933], in Literaturnoye nasledstvo [Literary Heritage]. Moscow, Izdaniye zhurnal'no-gazetnovo ob"yedineniya. Issue No. 15 (1934), pp. 258–81.

—— "Mirovaya garmoniya" [World Harmony], Atènei [Athenaeum] (Leningrad), No. 1–2 (1924), pp. 112–42.

—— "Neizdannaya glava romana 'Besy' F. M. Dostoyevskovo" [An Unpublished Chapter of F. M. Dostoyevski's Novel The Devils], Byloye [The Past] (Petrograd), No. 18 (1922), pp. 219–26.

—— "Nenapisannaya poema Dostoyevskovo." See Dolinin, A. S., ed., Dostoyevskii: Stat'i i materialy, Vol. I.

—— "Neue Probleme der Dostojewskij-Forschung 1925–1930," Zeitschrift für slavische Philologie (Leipzig), Bd. 10 (1933), pp. 402–28; Bd. 11 (1934), pp. 193–236.

—— "Roman 'Podrostok' kak khudozhestvennoye yedinstvo." See Dolinin, A. S., ed., Dostoyevskii: Stat'i i materialy, Vol. II.

— "Yunost' Dostoyevskovo" [The Youth of Dostoyevski], Byloye [The Past] (Leningrad), No. 23 (1924), pp. 3–42.

Komarovich, V. L., ed. See Grigorovich, D. V., Literaturnye vospominaniya.

Koni, Anatoli F. Na zhiznennom puti [On Life's Way]. St. Petersburg, "Trud." Vol. II (1912).

—— Nekrasov, Dostoyevskii po lichnym vospominaniyam [Nekrasov and Dostoyevski from Personal Reminiscences]. Petrograd, Kooperativnoye izdatel'stvo literatorov i uchonykh, 1921.

—— Ocherki i vospominaniya [Sketches and Memoirs]. St. Petersburg, 1906. Pages 73–90.

—— "Voprosy o prestuplenii i nakazanii v proizvedeniyakh Dostoyevskovo." See Priluko-Prilutski, N. G., comp., F. M. Dostoyevskii: Zhizn' i tvorchestvo.

Konovalova, K. "Novye tipy i sovremennye kharaktery" [New Types and Contemporary Characters], *Rezets* [Cutter] (Leningrad), No. 41 (1929), pp. 14–15.

Konshina, Ye. N., ed. *See* Dostoyevski, F. M., Zapisnye tetradi F. M. Dostoyevskovo.

Korobka, N. I. "Merezhkovskii o Tolstom i Dostoyevskom" [Merezhkovski on Tolstoi and Dostoyevski], *Obrazovaniye* [Education] (St. Petersburg), No. 11 (1901).

—— Opyt obzora istorii russkoi literatury dlya shkol i samoobrazovaniya [Attempt at a Survey of the History of Russian Literature for Schools and Self-Education]. St. Petersburg, 1907. Part 3.

Koteliansky, S. S., ed. and trans. *See* Dostoyevskaya, A. G., Dostoyevsky Portrayed by His Wife.

Koz'min, B. P. "Br. Dostoyevskiye i proklamatsii 'Molodaya Rossiya' " [The Dostoyevski Brothers and the "Young Russia" Proclamations], *Pechat' i revolyutsiya* [Press and Revolution] (Moscow), No. 2–3 (1929), pp. 69–76.

Kranikhfel'd, V. B. "Preodoleniye Dostoyevskovo" [Overcoming Dostoyevski], *Teatr i iskusstvo* [Theater and Art] (St. Petersburg), Nos. 14 and 16 (1911). Republished in the anthology *V mire idei i obrazov* [In the World of Ideas and Images] (Petrograd, "Zhizn' i znaniye," 1917), Vol. III.

Kubikov, I. N. "Obraz Smerdyakova i yevo obobshchayushchii smysl." *See* Dostoyevskii (Moscow, 1928).

Kulikov, S. N. "K biografii F. M. Dostoyevskovo" [More on F. M. Dostoyevski's Biography], *Katorga i ssylka* [Penal Servitude and Exile] (Moscow), No. 112 (1934), pp. 108–14.

Ladyzhenski, A. M. "F. M. Dostoyevskii kak filosof" [F. M. Dostoyevski as Philosopher], *Izvestiya Donskovo Gosudarstvennovo Universiteta* [News of the Don State University] (Rostov-on-Don, 1923).

Lapshin, I. "Estetika Dostoyevskovo." *See* Dolinin, A. S., ed., Dostoyevskii: Stat'i i materialy, Vol. I.

Lastoŭski, Vatslaŭ. *See* Peregrinus, pseud.

Lebedev, Z. "F. M. Dastaeŭski: Da 75-godzya z dnya smertsi" [F. M. Dostoyevski: On the Seventy-fifth Anniversary of His Death], *Belarus'* [Byelorussia] (Minsk), No. 2 (1956), p. 28.

Lenin, V. I. "Lev Tolstoi kak zerkalo russkoi revolyutsii" [Lev Tolstoi as a Mirror of the Russian Revolution], *Proletarii* [The Proletarian]

(Geneva, September 11, 1908). Reprinted in Lenin, *Sochineniya* [Works] (4th ed.; Moscow, Gospolitizdat), XV (1947), 179–86.

Lensu, Ye. "F. M. Dostoyevskii," *Sovetskaya Belorussiya* [Soviet Byelorussia] (Minsk, February 9, 1956).

Leont'yev, K. N. "Dostoyevskii o russkom dvoryanstve" [Dostoyevski on the Subject of the Russian Nobility], in Sobraniye sochinenii [Collected Works]. Moscow, Sablin, 1912. Vol. VII, pp. 438–48. Originally published in *Grazhdanin* [The Citizen] (St. Petersburg, 1896).

—— "Nashi novye khristiane: F. Dostoyevskii i L. Tolstoi" [Our New Christians: F. Dostoyevski and L. Tolstoi], *Varshavskii dnevnik* [Warsaw Journal] (Warsaw), Nos. 162, 169, and 173 (1880). Included in his *Sobraniye sochinenii* [Collected Works] (Moscow, Sablin, 1912), VIII, 175–215 (section entitled "O vsemirnoi lyubvi: Rech' F. M. Dostoyevskovo na Pushkinskom prazdnike" [On Universal Love: F. M. Dostoyevski's Speech at the Pushkin Celebration]).

Lerner, N. O. "Tainstvennye uzelki: Sluchai s Dostoyevskim" [Mysterious Complications: A Dostoyevski Episode], in Literaturno-khudozhestvennyi sbornik Krasnoi Panoramy [Literature and Art Miscellany of *Red Panorama*]. Moscow, Molodaya gvardiya, October, 1928. Pages 36–42.

Levidov, Mikhail Yul'yevich. "Mif o Dostoyevskom: Razroznennye mysli" [The Myth About Dostoyevski: Random Thoughts], *Literaturnaya gazeta* [Literary Gazette] (Moscow, February 9, 1931).

Lunacharski, A. V. "Dostoyevskii, F. M.," in Bol'shaya sovetskaya entsiklopediya [Large Soviet Encyclopedia]. 1st ed. Moscow, Gosudarstvennyi Nauchnyi Institut "Sovetskaya Entsiklopediya." Vol. XXIII (1931), cols. 332–45.

—— "Dostoyevskii i pisateli" [Dostoyevski and Writers], *Literaturnaya gazeta* [Literary Gazette] (Moscow, February 9, 1931).

—— "Dostoyevskii kak khudozhnik i myslitel' " [Dostoyevski as Artist and Thinker], *Krasnaya nov'* [Red Virgin Soil] (Moscow), No. 4 (1921), pp. 204–12. Republished in Lunacharski, *Literaturnye siluety* [Literary Silhouettes] (2d ed.; Leningrad, GIZ, 1925), pp. 155–69; and in the compilation *F. M. Dostoyevskii* (*q.v.*).

—— "Dostoyevskii kak myslitel' i khudozhnik" [Dostoyevski as Thinker and Artist], in Dostoyevski, F. M., Sochineniya [Works], ed. Lunacharski. Moscow and Leningrad, GIKhL, 1931. Pages v–xiv. Republished in Lunacharski, *Klassiki russkoi literatury* (*q.v.*), pp. 295–311; and in the compilation *F. M. Dostoyevskii v russkoi kritike: Sbornik statei* (*q.v.*).

—— Etyudy: Kriticheskiye i polemicheskiye stat'i [Studies: Critical and Polemical Articles]. St. Petersburg, "Pravda," 1905.

—— Klassiki russkoi literatury [Classics of Russian Literature], ed. and with commentaries by N. F. Bel'chikov. Moscow, GIKhL, 1937.

—— "O Dostoyevskom" [On Dostoyevski], *Rost* [Growth] (Moscow), No. 4 (1931). Republished in Lunacharski, *Russkaya literatura* [Russian Literature], ed. and with commentaries by N. F. Bel'chikov (Moscow, OGIZ, 1947), pp. 241–46; and in the compilation *F. M. Dostoyevskii v russkoi kritike: Sbornik statei* (*q.v*).

—— "O mnogogolosnosti Dostoyevskovo (po povodu knigi M. M. Bakhtina 'Problemy tvorchestva Dostoyevskovo')" [On the Polyphony of Dostoyevski (in Connection with M. M. Bakhtin's Book *Problems of Dostoyevski's Writing*)], *Novyi mir* [New World] (Moscow), No. 10 (1929), pp. 195–209. Republished in Lunacharski, *Klassiki russkoi literatury* (*q.v.*), pp. 312–34; and in the compilation *F. M. Dostoyevskii v russkoi kritike: Sbornik statei* (*q.v.*).

—— "Russkii Faust" [The Russian Faust], *Voprosy psikhologii i filosofii* [Questions of Psychology and Philosophy] (Moscow), No. 3 (May–June 1902), pp. 783–95.

Lunacharski, A. V., ed. *See* Dostoyevski, F. M., Sochineniya (1931).

L'vov-Rogachevski, V. (pseud. of Vasili L'vovich Rogachevski). Noveishaya russkaya literatura [Modern Russian Literature]. 6th ed., rev. Moscow, "Mir," 1927. Pages 113–37.

—— "Novoye khudozhestvennoye slovo." *See* the compilation F. M. Dostoyevskii.

Lyubimov, S. "F. M. Dostoyevskii (vopros ob yevo proiskhozhdenii)" [F. M. Dostoyevski: The Question of His Origin], *Literaturnaya mysl'* [Literary Thought] (Petrograd), No. 1 (1923), pp. 208–10.

—— "K voprosu o genealogii Dostoyevskovo." *See* Dolinin, A. S., ed., Dostoyevskii: Stat'i i materialy, Vol. II.

Maikov, V. N. "Nechto o russkoi literature v 1846 godu" [Something on Russian Literature in 1846], in Kriticheskiye opyty [Essays in Criticism]. St. Petersburg, Panteon literatury, 1889.

Matuzova, Nadiya. "Velikii rosiis'skii pis'mennik" [A Great Russian

Writer], *Radyans'ka zhinka* [Soviet Woman] (Kiev), No. 2 (1956), p. 22.

Mazon, André. "Quelques Lettres de Dostoevsky à Turgenev," *Revue des Etudes Slaves* (Paris), No. 1 (1921), pp. 117–37.

Meilakh, B. "Sila khudozhnika" [Power of the Artist], *Literaturnaya gazeta* [Literary Gazette] (Moscow, February 9, 1956).

Merezhkovski, D. S. "Dostoyevskii," in Polnoye sobraniye sochinenii [Complete Works]. St. Petersburg and Moscow, Vol'f. Vol. XIII (1911), pp. 210–36; and in Polnoye sobraniye sochinenii. Moscow, Sytin. Vol. XVIII (1914), pp. 5–32.

—— "Gor'kii i Dostoyevskii" [Gorki and Dostoyevski], in Bylo i budet [Past and Future]. Petrograd, 1915. Pages 269–83.

—— L. Tolstoi i Dostoyevskii [L. Tolstoi and Dostoyevskii]. 2 vols. St. Petersburg, Mir iskusstva, 1901–2; and several later editions. Published in English translation under the title *Tolstoy as Man and Artist, with an Essay on Dostoyevsky* (New York, 1902).

—— "O 'Prestuplenii i nakazanii' Dostoyevskovo" [On Dostoyevski's *Crime and Punishment*], *Russkoye obozreniye* [Russian Review] (St. Petersburg), II, No. 3 (1890), 155–86. Republished under the title "Dostoyevskii" (*q.v.*) in Merezhkovski, *Polnoye sobraniye sochinenii. See also* Priluko-Prilutski, N. G., comp., F. M. Dostoyevskii: Zhizn' i tvorchestvo.

—— "O prichinakh upadka i o novykh techeniyakh sovremennoi russkoi literatury" [On the Causes of the Decline and the New Trends in Contemporary Russian Literature], in the book of the same title. St. Petersburg, 1893. Republished in his *Polnoye sobraniye sochinenii* [Complete Works] (Moscow, Sytin), Vol. XVIII (1914).

—— "Prorok russkoi revolyutsii" [Prophet of the Russian Revolution], *Vesy* [The Scales] (Moscow), No. 3–4 (1906), pp. 19–47. Republished in his *Polnoye sobraniye sochinenii* [Complete Works] (St. Petersburg and Moscow, Vol'f), XI (1911), 173–224.

—— Vechnye sputniki [Eternal Companions]. St. Petersburg, Pirozhkov, 1897. Republished as Vol. XIII of *Polnoye sobraniye sochinenii* [Complete Works] (St. Petersburg and Moscow, Vol'f, 1911), and in Vol. XVIII of *Polnoye sobraniye sochinenii* [Complete Works] (Moscow, Sytin, 1914).

Mikhailovski, N. K. "Kommentarii k 'Besam' " [Commentaries on *The*

Devils], *Otechestvennye zapiski* [National Notes] (St. Petersburg, February, 1873). Reprinted in his *Sochineniya* [Works] (St. Petersburg, "Russkoye bogatstvo"), I (1896), 840–72.

—— "O Pisemskom i Dostoyevskom" [On Pisemski and Dostoyevski], *Otechestvennye zapiski* [National Notes] (St. Petersburg, February, 1881). Reprinted in his *Sochineniya* [Works] (St. Petersburg, "Russkoye bogatstvo"), V (1897), 410–31.

—— "Pis'ma postoronnevo v redaktsiyu 'Otechestvennykh zapisok' " [Letters from an Outsider to the Editors of *National Notes*], *Otechestvennye zapiski* [National Notes] (St. Petersburg, February, 1881). Reprinted in his *Sochineniya* [Works] (St. Petersburg, "Russkoye bogatstvo"), V (1897), 874–901.

—— "Zhestokii talant" [A Cruel Talent], *Otechestvennye zapiski* [National Notes] (St. Petersburg, September–October, 1882). Reprinted in his *Sochineniya* [Works] (St. Petersburg, "Russkoye bogatstvo"), V (1897), 1–78; and in the compilation *F. M. Dostoyevskii v russkoi kritike: Sbornik statei* (*q.v.*).

Mikulich, V. Vstrechi s pisatelyami. Lev Tolstoi, Dostoyevskii, Leskov, Vsevolod Garshin [Encounters with Writers: Lev Tolstoi, Dostoyevski, Leskov, and Vsevolod Garshin]. Leningrad, Izd. pisatelei, 1929.

Miller, Orest F. "Obshchestvennoye znacheniye 'Zapisok iz Myortvovo Doma.' " *See* Priluko-Prilutski, N. G., comp., F. M. Dostoyevskii: Zhizn' i tvorchestvo.

—— Russkiye pisateli posle Gogolya: Chteniya, rechi i stat'i Oresta Miller [Russian Writers after Gogol: Lectures, Speeches and Articles of Orest Miller]. St. Petersburg, Vol'f, 1886; and several later editions.

Miller, Orest F., and N. N. Strakhov. Biografiya, pis'ma, zametki iz zapisnoi knizhki F. M. Dostoyevskovo [Biography of F. M. Dostoyevski, Letters, and Notes from His Notebook]. St. Petersburg, Suvorin, 1883. Published previously in Dostoyevski, *Polnoye sobraniye sochinenii* [Complete Works] (St. Petersburg, A. G. Dostoyevskaya), Vol. I (1882).

Milyukov, A. P. "Katorga." *See* Priluko-Prilutski, N. G., comp., F. M. Dostoyevskii: Zhizn' i tvorchestvo.

—— "Vospominaniya o F. Dostoyevskom" [Reminiscences of F. Dostoyevski], in Literaturnye vstrechi i znakomstva [Literary Encounters and Acquaintances]. St. Petersburg, 1890.

Nazarenko, Yakov Antonovich. Istoriya russkoi literatury XIX veka [History of Russian Literature in the Nineteenth Century]. Leningrad, GIZ, 1925. 2d ed., rev., Moscow and Leningrad, GIZ, 1926. 3d ed., Moscow and Leningrad, GIZ, 1927.

Nechayeva, V. S. "Dva litsa meshchanskoi intelligentsii v rannikh povestyakh Dostoyevskovo" [Two Characters of the Petit-Bourgeois Intelligentsia in Dostoyevski's Early Stories], Russkii yazyk v sovetskoi shkole [Russian Language in Soviet Schools] (Moscow), No. 1 (1930), pp. 12–26.

—— "Iz rannikh let Dostoyevskovo" [From Dostoyevski's Early Years], Atènei [Athenaeum] (Leningrad), No. 1–2 (1924), pp. 143–50.

—— "Neopublikovannye rukopisi" [Unpublished Manuscripts], Literaturnaya gazeta [Literary Gazette] (Moscow, February 9, 1941).

—— "Poyezdka v Darovoye" [Trip to Darovoye], Novyi mir [New World] (Moscow), No. 2 (1926), pp. 128–44.

—— "Sravneniya v rannikh povestyakh Dostoyevskovo." See Dostoyevskii (Moscow, 1928).

—— V sem'ye i usad'be Dostoyevskikh [In the Family and Homestead of the Dostoyevskis]. Moscow, Gosudarstvennoye sotsial'no-ekonomicheskoye izdatel'stvo, 1939.

Nechayeva, V. S., ed. See Dostoyevski, F. M., Sobraniye sochinenii (1956).

Neifel'd, I. (Neufeld, J.). Dostoyevskii: Psikhoanaliticheskii etyud [Dostoyevski: A Psychoanalytical Study], trans. Ya. Druskin from a German edition ed. S. Freud. Leningrad, "Petrograd," 1925.

"Neizdannyi Dostoyevskii" [Unpublished Dostoyevski], Literaturnaya gazeta [Literary Gazette] (Moscow, February 7, 1956).

Nel's, S. "Sotsial'nye korni i sotsial'nye funktsii tvorchestva Dostoyevskovo" [The Social Roots and Social Functions of Dostoyevski's Writing], Krasnaya nov' [Red Virgin Soil] (Moscow), No. 3 (1931), pp. 156–71.

Neufeld, J. See Neifel'd, I.

Nikitenko, A. V. "Peterburgskii sbornik izdannyi N. Nekrasovym" [The Petersburg Miscellany Published by N. Nekrasov], Biblioteka dlya chteniya [Library for Reading] (St. Petersburg), No. 75 (1846).

Nikitin, Mikhail. Zdes' zhil Dostoyevskii [Here Lived Dostoyevski]. Moscow, Sovetskii pisatel', 1956.

Nikol'ski, Yu. Turgenev i Dostoyevskii: Istoriya odnoi vrazhdy [Turgenev and Dostoyevski: The Story of an Enmity]. Sofia, Ross.-Bolg. Knigoizdatel'stvo, 1921.

Nikulin, L. "Fyodor Mikhailovich Dostoyevsky," *Soviet Woman* (Moscow), No. 2 (February, 1956), p. 28.

N. L. "Dostoyevskii o Germanii i nemtsakh" [Dostoyevski on Germany and the Germans], *Rech'* [Speech] (St. Petersburg), No. 290 (October 27, 1914), p. 3.

Oksman, Yu. G. "Dostoyevskii v redaktsii 'Grazhdanina.'" *See* Grossman, Leonid P., ed., Tvorchestvo Dostoyevskovo.

Oktyabr' [October] (Moscow), No. 11 (1929), pp. 195–97. Unsigned review of M. M. Bakhtin's *Problemy tvorchestva Dostoyevskovo*.

"Ot redaktsii" [From the Editors], *Literaturnaya gazeta* [Literary Gazette] (Moscow, February 9, 1931).

Otverzhennyi, N. Shtirner i Dostoyevskii [Stirner and Dostoyevski]. Moscow, "Golos Truda," 1925.

"O vypade g. Gor'kovo protiv Dostoyevskovo" [On Mr. Gorki's Attack on Dostoyevski], *Birzhevye vedomosti* [Stock Exchange News] (St. Petersburg, October 8 and 9, 1913).

"Pamyati velikovo russkovo pisatelya: Vecher v Kolonnom zale, posvyashchonnyi 75-letiyu so dnya smerti F. M. Dostoyevskovo" [In Memory of a Great Russian Writer: An Evening in Hall of Columns in Observance of the Seventy-fifth Anniversary of the Death of F. M. Dostoyevski], *Izvestiya* (Moscow, February 10, 1956).

Peregrinus (pseud. of Vatslaŭ Lastoŭski). "Todar Dastaeŭski i Adam Mitskevich, syny kryvitskaha narodnaha heniya" [Fyodor Dostoyevski and Adam Mickiewicz, Sons of the Kryvichian National Genius], *Kryvich* (Kaunus), No. 1 (11) (1926), pp. 79–81.

Pereverzev, V. F. "Dostoyevskii, Fyodor Mikhailovich," in Literaturnaya entsiklopediya [Literary Encyclopedia]. Moscow, Izdatel'stvo Kommunisticheskoi Akademii. Vol. III (1930), cols. 396–408.

—— "Dostoyevskii i revolyutsiya (k stoletiyu so dnya rozhdeniya)" [Dostoyevski and Revolution (on the One-hundredth Anniversary of His Birth)], *Pechat' i revolyutsiya* [Press and Revolution] (Moscow), No. 3 (1921), pp. 3–10. Republished in lieu of Foreword to Pereverzev, *Tvorchestvo Dostoyevskovo*, 2d ed. (*q.v.*).

—— "Dostoyevskii v kritike" [Dostoyevski in Criticism], in F. M. Dos-

toyevski, Sochineniya [Works], ed. A. V. Lunacharski. Moscow and Leningrad, GIKhL, 1931. Pages xiv–xxxiv.
—— F. M. Dostoyevskii. Moscow and Leningrad, Gosizdat, 1925. 3d ed., 1928.
—— "Neobkhodimye predposylki marksistskovo literaturovedeniya" [The Necessary Premises of the Marxist Study of Literature], in Pereverzev, ed., Literaturovedeniye [Literary Scholarship]. Moscow, GAKhN, 1928.
—— "Problemy marksistskovo literaturovedeniya" [Problems of Marxist Literary Scholarship], Literatura i Marksizm [Literature and Marxism] (Moscow), No. 2 (1929), pp. 20–34.
—— Tvorchestvo Dostoyevskovo: Kriticheskii ocherk [Dostoyevski's Writing: A Critical Sketch], with a Foreword by P. N. Sakulin. Moscow, "Sovremennye problemy," 1912. 2d ed., rev., Moscow, Gosizdat, 1922. 3d ed., Moscow, Gosizdat, 1928.
Pereverzev, V. F., ed. See Dostoyevski, F. M., Pis'ma F. M. Dostoyevskovo k zhene.
Peshkov, Aleksei Maksimovich. See Gorki, Maxim, pseud.
Petrovski, M. A. "Kompozitsiya 'Vechnovo muzha.'" See Dostoyevskii (Moscow, 1928).
Petukhov, V. Ye. "Iz serdechnoi zhizni Dostoyevskovo (A. P. Suslova)" [From Dostoyevski's Affaires de Coeur], Izvestiya Krymskovo Pedagogicheskovo Instituta im. Frunze [News of the Frunze Crimean Pedgagogical Institute], Simferopol', No. 2 (1928), Section 2, pp. 4–16.
Piksanov, N. K. "Dostoyevskii i fol'klor" [Dostoyevski and Folklore], Sovetskaya etnografiya [Soviet Ethnography] (Leningrad), No. 1–2 (1934), pp. 152–80.
—— "Dostoyevskii v russkoi literature" [Dostoyevski in Russian Literature], Byulleten' "Khudozhestvennaya literatura" [Bulletin of "Khudozhestvennaya literatura" ("Imaginative Literature")] (Moscow), No. 2 (1931), pp. 12–15.
—— "Iz perepiski F. M. Dostoyevskovo" [From F. M. Dostoyevski's Correspondence], Pechat' i revolyutsiya [Press and Revolution] (Moscow), No. 6 (1926), pp. 55–72.
—— See also Dostoyevski, F. M., Iz arkhiva F. M. Dostoyevskovo: Pis'ma russkikh pisatelei.

Piksanov, N. K., ed. Shestidesyatye gody [The Sixties]. Moscow, Izd. Akademii Nauk SSSR, 1940.

Pisarev, D. I. "Bor'ba za zhizn'" [Struggle for Life], in his Polnoye sobraniye sochinenii v shesti tomakh [Complete Works in Six Volumes]. St. Petersburg, Pavlenko, 1897. Vol. VI, pp. 283–344. The first part of the article was published in 1867 under the title "Budnichnye storony zhizni" [The Everyday Sides of Life], in the periodical *Delo* [The Cause] (St. Petersburg) ; and the second part, under the title "Bor'ba za sushchestvovaniye" [The Struggle for Existence], in the same periodical in 1868. Republished in Priluko-Prilutski, N. G., comp., *F. M. Dostoyevskii: Zhizn' i tvorchestvo* (*q.v.*), and in *F. M. Dostoyevskii v russkoi kritike: Sbornik statei* (*q.v.*).

—— "Pogibshiye i pogibayushchiye" [The Perished and the Perishing], in Polnoye sobraniye sochinenii v shesti tomakh [Complete Works in Six Volumes]. St. Petersburg, Pavlenko, 1897. Vol. V, pp. 254–314. *See also* F. M. Dostoyevskii v russkoi kritike: Sbornik statei.

Pogozheva, L. "Kompozitsiya romana 'Prestupleniye i nakazaniye'" [Composition of the Novel *Crime and Punishment*], *Literaturnaya uchoba* [Literary Studies] (Moscow), No. 8–9 (August–September, 1939), pp. 110–20.

—— "Masterstvo kolorita u Dostoyevskovo" [Dostoyevski's Skill in Creating Atmosphere], *Literaturnaya uchoba* [Literary Studies] (Moscow), No. 4 (1939), pp. 51–61.

—— "Mechta Dostoyevskovo o 'zolotom veke'" [Dostoyevski's Dream of the "Golden Age"], *Krasnaya nov'* [Red Virgin Soil] (Moscow), No. 2 (1941), pp. 173–81.

Pokrovskaya, Ye. "Dostoyevskii i petrashevtsy." *See* Dolinin, A. S., ed., Dostoyevskii: Stat'i i materialy, Vol. I.

Pokrovski, G. A. Muchenik bogoiskatel'stva: F. Dostoyevskii i religiya [Martyr to God-Seeking: F. Dostoyevski and Religion]. Moscow, "Ateist," 1929.

Pokrovski, V. I., comp. Dostoyevskii, yevo zhizn' i sochineniya [Dostoyevski, His Life and Writings]. 2 vols. Moscow, 1908–12.

Polonski, Vyacheslav P. "Nikolai Stravrogin i roman 'Besy'" [Nikolai Stravrogin and the Novel *The Devils*], *Pechat' i revolyutsiya* [Press and Revolution] (Moscow), No. 2 (1925). Republished in the compilation *F. M. Dostoyevskii* (*q.v.*).

—— See also Grossman, Leonid P., and Vyacheslav Polonski.

Polyakova, M. M. "Dostoyevskii v otrazhenii sovremennosti" [Dostoyevski as Reflected in the Present], *Literatura i marksizm* [Literature and Marxism] (Moscow), No. 6 (1929), pp. 117–45.

—— "Sotsial'naya priroda geroyev Dostoyevskovo" [The Social Nature of Dostoyevski's Heroes], *Novyi mir* [New World] (Moscow), No. 4 (1931), pp. 145–54.

Popov, P. S. " 'Ya' i 'Ono' v tvorchestve Dostoyevskovo." *See* Dostoyevskii (Moscow, 1928).

Priluko-Prilutski, N. G., comp. F. M. Dostoyevskii: Zhizn' i tvorchestvo [F. M. Dostoyevski: Life and Work]. St. Petersburg and Warsaw, "Oros" [1912?]. Vol. XII of the series Korifei russkovo slova [Coryphaei of the Russian Word]. *Contents:* A. Kirpichnikov, "Fyodor Mikhailovich Dostoyevskii (Biograficheskii ocherk)" [Fyodor Mikhailovich Dostoyevski (Biographical Sketch)], pp. 3–25; B. V. Annenkov, "Uspekh 'Bednykh lyudei' " [The Success of *Poor Folk*], pp. 25–27; V. G. Belinski, "Bednye lyudi" [*Poor Folk*], pp. 27–39; Mel'-khior de Vogyue (Melchior de Vogüé), "Bednye lyudi" [*Poor Folk*], pp. 39–45; N. A. Dobrolyubov, "Makar Devushkin," pp. 45–51; Arseni I. Vvedenski, "Akakii Akakiyevich i Makar Alekseyevich" [Akaki Akakiyevich and Makar Alekseyevich], pp. 51–54; Ye. Zarin, "Zapiski iz Myortvovo Doma" [*Notes from the House of the Dead*], pp. 55–71; A. P. Milyukov, "Katorga" [Penal Servitude], pp. 71–78; Orest F. Miller, "Obshchestvennoye znacheniye 'Zapisok iz Myortvovo Doma' " [The Social Significance of *Notes from the House of the Dead*], pp. 78–88; D. I. Pisarev, "Bor'ba za zhizn' " [Struggle for Life], pp. 88–153; D. S. Merezhkovski, "Prestupleniye i nakazaniye" [*Crime and Punishment*], pp. 153–77; Arseni I. Vvedenski, "Glavnye geroi 'Prestupleniye i nakazaniye' " [The Main Characters of *Crime and Punishment*], pp. 178–82; Anatoli F. Koni, "Voprosy o prestuplenii i nakazanii v proizvedeniyakh Dostoyevskovo" [Questions of Crime and Punishment in the Works of Dostoyevski], pp. 188–200; Yuli I. Aikhenval'd, "Noch' russkoi literatury" [The Night of Russian Literature], pp. 200–220; Yevgeni A. Solov'yov, "Dostoyevskii kak khudozhnik i publitsist" [Dostoyevski as Artist and Publicist], pp. 221–43; Vladimir F. Chizh, "Dostoyevskii kak psikhopatolog" [Dostoyevski as a Psychopathologist], pp. 243–51.

Prokhorov, G. "Pochemu Dostoyevskii vyshel v otstavku" [Why Dosto-yevski Retired], in Literaturno-khudozhestvennyi sbornik "Krasnoi Panoramy" [Literature and Art Miscellany of *Red Panorama*]. Mos-cow, Molodaya gvardiya, December, 1929. Pages 46–48.

—— "Romany Dostoyevskovo (Isayeva, Suslova, Braun, Snitkina)" [Dostoyevski's Love Affairs (Isayeva, Suslova, Braun, Snitkina)], in Literaturno-khudozhestvennyi sbornik "Krasnoi Panoramy" [Literary and Art Miscellany of *Red Panorama*]. Moscow, Molodaya gvardiya, July, 1928. Pages 56–64.

Protopopov, M. A. *See* Gorshkov, Aleksandr, pseud.

Pyatakov, I. "Velikii rossiis'kii pis'mennik" [A Great Russian Writer], *Radyan'ska Ukraina* [Soviet Ukraine] (Kiev), No. 34 (February 9, 1956).

Raskol'nikov, S. "Zabytoye pis'mo F. M. Dostoyevskovo moskovskim studentam" [A Forgotten Letter of F. M. Dostoyevski to Moscow Stu-dents], *Krasnaya nov'* [Red Virgin Soil] (Moscow), No. 4 (1932), pp. 149–55.

Reizov, B. G. "K istorii zamysla 'Brat'yev Karamazovykh.'" *See* "Dos-toyevskii i o Dostoyevskom."

—— Konspekt doklada "O zapadnom vliyanii v romane Dostoyevskovo 'Brat'yev Karamazovykh'" [Conspectus of a Lecture "On the Western Influence in Dostoyevski's Novel *The Brothers Karamazov*"]. Offprint from *Izvestiya Severo-Kavkazskovo Gosudarstvennovo Universiteta* [News of the North Caucasus State University] (Rostov-on-Don), No. 3 (16) (1928), pp. 15–16.

—— "O zapadnom vliyanii v tvorchestve Dostoyevskovo (Nekotorye zapadnye istochniki romana 'Unizhonnye i oskorblyonnye')" [Con-cerning the Western Influence in Dostoyevski's Writing (Certain Western Sources of the Novel *The Insulted and Injured*)], *Izvestiya Severo-Kavkazskovo Gosudarstvennovo Universiteta* [News of the North Caucasus State University] (Rostov-on-Don), No. 1 (12) (1926), pp. 95–104.

Remizov, A. M. *See* Gornfel'd, A. G., and A. M. Remizov.

Riza-Zade, F. D. "Dostoyevskii i sovremennaya frantsuzskaya literatura" [Dostoyevski and Contemporary French Literature], *Pechat' i revo-lyutsiya* [Press and Revolution] (Moscow), No. 6 (1927), pp. 34–52.

—— "Dostoyevskii v zapadnoi kritike" [Dostoyevski in Western Criti-

cism], *Literatura i marksizm* [Literature and Marxism] (Moscow),
No. 3 (1929), pp. 139–76.

Rodzevich, S. I. "K istorii russkovo romantizma (Gofman v 30–40 g.g.
v nashei literature)" [On the History of Russian Romanticism: Hoffmann in the Thirties and Forties of Our Literature], *Russkii filologicheskii vestnik* [Russian Philological Courier] (Petrograd),
LVII, No. 1–2 (1917), 223–30.

Rogachevski, Vasili L'vovich. *See* L'vov-Rogachevski, V., pseud.

Rozanov, V. V. Legenda o Velikom Inkvizitore F. M. Dostoyevskovo:
Opyt kriticheskovo kommentariya [F. M. Dostoyevski's "Legend of
the Grand Inquisitor": An Essay in Critical Commentary]. Berlin,
"Razum," 1924. First published in *Russkii vestnik* [Russian Courier]
(Moscow, 1890); also in book form St. Petersburg, 1894 (3d ed.,
St. Petersburg, Pirozhkov, 1906).

—— *See also* Dostoyevski, F. M., Sochineniya (1894–95).

Rozenblyum, L. M. "Roman F. M. Dostoyevskovo 'Unizhonnye i oskor-
blyonnye' " [F. M. Dostoyevski's Novel *The Insulted and Injured*], in
Dostoyevski, *Unizhonnye i oskorblyonnye* [The Insulted and Injured].
Moscow, GIKhL, 1955. Pages 3–22.

Rozhkov, N. "Eticheskiye i esteticheskiye kharaktery" [Ethical and
Aesthetic Qualities], *Obrazovaniye* [Education] (St. Petersburg),
No. 10–11 (1900).

Ryabov, I. "Fyodor Mikhailovich Dostoyevskii: K 75-letiyu so dnya
smerti" [Fyodor Mikhailovich Dostoyevski: On the Seventy-fifth Anniversary of His Death], *Komsomol'skaya pravda* [Komsomol Truth]
(Moscow, February 9, 1956).

—— "Velikii pisatel': K 75-letiyu so dnya smerti F. M. Dostoyevskovo"
[A Great Writer: On the Seventy-fifth Anniversary of the Death of F.
M. Dostoyevski], *Ogonyok* [The Light] (Moscow), No. 6 (February,
1956), p. 21.

Ryurikov, B. S. "Nekotorye voprosy izucheniya tvorchestva Gor'kovo"
[Certain Questions concerning the Study of Gorki's Writing], *Literaturnaya gazeta* [Literary Gazette] (Moscow, May 6, 1954).

—— "O romane 'Prestupleniye i nakazaniye' " [Concerning the Novel
Crime and Punishment], in Dostoyevski, Prestupleniye i nakazaniye
[Crime and Punishment]. Moscow, GIKhL, 1955. Pages 525–51.

—— "Velikii russkii pisatel' F. M. Dostoyevskii" [The Great Russian

Writer F. M. Dostoyevski], *Kommunist* [Communist] (Moscow), No. 2 (February, 1956), pp. 89–103.

Ryurikov, B. S., ed. *See* Dostoyevski, F. M., Sobraniye sochinenii (1956).

Sakulin, P. N. Russkaya literatura i sotsializm [Russian Literature and Socialism]. Moscow, Gosizdat, 1922. Part I, pages 352–58.

—— *See also* Pereverzev, V. F., Tvorchestvo Dostoyevskovo.

Sakulin, P. N., ed. *See* Dostoyevski, F. M., Iz arkhiva F. M. Dostoyevskovo: "Idiot."

Saltykov, M. Ye. *See* Shchedrin, N., pseud.

Segalov, T. E. "Bolezn' Dostoyevskovo" [Dostoyevski's Sickness], *Nauchnoye slovo* [The Word of Learning] (Moscow), No. 4 (1929), pp. 88–98.

Seidman, Moisei. F. M. Dostoyevskii v zapadnoi literature [F. M. Dostoyevski in Western Literature]. Odessa, Kulberg & Kaplan, 1911.

Sharapov, S., ed. Moskovskii sbornik [Moscow Miscellany]. Moscow, 1887.

Shchedrin, N. (pseud. of M. Ye. Saltykov). O literature [On Literature]. Moscow, GIKhL, 1952. Pages 229–50, 491–92.

Shchogolev, P. Ye., comp. Petrashevtsy v vospominaniyakh sovremennikov: Sbornik materialov [The Petrashevtsy in Reminiscences of Contemporaries: A Collection of Materials]. 3 vols. Moscow, Gosizdat, 1926–28.

Shchukin, S. Ye. Dve kritiki: Plekhanov i Pereverzev [Two Critiques: Plekhanov and Pereverzev]. Moscow, Gosizdat RSFSR, 1930. Chap. 10 (Dostoyevski, Pereverzev, and Revolution).

Shestov, Lev I. Dostoyevskii i Nitsshe: Filosofiya tragedii [Dostoyevski and Nietzsche: The Philosophy of Tragedy]. St. Petersburg, 1903. 2d ed., St. Petersburg, Stasyulevich, 1909.

—— "Prorocheskii dar (K 25-letiyu so dnya smerti F. M. Dostoyevskovo)" [Prophetic Gift (on the Twenty-fifth Anniversary of the Death of F. M. Dostoyevski)], in Nachala i kontsy [Beginnings and Endings]. St. Petersburg, Stasyulevich, 1908. Pages 69–91.

Shevyryov, Stepan P. "Peterburgskii sbornik izdannyi N. Nekrasovym" [The *Petersburg Miscellany* Published by N. Nekrasov], *Moskvityanin* [The Muscovite] (Moscow), No. 2 (1846), pp. 170–72.

Shiller, F. P. "Legenda o Dostoyevskom v zapadno-yevropeiskoi kritike" [The Legend of Dostoyevski in Western European Criticism], *Literatura i marksizm* [Literature and Marxism] (Moscow), No. 5 (1928), pp. 95–106.

Shklovski, Viktor. O teorii prozy [On the Theory of Prose]. Moscow, Krug, 1925.

—— "Syuzhet u Dostoyevskovo" [Plot in Dostoyevski], *Letopis' Doma literatorov* [Annals of the House of Men of Letters] (St. Petersburg [*sic*]), No. 4 (December 20, 1921), pp. 4–5.

Shul'man, R. Ye. "Tvorchestvo rannevo Dostoyevskovo" [The Writing of the Early Dostoyevski], in Uchonye zapiski Stalingradskovo pedagogicheskovo instituta [Scholarly Papers of the Stalingrad Pedagogical Institute]. Stalingrad. Vol. I (1939), pp. 3–70.

Shulyatikov, V. M. "Kriticheskiye etudy: Nazad k Dostoyevskomu" [Critical Studies: Back to Dostoyevski], *Kur'yer* [Courier] (St. Petersburg), No. 287 (1903).

Shumski, A. "Genial'nyi russkii pisatel': K 75-letiyu so dnya smerti F. M. Dostoyevskovo" [A Russian Genius Writer: On the Seventy-fifth Anniversary of the Death of F. M. Dostoyevski], *Gudok* [Whistle] (Moscow, February 9, 1956).

Sidorov, V. "O 'Dnevike pisatelya.'" *See* Dolinin, A. S., ed., Dostoyevskii: Stat'i i materialy, Vol. II.

Simmons, Ernest J. Dostoevsky: The Making of a Novelist. New York, Oxford, 1940. London, John Lehmann, 1950.

Skabichevski, A. M. "Katorga pyat'desyat let tomu nazad i nyne: 'Zapiski iz myortvovo doma' F. M. Dostoyevskovo" [Penal Servitude Fifty Years Ago and Now: F. M. Dostoyevski's *Notes from the House of the Dead*], in Sochineniya [Works]. 3d ed. St. Petersburg, 1903. Vol. II, pp. 684–746.

—— *See also* Zauryadnyi chitatel', pseud.

Skaftymov, A. P. "Tematicheskaya kompozitsiya romana 'Idiot.'" *See* Brodski, N. L., ed., Tvorcheskii put' Dostoyevskovo.

Slonimski, A. L. F. M. Dostoyevskii: Ocherk [F. M. Dostoyevski: A Sketch]. Petrograd, Benke, 1915.

Sluchevski, K. K. *See* Dostoyevski, F. M., Polnoye sobraniye sochinenii (1889).

Smidovich, Vikenti Vikent'yevich. *See* Veresayev, V. V., pseud.

Sokolov, N. A. "Bibliografiya Dostoyevskovo." *See* Dolinin, A. S., ed., Dostoyevskii: Stat'i i materialy, Vol. II.

Soloviev, Evgenii. *See* Solov'yov, Yevgeni A.

Solov'yov, Vladimir S. "Chteniya o bogochelovechestve" [Lectures on Godmanhood], in Sobraniye sochinenii [Collected Works]. 2d ed. St. Petersburg, "Obshchestvennaya pol'za." Vol. III (1912), pp. 1–168.

—— "Tri rechi v pamyat' Dostoyevskovo" [Three Speeches in Memory of Dostoyevski], in Sobraniye sochinenii [Collected Works]. 2d ed. St. Petersburg, "Obshchestvennaya pol'za." Vol. III (1912), pp. 186–223.

Solov'yov, Vsevolod. "Fyodor Mikhailovich Dostoyevskii," *Niva* [Ploughland] (St. Petersburg), No. 1 (1878), pp. 2–3.

—— "Nashi zhurnaly" [Our Periodicals], *St.-Peterburgskiye vedomosti* [St. Petersburg News] (St. Petersburg), Nos. 32 and 58 (1875).

—— "Novye glavy romana 'Podrostka' " [New Chapters of the Novel *A Raw Youth*], *Russkii mir* [The Russian World] (St. Petersburg), No. 237 (1875).

—— "Pamyati F. M. Dostoyevskovo" [Memories of F. M. Dostoyevski] *Niva* [Ploughland] (St. Petersburg), No. 7 (1881), pp. 162–63.

—— "Sovremennaya literatura: 'Dnevnik pisatelya' F. M. Dostoyevskovo" [Contemporary Literature: F. M. Dostoyevski's *Diary of a Writer*], *Russkii mir* [The Russian World] (St. Petersburg), No. 38, (1876).

—— "Sovremennaya literatura: F. M. Dostoyevskii i Emil' Zola o Zhorzh Zand" [Contemporary Literature: F. M. Dostoyevski and Emile Zola concerning George Sand], *Russkii mir* [The Russian World] (St. Petersburg), No. 189 (1876).

—— "Sovremennaya literatura: Nasha nadezhda na narod—F. M. Dostoyevskii o narode" [Contemporary Literature: Our Hope of the People—F. M. Dostoyevski on the People], *Russkii mir* [The Russian World] (St. Petersburg), No. 65 (1876).

—— "Vospominaniya o F. M. Dostoyevskom" [Reminiscences of F. M. Dostoyevski], *Istoricheskii vestnik* [Historical Courier] (St. Petersburg, 1881), No. 3, pp. 602–16; No. 4, pp. 839–53.

Solov'yov, Yevgeni A. (pseud. Andreyevich). F. Dostoyevskii: Yevo zhizn' i literaturnaya deyatel'nost' [F. Dostoyevski: His Life and

Literary Activity]. St. Petersburg, Obshchestvennaya pol'za, 1891. 2d ed., 1898. 3d ed., 1907. Also, Kazan', Molodye sily, 1922. An English translation was published under the name Evgenii Soloviev, Dostoievsky: *His Life and Literary Activity*, trans. C. J. Hogarth (London, Allen & Unwin, 1916; New York, Macmillan, 1916).

—— "F. M. Dostoyevskii" (same as his "F. M. Dostoyevskii, kak khudozhnik i publitsist"), in the compilation F. M. Dostoyevskii (*q.v.*).

—— "F. M. Dostoyevskii, kak khudozhnik i publitsist" [F. M. Dostoyevski as Artist and Publicist], an abridgement of his F. Dostoyevskii: Yevo zhizn' i literaturnaya deyatel'nost', in Solov'yov, Ocherki po istorii russkoi literatury XIX veka [Studies in the History of Russian Literature in the Nineteenth Century], St. Petersburg, 1902; and in N. G. Priluko-Prilutski, comp., F. M. Dostoyevskii: Zhizn' i tvorchestvo (*q.v.*).

Stepanov, N. "Kak rabotal Dostoyevskii nad romanami" [How Dostoyevski Worked on Novels], *Literaturnaya uchoba* [Literary Studies] (Moscow), No. 6 (1932), pp. 46–85.

—— "Tvorchestvo Dostoyevskovo" [Dostoyevski's Writing], *Literaturnaya uchoba* [Literary Studies] (Moscow, 1931), No. 9, pp. 77–94; No. 10, pp. 36–90.

—— "Velikii russkii pisatel': K 75-letiyu so dnya smerti F. M. Dostoyevskovo" [A Great Russian Writer: On the Seventy-fifth Anniversary of the Death of F. M. Dostoyevski], *Trud* [Labor] (Moscow, February 9, 1956).

Stonov, D. "Sel'tso Darovoye" [Hamlet of Darovoye], *Krasnaya niva* [Red Field] (Moscow), No. 16 (1926).

Straikh, S. "Dostoyevskii i syostry Korvin-Krukovskiye" [Dostoyevski and the Korvin-Krukovski Sisters], *Krasnaya nov'* [Red Virgin Soil] (Moscow), No. 7 (1931), pp. 144–50.

Strakhov, N. N. " 'Prestupleniye i nakazaniye' F. M. Dostoyevskovo" [F. M. Dostoyevski's *Crime and Punishment*], *Otechestvennye zapiski* [National Notes] (St. Petersburg), Vol. CXXI, No. 3–4 (1867), pp. 544–56.

—— *See also* Miller, Orest F., and N. N. Strakhov.

Suslova, A. P. Gody blizosti s Dostoyevskim [Years of Intimacy with Dostoyevski], with an Introduction and commentaries by A. S. Dolinin. Moscow, Sabashnikovy, 1928.

Tkachov, P. N. "Bol'nye lyudi. 'Besy' Dostoyevskovo" [Sick People: Dostoyevski's *The Devils*], *Delo* [The Cause] (St. Petersburg), No. 3–4 (1873).

—— (under the pseud. M. Vovchek). "Literaturnoye popuri" [Literary Potpourri], *Delo* [The Cause] (St. Petersburg), Nos. 4–6 and 8 (1876).

Tomashevski, B. V. *See* Dolinin, A. S., ed., Dostoyevskii: Materialy i issledovaniya; and Dostoyevskii, F. M., Izbrannye sochineniya, and Polnoye sobraniye khudozhestvennykh proizvedenii.

Trofimov, I. "F. M. Dostoyevskii: K 75-letiyu so dnya smerti" [F. M. Dostoyevski: On the Seventy-fifth Anniversary of His Death], *Narod-noye obrazovaniye* [Public Education] (Moscow), No. 2 (February, 1956), pp. 10–15.

Tseitlin, A. G. "Dostoyevskii i revolyutsiya" [Dostoyevski and Revolution], *Literaturnaya gazeta* [Literary Gazette] (Moscow, February 9, 1931).

—— Povesti o bednom chinovnike Dostoyevskovo (k istorii odnovo syuzheta) [Stories about Dostoyevski's Poor Civil Servant: On the History of a Plot]. Moscow, Gosizdat, 1923.

—— " 'Prestupleniye i nakazaniye' i 'Les Misérables': Sotsiologicheskiye parallely" [*Crime and Punishment* and *Les Misérables:* Sociological Parallels], *Literatura i marksizm* [Literature and Marxism] (Moscow), No. 5 (1928), pp. 20–58.

—— "Vremya v romanakh Dostoyevskovo" [Time in the Novels of Dostoyevski], *Rodnoi yazyk v shkole* [Native Language in the School] (Moscow, 1929), No. 2, pp. 9–36; No. 3, pp. 134–51.

Tsekhnovitser, O. V. "Dostoyevskii i sotsial'no-kriminal'nyi roman 1860–1870 godov" [Dostoyevski and the Social Crime Novel of the 1860s and 1870s], in Uchonye zapiski Leningradskovo universiteta [Scholarly Papers of Leningrad University]. Leningrad. Vol. IV (1939), pp. 272–303.

—— "F. M. Dostoyevskii," *Oktyabr'* [October] (Moscow), No. 2 (1941), pp. 171–87.

—— "Povesti Dostoyevskovo" [Dostoyevski's Short Novels], in Dostoyevski, F. M., Povesti [Short Novels], ed. Tsekhnovitser. Leningrad, GIKhL, 1940. Pages 461–80.

—— "Velikii master tragicheskovo iskusstva" [A Great Master of

Tragic Art], *Iskusstvo i zhizn'* [Art and Life] (Leningrad), No. 2 (1941), pp. 38–39.

Tsveig [Zweig], S. Tri mastera: Bal'zak, Dikkens, Dostoyevskii [Three Masters: Balzac, Dickens, and Dostoyevski], trans. from the German. Leningrad, 1929. Vol. VII of his Sobraniye sochinenii [Collected Works].

Turbin, V. "Velikii russkii pisatel': K 75-letiyu so dnya smerti F. M. Dostoyevskovo" [A Great Russian Writer: On the Seventy-fifth Anniversary of the Death of F. M. Dostoyevski], *Krasnaya zvezda* [Red Star] (Moscow, February 9, 1956).

Tynyanov, Yuri N. Dostoyevskii i Gogol': K teorii parodii [Dostoyevski and Gogol: On the Theory of Parody]. Petrograd, "Opoyaz," 1921. Republished in Tynyanov, *Arkhaisty i novatory* [Archaists and Innovators] (Leningrad, "Priboi," 1929), pp. 412–56.

Uralov, R. "Pravda o Dostoyevskom (o knige V. Kirpotina 'Molodoi Dostoyevskii')" [The Truth about Dostoyevski: On V. Kirpotin's Book *The Young Dostoyevski*], *Literaturnaya gazeta* [Literary Gazette] (Moscow, November 26, 1947).

Uspenski, G. I. "Prazdnik Pushkina" [The Pushkin Celebration], in Polnoye sobraniye sochinenii [Complete Works]. Kiev, V. K. Fuks, 1903. Vol. IX, pp. 250–70. *See also* F. M. Dostoyevskii v russkoi kritike: Sbornik statei.

—— "Sekret" [A Secret], in Polnoye sobraniye sochinenii [Complete Works], Kiev, V. K. Fuks, 1903. Vol. IX, pp. 271–84. *See also* F. M. Dostoyevskii v russkoi kritike: Sbornik statei.

Veinberg, L. Kriticheskoye posobiye: Sbornik vydayushchikhsya statei russkoi kritiki [Critical Handbook: A Collection of Outstanding Articles of Russian Criticism]. Vol. II: Dostoyevskii i drugiye [Dostoyevski and Others]. Moscow, Sytin, 1913.

"Velikii pisatel' " [A Great Writer], *Literaturnaya gazeta* [Literary Gazette] (Moscow, February 9, 1956).

"Velikii russkii pisatel': K 75-letiyu so dnya smerti F. M. Dostoyevskovo" [A Great Russian Writer: On the Seventy-fifth Anniversary of the Death of F. M. Dostoyevski], *Pravda* (Moscow, February 6, 1956).

Veresayev, V. V. (pseud. of Vikenti Vikent'yevich Smidovich). "Chelovek proklyat" [Man under a Curse], *Sovremennyi mir* [Contemporary World] (St. Petersburg, 1910), No. 1, pp. 186–213; and No. 2, pp. 180–209.

—— Zhivaya zhizn' [Living Life]. Moscow, Popova, 1911. 3d ed., Moscow, Knigoizdatel'stvo Pisatelei, 1922. 4th ed., Moscow, 1928.

Verhaeren, Emile. *See* Verkharn, E.

Verkharn, E. (Emile Verhaeren). "O Dostoyevskom" [Concerning Dostoyevski], *Literaturnaya gazeta* [Literary Gazette] (Moscow, February 9, 1941).

Vetrinski, Ch. (pseud. of Vasili Yevgrafovich Cheshikhin). Dostoyevskii v vospominaniyakh sovremennikov, v pis'makh i zametkakh [Dostoyevski in Reminiscences of His Contemporaries and in Letters and Notes]. Moscow, Svetin. Vol. I, 1912. Vol. II, 1914. 2d ed. (revised and enlarged under the title F. M. Dostoyevskii v vospominaniyakh sovremennikov i v yevo pis'makh [F. M. Dostoyevski in Reminiscences of His Contemporaries and in His Letters]). Moscow, Dumnov. Vol. I, 1923. Vol. II, 1924.

Vinogradov, Viktor V. Evolyutsiya russkovo naturalizma: Gogol' i Dostoyevskii [The Evolution of Russian Naturalism: Gogol and Dostoyevski]. Moscow, "Academia," 1929.

—— "Stil' peterburgskoi poemy 'Dvoinik.'" *See* Dolinin, A. S., ed., Dostoyevskii: Stat'i i materialy, Vol. I.

—— "Syuzhet i arkhitektonika romana Dostoyevskovo 'Bednye lyudi' v svyazi s voprosom o poetike natural'noi shkoly." *See* Brodski, N. L., ed., Tvorcheskii put' Dostoyevskovo.

Vogüë, Melchior de. "Bednye lyudi." *See* Priluko-Prilutski, N. G., comp., F. M. Dostoyevskii: Zhizn' i tvorchestvo.

Voitolovski, L. N. "F. M. Dostoyevskii: K tridtsatiletiyu so dnya konchiny" [F. M. Dostoyevski: On the Thirtieth Anniversary of His Death], *Kiyevskaya mysl'* [Kievan Thought] (Kiev), No. 28 (1911).

—— Istoriya russkoi literatury XIX i XX vekov [History of Russian Literature in the Nineteenth and Twentieth Centuries]. Moscow, GIZ. Vol. I (1926), pp. 232–48.

"Vokrug Dostoyevskovo i Gor'kovo" [Around Dostoyevski and Gorki], *Byulleteni literatury i zhizni* [Bulletins of Literature and Life] (Moscow), No. 11 (1913), pp. 210–13; No. 12 (1913), pp. 393–400; No. 1 (1914), pp. 586–92.

Volotskoi, M. V. Khronika roda Dostoyevskovo, 1506–1933 [Chronicle of the Dostoyevski Family, 1506–1933]. Moscow, Sever, 1933.

Volynski, A. L. (pseud. of A. L. Flekser). F. M. Dostoyevskii: Kriticheskiye stat'i [F. M. Dostoyevski: Critical Articles]. St. Petersburg, Energiya, 1906.

—— Kniga velikovo gneva [A Book of Great Rage]. 2d ed. St. Petersburg, "Trud," 1904.

—— Tsarstvo Karamazovykh [The Kingdom of the Karamazovs]. St. Petersburg, Stasyulevich, 1901.

—— "Velikii bezumets" [The Great Madman], in Bor'ba za idealizm [The Struggle for Idealism]. St. Petersburg, Molostvov, 1900. Pages 493–530.

Volynski, A. L., ed. Dostoyevskii i Pushkin [Dostoyevski and Pushkin]. Petrograd, Parfenon, 1921.

Vovchek, M., pseud. See Tkachov, P. N., "Literaturnoye popuri."

Vrangel', A. Ye. Vospominaniya o F. M. Dostoyevskom v Sibiri (1854–56) [Reminiscences of F. M. Dostoyevski in Siberia (1854–1856)]. St. Petersburg, Suvorin, 1912.

Vvedenski, Arseni I. "Akakii Akakiyevich i Makar Alekseyevich." See Priluko-Prilutski, N. G., comp., F. M. Dostoyevskii: Zhizn' i tvorchestvo.

—— "F. M. Dostoyevskii," in Obshchestvennoye samosoznaniye v russkoi literature [Social Self-awareness in Russian Literature]. St. Petersburg, Mel'nikov, 1909. Pages 161–207.

—— "Glavnye geroi 'Prestupleniye i nakazaniye.'" See Priluko-Prilutski, N. G., comp., F. M. Dostoyevskii: Zhizn' i tvorchestvo.

Vyatkin, G. "Dostoyevskii v Omskoi katorge" [Dostoyevski in Omsk Prison], Sibirskiye ogni [Siberian Fires] (Novonikolayevsk [now Novosibirsk]), No. 1 (1925), pp. 155–80.

Yanovski, S. D. "Vospominaniya o Dostoyevskom" [Reminiscences of Dostoyevski], Russkii vestnik [Russian Courier] (Moscow), No. 176 (1885), pp. 796–819.

Yaroslavski, Yem. "Fyodor Mikhailovich Dostoyevskii protiv nemtsev" [Fyodor Mikhailovich Dostoyevski against the Germans], Bol'shevik (Moscow), No. 16 (August, 1942), pp. 38–43.

Yefimova, Z. S. "Problema groteska v tvorchestve Dostoyevskovo" [The

Question of the Grotesque in Dostoyevski's Writing], in *Nauchnye zapiski nauchnoissledovatel'skoi kafedry istorii yevropeiskoi kul'tury, Dal'ne-Vostochnyi Universitet* [Scholarly Papers of the Department of Research in the History of European Culture, Far Eastern University]. Vladivostok. Vol. II (1927), pp. 145–70.

Yemel'yanov, K. "Dostoyevskii v Tveri" [Dostoyevski in Tver'], in *Pisateli v Tverskoi gubernii* [Writers in Tver' Province]. Kalinin, Oblastnoye izdatel'stvo, 1941. Pages 52–76.

Yermilov, V. V. *F. M. Dostoyevskii.* Moscow, GIKhL, 1956.

—— "F. M. Dostoyevskii" (chapters from his monograph F. M. Dostoyevski), *Novyi mir* [New World] (Moscow), No. 12 (1955), pp. 159–222.

—— "F. M. Dostoyevskii i nasha kritika" [F. M. Dostoyevski and Our Criticism], *Literaturnaya gazeta* [Literary Gazette] (Moscow, December 24, 1947).

—— "F. M. Dostoyevskii: Ocherk tvorchestva" [F. M. Dostoyevski: Outline of His Work], in Dostoyevski, *Sobraniye sochinenii* [Collected Works]. Moscow, GIKhL. Vol. I (1956), pp. 7–76.

—— "Gor'kii i Dostoyevskii" [Gorki and Dostoyevski], *Krasnaya nov'* [Red Virgin Soil] (Moscow), No. 4 (April, 1939), pp. 157–77; No. 5–6 (May–June, 1939), pp. 240–72.

—— "Gorky and Dostoyevsky," *International Literature* (Moscow, 1940), No. 3, pp. 40–66; No. 4, pp. 107–54.

—— "Molodoi Dostoyevskii" [The Young Dostoyevski] (a chapter from his book F. M. Dostoyevskii), *Neva* (Leningrad and Moscow), No. 2 (February, 1956), pp. 162–76.

—— " 'Podrostok' Dostoyevskovo" [Dostoyevski's *A Raw Youth*] (a chapter from his book F. M. Dostoyevski), *Literaturnaya gazeta* [Literary Gazette] (Moscow, January 17, 1956).

—— Protiv reaktsionnykh idei v tvorchestve Dostoyevskovo [Against the Reactionary Ideas in Dostoyevski's Writing]. Moscow, Pravda, 1948.

—— "Spor o cheloveke" [Dispute over Man], *Literaturnaya gazeta* [Literary Gazette] (Moscow, June 15, 1939).

—— "Tema Dostoyevskovo" [Dostoyevski Theme], *Literaturnaya gazeta* [Literary Gazette] (Moscow, February 9, 1941).

—— "Velikii russkii pisatel' F. M. Dostoyevskii" [The Great Russian

Writer F. M. Dostoyevski], *Literatura i iskusstvo* [Literature and Art] (Moscow, September 5, 1942).

Yermilov, V. V., ed. *See* Dostoyevski, F. M., Sobraniye sochinenii (1956).

Yerusalimchik, M. "F. M. Dostoyevskii," *Molodaya gvardiya* [Young Guard] (Moscow), No. 2 (1941), pp. 159–60.

Yevnin, F. "Novaya kniga o Dostoyevskom (o knige V. Kirpotina 'F. M. Dostoyevskii')" [A New Book on Dostoyevski: On V. Kirpotin's Book *F. M. Dostoyevski*], *Novyi mir* [New World] (Moscow), No. 10 (October, 1947), pp. 261–65.

—— "Vydayushchiisya master romana" [Outstanding Master of the Novel], *Oktyabr'* [October] (Moscow), No. 1 (1956), pp. 154–68.

Yurman, N. A. "Bolezn' Dostoyevskovo" [Dostoyevski's Sickness], *Klinicheskii arkhiv genial'nosti i odaryonnosti* [Clinical Archive of Genius and Talent] (Moscow), No. 9 (1928), pp. 61–85.

Yuzovski, Yu. "Rostovskiye spektakli" [Rostov Plays], *Teatral'nyi al'-manakh* [Theatrical Almanac] (Moscow), No. 1 (1946).

—— "Tolstoi i Dostoyevskii na stsene" [Tolstoi and Dostoyevski on the Stage], *Molodaya gvardiya* [Young Guard] (Moscow), No. 1 (1933), pp. 145–51.

Zakrevskii, A. Religiya, psikhologicheskiye paralleli [Religion and Psychological Parallels]. Kiev, Zhurnal "Iskusstvo Yuzhnoi Rossii," 1913.

Zamotin, I. I. F. M. Dostoyevskii v russkoi kritike [F. M. Dostoyevski in Russian Criticism]. Warsaw, 1913. Part I.

Zarin, Ye. "Zapiski iz Myortvovo Doma." *See* Priluko-Prilutski, N. G., comp., F. M. Dostoyevskii: Zhizn' i tvorchestvo.

Zaslavski, D. I. "Burzhuaznye kritiki o Dostoyevskom" [Bourgeois Critics on the Subject of Dostoyevski], *Inostrannaya literatura* [Foreign Literature] (Moscow), No. 7 (July, 1956), pp. 170–74.

—— F. M. Dostoyevskii: Kritikobiograficheskii ocherk [F. M. Dostoyevski: A Critical and Biographical Sketch]. Moscow, Goslitizdat, 1956.

—— "Fyodar Mikhailavich Dastaeŭski: Da 75-godz'dzya z dnya s'mertsi" [Fyodor Mikhailovich Dostoyevski: On the Seventy-fifth Anniversary of His Death], *Nastaŭnitskaya hazeta* [Teachers' Gazette] (Minsk, February 9, 1956).

—— "O Dostoyevskom: 125 let so dnya rozhdeniya" [Concerning Dos-
toyevski: The 125th Anniversary of His Birth], *Literaturnaya gazeta*
[Literary Gazette] (Moscow, November 16, 1946).
—— "Protiv idealizatsii reaktsionnykh vzglyadov Dostoyevskovo"
[Against Idealization of the Reactionary Views of Dostoyevski], *Kul'-
tura i zhizn'* [Culture and Life] (Moscow, December 20, 1947).
—— "Velikii russkii pisatel': 75 let so dnya smerti F. M. Dostoyevskovo"
[A Great Russian Writer: The Seventy-fifth Anniversary of the Death
of F. M. Dostoyevski], *Kazakhstanskaya pravda* [Kazakhstan Truth]
(Alma-Ata, February 9, 1956).
Zauryadnyi chitatel' [Ordinary Reader] (pseud. of A. M. Skabichevski).
" 'Brat'ya Karamazovy.' Novyi roman g. Dostoyevskovo" [*The
Brothers Karamazov:* Mr. Dostoyevski's New Novel], *Molva* [Report]
(St. Petersburg), No. 45 (1879).
—— " 'Dnevnik pisatelya' g. Dostoyevskovo" [Mr. Dostoyevski's *Diary
of a Writer*], *Birzhevye vedomosti* [Stock Exchange News] (St.
Petersburg), Nos. 36 and 70 (1876) ; and No. 239 (1877).
—— "Nechto o predskazaniyakh g. Dostoyevskovo, o tom, pochemu oni
ne mogut sbyt'sya, i chto bylo by, yesli oni sbylis' " [Something on
Mr. Dostoyevski's Predictions, on Why They Cannot Come True, and
What Would Be If They Were to Come True], *Birzhevye vedomosti*
[Stock Exchange News] (St. Petersburg), No. 267 (1877).
—— "O g. Dostoyevskom voobshche i yevo romane 'Podrostok' " [Con-
cerning Mr. Dostoyevski in General and concerning His Novel *A Raw
Youth*], *Birzhevye vedomosti,* [Stock Exchange News] (St. Peters-
burg), No. 8 (1876).
—— "Sravneniye cheloveka s sharmankoi: Sharmanka g. Dostoyevskovo
zavedennaya na luchshuyu i naiboleye simpatichnuyu yeyo ariyu"
[Comparison of Man to a Hurdy-Gurdy: Mr. Dostoyevski's Hurdy-
Gurdy Wound Up to Its Best and Most Sympathetic Aria], *Molva*
[Report] (St. Petersburg), No. 141 (1879).
Zelinski, V. A. Kriticheskii kommentarii k sochineniyam F. M. Dostoyev-
skovo [Critical Commentary to the Works of F. M. Dostoyevski]. 3d
ed., Moscow, Kol'chugin, 1901. 4th ed., 1911.
Zevina, V. "Zdes' zhil Dostoyevskii" [Here Lived Dostoyevski], *Neva*
(Leningrad and Moscow), No. 2 (February, 1956), p. 188.
Zhukov, L. A. "Kritika kapitalizma u Dostoyevskovo" [Criticism of

Capitalism in Dostoyevski], in Trudy Moskovskovo bibliotechnovo instituta [Papers of the Moscow Library Institute]. Moscow. Vol. I (1938), pp. 138–58.
Zil'bershtein, I. S., ed. *See* Dostoyevski, F. M., and I. S. Turgenev, F. M. Dostoyevskii i I. S. Turgenev: Perepiska.
Zweig, Stefan. *See* Tsveig, S.

INDEX